SCREENING THE MALE

Screening the Male challenges the traditional understanding of the male's position in Hollywood cinema. Gathering together thirteen original essays by scholars in the US, UK, and Australia, as well as Steve Neale's ground-breaking article on male spectacle, this collection looks beyond the seemingly unassailable monolithic understanding of the 'masculine' which has previously dominated most film criticism.

Ranging from Valentino to Schwarzenegger, from the musical to the horror film, from close readings to 'queer' readings, the essays all differ in their critical method and historical focus. But whatever their specific interest, each essay holds a strong concern with issues that film studies has repeatedly linked to the feminine without considering how they relate as well to the masculine: spectacle, masochism, passivity, masquerade and, most of all, the body as it signifies gendered, racial, class, and generational differences.

Demonstrating that Hollywood's representation of the male and his masculinity deserves the same kind of critical attention devoted to the problem posed by the female and her femininity, *Screening the Male* will interest scholars, students, and fans of cinema who want to understand the textual complexity and cultural purchase of male imagery on the screen.

SCREENING THE MALE

Exploring masculinities in Hollywood cinema

Edited by

Steven Cohan and Ina Rae Hark

London and New York

First published 1993
by Routledge
11 New Fetter Lane, London EC4P 4EE

Simultaneously published in the USA and Canada
by Routledge
29 West 35th Street, New York, NY 10001

Reprinted 1994

Phototypeset in 10 on 12 point Times by
Intype, London
Printed and bound in Great Britain by
Butler & Tanner Ltd, Frome and London

British Library Cataloguing in Publication Data
Screening the Male: Exploring Masculinities in Hollywood Cinema
I. Cohan, Steven II. Hark, Ina Rae
791.4309

Library of Congress Cataloging in Publication Data
Screening the male : exploring masculinities in Hollywood cinema / edited by
Steven Cohan and Ina Rae Hark.
p. cm.
1. Men in motion pictures. 2. Sex in motion pictures. I. Cohan, Steven.
II. Hark, Ina Rae.
PN1995.9.M46S36 1993
791.43'652041—dc20 92–5815

ISBN 0–415–07758–3
ISBN 0–415–07759–1 (pbk)

Dedicated to the memory of our fathers

Albert Cohan 1923–1991
Hershel Hark 1914–1988

CONTENTS

Notes on contributors   ix

INTRODUCTION   1
Steven Cohan and Ina Rae Hark

PROLOGUE: MASCULINITY AS SPECTACLE   9
Reflections on men and mainstream cinema
Steve Neale

Part I Star turns

1 VALENTINO, 'OPTIC INTOXICATION,' AND DANCE
   MADNESS   23
   Gaylyn Studlar

2 'FEMINIZING' THE SONG-AND-DANCE MAN   46
   Fred Astaire and the spectacle of masculinity in the Hollywood
   musical
   Steven Cohan

3 MAMA'S BOY   70
   Filial hysteria in *White Heat*
   Lucy Fischer

Part II Men in women's places

4 THE DIALECTIC OF FEMALE POWER AND MALE
   HYSTERIA IN *PLAY MISTY FOR ME*   87
   Adam Knee

5 'DON'T BLAME THIS ON A GIRL'   103
   Female rape-revenge films
   Peter Lehman

6 DARK DESIRES   118
Male masochism in the horror film
Barbara Creed

7 'MORE HUMAN THAN I AM ALONE'   134
Womb envy in David Cronenberg's *The Fly* and *Dead Ringers*
Helen W. Robbins

Part III   Man to man

8 ANIMALS OR ROMANS   151
Looking at masculinity in *Spartacus*
Ina Rae Hark

9 FEMINISM, 'THE BOYZ,' AND OTHER MATTERS
REGARDING THE MALE   173
Robyn Wiegman

10 THE BUDDY POLITIC   194
Cynthia J. Fuchs

Part IV   Muscular masculinities

11 MASCULINITY AS MULTIPLE MASQUERADE   213
The 'mature' Stallone and the Stallone clone
Chris Holmlund

12 DUMB MOVIES FOR DUMB PEOPLE   230
Masculinity, the body, and the voice in contemporary action
cinema
Yvonne Tasker

13 CAN MASCULINITY BE TERMINATED?   245
Susan Jeffords

Index of films   263
General index   267

NOTES ON CONTRIBUTORS

Steven Cohan teaches narrative theory, the novel, and film at Syracuse University. In addition to writing extensively on the British novel, he is co-author with Linda Shires of *Telling Stories: a Theoretical Analysis of Narrative Fiction*, and has recently published on film in *Camera Obscura* and *Screen*. At present he is writing a book on American masculinity and the movies during the 1950s.

Barbara Creed lectures in cinema studies at La Trobe University, Melbourne. Her articles have appeared in *Screen, New Formations, Camera Obscura*, and *Continuum*. Her book *The Monstrous-Feminine in Film: Feminism, Psychoanalysis, Horror* has just been published by Routledge.

Lucy Fischer is a professor of film and English at the University of Pittsburgh where she directs the film studies program. She is the author of *Jacques Tati: a Guide to References and Resources*; *Shot/Countershot: Film Tradition and Women's Cinema*, and *Imitation of Life*. She has published extensively in the major film journals and is currently working on a book on motherhood and the cinema.

Cynthia J. Fuchs, assistant professor of English and film and media studies at George Mason University, teaches courses in American film, literature, and television. She is working on a book about gender hysteria in recent American culture.

Ina Rae Hark, professor of English at the University of South Carolina, has published on film in *Cinema Journal, The Journal of Popular Film, South Atlantic Quarterly, New Orleans Review*, and *Literature/Film Quarterly*. She has also written widely on her other teaching areas, Victorian literature and modern drama. She has just completed a book, *There's No Place Like Home: Hollywood Narratives and Their Sites of Consumption*.

Chris Holmlund is an assistant professor at the University of Tennessee, teaching in the Department of Romance languages and the programs of cinema studies and women's studies. She has published articles on French feminist philosophy, and French and American mainstream and experimental film in *Cinema Journal, New Formations, Jump Cut, Quarterly Review of Film and Video, Velvet Light Trap, Social Text*, and *Camera Obscura*.

Susan Jeffords is chair of the women's studies department at the University of Washington. She is author of *The Remasculinization of America* and the forthcoming *Hard Bodies: Hollywood Masculinity in the Reagan Era*.

Adam Knee teaches film history and theory at New York University and the School of visual arts. His essays have appeared in *Film Quarterly, Wide Angle, Film Criticism*, and *Post Script*.

Peter Lehman is a professor and director of graduate studies in the Department of media arts at the University of Arizona. He is editor of *Close Viewings: an Anthology of New Film Criticism* and author of *Running Scared: Sexuality and the Representation of the Male Body*.

Steve Neale is senior lecturer in film studies at the University of Kent. He is the author of *Genre, Cinema and Technology*, a number of articles published in *Screen* and *Framework* and, with Frank Krutnik, of *Popular Film and Television Comedy*.

Helen W. Robbins is an assistant professor of English at Arkansas College. Her research interests, in addition to film, include Victorian literature.

Gaylyn Studlar, associate professor of film studies at Emory University, has published articles in numerous journals and some dozen anthologies. The author of *In the Realm of Pleasure: Von Sternberg, Dietrich, and the Masochistic Aesthetic*, she has recently completed two books, *Shadow Boxing: John Huston and the American Experience*, co-edited with David Desser, and *This Mad Masquerade: Masculinity and Stardom in the Jazz Age*.

Yvonne Tasker lectures in film studies at Sheffield Polytechnic. She is currently completing, with Duncan Webster, a book on masculinity and popular culture.

Robyn Wiegman is an assistant professor of English and women's studies at Indiana University. Her articles on gender, race, and US culture have appeared in *Cultural Critique, American Literary History*, and *Bucknell Review*. She is completing a book, *Economics of Visibility: Race and Gender in US Culture*.

INTRODUCTION

Steven Cohan and Ina Rae Hark

Perhaps the most extensively argued premise of film theory is that the structures of pleasure which Hollywood cinema offers male and female viewers alike ultimately work to prop up the phallocentric bias of its representational system. Starting with Laura Mulvey's much reprinted essay on visual pleasure and narrative film, in the past two decades numerous critics have analyzed classical Hollywood cinema as a pleasure machine which manufactures a masculinized viewer through the ideological apparatus of cinematic address. There is now a coherent body of strong feminist criticism which has repeatedly shown how difficult it is for a woman to resist becoming implicated in the representational system that is Hollywood cinema: the apparatus not only uses the female figure to signify a male desire that disavows difference, but it excludes her from its masculine address as well.

In concentrating on the female body as the primary stake of cinematic representation, however, even the most acute and insightful of those discussions have ignored the problem of masculinity which motivates that system. There have been some exceptions, of course – such as the discussions of 'male trouble' in several issues of the feminist journal *Camera Obscura* as well as scattered analyses of men and masculinity in various films, most of them cited in the bibliographies of the essays to follow – but even these are symptomatic. Generally speaking, the feminist film theory based in Mulvey's analysis of visual pleasure, though critiquing both the feminine spectator implied by her theoretical model and the psychoanalytic assumptions that inspired it, has by and large minimized or taken for granted the complex and considerable cultural investment which classical Hollywood cinema has historically expended in the display of the male, especially as his figure on screen calls into question the stability and unity equated with 'masculinity' and epitomized in the diegesis by the gaze of the male actor.

Until recently, at least, while it has been recognized that orthodox masculine subjectivity functions as the central problem raised by classic Hollywood film, the status of the male in both the cinema auditorium

1

and on screen has also, oddly enough, been too eagerly accepted as the unproblematic given of the system (and of the theory, too). Arguing that the preoccupation with lack and castration which underlies the narrative and visual regimes of Hollywood film arises from the problem of masculine subjectivity in patriarchy, most of this criticism does not pursue that problem very far. On the contrary, in much of it the male spectator and his cinematic surrogate appear, not only unified and coherent, but quite comfortable as well, thank you, secure with their life on the screen as voyeur and fetishist. Film criticism in the wake of Mulvey's influential article has thus pretty much expanded upon her thesis about visual pleasure while retaining the binary of masculine activity versus feminine passivity that motivates her reading of Hollywood cinema as a representational system. And that kind of thinking has turned the screen's representation of masculinity into an easy target of attack, too much the straw man. Note, for instance, the sweeping claim of Lorraine Gamman and Margaret Marshment, on the first page of their introduction to *The Female Gaze* (London: The Women's Press, 1988), a collection of essays on female spectatorship: 'Men act; women are acted upon. This is patriarchy.'

As a result, not much attention has been paid to the problems arising – in texts and for audiences – from the secure and comfortable 'norm' of masculinity which, according to the theoretical model that continues to circulate in film theory, drives the representational system and its institutional apparatus only by being *disabled*. Rather than examine the paradox of a masculinity that derives considerable social and sexual – not to say spectatorial – power from being castrated, wounded, and lacking, film theory has for the most part confidently equated the masculinity of the male subject with activity, voyeurism, sadism, fetishism, and story, and the femininity of the female subject with passivity, exhibitionism, masochism, narcissism, and spectacle. In this scheme of homologous differences the power, stability, and wholeness of masculine subjectivity at the expense of femininity seem all too axiomatic and, thus, universal and uncontestable. But insofar as film theory also maintains that this representational system works by disturbing the symbolic order of patriarchy in order to motivate audience assent to its restoration, just how singular and unified, let alone secure and comforting, is that orthodox masculine position? For that matter, what are we to make of a masculinity that can preserve its hegemony only by confessing its anxieties at every turn? These questions are difficult to answer so long as masculinity and femininity continue to be differentiated in only those monolithic, homologous terms.

While we certainly do not minimize the importance of exposing the disadvantaged positioning of the female spectator and the woman within the diegesis in Hollywood cinema, the scant attention paid to the spec-

tacle of men ends up reinforcing the apparent effacement of the masculine as a social construction in American culture. The male's seeming
exemption from visual representation may work very hard to preserve
the cultural fiction that masculinity is not a social construction, but
American movies have always served as one of the primary sites through
which the culture, in the process of promulgating that fiction, has also
exposed its workings as a mythology. The male image on the cinema
screen is therefore as significant a representational stake as the female;
and the essays we have collected for this volume examine that imagery
from a variety of perspectives to look at its complexity, its historicity,
and (as our subtitle recognizes) its multiplicity.

Indeed, with this goal in mind, the title of our volume intends to
raise a multiple pun that captures the considerable force of the male in
Hollywood cinema: the apparatus puts him on screen, it hides him behind
a screen, it uses him as a screen for its ideological agenda, and it screens
out socially unacceptable and heterogeneous cultural constructions of
masculinity. The thirteen original essays that comprise this book may
thus differ in their arguments, critical methods, historical focus, and
generic interests, but they share as a group a concern with issues that
film theory has repeatedly linked to the feminine and not the masculine:
spectacle, masochism, passivity, masquerade, and, most of all, the body
as it signifies gendered, racial, class, and generational differences. Instead
of the unperturbed monolithic masculinity produced by a de-contextual-
ized psychoanalysis, this volume portrays filmed men and male film
characters overtly performing their gender, in neurotic (and even psychotic) relationships to it, or seeking alternatives to masculinity as their
culture defines it. Any male performer who has offered up his body to
the gaze of the apparatus has clearly forfeited an unassailable masculinity,
and the essays in *Screening the Male* demonstrate that the business of
representing men is a precarious one indeed. For Hollywood film texts
rarely efface the disturbances and slippages that result from putting men
on screen as completely and as seamlessly as the culture – and the
criticism – has assumed.

As a prologue to this collection and historical referent for many of
the essays, we reprint Steve Neale's 1983 essay, 'Masculinity as spectacle,'
a pioneering attempt to put Mulvey's arguments in the context of those
films that obviously represent a spectacular form of masculinity, particularly through elaborately staged rituals of conflict between men, such as
Western gunfights, gangland shootouts, or coliseum combats in Roman
epics, or the avowed performative display of men in musicals. Neale
argues that 'the elements [Mulvey] considers in relation to images of
women can and should also be considered in relation to images of men'
and that because the spectatorial look is so insistently male 'the erotic

3

elements involved in the relations between the spectator and the male image have constantly to be repressed and disavowed.'

Following Neale's article, the first group of original essays, 'Star Turns,' examines the Hollywood personae of three male dancers whose display of their bodies as spectacle in studio-era films is not covert or disavowed but, on the contrary, made inextricable from their star images. In 'Valentino, "optic intoxication," and dance madness,' Gaylyn Studlar examines, as a context for Rudolph Valentino's stardom, the cultural discourse of gender and ethnicity that arose from the craze for dance, primarily among women, that swept America in the 1910s and 1920s. The male dancer, representing a 'utopian' masculinity as fantasized by women, drew scorn in the popular press as the 'woman-made man.' Valentino, Studlar asserts, 'seemed to represent the racial/ethnic misplacement of female desire, but the star also stood for the many American males of the late 1910s and 1920s who perceived themselves as being in danger of being desired and dominated rather than desiring and dominating.'

The next two essays examine stars of the 1930s whose images became more noticeably inflected by gender concerns in their post-World War II films. Steven Cohan's ' "Feminizing" the song-and-dance man: Fred Astaire and the spectacle of masculinity in the Hollywood musical' explores through Astaire's star persona those show-stopping numbers in the MGM musical when 'the Hollywood song-and-dance man' performs 'a socko number and fulfill[s] what the genre takes to be his destiny as a star' and simultaneously signifies the spectacularity that classical Hollywood cinema has traditionally coded as feminine. Yet because these numbers exceed and stop narrativity, Astaire's male spectacle does not simply reverse his active position as a man in patriarchy. Sadism, as Mulvey tells us, demands a *story*, and by stopping show and story, the spectacularized male dancer could escape the binarized economy of sadistic viewing and masochistic spectacle. 'In contrast to the more oppressive, often hysterical, depiction of postwar America's restoration of binarized gender roles in *film noir*,' Cohan concludes, 'the musical imagined an alternative style of masculinity, one grounded in spectacle and spectatorship, which was literally made visible and given body by Fred Astaire.'

James Cagney, Lucy Fischer tells us in 'Mama's boy: Filial hysteria in *White Heat*,' was at heart a song-and-dance man who, on-screen and off, loved and admired his mother. Movie audiences, however, relished him above all as a tough-guy, sadistic killer. When Cagney returned to this gangster image in 1949 after unsuccessful efforts to escape it during the earlier years of the decade, his psychotic Cody Jarrett showed the strain. Although a macho criminal, Cody is also a feminized hysteric, who suffers migraine headaches linked to his unnaturally strong attachment to his mother. Studying those oppressive and hysterical discourses of masculinity in the late 1940s to which Cohan refers, Fischer uncovers a wealth of material to demonstrate that this 'crazed hero' is in fact 'a figure that registers myriad cultural fears' of returned war veterans transformed either into criminal killing machines or psychoneurotic cripples as well as of a 'Momism' perceived to have generated a wide-ranging perversion of 'manhood within the American nuclear family.'

If the cultural anxiety about feminized men traced in these three essays stemmed from a belief in a natural masculinity and femininity that those who stepped beyond their conventional gender roles *un*naturally transgressed, then the advent of feminist discourses in the 1970s and 1980s that pointed up the cultural constructedness of gender and examined the assumptions about the nature of men's and women's 'places' created a new set of anxieties. Film texts began to point out the attraction for men of the narrative, biological, and spectatorial positions regarded as woman's. Yet a simultaneous repulsion accompanied the attraction.

In the first essay of our section 'Men in women's places' Adam Knee traces 'The dialectic of female power and male hysteria in *Play Misty for Me*.' Here the laconic Western star Clint Eastwood, taking his first leading role without a horse (and his first directorial assignment), faces up uncomfortably to changing gender relations in the 1970s, in the process assuming the female role in a slasher-stalker narrative and being reduced to a near-hysterical speechlessness: 'A further oxymoronic characteristic of David's [Eastwood] already problematic persona is that he is an *inarticulate* DJ.' Ultimately the film represents for Eastwood, according to Knee, 'a passing moment of progressive questioning of traditional constructions of male identity prior to the conservative reaction which launched him to greater macho stardom.'

Vengeful women like *Misty*'s Evelyn stalk the plots of the female rape-revenge sub-genre Peter Lehman surveys in ' "Don't blame this on a girl": Female rape-revenge films.' Although dismissive critics assume that such films offer pleasures 'sadistic in a simple manner, whereby men enjoy watching women getting raped and women enjoy watching men get blown away,' Lehman demonstrates that the films address themselves primarily to a masochistic male spectator who identifies with the gruesome mutilations of other men.

Male masochism also underlies the construction of the monstrous males of the horror film, says Barbara Creed in 'Dark desires: Male masochism in the horror film.' Using Julia Kristeva's notion of the abject, Creed finds that the supernatural, physiologically deviant movie monsters such as Dracula and the werewolf take on female biological traits while the psychotic, mentally deviant serial killer, from *Psycho* to *Dressed to Kill* to *The Silence of the Lambs*, attempts to clothe himself in the woman's body. These abject, monstrous bodies address 'most clearly the masochistic desires of the spectator. As a consequence, the male spectator is punished, as he looks at the abject body of the other – his monstrous, feminised gender counterpart.'

Examining two films that Creed notes in passing, Helen W. Robbins's ' "More human than I am alone": Womb envy in David Cronenberg's *The Fly* and *Dead Ringers*' reveals males obsessed with controlling and appropriating women's ability to reproduce out of their own fears of a loss of control over the 'dissemination' of intellectual and scientific discoveries. In the end, however, 'the womb envy of Cronenberg's men is often indistinguishable from their masochistic, regressive desire to return to the pre-symbolic connection with the maternal real,' and Seth Brundle and the Mantle twins eventually become far more monstrous in body and spirit than the 'mutant' women they both fear and hope will engulf them.

The third section of the volume, 'Man to man,' deals with films in which a character's masculinity is primarily constructed not in relation to woman, but to other men. Such films raise issues of male bonding, homoeroticism, and a reconfiguration of the structures of gender difference along the lines of racial, class, and economic differences. Ina Rae Hark in 'Animals or Romans: Looking at masculinity in *Spartacus*' maintains that the film offers its male characters either a narcissistic, materialist, and aggressively phallic masculinity appropriate to slaves or a symbolic, perversely bloodless, subjectivity propped up on the objectification of all save the Roman patrician class. Within its political plot, *Spartacus* traces its hero's search for an alternative masculinity that avoids these twin traps; but, Hark argues, 'While *Spartacus* allows its protagonists to oscillate among all these positions, it cannot imagine a space in which such binarism collapses. The future perfect solution to masculine subjectivity, unattainable within the diegesis, is no more possible for 1960 Hollywood than for 73 BC Rome.'

Finding an alternative masculinity is also the project of *Boyz N the Hood*, according to Robyn Wiegman's 'Feminism, "the Boyz," and other matters regarding the male.' Wiegman seeks to collapse the binarism which dominates (and erases race from) most feminist theories of gender in order 'to approach not simply relations of identity and difference but, most crucially, their embodied asymmetries as well' and so reveal 'various complexities within the race/gender nexus.' Her analysis of the 'mediated' black masculinity advocated by *Boyz*'s father/prophet Furious Styles aims to provide a model for such non-binaristic inquiry.

Interracial bonding between men has become increasingly evident during the 1980s in what Cynthia Fuchs calls 'The buddy politic.' By foregrounding the erasure of racial differences via bonds formed during episodes of explosive penetration, the buddy film works to disguise the homoeroticism always implicit in its formulaic structure. Fuchs notes that 'Mapping the formula's evolution from the cultural trauma of Vietnam through the farce of the Reagan–Bush drug wars, these films efface the intimacy and vulnerability associated with homosexuality by the "marriage" of racial others, so that this transgressiveness displaces homosexual anxiety.'

Our final section, 'Muscular masculinities,' deals with some of the same issues raised in 'Man to Man' but focuses more narrowly on a specific, historicized genre, the action film of the 1980s that starred such pumped-up icons as Sylvester Stallone and Arnold Schwarzenegger and in which, Susan Jeffords observes, 'the male body – principally the white male body – became increasingly a vehicle of display – of musculature, of beauty, of physical feats, and of a gritty toughness.'

Chris Holmlund's 'Masculinity as multiple masquerade: the "mature" Stallone and the Stallone clone' applies theories of the masquerade developed around the figures of gendered or racial others to the representation of white, male heterosexuality in *Tango and Cash* and *Lock Up*. She further distinguishes three different forms of masquerading: 'dressing up (embellishment) . . . putting on (parody, critique) . . . stepping out (affirmation, contestation).' Her 'queer reading' of the Stallone films then proceeds 'to question the body as base' by acknowledging 'all matrices of masquerade.'

Yvonne Tasker analyzes these same two films, along with *Die Hard* and *Die Hard 2*, from the perspective of the marketability of the male body in a bureaucratized consumer culture where gender roles in the world of work are changing. The resultant anxieties, she explains in 'Dumb movies for dumb people: Masculinity, the body and the voice in contemporary action cinema,' are worked out over a beleaguered male body commodified as spectacle: 'Resorting either to images of physical torture and suffering or to comedy, the body of the hero, his excessive "musculinity", is subjected to humiliation and mockery at some level.'

In the volume's concluding essay, 'Can masculinity be terminated?' Susan Jeffords notes the turn away from externalized muscular masculinity in the more internalized male-centered narratives of the 1990s. Using the two *Terminator* films, she charts a shift that began in the late 1980s to make 'fathering . . . a key characterization and narrative device for displaying the "new" Hollywood masculinities.' She also notes some dangers of this apparently positive evolution: the displacement of the mother by the father as the parental signifier and the recuperation of macho, destructive masculinity even as it dissolves itself.

Each in their own way, then, the essays written for *Screening the Male* take pains to establish that masculinity is an effect of culture – a construction, a performance, a masquerade – rather than a universal and unchanging essence. A recent *Hi and Lois* comic strip makes this important point about the meaning of masculinity in the movies perfectly if

7

Figure 1 Hi and Lois comic strip. By permission of King Features Syndicate

humorously clear by poking fun at the way fashions have changed when it comes to playing out games of power and gender.

In their playing, Dot and Ditto, the two young children, register the ascendancy of Schwarzenegger's muscular masculinity, and their older brother and father then historicize it with reference to another generation's model of virility. Since the children involved are a boy and a girl, this child's game also hints at the cross-gendered implications of such play. If the signifier changes – Arnold in the place of the Duke – does what he signifies alter too? Though the suspicion lingers that the more things change in outward appearance, the more they have thus far stayed the same in their fundamental political structure, with the game fixed so as always to produce a white heterosexual male winner, who routinely overcomes the other – the Indians, the aliens, the feminine – the essays collected here show that this state of affairs by no means lessens the need to look closely at Hollywood's representations of masculinity. On the contrary, it means that putting the male on view and under analysis is all the more urgent a task at this moment in film studies. For this reason, one important aim in organizing this book is to help prepare the ground for further research into the cultural significance of male stars and their movies: more historical as well as theoretical examinations of specific masculine star images, of male genres modified by social and political changes, of the commodification of the male body in consumer culture, of the complexities of shifting racial and gender alignments. We hope, in short, that *Screening the Male* will help to bring into focus the diversity with which Hollywood cinema has in the past and continues in the 1990s to make masculinity highly visible and central to the cultural politics of gendered representations.

PROLOGUE

MASCULINITY AS SPECTACLE
Reflections on men and mainstream cinema
Steve Neale

Since the early 1970s, numerous books and articles have appeared discussing the images of women produced and circulated by the cinematic
institution. Motivated politically by the development of the women's
movement, and concerned therefore with the political and ideological
implications of the representations of women offered by the cinema, a
number of these books and articles have taken as their basis Laura
Mulvey's 'Visual Pleasure and Narrative Cinema', first published in
Screen in 1975. Mulvey's article was highly influential in its linking
together of psychoanalytic perspectives on the cinema with a feminist
perspective on the ways in which images of women figure within mainstream film. She sought to demonstrate the extent to which the psychic
mechanisms cinema has basically involved are profoundly patriarchal,
and the extent to which the images of women mainstream film has
produced lie at the heart of those mechanisms.

Inasmuch as there has been discussion of gender, sexuality, representation, and the cinema over the past decade then, that discussion has
tended overwhelmingly to center on the representation of women, and
to derive many of its basic tenets from Mulvey's article. Only within the
gay movement have there appeared specific discussions of the representation of men. Most of these, as far as I am aware, have centered on
the representations and stereotypes of gay men. Both within the women's
movement and the gay movement, there is an important sense in which
the images and functions of heterosexual masculinity within mainstream
cinema have been left undiscussed. Heterosexual masculinity has been
identified as a structuring norm in relation both to images of women and
gay men. It has to that extent been profoundly problematized, rendered
visible. But it has rarely been discussed and analyzed as such. Outside
these movements, it has been discussed even less. It is thus very rare to
find analyses that seek to specify in detail, in relation to particular films
or groups of films, how heterosexual masculinity is inscribed and the
mechanisms, pressures, and contradictions that inscription may involve.
Aside from a number of recent pieces in *Screen*[1] and *Framework*,[2] Ray-

9

mond Bellour's article on *North by Northwest* (Bellour 1975) is the only example that springs readily to mind. Bellour's article follows in some detail the Oedipal trajectory of Hitchcock's film, tracing the movement of its protagonist, Roger Thornhill (Cary Grant) from a position of infantile dependence on the mother to a position of 'adult', 'male', heterosexual masculinity, sealed by his marriage to Eve Kendall (Eva Marie Saint) and by his acceptance of the role and authority of the father. However, the article is concerned as much with the general workings of a classical Hollywood film as it is with the specifics of a set of images of masculinity.

Although, then, there is a real need for more analyses of individual films, I intend in this article to take another approach to some of the issues involved. Using Laura Mulvey's article as a central, structuring reference point, I want to look in particular at identification, looking, and spectacle as she has discussed them and to pose some questions as to how her remarks apply directly or indirectly to images of men, on the one hand, and to the male spectator on the other. The aim is less to challenge fundamentally the theses she puts forward, than to open a space within the framework of her arguments and remarks for a consideration of the representation of masculinity as it can be said to relate to the basic characteristics and conventions of the cinematic institution.

IDENTIFICATION

To start with, I want to quote from John Ellis's book *Visible Fictions*. Written very much in the light of Mulvey's article, Ellis is concerned both to draw on her arguments and to extend and qualify some of the theses she puts forward vis-à-vis gender and identification in the cinema. Ellis argues that identification is never simply a matter of men identifying with male figures on the screen and women identifying with female figures. Cinema draws on and involves many desires, many forms of desire. And desire itself is mobile, fluid, constantly transgressing identities, positions, and roles. Identifications are multiple, fluid, at points even contradictory. Moreover, there are different forms of identification. Ellis points to two such forms, one associated with narcissism, the other with phantasies and dreams. He sums up as follows:

> Cinematic identification involves two different tendencies. First, there is that of dreaming and phantasy that involve the multiple and contradictory tendencies within the construction of the individual. Second, there is the experience of narcissistic identification with the image of a human figure perceived as other. Both these processes are invoked in the conditions of entertainment cinema. The spectator does not therefore 'identify' with the hero or heroine: an identifi-

cation that would, if put in its conventional sense, involve socially constructed males identifying with male heroes, and socially constructed females identifying with women heroines. The situation is more complex than this, as identification involves both the recognition of self in the image on the screen, a narcissistic identification, and the identification of self with the various positions that are involved in the fictional narration: those of hero and heroine, villain, bit-part player, active and passive character. Identification is therefore multiple and fractured, a sense of seeing the constituent parts of the spectator's own psyche paraded before her or him.

(Ellis 1982: 43)

A series of identifications are involved, then, each shifting and mobile. Equally, though, there is constant work to channel and regulate identification in relation to sexual division, in relation to the orders of gender, sexuality, and social identity and authority marking patriarchal society. Every film tends both to assume and actively to work to renew those orders, that division. Every film thus tends to specify identification in accordance with the socially defined and constructed categories of male and female.

In looking specifically at masculinity in this context, I want to examine the process of narcissistic identification in more detail. Inasmuch as films *do* involve gender identification, and inasmuch as current ideologies of masculinity involve so centrally notions and attitudes to do with aggression, power, and control, it seems to me that narcissism and narcissistic identification may be especially significant.

Narcissism and narcissistic identification both involve phantasies of power, omnipotence, mastery, and control. Laura Mulvey makes the link between such phantasies and patriarchal images of masculinity in the following terms:

As the spectator identifies with the main male protagonist, he projects his look on to that of his like, his screen surrogate, so that the power of the male protagonist as he controls events coincides with the active power of the erotic look, both giving a satisfying sense of omnipotence. A male movie star's glamorous characteristics are thus not those of the erotic object of his gaze, but those of the more perfect, more complete, more powerful ideal ego conceived in the original moment of recognition in front of the mirror.

(Mulvey 1975: 12)

I want to turn to Mulvey's remarks about the glamorous male movie star below. But first it is worth extending and illustrating her point about the male protagonist and the extent to which his image is dependent

11

upon narcissistic phantasies, phantasies of the 'more perfect, more complete, more powerful ideal ego'.

It is easy enough to find examples of films in which these phantasies are heavily prevalent, in which the male hero is powerful and omnipotent to an extraordinary degree: the Clint Eastwood character in *A Fistful of Dollars* (1964), *For a Few Dollars More* (1965), and *The Good, the Bad, and the Ugly* (1967), the Tom Mix Westerns, Charlton Heston in *El Cid* (1961), the Mad Max films, the Steve Reeves epics, *Superman* (1978), *Flash Gordon* (1980), and so on. There is generally, of course, a drama in which that power and omnipotence are tested and qualified (*Superman 2* (1980) is a particularly interesting example, as are Howard Hawks's Westerns and adventure films), but the Leone trilogy, for example, is marked by the extent to which the hero's powers are rendered almost godlike, hardly qualified at all. Hence, perhaps, the extent to which they are built around ritualized scenes which in many ways are devoid of genuine suspense. A film like Melville's *Le Samourai* (1967), on the other hand, starts with the image of self-possessed, omnipotent masculinity and traces its gradual and eventual disintegration. Alain Delon plays a lone gangster, a hit-man. His own narcissism is stressed in particular through his obsessive concern with his appearance, marked notably by a repeated and ritualized gesture he makes when putting on his hat, a sweep of the hand across the rim. Delon is sent on a job, but is spotted by a black female singer in a club. There is an exchange of looks. From that point on his omnipotence, silence, and inviolability are all under threat. He is shot and wounded; his room is broken into and bugged; he is nearly trapped on the Metro. Eventually, he is gunned down, having returned to the club to see the singer again. The film is by no means a critique of the male image it draws upon. On the contrary, it very much identifies (and invites us to identify) with Delon. Nevertheless, the elements both of that image and of that to which the image is vulnerable are clearly laid out. It is no accident that Delon's downfall is symptomatically inaugurated in his encounter with the black woman. Difference (double difference), is the threat. An exchange of looks in which Delon's cold commanding gaze is troubled, undermined, and returned is the mark of that threat.

The kind of image that Delon here embodies, and that Eastwood and the others mentioned earlier embody too, is one marked not only by emotional reticence, but also by silence, a reticence with language. Theoretically, this silence, this absence of language can further be linked to narcissism and to the construction of an ideal ego. The acquisition of language is a process profoundly challenging to the narcissism of early childhood. It is productive of what has been called 'symbolic castration.' Language is a process (or set of processes) involving absence and lack, and these are what threaten any image of the self as totally enclosed, self-sufficient, omnipotent. The construction of an ideal ego, meanwhile, is a process involving profound contradictions. While the ideal ego may be a 'model' with which the subject identifies and to which it aspires, it may also be a source of further images and feelings of castration, inasmuch as that ideal is something to which the subject is never adequate.[3]

If this is the case, there can be no simple and unproblematic identification on the part of the spectator, male or female, with Mulvey's 'ideal ego' on the screen. In an article published in *Wide Angle*, D. N. Rodowick has made a similar point. He goes on to argue both that the narcissistic male image – the image of authority and omnipotence – can entail a concomitant masochism in the relations between the spectator and the image, and further that the male image can involve an eroticism, since there is always a constant oscillation between that image as a source of identification, and as an other, a source of contemplation. The image is a source both of narcissistic processes and drives, and, inasmuch as it is other, of object-oriented processes and drives:

> Mulvey discusses the male star as an object of the look but denies him the function of an erotic object. Because Mulvey conceives the look to be essentially active in its aims, identification with the male protagonist is only considered from a point of view which associates it with a sense of omnipotence, of assuming control of the narrative. She makes no differentiation between identification and object choice in which sexual aims may be directed toward the male figure, nor does she consider the signification of authority in the male figure from the point of view of an economy of masochism.
>
> (Rodowick 1982: 8)

Given Rodowick's argument, it is not surprising either that 'male' genres and films constantly involve sado-masochistic themes, scenes, and phantasies or that male heroes can at times be marked as the object of an erotic gaze. These are both points I wish to discuss below. However, it is worth mentioning here that they have also been discussed in Paul Willemen's article 'Anthony Mann: Looking at the Male.'

Willemen argues that spectacle and drama in Mann's films tend both to be structured around the look at the male figure: 'The viewer's experience is predicated on the pleasure of seeing the male "exist" (that is walk, move, ride, fight) in or through cityscapes, landscapes or, more abstractly, history. And on the unquiet pleasure of seeing the male mutilated (often quite graphically in Mann) and restored through violent brutality' (Willemen 1981: 16). These pleasures are founded upon a repressed homosexual voyeurism, a voyeurism 'not without its problems: the look at the male produces just as much anxiety as the look at the female, especially when it's presented as directly as in the killing scenes in *T-Men* (1947) and *Border Incident* (1949)' (Willemen 1981: 16). The

13

(unstated) thesis behind these comments seems to be that in a heterosexual and patriarchal society, the male body cannot be marked explicitly as the erotic object of another male look: that look must be motivated in some other way, its erotic component repressed. The mutilation and sadism so often involved in Mann's films are marks both of the repression involved and of a means by which the male body may be disqualified, so to speak, as an object of erotic contemplation and desire. The repression and disavowal involved are figured crucially in the scenes in *T-Men* and *Border Incident* to which Willemen refers, in which 'an undercover agent must look on, impassively, while his close (male) friend and partner is being killed' (Willemen 1981: 16).

There is one final and important contradiction involved in the type of narcissistic images of masculinity discussed above to which I'd like to refer. It is the contradiction between narcissism and the law, between an image of *narcissistic* authority on the one hand and an image of *social* authority on the other. This tension or contradiction is discussed at some length by Laura Mulvey in an article seeking to re-consider her 'Visual Pleasure' piece with particular reference to *Duel in the Sun* (1946). It is a tension she sees as especially evident in the Western. Using a narrative model from Vladimir's Propp's analyses of folktales (Propp 1968), Mulvey points to two narrative functions, 'marriage' (and hence social integration) and 'not marriage,' a refusal by the hero to enter society, a refusal motivated by a nostalgic narcissism:

> In the Proppian tale, an important aspect of narrative closure is 'marriage', a function characterised by the 'princess' or equivalent. This is the only function that is sex specific and thus essentially relates to the sex of the hero and his marriageability. This function is very commonly reproduced in the Western, where once again 'marriage' makes a crucial contribution to narrative closure. However, the function's presence also has come to allow a complication in the Western, its complementary opposite 'not marriage'. Thus, while the social integration represented by marriage is an essential aspect of the folk-tale, in the Western it can be accepted . . . or not. A hero can gain in stature by refusing the princess and remaining alone (Randolph Scott in the Ranown series of movies). As the resolution of the Proppian tale can be seen to represent the resolution of the Oedipus complex (integration into the symbolic), the rejection of marriage personifies a nostalgic celebration of phallic, narcissistic omnipotence.
>
> (Mulvey 1981: 14)

There are thus two diverging images of masculinity commonly at play in the Western:

The tension between two points of attraction, the symbolic (social integration and marriage) and nostalgic narcissism, generates a common splitting of the Western hero into two, something unknown in the Proppian tale. Here two functions emerge, one celebrating integration into society through marriage, and the other celebrating resistance to social standards and responsibilities, above all those of marriage and the family, the sphere represented by women.

(Mulvey 1981: 18)

Mulvey goes on to discuss John Ford's Western *The Man who Shot Liberty Valance* (1962), noting the split there between Tom Doniphon, played by John Wayne, who incarnates the narcissistic function of the anachronistic social outsider, and Ranse Stoddart, played by James Stewart, who incarnates the civilizing functions of marriage, social integration, and social responsibility. The film's tone is increasingly nostalgic, in keeping with its mourning for the loss of Doniphon and what he represents. The nostalgia, then, is not just for an historical past, for the Old West, but also for the masculine narcissism that Wayne represents.

Taking a cue from Mulvey's remarks about nostalgia in *Liberty Valance*, one could go on to discuss a number of nostalgic Westerns in these terms, in terms of the theme of lost or doomed male narcissism. The clearest examples would be Peckinpah's Westerns: *Guns in the Afternoon* (1962), *Major Dundee* (1965) (to a lesser extent), *The Wild Bunch* (1969), and, especially, *Pat Garrett and Billy the Kid* (1973). These films are shot through with nostalgia, with an obsession with images and definitions of masculinity and masculine codes of behaviour, and with images of male narcissism and the threats posed to it by women, society, and the law. The threat of castration is figured in the wounds and injuries suffered by Joel McCrea in *Guns in the Afternoon*, Charlton Heston in *Major Dundee*, and William Holden in *The Wild Bunch*. The famous slow-motion violence, bodies splintered and torn apart, can be viewed at one level at least as the image of narcissism in its moment of disintegration and destruction. Significantly, Kris Kristofferson as Billy in *Pat Garrett and Billy the Kid*, the ultimate incarnation of omnipotent male narcissism in Peckinpah's films, is spared any bloody and splintered death. Shot by Pat Garrett, his body shows no sign either of wounds or blood: narcissism transfigured (rather than destroyed) by death.

I want now to move on from identification and narcissism to discuss in relation to images of men and masculinity the two modes of looking addressed by Mulvey in 'Visual Pleasure', voyeuristic looking, on the one hand, and fetishistic looking on the other.

15

Voyeuristic + fetishestic

STEVE NEALE

LOOKING AND SPECTACLE

In discussing these two types of looking, both fundamental to the cinema, Mulvey locates them solely in relation to a structure of activity/passivity in which the look is male and active and the object of the look female and passive. Both are considered as distinct and variant means by which male castration anxieties may be played out and allayed.

Voyeuristic looking is marked by the extent to which there is a distance between spectator and spectacle, a gulf between the seer and the seen. This structure is one which allows the spectator a degree of power over what is seen. It hence tends constantly to involve sado-masochistic phantasies and themes. Here is Mulvey's description:

> voyeurism . . . has associations with sadism: pleasure lies in ascertaining guilt (immediately associated with castration), asserting control and subjecting the guilty person through punishment and forgiveness. This sadistic side fits in well with narrative. Sadism demands a story, depends on making something happen, forcing a change in another person, a battle of will and strength, victory and defeat, all occurring in a linear time with a beginning and an end.
>
> (Mulvey 1975: 14)

Mulvey goes on to discuss these characteristics of voyeuristic looking in terms of the *film noir* and of Hitchcock's movies, where the hero is the bearer of the voyeuristic look, engaged in a narrative in which the woman is the object of its sadistic components. However, if we take some of the terms used in her description – 'making something happen', 'forcing a change in another person,' 'a battle of will and strength,' 'victory and defeat' – they can immediately be applied to 'male' genres, to films concerned largely or solely with the depiction of relations between men, to any film, for example, in which there is a struggle between a hero and a male villain. War films, Westerns, and gangster movies, for instance, are all marked by 'action,' by 'making something happen.' Battles, fights, and duels of all kinds are concerned with struggles of 'will and strength,' 'victory and defeat,' between individual men and/or groups of men. All of which implies that male figures on the screen are subject to voyeuristic looking, both on the part of the spectator and on the part of other male characters.

Paul Willemen's thesis on the films of Anthony Mann is clearly relevant here. The repression of any explicit avowal of eroticism in the act of looking at the male seems structurally linked to a narrative content marked by sado-masochistic phantasies and scenes. Hence both forms of voyeuristic looking, intra- and extra-diegetic, are especially evident in those moments of contest and combat referred to above, in those moments at which a narrative outcome is determined through a fight or gun-battle, at which male struggle becomes pure spectacle. Perhaps the most extreme examples are to be found in Leone's Westerns, where the exchange of aggressive looks marking most Western gun-duels is taken to the point of fetishistic parody through the use of extreme and repetitive close-ups. At which point the look begins to oscillate between voycurism and fctishism as the narrative starts to freeze and spectacle takes over. The anxious 'aspects' of the look at the male to which Willemen refers are here both embodied and allayed not just by playing out the sadism inherent in voyeurism through scenes of violence and combat, but also by drawing upon the structures and processes of fetishistic looking, by stopping the narrative in order to recognize the pleasure of display, but displacing it from the male body as such and locating it more generally in the overall components of a highly ritualized scene.

John Ellis has characterized fetishistic looking in the following terms:

> where voyeurism maintains (depends upon) a separation between the seer and the object seen, fetishism tries to abolish the gulf. . . . This process implies a different position and attitude of the spectator to the image. It represents the opposite tendency to that of voyeurism. . . . Fetishistic looking implies the direct acknowledgement and participation of the object viewed . . . with the fetishistic attitude, the look of the character towards the viewer . . . is a central feature. . . . The voyeuristic look is curious, inquiring, demanding to know. The fetishistic gaze is captivated by what it sees, does not wish to inquire further, to see more, to find out. . . . The fetishistic look has much to do with display and the spectacular.
>
> (Ellis 1982: 47)

Mulvey again centrally discusses this form of looking in relation to the female as object: 'This second avenue, fetishistic scopophilia, builds up the physical beauty of the object, transforming it into something satisfying in itself' (Mulvey 1975: 14). 'Physical beauty' is interpreted solely in terms of the female body. It is specified through the example of the films of Sternberg:

> While Hitchcock goes into the investigative side of voyeurism, Sternberg produces the ultimate fetish, taking it to the point where the powerful look of a male protagonist is broken in favour of the image in direct erotic rapport with the spectator. The beauty of the woman as object and the screen space coalesce; she is no longer the bearer of guilt but a perfect product, whose body, stylised and fragmented by close-ups, is the content of the film and the direct recipient of the spectator's look.
>
> (Mulvey 1975: 14)

If we return to Leone's shoot-outs, we can see that some elements of the fetishistic look as here described are present, others not. We are offered the spectacle of male bodies, but bodies unmarked as objects of erotic display. There is no trace of an acknowledgment or recognition of those bodies as displayed solely for the gaze of the spectator. They are on display, certainly, but there is no cultural or cinematic convention which would allow the male body to be presented in the way that Dietrich so often is in Sternberg's films. We see male bodies stylized and fragmented by close-ups, but our look is not direct, it is heavily mediated by the looks of the characters involved. And those looks are marked not by desire, but rather by fear, or hatred, or aggression. The shoot-outs are moments of spectacle, points at which the narrative hesitates, comes to a momentary halt, but they are also points at which the drama is finally resolved, a suspense in the culmination of the narrative drive. They thus involve an imbrication of both forms of looking, their intertwining designed to minimize and displace the eroticism they each tend to involve, to disavow any explicitly erotic look at the male body.

There are other instances of male combat which seem to function in this way. Aside from the Western, one could point to the epic as a genre, to the gladiatorial combat in *Spartacus* (1960), to the fight between Christopher Plummer and Stephen Boyd at the end of *The Fall of the Roman Empire* (1964), to the chariot race in *Ben-Hur* (1959). More direct displays of the male body can be found, though they tend either to be fairly brief or else to occupy the screen during credit sequences and the like (in which case the display is mediated by another textual function). Examples of the former would include the extraordinary shot of Gary Cooper lying under the hut toward the end of *Man of the West* (1958), his body momentarily filling the CinemaScope screen. Or some of the images of Lee Marvin in *Point Blank* (1967), his body draped over a railing or framed in a doorway. Examples of the latter would include the credit sequence of *Man of the West* again (an example to which Willemen refers), and *Junior Bonner* (1972).

The presentation of Rock Hudson in Sirk's melodramas is a particularly interesting case. There are constantly moments in these films in which Hudson is presented quite explicitly as the object of an erotic look. The look is usually marked as female. But Hudson's body is *feminized* in those moments, an indication of the strength of those conventions which dictate that only women can function as the objects of an explicity erotic gaze. Such instances of 'feminization' tend also to occur in the musical, the only genre in which the male body has been unashamedly put on display in mainstream cinema in any consistent way. (A particularly clear and interesting example would be the presentation of John Travolta in *Saturday Night Fever* (1977).)

It is a refusal to acknowledge or make explicit an eroticism that marks all three of the psychic functions and processes discussed here in relation

18

to images of men: identification, voyeuristic looking, and fetishistic looking. It is this that tends above all to differentiate the cinematic representation of images of men and women. Although I have sought to open up a space within Laura Mulvey's arguments and theses, to argue that the elements she considers in relation to images of women can and should also be considered in relation to images of men, I would certainly concur with her basic premise that the spectatorial look in mainstream cinema is implicitly male: it is one of the fundamental reasons why the erotic elements involved in the relations between the spectator and the male image have constantly to be repressed and disavowed. Were this not the case, mainstream cinema would have openly to come to terms with the male homosexuality it so assiduously seeks either to denigrate or deny. As it is, male homosexuality is constantly present as an undercurrent, as a potentially troubling aspect of many films and genres, but one that is dealt with obliquely, symptomatically, and that has to be repressed. While mainstream cinema, in its assumption of a male norm, perspective and look, can constantly take women and the female image as its object of investigation, it has rarely investigated men and the male image in the same kind of way: women are a problem, a source of anxiety, of obsessive enquiry; men are not. Where women are investigated, men are tested. Masculinity, as an ideal, at least, is implicitly known. Femininity is, by contrast, a mystery. This is one of the reasons why the representation of masculinity, both inside and outside the cinema, has been so rarely discussed. Hopefully, this article will contribute toward such a discussion.

NOTES

This article was first published in *Screen* 24, 6 (1983).

I would like to thank John Ellis and Andrew Higson for their comments on an earlier draft of this article, which is based on a talk given during the course of a SEFT Day Event on Masculinity held at Four Corners Film Workshop, London, March 19, 1983.

1 See Cook (1982), Neale (1982), Caughie and Skirrow (1982), and Modleski (1982).
2 See Willemen (1981).
3 For further elaboration of these two related points see Safouan (1981).

BIBLIOGRAPHY

Bellour, R. (1975) 'Le Blocage Symbolique,' *Communications* 23: 235–350.
Caughie, J. and Skirrow, G. (1982) 'Ahab, Ishmael, and . . . Mo,' *Screen* 23, 3–4: 54–9.
Cook, P. (1982) 'Masculinity in Crisis?' *Screen* 23, 3–4: 39–46.
Ellis, J. (1982) *Visible Fictions*, London: Routledge.

Modleski, T. (1982) 'Film Theory's Detour,' *Screen* 23, 5: 72–9.
Mulvey, L. (1975) 'Visual Pleasure and Narrative Cinema,' *Screen* 16, 3: 6–18.
_____ (1981) 'Afterthoughts . . . Inspired by *Duel in the Sun*,' *Framework* 15–17: 12–15.
Neale, S. (1982) 'Chariots of Fire, Images of Men,' *Screen* 23, 3–4: 47–53.
Propp, V. (1968) *Morphology of the Folktale*, Austin: University of Texas Press.
Rodowick, D. N. (1982) 'The Difficulty of Difference,' *Wide Angle* 5: 4–15.
Safouan, M. (1981) 'Is the Oedipus Complex Universal?' *m/f* 5–6: 85–7.
Willemen, P. (1981) 'Anthony Mann: Looking at the Male,' *Framework* 15–17: 16–20.

Part I

STAR TURNS

Figure 2 Fred Astaire in *Royal Wedding*

1

VALENTINO, 'OPTIC INTOXICATION,' AND DANCE MADNESS

Gaylyn Studlar

Dance critic Sigmund Spaeth once noted that 'the decade between 1910 and 1920 can be identified primarily as the period in which America went dance mad' (quoted in Stearns 1968: n.p.). The American cultural scene was transformed by a virtually unprecedented interest in dance. Dance madness was characterized by the popularity of new, social dance forms perceived as indecent. At the same time 'art dance' brought a decadent sensuality to the American concert stage, to vaudeville, and to hundreds of local halls across the country as dancers like Ruth St Denis and Roshanara performed interpretive 'ethnic' dances that invariably linked Orientalism and eroticism in capitalizing on a longstanding American fascination with the East and eastern dancing.

As a consequence, by the time Diaghilev's Ballets Russes arrived in the United States in 1916, Americans were already familiar with dance's capacity to disturb sexual and ethnic conventions. In true American entrepreneurial spirit, Gertrude Hoffman's Les Saisons De Ballet Russes had not only proceeded to rip off the Diaghilev/Fokine *Schéhérazade* as early as 1911, but she also co-opted Diaghilev's *Cleopâtre* and Strauss's opera *Salome*. The latter had an aborted debut at the Metropolitan Opera House, killed by censorship, but Hoffman's dance version persisted nicely, with one critic remarking: 'It grovels, it rolls in horrible sensuality . . . can we endure this indecent physical display' (Kendall 1979: 75)? How indeed? Dance was developing an astonishing physicality: nationwide it was regarded as 'slightly dangerous,' or as one critic called it, an 'optic intoxication,' that was 'awakening all our latent and barbaric sensibilities' (Kendall 1979: 119).[1]

Elizabeth Kendall notes that dance's shocking displays of the body possessed 'a special appeal for women – perhaps because of their very unrestraint' (Kendall 1979: 80). After the turn of the century, women filled concert halls to view matinée dance performances. They enthusiastically responded to the demonstrations of physical freedom offered to them by female dancers who, in embracing modern idioms of dance, appeared bare-legged and bare-footed, sometimes in defiance of censors. In 1920, one female commentator pointedly criticized Americans for being 'below par in appreciation of dancing' because:

We are still prudes . . . the minute a dancer appears there is a tightening of the muscle and a closing of the mind, as prone as we are to be ashamed of the body. We are still shocked by bare feet.

(Russell 1920: n.p.)

Women were so dominant in American dance that it was suggested that the participation of more men 'would help relieve the dance of the curse of femininity and cure us of the false idea that dancing is female and frippery' (Caspary 1926: 60). Nevertheless, when male dancers did appear, they often were derided. Vaslav Nijinsky provoked special antagonism among the nation's male critics who dismissed him for his 'lack of virility' and 'unprepossessing effeminacy' (MacDonald 1975: 174–5);[2] yet, it was assumed that he appealed to women; a *New York Journal* reporter asked: 'what is it . . . that exercises such an extraordinary fascination? His charms appear to lie entirely in his figure. His face can hardly be an attraction, unless there are some women who love ugliness' (MacDonald 1975: 179).[3]

Because dance was so closely associated with a heightened awareness of the body, its fascination for women was noted with varying degrees of alarm. In spite of art dance's controversial inscriptions of the human body, aesthetic motivation (and European inspiration) often provided an adequate excuse for the shock of the new. As a result, condemnations of dance were frequently directed beyond the proscenium arch, at American social dancing, which was fostering a startling casual intimacy between men and women (Erenberg 1981: 154).[4] Objectionable dances like the tango, turkey trot, and grizzly bear were denounced by one Catholic clergyman as being 'as much a violation of the seventh commandment as adultery' (Loxley 1939: 8).

Angela McRobbie has suggested that dance evokes strong emotional response from females and occupies a unique place in many women's fantasies (McRobbie 1990: 41–4), yet film scholars have paid scant attention to the link between film, dance, and female-centered spectatorship. One notable convergence of these elements was played out in complex intertextual terms through the career of dancer turned actor Rudolph Valentino. Recently Valentino has become the center of scholarly interest, largely because of his overwhelming popularity among female film audiences of the 1920s. His great number of women fans were counterpointed in their devotion by his well-documented rejection by American men: in terms of popular discourse, he was a 'pink powder puff,' a 'wop,' and, in the opinion of the *Chicago Tribune*, the most influential instructor in Hollywood's effeminate 'national school of masculinity' (Anger 1981: 107).

The female cult surrounding Valentino's 'ambiguous and deviant identity' has been read as a radical subversion of traditional American gender ideals (Hansen 1986: 20–1). Certainly he appeared to violate twentieth-century codes of American masculinity rooted in a Rooseveltian virility cult, and his popularity as a 'Latin Lover' also seemed to contradict the virulent xenophobia directed during the 1920s at immigrants from southern and eastern Europe. That xenophobia has led Sumiko Higashi to ask: 'Was it coincidental that Valentino achieved stardom as a Latin lover during the same years that Italian anarchists Sacco and Vanzetti were unjustly tried and executed?' She concludes that 'Such questions require a more detailed probing of history than has been provided by previous scholarly work on Valentino' (Higashi 1991: 116). But what aspects of history should we probe to understand the relationship between Valentino and the historical moment in which he achieved fame?

As I have argued elsewhere, Valentino's appeal to women spectators cannot be understood in isolation from the intertextual web of discourses that supports and shapes films (Studlar 1989; Studlar 1991). As contradictory as Valentino's stardom may seem, it was the logical result of trends already apparent in film and other cultural arenas. In this article, I wish to explore how one of these arenas – dance – figures as an important dimension of Valentino's controversial masculinity. I will argue that Valentino's dance background was a significant factor in shaping his textual and extratextual 'construction' (and reception) as a male matinée idol for women, and that dance conventions figured heavily in his representation of masculinity. Thus, I am suggesting that the paradoxical rise to fame of Rudolph Valentino can only be understood by reference to the codification of masculinity pre-existent in dance, in both its 'high' and 'low' cultural manifestations. Nevertheless, dance has been all but ignored in attempts to delineate the source and meaning of Valentino's enormous popularity with female audiences or to account for the problematic status of his masculinity within American culture of the 1920s.

THE MELTING POT SIZZLES

The rise of dance culture in the United States between 1910 and 1920 took place within a broader ideological framework marked by women's growing economic and sexual emancipation. To many observers, American women's challenge to traditional sexual roles and male domestic authority was exemplified by the popularity of tango teas and nightclub dancing. In the 1910s, dancers like Maurice Mouvet, Vernon and Irene Castle, Mr and Mrs Douglas Crane, Joan Sawyer and Carlo Sebastian, and Bonnie Glass and Rudolph Valentino appeared in nightclubs that catered to both men and women. However, in nightclub ballroom dance exhibitions, the sexually transgressive aspects of popular dance, as well as its all too obvious violations of class and ethnic norms, still could be controlled. One demonstration of how that regulation might be achieved occurred with the tango.

Credited with bringing both the tango and the apache dance to the United States, cabaret dancer Maurice Mouvet consciously exploited the sensual, lower-class origins of these dances. Establishing a precedent for other dance teams, Maurice also exploited the apparent ethnic contrast between himself as a dark 'foreigner' (he was really from Brooklyn) and his female partners, particularly blonde Madeleine d'Arville (Mouvet 1915: 35–46; Erenberg 1981: 165). As with Valentino, the dangerous 'Latin gigolo' aspect of Maurice's appeal was inseparable from his association with dances (like the tango and apache) that played out ritualized extremes of sexual domination and submission. It was no surprise then that Maurice was regarded as a 'tiger' for women to 'both desire and fear' (Erenberg 1981: 165), an ambivalence of response later exploited with even greater success in Valentino's career. Ted Shawn cynically suggested that Americans' extreme self-consciousness and their fear of being different contributed to the toning down of dances like the tango (Shawn 1936: 47).[5] Public discourse usually cited moral concerns behind the demand that suggestive and barbaric dances be cleaned up. In any case, the era's most popular dancing team, British-born Vernon Castle and his fashion-setting American wife, Irene, happily obliged. Irene commented in their autobiography: 'If Vernon had ever looked into my eyes with smoldering passion during the tango, we should have both burst out laughing' (Castle 1914: 164).

Less amenable to moral safeguards than cabaret dancing and accordingly regarded with disdain by social commentators were the afternoon 'tango teas' in which women rented male escorts to take them through the new steps. These teas were condemned as a dangerous violation of sexual, ethnic, and class norms: middle-class women were participating in the 'careless forming of undesirable acquaintants, the breaking down of barriers of necessary caution' (Erenberg 1981: 82). The paid dance partners at tango teas were often immigrant, lower-class Italians and Jews who had acquired a sufficient veneer of clothes and manners to allow them to cater to American women's new preoccupation with the pleasure of dance (Erenberg 1981: 83). If, as Irene Castle declared, 'dancing is the language of the body' (Erenberg 1981: 166), then the women who frequented tango teas were learning to speak in a foreign dialect. Dance was making the American melting pot sizzle.

Tango teas were regarded as evidence of how, more generally, American women were changing gendered norms of behavior. Although worrisome in the 1910s, these changes were thought to be spiraling out of

26

control in the postwar period. Women's active search for public (and private) pleasure was replacing their traditional role as spiritual and maternal guardian of the domestic sphere. While women were swooning in the embraces of tango pirates, their 'husbands and sons [were] slaving away in downtown offices,' but even these dutiful husbands and sons were not immune from the debilitating influence of dance as a social phenomenon: it was believed that women's '[p]leasure would ultimately force respectable men to ape the manners of these menial and sensual men to hold their own women . . . and this process would leave them lost and adrift, incapable of success' (Erenberg 1981: 83). One editorial remarked ironically that young men should stop worrying about studying law or business: 'why slave in an office or behind a counter when one may dance with the wives of tired businessmen or their youthful daughters and get from $30 to $100 a week for doing it?' ([Tango] clipping 1914: n.p.). Women's pleasure, dance, and the future of American male identity were united in popular discourse even as Rudolph Valentino, film star, would be grafted on to this same controversy.

WOMAN-MADE MAN AND THE 'MALE BUTTERFLY'

With their reversal of the expected gender alignment of sexual commodification, the tango teas vividly demonstrated the dreaded possibilities of a 'woman-made' masculinity, much discussed and denounced in antifeminist tracts, general interest magazines, and popular novels. In 1914, at the height of dance madness in the United States, Michael Monahan warned readers of the magazine *Forum* that Americans were 'suffering from too much womanism,' a situation that was 'preparing the way for a nation of mollycoddles.' Already, Monahan declared, 'the tradition of great men' was lost; taking its place was 'an epicene type [of man] which unites the weakness of both sexes, a sort of man-woman' (Monahan 1914: 878–9). By 1927, Lorine Pruette was telling readers of *The Nation*: 'If it is true that man once shaped woman to be the creature of his desires and needs, then it is true that woman is now remodeling man. . . . the world is fast becoming woman-made' (Pruette 1927: 200).

Rudolph Valentino seemed to exemplify the epicene results of women's perverse search for a new model of masculinity that defied normative American models. As a former paid dancing partner to café society matrons, he was easily dismissed as one of the 'menial and sensual' immigrants who made their living by exploiting women's desire for pleasure. His commodification as a dancer threw him into the category of 'male butterflies,' the ultimate in 'woman-made' masculinity described by one novelist as 'young men of extremely good looks . . . [who are adopted by women] for amusement much as kings in olden times attached jesters to their persons' (Wiley 1926: 8). Valentino, in the words of

27

Adela Rogers St John, represented 'the lure of the flesh,' the male equivalent of the vamp (St John 1924: 21).

Valentino's good looks, however, did not immediately catapult him into film stardom. After playing assorted ethnic villains in the late 1910s, Valentino's first leading role came in *The Four Horsemen of the Apocalypse* (1921), an epic family melodrama that became the biggest box office hit of the 1920s. The notion that such an epic production necessitated the casting of ethnic actors like Valentino to insure its authenticity was implied by promotion and quickly picked up by reviewers. A *New York World* review noted that 'The characters [are] used primarily to give color to the picture – South American natives, Spanish, French, and German specimens – are all strikingly individualized . . .' (*New York World c.* 1921: n.p.); another reviewer remarked of Valentino: 'Here is a particularly well chosen player for type. Especially so since the part calls for an adept dancer of the Argentine tango, for Valentino was a dancer before he was a movie actor' ('*Four Horsemen* Enthralls' 1921: n.p.).

Chosen 'for type,' Valentino was cast as Julio Desnoyers, a character described as a 'romantic South-American hero' and a 'picturesque figure' (*Newark American Tribune* 1921: n.p.). The film exploited the exoticism of non-Anglo ethnicity as well as the audience's familiarity with deviant forms of masculinity, including the 'male butterfly' and the tango tea gigolo. Before he is ever shown on camera, Julio is described as the spoiled heir to an Argentine ranching family. But he is not to blame, for, as the intertitles tell us: 'What chance had Julio Desnoyers to be other than a youthful libertine?' His 'wild ways' are encouraged by his indulgent grandfather, Madariaga. At his grandfather's death, Julio moves with his parents to Paris, where he becomes an artist whose only visible talents are collecting female models and dancing. He relies on the latter, his 'boyhood pastime,' to secure the funds he needs 'to satisfy his extravagant tastes': he teaches aging dowagers how to tango.

In spite of the film's complex family-centered narrative, many of its advertisements were focused on what was assumed to be its primary box office attraction: 'You cannot have known how the tango can be danced until you have seen: *The Four Horsemen of the Apocalypse*,' proclaimed one, while another declared: 'It is a dance for the hot countries, a dance of tropic passion! At first seductively slow then abruptly changing to steps of lightning quickness and lithe grace' ([*Four Horsemen* ad] *c.* 1921: n.p.). Not surprisingly, Valentino's first appearance in the film occurs in a 'stunningly designed' (Walker 1977: 22) dance scene that crystallizes the era's fascination with (and fear of) dance as a stimulus on the sexual imaginations of American women. Dressed in gaucho costume, Valentino/Julio appears in close up, puffing on a cigarette as he stares at a woman in a Buenos Aires dance hall. The foreign setting and costuming are important because they serve to momentarily naturalize and normalize Julio's masculinity by distancing it from the potential feminizing traits (sartorial excess, love of pleasure, avoidance of work, consumption) that were associated with the tango pirate in the United States.

Julio cannot be accused of being a tango pirate at this point in the narrative since he is a native son whose ability to dominate women finds a thoroughly masculine outlet in 'el tango.' The disreputable low origins of the tango as a dance of Argentine pimps and prostitutes are re-asserted through the setting and in the heavily made-up female with whom Julio dances. Displaying a barely constrained animal sexuality, Valentino proceeds to whip the woman's dance partner into submission, then slides her across the dance floor in the sensuous maneuvers of the tango. The woman is far from beautiful, the saloon, obviously working-class, but in spite of this – or rather *because* of this – the effect is devastating: Julio's beauty and sexual appeal are inscribed in terms of the tango's ritualized grace and blatant machismo. Julio is the master of the woman's body in the tango's controversial 'hot hip contact' (Hanna 1988: 164–5), but just as important, he is master of his own. Valentino's body becomes the authoritative instrument through which his character's exotic menace is combined with the erotic potential of a dancer's refined physical expressivity.

This combination of refinement with the dangerous or 'barbaric' was a staple element in Mouvet's cabaret dancing as well as Diaghilev's Ballets Russes. As a concept, it was already being exploited in Hollywood miscegenation dramas of the late 1910s, especially those starring Sessue Hayakawa in which the Oriental male's despotism is played against his overrefinement to help produce, in the words of one ad, the 'delectable romance so inseparably associated with Oriental subjects of the higher class' ([*City of Dim Faces* ad] c. 1918: n.p.).[6] However, in *The Four Horsemen of the Apocalypse*, the barbaric and the refined are expressed through dance, a form linked in popular discourse of the time to women's pleasure and, as Judith Lynne Hanna asserts, a mode of communication that may play to women's superior sensitivity to nonverbal communi-cation (Hanna 1988: 14–15).

The next appearance of dance in *The Four Horsemen of the Apocalypse* occurs in connection with Julio's calculating, self-interested seduction of Marguerite Laurier (Alice Terry), an attractive young woman married to one of his father's friends. The beginning of their affair is set against the backdrop of a decadent Parisian tango 'palace' where dance mad dowagers and their male escorts share space with lesbians in drag. In this debauched atmosphere, Julio displays the suave duplicity associated with the lascivious ethnic seducer, a stereotyped role that Valentino earlier had essayed in films like *Eyes of Youth* (1919). Julio invites

Figure 3 The Four Horsemen of the Apocalypse

Marguerite to his studio. There, after a number of her visits, he ignores her protests and employs a blend of physical force and verbal persuasion to initiate sexual intimacy.

Because of this conventionally 'villainous' behavior, Julio must atone for his sexual transgression and be redeemed through suffering and the realization of true love. Julio and Marguerite's affair is discovered, and they are forced to part. With the advent of the Great War and the loss of Marguerite, Julio realizes a purer love for her, but also a greater responsibility. He dies on a muddy battlefield in France, but effects a ghostly return to encourage Marguerite to fulfill her duty to her now blind husband.

This movement from Julio's apparent misogyny and brutality displayed at the beginning of the film to love and self-sacrifice is not indicative of an 'oscillation of his persona between sadistic and masochistic positions,' as Hansen has claimed of Valentino's films (Hansen 1986: 20–1).[7] Instead, *Four Horsemen of the Apocalypse*, like many other of the star's vehicles, foregrounds a *transformation* of masculinity that resembles Janice Radway's description of the construction of the hero in the modern romance novel (Radway 1984). This literary phenomenon, Carol Thurston suggests, may have had its prototype in Edith M. Hull's sensational novel,

Figure 4 The Four Horsemen of the Apocalypse

The Sheik, made into Valentino's most influential film in 1921 (Thurston 1987: 38–9).

Radway argues that, in Harlequin romances, the male object of desire must undergo 'the imaginative transformation of masculinity to conform to female standards.' Initially possessed of a 'terrorizing effect,' the hero must be revealed to be other than he originally seems since the narrative must prove that male behavior (and, therefore, heterosexual romance) 'need not be seen as contradictory to female fulfillment' (Radway 1984: 147). This is accomplished by showing that the hero has the 'quite unusual ability to express his devotion gently and with concern for his heroine's pleasure' (Radway 1984: 70).

In *The Four Horsemen of the Apocalypse*, the hero's 'terrorizing effect' is inscribed in the opening tango scene, but it should be remembered that misogyny and 'sadomasochism' were highly conventionalized elements in the tango and apache dances promulgated by familiar ethnic dancers like Maurice Mouvet. Thus, the tango can be seen as metaphorically representing the essential reality of patriarchal relations through its dramatic exaggeration of masculine domination and female submission. Its conventions permit the female spectator to enjoyably experience a ritual confrontation with male brutality. Within the suspended time and space

31

of the dance performance, sexual violence is carefully controlled, just as it is in the romance novel so that a reconciliation with masculinity can occur (Radway 1984: 71–3).

As a consequence of this process, the female spectator of *The Four Horsemen of the Apocalypse* did not necessarily participate in a simple masochistic fantasy reproducing the dance partner's submission to the dark, mysterious, brutal man. She may savor the tango as a '*safe* display' (Radway 1984: 70–3) of dangerously eroticized heterosexual relations because she can rely on the conventionalized patriarchal dynamics of dance to displace responsibility for her own arousal on to the powerful male dancer (Radway 1984: 70–3). The actualities of casting and presentation also offer the spectator the imaginative space to enjoy being superior – in class, ethnicity, and/or physical beauty – to the woman in Valentino's arms.

Her presumed superiority also allows the spectator to re-interpret the hero's misogynistic male behavior in a sympathetic light that prepares the way for the reconciliation of masculinity with feminine ideals. For example, when Julio returns to his table with his dance partner, his grandfather suddenly collapses to the floor. Julio roughly discards the woman on his lap when she (thinking, perhaps, that the old man is drunk) laughs at him. However, the female spectator may regard Julio's rejection of the inadequate (i.e. slovenly, lower-class, insensitive) woman as appropriate. Ironically, what the film accomplishes at this moment is the revelation of Julio's 'feminine' side in his tender concern for his grandfather. That tenderness will later be evident in Julio's interaction with his mother and, finally, in his relationship with Marguerite.[8]

Female spectators may have been sensitive to the promise of dance as a transformative experience, one in which they, as well as the hero, might readily participate,[9] In *The Four Horsemen of the Apocalypse*, dance provides a complexly nuanced physical revelation suggesting that the beautiful but apparently misogynistic man possesses a latent capacity to be another kind of lover, one who combines strength and tenderness. The hero's authoritative masculinity promises sexual excitement, but women spectators, like romance readers, may see something else in his refined grace. They may see, in Radway's words, that he is also 'a man who is capable of the same attentive observation and intuitive "understanding" that they believe women regularly accord to men' (Radway 1984: 83). It is of no little interest that an interview with Valentino for *Dance Lover's Magazine* stresses some of these very same qualities in dance: 'Would-be tangoers,' Valentino is quoted as saying, 'should remember that the good dancer gives his exclusive attention to his partner' (Kutner 1925: 22).

Radway argues that such a transformation of masculinity particularly appeals to women unsure of their equality (Radway 1984: 78), a situation surely applicable to many American women in the 1920s. However, it is another aspect of the transformation of masculinity in *The Four Horsemen of the Apocalypse* that probably solidified a wide audience for the film. Promotion capitalized on the spectacle of Julio's transformation from male butterfly into sacrificing war hero. One ad described the situation that requires a transformation: 'Their [the lovers'] butterfly mentalities do not even respond at first to the sudden shock of war that breaks about them'; another declared: 'And when he did enlist it was from a greater force than merely being lonely without his boulevard companions. It was the first time in his life anything but pleasure had actuated him.' Of course, men who danced instead of working for a living were regarded as prime candidates for a little war service, and Julio's attainment of manhood certainly would have provided a measure of wish-fulfillment for a broad segment of the American public: Americans had regarded the Great War as a moral crusade that, in the words of the *Washington Post*, could turn any 'slacking, dissipated, impudent lout' into a man (quoted in Filene 1980: 324). Not surprisingly, Julio would not be the only Valentino character to require such a transformation. This very same approach to masculinity would be continued in publicity for another Valentino film, released the following year, *Moran of the Lady Letty* (1922), a seafaring adventure advertised as the story of 'a soft society dandy whom love made a man' ([*Moran* ad] *c.* 1922: n.p.).

REFIGURING THE 'CULT OF THE BODY'

It has been claimed that Valentino 'inaugurated an explicitly sexual discourse on male beauty' and destabilized 'standards of masculinity with connotations of sexual ambiguity, social marginality and ethnic/racial otherness' (Hansen 1986: 23, 7). However, by the time Valentino brought a dancer's grace and exotic sensuality to film, not only had the tango pirate accomplished all these things but concert dance was imbricated in these same trends. In fact, the latter's iconography literally set the stage for the filmic representation of Valentino.

Influenced by European ballet tastes, dance in the United States was offering a startling transformation of gender norms through androgynous inscriptions of the male body and reversals of sexual role playing, often mediated through the iconography of the Orient that reversed the long-standing male fascination with the culturally taboo (i.e., darker) woman and that conflated a wide range of foreignness, Mediterranean, Middle Eastern, Russian, and Asiatic. Confirmed by the success of Diaghilev's Ballets Russes, high art dance narratives, like tango teas, were often semiotically loaded with ritualized violence within a libidinal economy of excess. As Peter Wollen notes, the Ballets Russes (and the company's many American imitators and precursors that Wollen ignores), not only unsettled gender norms, but helped solidify a cultural fantasy revolving around the Orient as the locus of decadent passion often characterized by a gender inversion of sexual power in which it is the woman who is desiring and the man who is desired (Wollen 1987: 18–20). Conjuring up male anxiety within an area of changing gender relations, Valentino, like *Schéhérazade*'s 'Golden Slave,' seemed to represent the racial/ethnic misplacement of female desire, but the start also stood for the many American males of the late 1910s and 1920s who perceived themselves as being in danger of being desired and dominated rather than desiring and dominating.

By offering up an eroticized and androgynous male body, dance appeared to be threatening an athletic, physically based American masculinity. This idea of masculinity, suggests Jeffrey Hantover, came into prominence early in the century because American middle-class men were having difficulty validating their masculinity through work. More and more of them were confined to bureaucratic and sedentary, i.e., 'feminine' jobs. To offset the lack of traditional masculine validation in the workplace, muscularity achieved through athletic leisure activities became the means for asserting a middle-class manly ideal (Hantover 1980: 285–9). However, dancers like Nijinsky, Ted Shawn, and Valentino undercut the foundation of the masculine ideal of this 'cult of the body' since they were obviously muscular and athletic yet, at the same time, they were regarded as 'effeminate' if not 'queer.'[10] In one of his numerous defenses of the male dancer's masculinity, Ted Shawn declared: 'there is a great difference between having some of the feminine qualities and in being effeminate' (Ryan 1921: 97), but that distinction was lost on most American men, at least in reference to dancers in general and to Valentino in particular.

'WHO SAID LOUNGE LIZARD?'[11]

The early star exploitation of Valentino as a romantic movie idol revolved around the film industry's manipulation of predictable negative reaction against the star as a 'woman-made' dance commodity of dubious foreign origin. In the wake of his appearance in *The Four Horsemen of the Apocalypse*, Valentino's extratextual persona was constructed squarely within the terms applied to male dancers, and his career as a dancer was simultaneously disavowed and exploited in fan magazines and film promotion. As early as 1922, *Motion Picture Magazine* published an article, 'The Perfect Lover,' which described Valentino in terms that both cater to the fascination with the tango pirate and simultaneously attempt to defuse Valentino's transgression of American gender norms. Author Willis Goldbeck describes the actor as 'suave, enigmatic, with a

34

glistening courtesy alien and disarming.' Immediately after this description befitting a gigolo, he advises the reader to: '[F]irst of all dismiss the idea of the sleek and the insidious. There is nothing repellent, nothing unmasculine about Valentino. Merely a heavy exoticism, compelling, fascinating, perhaps a little disturbing . . .' (Goldbeck 1922: 40). In the same year, a Paramount-produced fan magazine reveals a direct (if heavy-handed) approach to the problematic implications of Valentino's former profession. Noting that 'most screen stars [are] capable of taking up other professions,' *Screenland* recites the work-centered accomplishments of other Paramount male stars, then defensively declares: 'Rudolph Valentino could make a good living as a dancer, though he doesn't like it as a profession, but his real qualifications, aside from his skill as an actor, is [*sic*] landscape gardening' ('Most Stars' 1922: 12). As late as 1924, a letter to a newspaper summed up a view of the star that obviously still had currency: 'And as for Rudolph Valentino, I doubt whether he could earn a living outside of a motion picture studio or a dance hall' (Sarason 1924: n.p.).

In spite of such reactions against Valentino and his violation of a functional, work-centered American masculinity, the star's films and their extratextual promotion continued to assume that his fascination for female audiences was inseparable from his association with dance. His films regularly featured a dance scene or scenes that incorporate dance-like movements and rhythms. An example of the latter worthy of discussion is the 'rape' scene in *The Son of the Sheik* (1926). At this point in the film's narrative, Ahmed (Valentino) believes the beautiful street dancer Yasmin (Vilma Banky) has betrayed him, an act resulting in his being brutally beaten. He kidnaps her. Inside his tent, she is defiant. She tries to escape, but he throws her to the ground in stylized apache dance fashion. She gets up to defend herself. They stand face to face as she repeatedly declares that she hates him. Suddenly, he grabs her and kisses her. She resists and runs away. With a measured pace, he very slowly stalks her into the bedroom as she retreats. He wordlessly holds his arms out to encircle her as he moves toward her. The scene ends with a fade out as Ahmed continues to advance on Yasmin.

This scene appears as a highly stylized balletic interpretation of rape. Because of the quality of movement displayed, the scene could hardly be read as being a realistic depiction of sexual assault. Through dance-like movement and repose (sometimes Valentino rests in an arabesque position), the scene may work to make violence acceptable to the film's female audience by controlling and containing the vicious and brutal aspects of male behavior that women might find objectionable or offensive. As Radway explains of Harlequin readers, '[V]iolence is acceptable to them only if it is described sparingly, if it is controlled carefully, or if it is *clearly* traceable to the passion or jealousy of the hero' (Radway

Figure 5 Son of the Sheik

1984: 76). Yasmin, like the romance novel heroines Radway describes, 'is misunderstood by the hero, mistreated and manhandled as a consequence of his misreading' (Radway 1984: 75), but reconciliation between Yasmin and Ahmed can ultimately take place to the satisfaction of the female spectator, in large part, because the conventions of dance have permitted a '*safe* display' of the dangers of masculine domination.

The role of dance in determining Valentino's popularity was most forcefully illustrated when Valentino walked out on his contract with Famous Players-Lasky in late 1922. He and second wife Natacha Rambova, a ballet-trained dancer, embarked on a highly successful dance exhibition tour under the sponsorship of Mineralava beauty clay. The tour no doubt was partly responsible for Valentino's being named the fourth most popular *dancer* in the United States in a poll taken in 1925 ('Who Are?' 1925: 64).[12] If the tour increased dancer lovers' appreciation of Valentino, by way of contrast, the star's endorsement of a cosmetic beauty clay in connection with that tour obviously accomplished little in modifying opinion regarding the actor's offensive woman-made masculinity; neither did newspaper reports of his relationship to Natacha, who had first come to Hollywood with Theodore Kosloff's ballet company. One newspaper article of 1924 reported that Natacha wielded 'a mighty hand over the head of Rudy' (Harrison 1924: 8). It was widely reported that she made unreasonable attempts to control all aspects of his film productions, including his leading ladies; her control over his publicity was considered to be self-evident.

Although his early publicity photos duplicated the starch-shirted attire of Anglo matinée idols like Wallace Reid and Anglicized ethnics like Antonio Moreno, Valentino's publicity photos increasingly displayed him in ethnic costumes from his films and/or assuming the costumes (or lack of them) and poses similar to those employed in dance studies of both interpretive and ballet dancers. His costumes for *The Young Rajah* (1922), designed by Natacha Rambova, resembled those assumed by male dancers in the decorative mode like Arthur Corey and the Marchon brothers, who performed Oriental fare everywhere from vaudeville to society balls like Chicago's Pageant of the East. Designer Adrian's cossack costumes for *The Eagle* (1925) bore an uncanny resemblance to those for Diaghilev's ballet *Thamar*; in addition, Valentino was frequently photographed by Nickolas Muray, whose soft focus 'pictorial' or painterly style was also used in studies for many American danseurs, including Pavlova's former partner, Hubert Stowitts.

The problematic link between dance representations and Valentino's 'woman-made' masculinity was crystallized in an infamous photograph by Helen MacGregor published in the fan magazine *Shadowland* in 1923 (MacGregor 1923: n.p.). In this publicity still, Valentino appears costumed as Nijinsky for his role in *L'Après-Midi d'un Faune*. Although she was not yet married to Valentino, Natacha was thought to be the guiding hand behind Valentino's emulation of the male dancer most criticized in the United States for his effeminacy.[13] Alexander Walker claims that the couple were so hard pressed to explain the photograph that they were forced to pretend that it was a costume test for a film about fauns (Walker 1977: 51).[14]

Rather than redeeming his humble immigrant beginnings in America, the well-known facts of Valentino's multifaceted personal and professional connection to dance, as well as the star's overwhelming popularity among female film audiences, merely confirmed his status as a 'woman-made' man. In spite of publicity pronouncements to the contrary, Valentino's link to the foreign tango pirate was exacerbated by interviews

Figure 6 Valentino's costume for *Young Rajah*

and fan magazine articles in which Valentino pointedly criticized American men as being obsessed with business and bad lovers as well (Valentino 1922). Although this kind of early exploitation of the star as a controversial figure was successful, publicity discourses surrounding Valentino failed to contain lingering questions about his transgressive masculinity.

In similar fashion as the tango's ethnically and sexually titillating effects were first tolerated within American social dance then tamed, Hollywood initially exploited Valentino's decadent differences then reversed itself during the last two years of his career and worked towards

38

a desperate reconciliation of his Otherness with masculine American norms. The reasons for this change can be traced to Hollywood's investment in numerous Valentino imitators and in disturbing rumors that the star's box-office appeal among women was slipping. In 1926, *Photoplay*'s Herbert Howe declared, 'The Valentino storm has blown over, leaving Rudy to paddle his bark by main strength of histrionic ability' (Howe 1926: 53). Textually, the push toward this reconciliation is apparent in Valentino's last three film vehicles. In *Cobra* (1925), Valentino is an aristocratic Italian who leaves his 'first pure love' to preserve his friendship with Jack, a naive American businessman. *The Eagle* (1926) successfully molds Valentino into a more athletic Fairbanks-style 'slavic' hero. His last film, *The Son of the Sheik* (1926), released posthumously, is, in some respects, a parody of the kind of vehicle that had brought Valentino to stardom with a largely female audience.

In early 1926, after newspapers reported that Valentino was aggressively seeking a male audience ('Rudolph Valentino to Change his Act?' 1925: n.p.), the star was interviewed for *Collier's*. In the interview, dance is portrayed as the last resort of an immigrant's honest attempts to make a living. Valentino recounts falling back on his dance talents *after* he has pursued all other alternatives: 'polishing brass, sweeping out stores, anything.' He is quoted as saying of his film career:

> I wanted to make a lot of money, and so I let them play me up as a lounge lizard, a soft, handsome devil whose only aim in life was to sit around and be admired by women. . . . And all the time I was a farmer at heart, and I still am.[15]
>
> (Valentino 1926: 28)

Not only had his stint as a paid dancing partner marked him as a parasitic 'lounge lizard,' but even Valentino's elevation to professional cabaret dancer had done little to make his masculinity less suspect since the professional dancer was regarded as being 'heavily involved in sensual expression, combining the traits of expressiveness, absence of work, love of luxury, and fascination with women' (Erenberg 1981: 85). Only those dancers who appeared to consider dance as purely a business enterprise could hope to be regarded as 'regular fellows'; yet the difficulty of any dancer to achieve a nontransgressive masculinity is illustrated by the fact that even Vernon Castle, the darling of café society until he went off to World War I to train pilots, could not escape slurs. A Detroit newspaper editorial, printed after the dancer's war-related death in 1918, bears uncanny resemblance in tone to the infamous *Chicago Tribune* Pink Powder Puff attack directed at Valentino shortly before his death eight years later:

> Here was a guy who combed his hair back flat an' then polish' it.

He hung around tea tables and wore soft shoes. Th' dames with kale used to pay him so much per second for lettin' 'em tred on his toes while a bunch o' crazy niggers beat a lot o' dishpans. . . . a guy that makes a business of it – you know, it's sort o' queer, ain't it, now . . . all I gotta say is – we was all wrong . . . My hat's off to Vernon Castle.

('The Office Roughneck' 1918: n.p.)

Another newspaper eulogized the dancer as 'the butterfly who became an eagle' ('Bury Capt. Castle' 1918: n.p.).[16] Like Julio in *The Four Horsemen of the Apocalypse*, Vernon's masculinity could be redeemed by death: Valentino would not be so lucky.

WHERE GOOD DANCERS GO

In October of 1926, *The Dance* magazine satirically declared that Hollywood was the heaven of opportunity 'where good dancers go when they die' ('A Dance Mappe' 1926: 25). Valentino's sudden death from peritonitis a little more than a month before the magazine's publication demonstrated a deep if no doubt unintended irony in that statement, and death would not end the debate over Valentino's symbolic place within the perceived crisis in American sexual and gender relations. Even as the Ballets Russes had been poised between old and new aesthetic orders, Valentino had been culturally poised between an old order of masculinity and a utopian feminine ideal, between a sensual excess ascribed to the Old World and the functional ideal of the New. Ultimately, the aesthetic implications of American efficiency, productivity, and economy brought formal changes to the arts in America, including film and dance (Tichi 1987: 75). But the textualization of the body as a kinetic machine would have to wait, at least for a moment, as Hollywood offered women the 'optic intoxication' of Rudolph Valentino and generated a fantastic vision of the reconciliation of masculinity and femininity through a privileging of the dancer's body as a site of expressive knowledge and sensual understanding.

NOTES

My thanks to Adrienne McLean for her invaluable insights into dance history and for her contribution to this article's development.
 1 The popularity in Britain of all-female Salome dinners in which guests dressed in appropriate costume and reproduced Maude Allan's version of the dance of the seven veils was supposedly the impetus for an attempt to prevent a similar Salome craze in the United States. Not only was President Theodore Roosevelt requested to intervene, but theater managers in New York City became 'exceptionally active in guarding against outbreaks of Salomania.'

Quotation from *New York Times*, August 16, 1908, cited in Hanna 1988: 183.

2 Mikhail Mordkin, sometimes called 'The Greek God of Dance,' was often contrasted with Nijinsky. The former's performances were regarded as an exemplar of dance as a manly art, but critics ran hot and cold when it came to Nijinsky's representation of masculinity and were especially hostile towards his 'effeminate' performances in *Narcisse* and *Le Spectre de la Rose.*

3 The racial nature of this particular attack on Nijinsky closely resembles a later commentary on Valentino by Adela Rogers St John. While the *New York Journal* went on to remark that Nijinsky 'has the high cheek bones, the broad flat nose and the thick lips of the Mongolian race,' St John told *Photoplay* readers that Valentino, 'with his small eyes, his flat nose and large mouth, fails to measure up to the standards of male beauty usually accepted in this country' (St John 1924: 21, 17).

4 One example of the American reaction against the moral dangers of concert dance can to be found in the Catholic Theatre Movement, founded in 1913 and devoted to censoring. Members of the organization took a pledge to 'avoid improper plays and exhibitions.' This committee was, of course, very interested in the American premiere of *L'Après-Midi d'un Faune*. See MacDonald 1975: 142.

5 Shawn also suggested a more mundane reason for the tango's decline, that '[T]he tango died because it was impossible in a crowded room to do the figures of the tango.'

6 Although Miriam Hansen gives the impression that Valentino was the first ethnic romantic hero, many of Sessue Hayakawa's films after his appearance in DeMille's *The Cheat* (1915) emphasized the romance between white and the racial Other in a sympathetic light that marks Hayakawa's character as the 'hero.' Often these films appear to rely on one of two solutions to the dilemma of miscegenation: death for the Oriental hero or the discovery of the heroine's mixed blood so that marriage may occur. It is racial ideology, then, that may contribute also to the several tragic endings to Valentino's films. I find this link to Hayakawa's films a promising line of future inquiry with regard to the intertextual status of Valentino's films in a xenophobic culture. However, Hansen finds her explanation for the unhappy endings to Valentino's films in 'the deep affinity between eros and death drive' (Hansen 1986: 29).

7 Hansen believes that Valentino's films (apparently regardless of production date, scenarist, studio, or director) evidence a shared textual inscription of 'the interchangeability of sadistic and masochistic positions within the diegesis'; in passing, she refers to the star as 'auteur,' but she does not follow up the implications of this assertion; instead, she focuses on building a paradigm of non-masochistic female spectatorial position from Freud's essay, 'A Child is Being Beaten' (1919). To do this, Hansen must ignore the fact that Freud concluded that the female subjects of his study found masochistic satisfaction even from the superficially 'sadistic' situation displayed in the third phase of their fantasies. Hansen reverses Freud's conclusion to argue for a 'sadistic' female spectatorial position arising from Valentino's films and from the star's placement in a position analogous to that of the 'whipping boy' described by Freud. See my reply to her article (Studlar 1987). Although its publication occurred too late to allow inclusion in my discussion here, Hansen's *From Babel to Babylon* (1991) does expand the terms of her con-

sideration of Valentino, but she retains this psychoanalytic explanation virtually intact from her 1986 article.

8 It is of no surprise that this same quality of tenderness would be emphasized in later Valentino vehicles. An advertisement for *The Eagle* (1925) declared its hero to be 'As rapacious as an eagle as a bandit, as soft as a woman when the heart rules, this ideal lover Rules Supreme' ([*The Eagle* ad] *c.* 1925: n.p.).

9 On the transformative capacity of dance see Sparshott 1988: 399. More than one fan magazine article caters to the fantasy of dancing with Valentino. In 'When Valentino Taught Me to Dance,' author Mary Winship gives a first-person account. She begins: 'Naturally, I was scared to death. Who wouldn't be?' . . .' [and progresses to this description]: 'His arm supported me like a brace. I swung myself back, closed my eyes, breathed in the music and – followed. I couldn't have been so proud if I'd swum the English channel. . . . The music stopped. Rudolph gallantly applauded. He's really awfully sweet.' See Winship 1922: 45. See also Kutner 1925: 22–3 and Hall 1923: 7–.

10 In film Douglas Fairbanks exemplified the manly 'cult of the body,' but he produced and starred in one of the most heavily dance-inspired films of the 1920s, *The Thief of Bagdad* (1924), a film that fairly reeks of the influence of the Ballets Russes. Michael Morris argues that Valentino's alleged homosexuality is the result of insinuations of recent origin (Morris 1991: 263–4). Although Miriam Hansen mentions 'rumors' of the star's homosexuality circulating in the 1920s (Hansen 1986: 19), I have as yet found no evidence of these rumors in any of my research: the question remains whether Valentino's 'sexual ambiguity' is textually inscribed or primarily the product of stereotypical assumptions about the sexuality of male dancers.

11 Caption to Valentino photo ('Who Said Lounge Lizard?' 1923).

12 Valentino trailed Ted Shawn, Laurent Novikoff, and Buster West in the voting. The article notes: 'Though Rudolph Valentino has not been seen dancing for two or three years, he still retains a following who loyally voted him the fourth most popular dancer in America and who put Mrs. Valentino's name on the gold star list. This is surprising since Mrs. Valentino has never sought fame as an individual artist . . .'

13 After Valentino's death, Adela Rogers St John characterized Natacha as 'dominating, artistic, fascinating' and noted that the couple's 'stormy matrimonial voyage' . . . 'is generally conceded to have greatly injured Rudy's career.' See St John 1927: 29. It is interesting that Natacha's influence on Valentino continues to be portrayed in similar terms. David Gill's and Kevin Brownlow's *Hollywood* documentary television series attributes Valentino's faun photographs and one in which he posed in loin cloth as a Native American spirit guide, 'Black Feather,' to Natacha's 'almost hypnotic influence' over her husband, who 'submitted' to the photographs 'because he loved and admired' his wife. The latter study bears some resemblance to pictures that circulated of Ted Shawn from his ballet *Invocation of the Thunderbird*. For a sympathetic re-evaluation of Natacha's impact on Valentino see Morris 1991.

14 A keen eye can detect that while Nijinsky is shown wearing tights and a leotard in his faun pictures, Valentino is not only nude from the waist up in his, but the actor's spots are merely painted on. The presence of a G-string preserves his modesty.

15 As if to emphasize Valentino's association with normative American masculinity, i.e., the middle-class businessman, a picture of Valentino accompanying

the interview shows the star flourishing a smoking pipe. In *Advertising the American Dream*, Roland Marchand suggests that in the 1920s, advertising for Edgeworth Smoking Tobacco 'suggested that the growing number of women smokers had effeminized cigarettes; men should respond by turning to pipes. . . . Edgeworth proclaimed: "A man looks like a man when he smokes a pipe." ' Marchand discusses the era's attempt to maintain the view of men as functional in contrast to women's decorative status. See Marchand 1985: 191.

16 On the tragic endings in films about dancers see McLean 1991: 1–19. A fascinating and hilarious sound film called *Bolero* (1934) focuses on a fictional male cabaret dancer whose life seems to be a composite of aspects of the lives of Valentino, Mouvet, and Vernon Castle. The film utilizes young George Raft's amazing resemblance to Valentino (maintained as long as the former's mouth is shut). Adding to the goofy fun is William Frawley as Raft's half-brother and Carole Lombard as his sometime dance partner. Following the examples of Vernon Castle and Julio Desnoyers, Raft's character goes off to fight in World War I. He survives, but just long enough to get in one more sexy tango before dying of a war-induced heart condition. Frawley's epitaph for him: 'He was too good for this joint.'

BIBLIOGRAPHY

Anger, K. (1981) *Hollywood Babylon*, New York: Bell Publishing.

'Bury Capt. Castle with War Honors' (1918) unidentified newspaper: n.p., New York Public Library Theater Arts Collection (hereafter cited as NYPLTA), Castle Scrapbooks, February 20.

Caspary, V. (1926) 'The Twilight of the Dance Gods: Merely a Theory Regarding Masculine Arms and Feminine Ankles,' *The Dance* 6, 2: 19, 60.

Castle, I. and V. (1914) *Modern Dancing*, New York: Harper.

City of Dim Faces [advertisement] (*c.* 1918) unidentified clipping, n.p., NYPLTA.

'A Dance Mappe of These U.S. Culture: Culture Made Pleasant' (1926) *The Dance* 6, 6: 24–5.

[*The Eagle* advertisement] for Rialto Theater, New York (*c.* 1925): n.p., unidentified clipping, NYPLTA.

Erenberg, L. (1981) *Steppin' Out: New York Nightlife and the Transformation of American Culture, 1890–1930*, Chicago, IL: University of Chicago Press.

Filene, P. (1980) 'In Time of War' in E. and J. Pleck (eds) *The American Man*, Englewood Cliffs, NJ: Prentice-Hall.

'*Four Horsemen* Enthralls Viewers' (1921) *San Francisco Call*: n.p., clipping, NYPLTA, June 28.

Goldbeck, W. (1922) 'The Perfect Lover,' *Motion Picture Magazine* 23, 4: 40–1, 94.

Hall, G. (1923) 'Women I like to Dance with, By Rudolph Valentino,' *Movie Weekly* 7, clipping file NYPLTA, January 27.

Hanna, J. L. (1988) *Dance, Sex and Gender*, Chicago, IL: University of Chicago Press.

Hansen, M. (1986) 'Valentino, Ambivalence, and Female Spectatorship,' *Cinema Journal* 25, 4: 6–32.

—— (1991) *From Babel to Babylon*, Cambridge, MA: Harvard University Press.

Hantover, J. (1980) 'The Boy Scouts and the Validation of Masculinity' in E.

Pleck and J. Pleck (eds) *The American Man*, Englewood Cliffs, NJ: Prentice-Hall.

Harrison, H. (1924) 'Rudolph Valentino Talks about his Poetry, Mash Notes and Sheiks,' *Brooklyn Eagle* 8, clipping file, NYPLTA, September 21.

Higashi, S. (1991) 'Ethnicity, Class, and Gender in Film: DeMille's *The Cheat*' in L. Friedman (ed.) *Unspeakable Images: Ethnicity and the American Cinema*, Urbana: University of Illinois Press.

Howe, H. (1926) 'Close ups and Long Shots,' *Photoplay* 29 February: 52.

Kendall, E. (1979) *Where She Danced*, New York: Knopf.

Kutner, M. (1925) 'Valentino's Own Version of The Tango,' *Dance Lover's Magazine* 3, 5: 22–3.

Loxley, E. (1939) 'The Turkey-trot and Dance America 1900–1920,' *U.S. History Magazine*, December: 8.

MacDonald, N. (1975) *Diaghilev Observed by Critics in England and the United States 1911–1929*, New York: Dance Horizons.

MacGregor, H. (1923) *Shadowland*: unpaginated clipping, NYPLTA [Photo of Valentino].

McLean, A. (1991) 'The Image of the Ballet Artist in Popular Film,' *Journal of Popular Culture* 25, summer: 1–19.

McRobbie, A. (1990) '*Fame, Flashdance*, and Fantasies of Achievement' in J. Gaines and C. Herzog (eds) *Fabrications: Costume and the Female Body*, New York: Routledge.

Marchand, R. (1985) *Advertising the American Dream*, Berkeley: University of California Press.

Monahan, M. (1914) 'The American Peril,' *Forum* 51: 878–82.

Moran of the Lady Letty [advertisement] unidentified newspaper (*c.* 1922): n.p., clipping file, NYPLTA.

Morris, M. (1991) *Madam Valentino: the Many Lives of Natacha Rambova*, New York: Abbeville Press.

'Most Screen Stars Capable of Taking Up Other Professions' (1922) *Screenland* (Dallas, Texas) 1, 2: 12.

Mouvet, M. (1915) *Art of Dancing*, New York: Schirmer.

New York World (*c.* Sept., 1921): n.p., clipping file, NYPLTA [Review of *Four Horsemen of the Apocalypse*].

Newark American Tribune (Sept., 1921): n.p., clipping file, NYPLTA. [Caption to *Four Horsemen of the Apocalypse* photo].

'The Office Roughneck Takes His Hat Off to Vernon Castle' (1918) *Detroit Journal*: n.p., NYPLTA, Castle Scrapbooks, Robinson Locke Collection.

Pruette, L. (1927) 'Should Men Be Protected?' *The Nation* 125: 200–1.

Radway, J. (1984) *Reading the Romance*, Chapel Hill: University of North Carolina Press.

'Rudolph Valentino to Change his Act?' (1925) *New York World*: n.p., clipping file NYPLTA, November 22.

Russell, O. (*c.* 1920) 'U.S. Below Par in Appreciation of Dancing,' unidentified newspaper, Cleveland, Ohio: n.p., Denishawn Dance Scrapbook, New York Public Library Dance Collection, Lincoln Center, hereafter cited as NYPLDC.

Ryan, V. (1921) 'Should Men Be Graceful?' *Physical Culture Magazine*, January: 36, 97.

St John, Adela Rogers (1924) 'What Kind of Men Attract Women Most?' *Photoplay* 25, 5: 40–1, 110–12.

—— (1927) 'Why do Great Lovers Fail as Husbands' *Photoplay* 32: 28–30, 116–17.

Sarason, C. (1924) *Daily News*: n.p., clipping file NYPLTA [Letter] September 9.

Shawn, T. (1936) *The American Ballet*, New York: Henry Holt and Company.

Sparshott, F. (1988) *Off the Ground: First Steps to a Philosophical Consideration of Dance*, Princeton, NJ: Princeton University Press.

Stearns, M. (1968) 'Jazz dance,' chapter 13, unidentified book: n.p., Tango file NYPLDC.

Studlar, G. (1987) 'Dialogue,' *Cinema Journal* 26, 2: 51–2.

_____ (1989) 'Discourses of Ethnicity and Gender: the Construction and De-(con)struction of Rudolph Valentino as Other,' *Film Criticism* 13, 2: 18–35.

_____ (1991) 'The Perils of Pleasure? Fan Magazine Discourse as Women's Commodified Culture in the 1920s,' *Wide Angle* 13, 1: 6–33.

[Tango] Unidentified newspaper clipping (*c.* 1914): n.p., Tango file, NYPLDC.

Thurston, C. (1987) *The Romance Revolution*, Urbana: University of Illinois Press.

Tichi, C. (1987) *Shifting Gears: Technology, Literature, Culture in Modernist America*, Chapel Hill: University of North Carolina Press.

Valentino, R. (1922) 'Woman and Love,' *Photoplay* 21: 41–2, 106–7.

_____ (1926) (with J. Winkler) ' "I'm tired of being a Sheik," ' *Collier's* 77: 28–9.

Walker, A. (1977) *Rudolph Valentino*, Harmondsworth: Penguin.

'Who are America's Favorite Dancers?' (1925) *The Dance* 5: 12–13.

'Who Said Lounge Lizard?' (1923) *Screenland*: n.p., clipping file, NYPLTA, [Caption to Valentino photo].

Wiley, J. (1926) *Triumph*, New York: Minton, Balch and Co.

Winship, M. (1922) 'When Valentino Taught Me to Dance,' *Photoplay* 21: 45, 118.

Wollen, P. (1987) 'Fashion/Orientalism/The Body,' *New Formations* 1: 5–33.

2

'FEMINIZING' THE SONG-AND-DANCE MAN

Fred Astaire and the spectacle of masculinity in the Hollywood musical

Steven Cohan

It's a truism of show business, which the Hollywood musical celebrates again and again, that a star performer can quite literally and quite spectacularly stop the show as proof of his or her extraordinary talent. The female performer's ability to stop the show (and the story) is a familiar enough feature of Hollywood cinema, extending from the musical genre itself to the nightclub or saloon setting of other genres, like the gangster story or the Western, which provides the star with a ready excuse to do a number. A recurring backdrop for the female star generally, Laura Mulvey has pointed out, the show setting equates femininity with spectacle; it crystallizes her position as a static icon of male desire, differentiating feminine exhibitionism and passivity from masculine voyeurism and agency. In particular, as Mulvey's own reference to Ziegfeld and Berkeley suggests, because of its reliance on spectacle the musical would appear to be the genre most responsible for reproducing this reductive binary opposition of female performer and male spectator, what with the kaleidoscopic array of chorus girls working so hard and so often to feminize spectacle for a masculine viewer on screen as well as off.[1] This division of labor, most obvious in the numerous gold diggers and sugar daddies who populate the genre from *Broadway Melody* (1929) to *Gentlemen Prefer Blondes* (1953), also makes itself felt in the narrative preoccupation, in musical after musical, with producing the ideal heterosexual couple.

However, as Steve Neale notes in passing when discussing male spectacle, the musical is 'the only genre in which the male body has been unashamedly put on display in mainstream cinema in any consistent way' (Neale 1983: 15). This Hollywood genre actually differs from others because it features men in showstopping numbers as well as women. In making such a blatant spectacle of men, the musical thus challenges the very gendered division of labor which it keeps reproducing in its generic plots. For when he stops the show (and the story) to perform a socko number and fulfill what the genre takes to be his destiny as a star, the Hollywood song-and-dance man also connotes, to use Mulvey's fine phrase, 'to-be-looked-at-ness' (Mulvey 1975: 19). He therefore finds himself in rather problematic territory – at least as far as film theory is concerned – for the genre has placed him in the very position which the representation system of classic Hollywood cinema has traditionally designated as 'feminine.'

Such 'feminization' of male musical stars involves more than simply making them, as Neale puts it, 'objects of an explicitly erotic gaze' in a pattern just reversing the gendered terms of sexual objectification (Neale 1983: 14–15). Rather, I am arguing here through the example of Fred Astaire, something other than a conventional objectification of the male body is at stake with the spectacle of a song-and-dance man in the musical, because his 'feminization' arises from a highly self-conscious and theatrical performance that constructs his masculinity out of the show-business values of spectatorship and spectacle.[2]

The complexity of male spectacle in the Hollywood musical results from several important factors, which I shall be treating in some detail as I discuss Fred Astaire in the context of the musical genre and its production of male stardom. But let me summarize my claims at the outset: To start with, when this most exemplary of male musical performers does a star turn, even if the number means to sustain his power as dominant male in the narrative (as when he dances in order to authorize his patriarchal position as teacher, director, or lover of a younger female co-star like Cyd Charisse or Jane Powell), because he halts the linearity of the story with his musical performance, he also stops the show to insist upon his own ability to signify 'to-be-looked-at-ness.' Whether relying on props and special effects or simply building off of the star's physical grace and agility, Astaire's solo numbers in particular were obviously engineered to do more than simply texture a characterization or advance a story's linear movement towards closure, since they interfere with the narrative economy of his films by foregrounding the value of his performance as spectacle. Astaire's numbers thus oftentimes exceed both linear narrativity and the heterosexual (that is, 'straight' in the cultural as well as the narrative sense) male desire that fuels it. At the same time, because of their relative extradiegetic autonomy, the numbers disrupt the politics of the erotic gaze; they break the diegetic illusion that maintains spectatorial distance from the image, and with it the conventional demarcation of sexual difference, in effect allowing the star to acknowledge being looked at by an audience and even, through direct address, to return the look too. As a result of his clearly marked spectacular value as a musical star, I am concluding, Astaire's screen persona makes full use of all the technology the industry has to offer, paradoxically enough, in order to authenticate the ground for the audience's fascination with his male image in the so-called 'feminine' tropes of narcissism, exhibitionism, and masquerade.

In sum, to see Hollywood's song-and-dance men connoting 'to-be-looked-at-ness' does not imply as a consequence that musical spectacle automatically 'feminizes' the male star to the point of erasing his masculinity (or sexual difference) altogether. In pointing out the *comparable* spectacularity of the male and female musical star, I therefore do not mean to suggest that their treatment is even-handed and symmetrical: she is neither 'masculinized' in turn nor is her spectacular value made exactly the same as his. A pretty girl remains a melody in the musical, so the showgirl and all that she implies about female spectacle do not diminish in importance for the genre's sexual differentiation of male and female stars.[3] But what the Hollywood musical does foreground above all else when numbers interrupt the flow of narrative is the production of masculinity and femininity alike out of highly theatricalized performances of gender.

STOPPING THE SHOW (AND THE STORY)

The Hollywood musical has always been seen as an expression of unbounded joy and physical liberation because the libidinal energy released in the numbers is not linear, that is, not consistent with the conservative, teleological economy of classical narrative. In *Silk Stockings* (1957), Astaire's last musical as a leading man, Cyd Charisse makes a sarcastic comment which well summarizes the uneasy relation between narrative and number. Trying to seduce her through Cole Porter's 'All of You,' Astaire (Steve Canfield) complains, 'Don't you ever let yourself go?' 'Go where?' Charisse (Ninotchka) wants to know, taking his question literally. 'I don't know,' he replies, 'Just go, go, *go!*' He lets go with a burst of dancing. 'Don't you ever feel so happy that you just want to dance all round the room?' he asks afterwards. 'Happiness is a reward of industry and labor,' she retorts. 'Dancing is a waste of time.' 'I like wasting time,' he responds, and then repeats his show of fancy footwork: 'Well?' 'You go, go, go,' Charisse concludes after watching him dance, 'but you don't get anywhere.'

Though Astaire replies, rather archly, 'You're telling *me*,' in order to place her comment back into its narrative context of seduction, Charisse's remark lingers, emblematic of what Astaire's numbers can do, do do (that is, interrupt, stall, and exceed) to the libidinal economy of linear narrative. For once he begins performing, twirling around the shiny parquet floors, his body's energy and motion redefine narrative space in completely visual terms as spectacle. His musical numbers exert a non-narrative, extradiegetic pressure – contemplation of the star performing

– that remains in excess of the conservative narrative activity of the film's plot.

Truth to tell, when all is said and done I do recognize that I am still talking about a Hollywood product. Most often the tension between the excesses of a film's musical numbers and its compacted narrative appears easily enough resolved in the closure; then the energy of a number does appear to have gone somewhere, namely into the linear direction of a story. Or at least this is the view of 'the ideally integrated musical,' always held up by the industry as the genre's highest aesthetic achievement, 'a musical where song, dance, and story are artfully blended to produce a combined effect' (Mueller 1984: 28). A frequently cited example of the perfect integration of narrative and number is 'Dancing in the Dark' in *The Band Wagon* (1953), where, as John Mueller has shown with his detailed analysis of the choreography, 'the change in the relationship between Astaire and [Cyd] Charisse, at once subtle and profound, is accomplished entirely in dance terms' (Mueller 1984: 35). Narratively speaking, their duet resolves the conflict in ages and musical styles which has stood in the way of their collaboration on stage, and in providing them with a basis for working together as a professional team, the number moves them on to the next segment of the narrative action, when they take the show out of town. In similar fashion, before he is through dancing to 'All of You' in *Silk Stockings*, Astaire gets 'somewhere' with Charisse because he does succeed in luring her into dancing with him, however stiffly, as the music swells to a lush string arrangement of the melody. Afterwards, as she reclines contentedly on a rug, he remarks, with an irony that transcends this scene – indeed, the entire picture – 'so, uh, dancing is a waste of time?'

When I claim that musical numbers go, go, go without necessarily getting anywhere in the story but without being a waste of time either, I am, therefore, intentionally reading *against* the value of integration; but, at the same time, I do not mean to suggest that musical numbers bear no relation at all to their narrative context. Rather, I want to revise our understanding of the kind of pressure a number exerts on the economizing drive of the narrative frame, especially when it concerns the spectacle of a *male* star peforming, since this situation also overturns the customary way in which masculinity is assumed to advance and dominate linear narrative.

In his analysis of the Hollywood musical, Rick Altman argues that a musical plot does not operate in the linear fashion one expects of other Hollywood genres but moves according to a vertical principle of formal economy. Instead of arranging its basic narrative units (scenes, settings, character traits, and most importantly, musical numbers) in simple succession, the musical plots them as a series of parallel relations.

[W]e alternate between the male focus and the female focus, working our way through a prepackaged love story whose dynamic principle remains the difference between male and female. *Each segment must be understood not in terms of the segments to which it is causally related but by comparison to the segment which it parallels.*

(Altman 1987: 20, his emphasis)

Building this dual focus around character (and a principle of comparability and simultaneity) rather than plot (and a principle of chronology and sequence), this paradigmatic structure defines sexual difference in terms of the primary opposition of masculinity and femininity, and this binary in turn generates a series of secondary opposing values (like age/youth, riches/beauty, rural/urban, nature/technology) which can be made more specific than the masculine/feminine binary to a given narrative context and as a consequence appear reconciled in the course of two hours. The harmonizing (in all senses) of those various oppositions then supplies both the cause and the effect of the heterosexual couple's successful formation as a union of complementary differences at the film's end.

Almost all Hollywood musicals follow this paradigm, which structurally organizes the numbers as well as the narrative. In *Royal Wedding* (1951) Astaire stars with Jane Powell as a brother–sister team modeled on his own act with sister Adèle in vaudeville and on Broadway. The stars perform two numbers together early in the film, one ('Ev'ry Night at Seven') which features him singing while she looks on mutely, and another ('Open Your Eyes') which reverses the labor, with Powell singing while Astaire stands by idly against the piano waiting for their waltz to begin. When it does, he dances primarily to support her – in what must be his most self-effacing musical performance since his debut opposite Joan Crawford in *Dancing Lady* in 1933. The two numbers balance each other with a display of different but complementary talents that equates the female's with singing, the male's with dancing.

The stars' solos then reinforce this homology. On board the ship taking them to London, Astaire rehearses an improvised dance with a hat rack in his sister's absence ('Sunday Jumps'), and two numbers later Powell rehearses a song in their hotel room ('The Happiest Day of My Life'). Similarly, in the second half of the film, Powell sings her declaration of love to Peter Lawford after the opening night of the show ('Too Late Now'), and moments later, Astaire articulates his feelings for Sarah Churchill by doing a spectacular dance up and down the walls and ceiling of his hotel room ('You're All the World to Me'). To underscore this dual focus, the overture playing behind the main titles is a medley of the music from these last two solos.

The final two show numbers then expand upon this dual focus to emphasize the theatricality of both the stars' performance style and their relationship in the diegesis as a heterosexual show business couple. Performed to represent the opening night of their show in London, 'How Can You Believe Me When I Said I Love You, When You Know I've Been a Liar All My Life?' casts Astaire as a gum-chewing, low-life cad and Powell, in a black wig and tight sweater, as the girl friend he has lied to, the number explicitly playing against – and so implying the similar theatricality of – their familiar screen images as debonair gentleman and blonde ingenue respectively. This is the only number in the film in which both stars sing as well as dance together, possibly because with its broad colorful strokes it aims to satirize binarized male/female roles by showing their basis in outlandish gender stereotypes. The number even ends with Powell punching out Astaire!

Their final duet together, 'I Left My Hat in Haiti,' rhymes with the opening as Astaire once again performs with a mute Powell, who doesn't appear until the second half. In contrast to that simpler first dance, which remained (by MGM standards) realistically stage-bound, this big production number – overblown, incoherent, and terrific to watch – emphasizes the value of cinema's version of theatricality. Awash with color on one of those MGM theater stages which seem to extend backwards for two city blocks, this final number fills no apparent plot function whatsoever and, indeed, goes even further to collapse whatever narrative line the verse tries to construct for itself (something about Astaire having forgotten his blue–grey fedora when leaving a one-night stand) in the interest of filling the screen with theatrical spectacle (scrims, moving stages, brightly costumed dancers, crayola-colored sets, a live monkey), which provides the background against which Astaire, in a cream-colored suit, always commands the viewer's eye.[5]

Representing sexual difference through its two stars, *Royal Wedding* operates in accordance with the dual focus of the musical genre, but upon close inspection the numbers pose something of a problem for that paradigmatic narrative structure. Many studies of the musical have explained quite well how dance functions as a metaphor for sexual differentiation, seduction, and consummation, nowhere more brilliantly, subtly, or consistently so than in Astaire's films.[6] Given the stress which the genre's dual focus places on the sexual relation of musical performers, *Royal Wedding* is an especially uncharacteristic Astaire musical since it does not have him romance his sexual partner through dance. The show numbers amplify a brother–sister relationship, placing teamwork over romance as the objective of male–female pairing. As the film ends, Alan Jay Lerner's script even implies, albeit very discreetly, that this musical teaming is indeed standing in for some other kind of sexual relation: when Astaire and Powell rush to tell their London agent that they want to get married, he exclaims, 'But I thought you two were related!'

Figure 7 Fred Astaire dancing to 'Sunday Jumps'

Exactly. Even though the plot recounts two romances (Astaire and Churchill, Powell and Lawford), the primary relation structuring the film – the one given musical density and specificity by the numbers – is the brother–sister act, with its stress on family sameness (and talent) over heterosexual difference (and desire). As a result of their function in elaborating upon the musical abilities, collaboration, and intimacy of the sibling team, the numbers in this film do not support either the narrative economy of conventional heterosexual romancing or the traditional sexual binary of the female as a show, the male as a spectator.[7]

Performed for an actual audience within the film, Astaire's four show

Figure 8 Fred Astaire dancing to 'You're All the World to Me'

numbers with Powell openly acknowledge the stars' comparable status as spectacle. During the shipboard dance to 'Open Your Eyes,' in fact, the dancers lose their balance because of the unstable movement of the ocean liner, which causes them to slip and slide across the tilting floor, even to fall into the laps of some spectators. In the context of these show numbers and their increasing appeal to spectacle over story, Astaire's two famous solos are worth a second look for the way they also focus attention on the spectacle of his body. 'Sunday Jumps' dispenses with its lyric altogether to serve as the most non-narrative of the eight numbers. Deriving its rhythm initially from a metronome, and its choreography

53

from Astaire's spontaneous interaction with the physical objects that surround him in the ship's gym, the number turns his dancing into pure physical play. His boundless energy moves him in all directions around the room for the sheer pleasure of it and, as he gets entangled in the various machines during the middle of the dance, his chiding of his own thin and decidedly unmuscular body also implicitly makes fun of the weighty body-builders who have nothing on the physical strength necessary for his brand of light stepping. One effect of this number is that Astaire's body appears to transcend the cinematic apparatus, which seems simply to be catching him in action; in comparison, 'You're All the World to Me' foregrounds the apparent ability of his body to defy gravity through dance, the number going to the other extreme of celebrating Astaire's relation to the apparatus (emphasized all the more by the publicity explaining the technology of the dance's complicated production). If the first solo makes an audience think, 'wow, look at what he can do!' the second makes them wonder, 'wow, how did they do that?'

In keeping with Astaire's style of choreography generally, neither number concludes with the kind of bravura finish that makes the rest of the dance diminish in intensity or effect. The first solo ends with him lifting the hat rack, twirling around with it on his shoulders, then quickly pressing it up over his head and swinging it around along the floor, so that he closes with it cradled along the line of his body; then he and his 'partner' bow to the silent applause of an imaginary audience. The second number ends even more quietly: after literally dancing all around the room, he concludes by simply sitting down and contemplating Sarah Churchill's photograph (purloined from the street display of his own show), in very much the same position he was in when the number opened and then again later when he paused to look at her photo halfway through. Nor, from a formalist consideration, is either number very economically designed as a linear structure meant to reach a climax with the minimum expenditure of energy (though both are impeccably timed in terms of the dancing itself and the technological difficulties of shooting the choreography to a prerecorded track, just as the musical scoring of each is structured to advance the movement of the dance through time and to regulate its rhythm in space). In the first solo, Astaire moves around the gym at random; it is only after he fails to lift the hat rack and starts 'working out' with the equipment, though in a highly self-mocking fashion, that the number can be said to have any kind of discernible direction insofar as it finishes with a lift that he couldn't perform before. In the second number, he goes around the room twice, the first time hopping from chair to wall to ceiling, the second time jumping around more vigorously and then tap dancing on the ceiling; this repetition of his tour round the room causes the number to redouble upon itself, the second half offering a kind of encore before the number is even over.

Both numbers, finally, rely on props (the hat rack and gym equipment in one, the photograph and, much more subtly, the cinematic apparatus producing the special effect, in the other) to compensate for the female partner's absence, and the fetishizing use of these props in the dancing raises a provocative suggestion of autoeroticism consistent with Linda Williams's proposed analogy between the musical and pornography: 'To a great extent, in fact, the hard-core feature film *is* a kind of musical, with sexual number taking the place of musical number' (L. Williams 1989: 124). Specifically, she compares the solo number of a musical to a masturbation number, 'a solo song or dance of self-love and enjoyment' (133). With this comparison in mind, it is important to appreciate that, far from being directed towards a slam-bang type of climax exclusively male in its libidinal orientation, Astaire's solo numbers disperse their autoerotic energy into extended foreplay – the duration of the number – so that the pleasure of the dance – not only for the performer but also, it can be assumed, for the viewer contemplating the dancer's image and identifying with the emotions and movements driving the dance – is bounded desire itself and not its consummation. That Astaire's musical numbers generally do not direct their energy towards a big, showy cumulative finish – indeed, they are actually planned out and then shot in segments so that the dancer's energy can be expended throughout the duration of the dance and not saved up for the finish – may begin to explain why they can be watched repeatedly without loss of pleasure.

'YOU GO, GO, GO, BUT DON'T GET ANYWHERE'

While both solo numbers in *Royal Wedding* might seem to glorify traditional – and, because of Astaire's age, patriarchal – male power as reinforcement of the binarism of the generic musical plot, the masculinity put on display is far from the phallic posturing of other types of Hollywood spectacle analyzed by Steve Neale, like the Western or gangster shoot-out. If anything, Astaire's numbers reverse the usual psychoanalytic terms for describing gender identification symbolically, since in their orchestration of the male body as a site of joy they display plenitude and not lack, presence and not absence. Rather than successfully binding the desire of the dance to the linear trajectory of classical plot, or working out a dual heterosexual focus that reaches fulfillment in the consummation symbolized by marriage, Astaire's solo numbers in this film confirm his status for cinema as an object of vision, a male spectacle driving the musical portions to exceed its narrative containment and closure.

The disrupting effect of the numbers in *Royal Wedding* may appear

Figure 9 Fred Astaire and Cyd Charisse dancing to 'All of You'

more immediately striking than in most musicals because of the coincidence of its show setting with an obvious disinclination to musicalize a romance plot, but the spectacular value of Astaire's two solos and four show numbers with Powell is consistent with the dancing in his films generally, even those with Ginger Rogers or Cyd Charisse, which tend to be more successfully bound to a narrative context of male–female seduction/education. In *Top Hat* (1935), to cite the quintessential partnership of Astaire and Rogers, the dance duet to 'Isn't This a Lovely Day (To Be Caught in the Rain)?' emphasizes the equality at the heart of their joy in dancing together. The narrative motivation for the number is Rogers's fear of thunder, which, in driving her into Astaire's arms,

Figure 10 Fred Astaire and Cyd Charisse dancing to 'Fated to be Mated'

allows her to overcome her half-hearted resistance to him. Once he begins to dance, she tries to feign lack of interest but quickly jumps in in perfect harmony to his steps. As the dance then takes its course, the two stars perfectly match their steps, timing, hand gestures, gazes so that their movement when dancing makes them comparable, not sexually differentiated, figures on screen (she is even wearing pants because she has been out riding). Then, as the dance starts to wind down and Astaire quickly spins Rogers over his feet and around his body in a very characteristic masculine ballroom dance gesture, she simply and effortlessly follows his example, and does the same to him. At the close of the dance, they shake hands and smile knowingly, as if perfectly aware

57

that their dance has enacted a sexual ritual, choreographing their sexual relation in terms of comparability and partnership without losing its romance and erotic charge.

Most commentaries on Astaire's duets emphasize the equality of his dancing with Rogers in contrast to the sexual hierarchy that defines his pairings with younger co-stars, particularly in his last decade as a musical leading man; but such a reading of his dancing in those later films is largely influenced by the narrative contexts of the numbers. The plot of *Silk Stockings* rechannels Charisse's initial sexual indifference to Astaire ('If we are to spend the day together,' she warns, 'forget I am a woman and forget you are a man') into a passive femininity that greatly depends upon binarized sexual differentiation – beginning with her acceptance of spectacle as the proper feminine sphere, measured by her growing interest in Paris fashions – in order to demonstrate her change of commitment from communism to capitalism. 'Without love, what is a woman?' she asks him in song after her conversion, and concludes, 'For a woman to a man is just a woman, / But a man to a woman is her life.' However, 'Fated to be Mated,' the big dance number celebrating the couple in the next scene, choreographs the sexual relation quite differently on a more egalitarian ground reminiscent of the Astaire–Rogers duet to 'Isn't This a Lovely Day.'

'Fated to be Mated,' which takes place on a movie studio lot, could easily be subtitled 'Sunday Jumps Times Two.' Astaire and Charisse boisterously accommodate their dancing to the properties that fill up the space: they twirl around poles, sit on a park bench, push off pillars, swoop under parallel bars. Beginning and ending with the dancers in the same position (a medium shot of them hugging closely), this number moves serially rather than sequentially, continuously rather than cumulatively. It could conceivably go on for as long as there is music and dance space – or it could conceivably be cut down without losing its choreographic coherence.[8] Astaire and Charisse bound from one sound-stage setting to another, each locale signaling a shift in the music and, accordingly, in the tempo and style of their dancing, as the accompanying melody changes from 'Fated to be Mated' to reprises of Astaire's earlier love songs, 'Paris Loves Lovers' and 'All of You.' Now, in contrast to the staging of those other two songs (when Astaire was trying to seduce Charisse into both the benefits of capitalism for the sake of the story *and* the pleasures of dancing for the sake of the numbers), the choreography and the framing of this number treat the dancers on visibly equal terms. A great deal of side-by-side dancing keeps them together in the frame spatially, and this relation is then reinforced by the precision with which they synchronize their movement while facing the camera. As a consequence, when the many lifts, spins, and bends of this rather athletic number physically differentiate the dancers' positions, they do not connote Astaire's male superiority so much as continue to keep reconfiguring the dancers in relation to each other as two equally spectacular bodies moving through cinematic space.

In confirmation of their comparable value for the film as sources of spectacle, Charisse and Astaire do not dance together in a finale (as one might expect from the romantic plot) but individually star in big, splashy, energetic production numbers. Astaire's 'Ritz Rock and Roll,' his last big dance number at MGM, pays homage to his 'Top Hat' signature number in the film of that name and also to 'Puttin' on the Ritz' from *Blue Skies* (his premature swan song to films in 1946), and it is performed to celebrate both the opening of his new nightclub and the success of his scheming to get Charisse out of Moscow and back to Paris. All along, the plot has been working to push Astaire and Charisse into a binary sexual relation that differentiates them in terms of his masculine activity as a narrative agent and her feminine passivity as an object of spectacle; and there are indeed numbers in the film which help to achieve this structuring of sexual difference through female spectacle (as in Charisse's 'Silk Stockings' and Janis Paige's 'Satin and Silk'), though, significantly enough, they do not occur in Astaire's presence. But if it has not been made clear enough before this last number, with a shot of Charisse looking at Astaire rapturously just before he begins performing, there is no doubt at this moment that the film makes her the viewer and *him* the show.

A STAR IS SHOWN

What kind of show does Astaire offer a spectator? At some point in his films almost every one of his female co-stars finds herself watching him perform. As Madonna could have said in her song 'Vogue,' Astaire gives good show. An excellent example, because it is just an ordinary solo number by his standards, is his song and dance to 'Let's Kiss and Make Up' in *Funny Face* (1957). Just prior to this number, Audrey Hepburn/Jo Stockton has (somewhat awkwardly if energetically) performed a number ('Basal Metabolism') in a club, and Astaire/Dick Avery has watched her dance with his hands to his face in dismay; with this number he now shows what *he* can do, which is to dance as 'Fred Astaire.' This number therefore functions for the narrative to delineate the traditional terms of sexual difference by re-establishing male authority through the same vehicle, dance. Of course, insofar as an audience knows 'Fred Astaire,' his superiority as a dancer in comparison to Hepburn is a foregone conclusion, so while in the story Dick Avery implores Jo Stockton to forget his rude behavior and kiss and make up, as shot and performed the number exceeds that specific narrative function because it presents the middle-aged Astaire in a star turn doing what he has done on screen for the past twenty-five years.

His number is thus a pleasure to watch, which is exactly what Hepburn does. Along with the camera's positioning of his body primarily in long and medium shot (the standard for all his dances), Astaire's choreography of the number draws particular attention to the spectacle of his body moving in a musical rather than narrative space, with the logic of the dancing emerging in response to his costume, a rather shapeless white red-lined raincoat with a grey suit underneath. As he dances, his powder-blue socks standing out to draw the eye to his feet, he uses an umbrella as a prop, tossing it in the air and against the ground, his coat whipping around him to emphasize his body's movement. The number, in short, achieves exactly the effect that Mulvey attributes to cinematic spectacle: 'to freeze the flow of action in moments of erotic contemplation' of a star's body (Mulvey 1975: 19). In this case, though, it is a female star who looks on and a male star who performs for her benefit, and the two close-ups of Hepburn watching (first when he sings, and then in the middle of his dance) feature her smiling to signify the pleasure she takes in looking at Astaire.

These close-ups align Hepburn's look with the spectator's to reverse the usual sexual division of the gaze; once the dance begins and Hepburn leaves the camera's field of vision, the visual address then detaches itself from her visual mediation of Astaire dancing. Astaire concludes the song's chorus, during which time he and Hepburn are both in the shot, her position higher than his, with the balcony rail separating them, and then he jumps down to the courtyard below. As he moves, the camera follows him, and so presumably does Hepburn's view, for after she gets out of the camera's sightline, the balcony rails initially filter his image to serve as a reminder of her viewing position; but then, with a cut to a full shot of him, the camera gets placed in front of the balcony (where Hepburn remains) and Astaire's dance begins in earnest in the yard below her window. During the dance, because the camera moves to and away from him to indicate a new location on the ground, it becomes evident that the spectator's extradiegetic view of Astaire has succeeded Hepburn's for the rest of the number. Thus the dance closes *without* a reverse shot of her looking, as Astaire takes his bow in acknowledgment of the audience's spectatorship more than hers.[9]

When Astaire performs this number, he looks directly at his audience (Hepburn in the diegesis, but also the spectator in the cinema auditorium), so his own gaze makes for a rather uncharacteristic type of spectatorial address. Usually the codes of realism which determine the address of Hollywood cinema require an actor to be positioned at an angle to the camera, so that he appears oblivious of the extradiegetic audience, who then identifies with his image indirectly, that is, through the character whose vision is in turn mediated by editing techniques such as shot/reverse shot. By contrast, here when Astaire sings and dances directly to the camera, his more direct style of address openly acknowledges the spectator's viewing position; it therefore prompts from the audience a much more intimate identification with the image itself, since it involves so little editing and, as in this example, only offers a token reverse shot of a viewer watching him in the diegesis.

The style of musical address in 'Let's Kiss and Make Up,' typical of almost any Astaire number that comes to mind, makes an explicit recognition of the star's visibility by momentarily disengaging his image from the mediation of narrative. Such layering of star persona over character serves to rupture the apparent transparency of the diegesis by calling attention to the star's personality and special talents over and above his or her acting of a fictional character bound to a narrative. The musical is the one genre which regularly allows a star to look so openly at the spectator: when performing a number, musical stars generally 'shift their identities from being actors in a drama to entertainers addressing the audience directly' (Schatz 1981: 217), this effect occurring because of the performing style fostered by studio technology, which in its prerecording of singing, postrecording of taps, and direct address to an extradiegetic spectator generally emphasizes performance over characterization in order to refer to the showstopping tradition of live entertainment (vaudeville and theater).[10] In no other Hollywood genre, in fact, does the star persona of a performer so overwhelm and thus overdetermine characterization because it is primarily through the spectacle of its stars, rather than through the course of its stories, that the musical makes most sense to audiences.

'SO, UH, DANCING'S A WASTE OF TIME?'

That the Hollywood musical routinely makes a spectacle of a male star, as I have been showing through my analysis of Fred Astaire, may go far in accounting for its great popularity in the late 1940s and early 1950s. Though always a significant factor in a studio's annual output since the invention of sound, the musical was most important during the ten-year period after World War II in large part because of the genre's emphasis on spectacle.[11] As Dana Polan comments, 'if musicals have seemed so typically a Hollywood art, this is not so much because they inevitably move a couple toward the finality of an ostensible productivity of an adult middle-class heterosexuality but because they propel characters toward an endless nonfinality, the spectacle as literally a showstopper' (Polan 1986: 293). More specifically, Hollywood musicals reimagined American masculinity for postwar audiences in the kind of spectacular terms that would later come to dominate a televisual popular culture, but with more mobility and flexibility.

To amplify what I mean, an understanding of the components that made up Astaire's star persona is crucial. For all his grace on the dance floor, he conformed to the marked ordinariness of almost every musical performer during the studio era. As Arlene Croce observes, 'The list of male singers and dancers who have become big stars in the movies is very largely an assortment of aging, balding, skinny, tubby, jug-eared, pug-faces and generally unprepossessing men' (Croce 1972: 8). With the exception of Gene Kelly,[12] none of the big musical stars – not Bing Crosby, Frank Sinatra, Dan Dailey, Donald O'Connor, Danny Kaye, or Fred Astaire – were likely candidates either for pin-ups or action heroes. So when musicals nevertheless made a spectacle of them, these male stars offered an alternative representation of masculinity which openly conflicted with the reductive binarism of active male/passive female that the generic romantic plots frequently promoted. The supposed evaluation of Astaire's first screen test – 'Can't act. Can't sing. Balding. Can dance a little' (Croce 1972: 14) – has continued to circulate in accounts of his career, including his AFI tribute, in order to show the myopia of studio heads, to be sure, but also, more significantly, to summarize how he revised the terms of male movie stardom by emphasizing talent over looks, dancing over action, spectacle over narrative.

This factor, I think, helps to explain the enormous attraction of both the musical genre and a middle-aged musical star like Fred Astaire for mainstream audiences during the postwar years. While Astaire may have connoted modernity and youth in his RKO films of the 1930s (where he represents the modernity of new and unpretentious popular musical sounds like jazz and swing), and tradition and maturity in the postwar era (where he now comes to represent just the opposite, the established tried-and-true show business tradition of the popular entertainer resisting the fads of postwar modernity), what authenticated his star persona on screen in either case was always spectacle, the sight of him performing as 'Fred Astaire.' Hence his star image was consistently represented by metonymies of his body, the source of his talent and charisma, through-out his career, most notably so during the 1950s when a shot of his legs (the opening of *Silk Stockings*), or his top hat (the opening of *The Band Wagon*), or even his voice (singing over the titles to *Funny Face*), could serve instantly to signal his star identity in a film.

While those iconic signs fetishize Astaire in a way unexpected of a longstanding Hollywood leading man, they are nonetheless consistent with the means through which all of his films repeatedly authenticate his star quality as an entertainer through his spectacularity. For example, his signature style of dress – ranging from the trademark top hat and tails that became instantly identifiable with 'Fred Astaire' in the RKO series, to the baggy flannels and brightly-colored matching scarf and socks worn in the Technicolor films at Metro – insists upon the spectacle of his body in ways that go against the grain of Hollywood's typical treatment of a leading man. What's quite remarkable about Astaire's appearance in the opening of *Easter Parade* (1948), his comeback vehicle for MGM after a two-year retirement, is not his singing and dancing so much as the fact that, from the very first shot of the film, the vibrant colors of his costume – grey suit, pink shirt, white vest, blue carnation, black tie, white hankie, pearl tie stud, spats – turn him into a spectacle quite worthy, as the title song says in the film's finale, of the rotogravure: clearly a costume no different in purpose than the bangles and beads of a showgirl outfit, this outfit sets Astaire in an explicit relation of comparability to the women in the fashion salon ('Happy Easter'), and to the little boy in knickers with whom he competes for the purchase of a toy in the drug store immediately afterwards ('Drum Crazy'). Subsequently, when Astaire finally stands next to two of his co-stars, Ann Miller and Peter Lawford, he still stands *out* as the primary spectacle drawing the filmgoer's eye, because his costume makes a vivid contrast to the monochrome colors worn by both Lawford (dressed in shades of brown) and Miller (wearing a peach gown).

As the opening of *Easter Parade* illustrates, far from objectifying him as an erotic object in the manner of a showgirl, what the spectacle of Astaire draws attention to, in addition to the movement of his body, is the theatricality of his musical persona, which is finally what gives that body its cinematic value. Specifically, the star text of 'Fred Astaire' builds his charismatic persona out of tropes normally considered 'feminine' – *narcissism* (in his solo performances and special-effects numbers), which defines his body in terms of boundless energy and joyful motion; *exhibitionism* (in his show numbers, challenge dance duets, or those dances performed for a bystander, sometimes for purposes of seduction), which defines his performance in terms of self-conscious spectacle and display of style; and *masquerade* (in his dandyish costuming, the levels of multiple personification required for some show numbers, the numerous plots of disguises or mistaken identities), which defines his identity in terms of theatrical play and social manners. These three elements intersect at the point of his star persona so that every characteristic of 'Fred Astaire' is an effect of their working in unison. His costuming in *Easter Parade*, for instance, has obvious implications of exhibitionism and narcissism as well as masquerade, just as his special effect number in *Royal Wedding* involves him in an exhibitionistic display of physical agility which actually serves to masquerade the technological fakery that enables him to dance on film. As a star text, all of this is to say, 'Fred Astaire' is a highly theatricalized representation of maleness on screen which oscillates between, on the one hand, a fictional character grounded in the static

63

and reductive binarism of traditional gender roles and, on the other, a musical persona whose energy choreographs a libidinal force that revises conventional masculinity and linear desire.

Although immediately famous in the 1930s when he made the extraordinary series of dance musicals with Rogers, Astaire's star persona was most resonant for American culture after his comeback with the smash success of *Easter Parade* in 1948. For then he not only continued to defy gravity as a dancing man, with all the considerable assets of MGM and the Arthur Freed unit at his disposal to support him, but he appeared uncannily able – in the grace, ease, and energy which with he still moved on screen – to hold back the sands of time as well. This is the reason I have paid so much attention to Astaire's films from the 1950s, even though one could easily argue that his star persona was pretty much put in place during the years at RKO. Historically, though, there is a significant difference between the two stages in his career, and it is largely due to Hollywood's transformation of the Astaire–Rogers dance film into the integrated dance musical produced at MGM.

The effect of the integrated musical on the relation of narrative and number, as I mentioned earlier, is usually misunderstood or at best misrepresented, even by the people who made them, as a narrativization of song and dance. When interviewed in the late 1950s Roger Edens – song writer, vocal arranger, and associate producer for the Freed unit at Metro – explained about the craft of integrating narrative and number: 'you have to be careful about music in films,' he said, ' – so many musicals have been made in which the plot and the songs have nothing to do with each other. . . . I believe that songs in film musicals should be part of the script itself, actually sung dialogue' (Johnson 1958: 180). The actual achievement of the integrated musical, though, was not simply to use the numbers to advance the plot along, which implies a subordinate relation of the musical portions to the narrative. More specifically, as Jerome Delameter explains:

> [T]he nature of integration of the film musical lies not simply with the idea that the musical numbers and dances, in particular, should advance the plot but also suggests an integration of the entire cinematic process. The way in which the dances in a particular film are photographed, for example, suggests a kind of integration of the film making process with the dance process and that *together* they contribute to the integrity of the film. . . . Certainly part of the process of integration as [Gene] Kelly viewed it was to move easily and naturally from the regular narrative portions of the films into the numbers and back again; that requires a dancing persona, though not necessarily a character within the diegesis who is explained to be a dancer.
>
> (Delameter 1981: 98, 150)

In a truly integrated musical, even though the language of 'integration' always means to suggest the opposite practice, the extradiegetic, anti-realist conventions of the numbers also purposefully shade into and influence the book portions, as when the soundtrack shifts aural registers to more closely miked sound for the dialogue before a number begins, or the music track begins to anticipate the melody of an upcoming number, or a star's movement in walking begins to take on the rhythmic dimensions of a dance. Thus whereas the numbers in 1930s musicals like the Astaire–Rogers series are by no means indifferently placed in terms of narrative development, they do differ from the story as distinctly marked moments of musical spectacle. By contrast, as I have already implied with my examples of narrative disruption and extradiegetic address, postwar musicals shift spectatorial interest from a musical film's narrativity to its continuous deployment of spectacle. This shift of interest lies behind the conventional structure of the postwar musical, one tending to build toward a big ballet (as in *An American in Paris* (1951)) which either interrupts the narrative with spectacle, or repeats it as dance, but rarely resolves a plot.

More to the point of what I have been arguing here, the integrated dance musical, which became synonymous with the names 'Fred Astaire' and 'Gene Kelly,' also determined a revaluation of the male star and his 'dancing persona' in terms of spectacle over narrative. *The Pirate* (1948) in particular exemplifies this new styling of masculinity in the way it leads Judy Garland/Manuela from her infatuation with the legendary pirate Mack the Black, whose phallic masculinity is based in narrativity (the accounts of his adventures in the book she reads), to her appreciation of Serafin the Clown/Gene Kelly, whose playful and performative masculinity is based in spectacle. While a key film in any reading of Kelly, *The Pirate* was a historically significant film for Astaire as well because *Easter Parade* was intended as the follow-up Kelly–Garland teaming, and when Kelly broke his ankle, Astaire came out of retirement and into the pages of the rotogravure.[13]

When all is said and done, because of the genre's 'feminization' of the song-and-dance man through spectacle, I don't think it is simply a coincidence of film history that the integrated Hollywood dance musical became so enormously popular for audiences and studios alike during roughly the same period as that other emblematic postwar genre, *film noir*. Though no *noir* detective ever looked so trim and dapper, or moved so swiftly and effortlessly through the city shadows, as Astaire's 'Rod Riley' in 'The Girl Hunt Ballet' that closes *The Band Wagon*, this witty and spectacular number implies some kind of an inverse relation existing between the two genres, from the number's tough-guy voice-over narration, styled parodically after Mickey Spillane, to the representation of femininity as a duality in the ballet scenario, danced with great verve by

Cyd Charisse for ironic effect, since here the blonde virgin, and not the brunette spider woman, turns out to be the killer. The comparison suggested by 'The Girl Hunt Ballet' actually makes considerable sense of both genres because, like *film noir*, the integrated dance musical represented urban experience in ways highly responsive to postwar anxieties about male authority and masculinity, though to be sure, the musical went to one extreme (visual excess), and *film noir* to the other (visual spareness).[14] But each in its own way commodified the materialism of cinematic spectacle, each celebrated technological innovation, and (as Lucy Fischer begins to suggest with her study of *White Heat* in this volume) each featured a particular type of 'feminized' male star performance, with the song-and-dance man the counterpart of the castrated vet or rogue detective of *noir* dramas.

In contrast to the more oppressive, often hysterical, depiction of postwar America's restoration of binarized gender roles in *film noir*, the musical imagined an alternative style of masculinity, one grounded in spectacle and spectatorship, which was literally made visible and given body by Fred Astaire, and this was surely no mean accomplishment for a popular mainstream genre. But the Hollywood musical could produce this effect so easily because it was the one genre which, through its numbers, could take the performance of a star's masculinity to heart so completely, so seriously, and so openly as spectacle.

NOTES

1 For further elaboration see Lucy Fischer's discussion of female spectacle in *Dames* (1934) (Fischer 1989: 132–48).

2 In my effort to move the male musical star beyond the simple reversal of male spectator/female erotic object, I should make clear that I do not mean to suggest that the sexual objectification which Neale describes does not apply in some cases (such as John Travolta, Neale's own example). Since my particular concern here is the Hollywood dance musical produced under the studio system, where someone like Fred Astaire most exemplifies the relation of the male star to spectacle, I have had to exclude from the scope of my discussion consideration of those teen music idols (Elvis Presley, Pat Boone, Cliff Richard, etc.), who came to musicals starting in the late 1950s, and whose stardom poses important questions about male spectacle in *and* out of film as conventional pin-up material.

3 Even so, some of the great female musical stars pose problems for that showgirl standard. The one who immediately comes to mind is Judy Garland. Her short-waisted body – unconventional by showgirl standards and uncontrollable, as it eventually turned out, by the studio – is a significant and transgressive element of her star image, as Richard Dyer explains (see Dyer 1986: 156–68). Too, recall the queen of spectacle at MGM, Esther Williams; when the camera lingers on the sight of her naked thighs in *Million Dollar Mermaid* (1952), the physical strength, awesome muscularity, and disciplined athleticism connoted by her body (which in this respect is comparable to that of her co-

star, Victor Mature) likewise transform the showgirl basis of her female star image into something quite different.

4 Robin Wood raises a similar argument about the numbers of *Silk Stockings*, when he states that their 'vitality . . . itself transcends their local ideological functions' (Wood 1975: 67). Significantly, though, he has very little to say about either Astaire's or Charisse's numbers, which is where the film's vitality primarily lies, as I will show later in this essay.

5 John Mueller, who reads all of Astaire's numbers through their narrative logic, thinks this is 'a garish, ghastly production number' and complains in particular about its *lack* of internal narrative coherence, concluding that 'the "Haiti" number betrays no thought processes whatever' (Mueller 1985: 329, 330). One might argue, though, that the purpose of this number, which delays the introduction of Powell for at least half its length, is to give the brother and sister one last chance to dance together, so in this respect the pattern behind the dance movement is the separation and reunion of the performing team; this may be why the fictional performers then break 'character' in their curtain call afterwards, acknowledging their mutual pleasure in the audience's applause. By contrast, they remain in low-life 'character' after the 'Liar' number on their opening night in London, possibly because for the post-performance party they plan to be each other's date and are still a team acting in perfect synchrony.

6 See, for example, the discussions of Astaire's dancing in Croce 1972, Delameter 1981, Mueller 1984 and 1985, and Mast 1987.

7 One might try to account for the casting of Astaire and Powell (in her first major adult role) as siblings not lovers by citing the age difference between them, but then wouldn't that explanation more logically result in a father–daughter team (thereby strengthening my claim)? Powell was actually the third actress cast in the role of Astaire's sister, replacing Judy Garland (this was the dismissal that ended her relation to Metro), who replaced June Allyson. The casting of Garland, who had starred opposite Astaire as a romantic lead in *Easter Parade* in 1948, and was due to play his wife in *The Barkleys of Broadway* the following year (the role went to Ginger Rogers), indicates that the age difference alone did not explain the script's focus on a sibling team. Rather, as a reference to Astaire's own professional teaming with his sister Adèle, the story situation continues the intertextual references to his star image in his MGM vehicles that began with *Easter Parade* and *The Barkleys of Broadway* and continued through *The Band Wagon*.

8 As indeed it has been cut down: the original MGM soundtrack album included an abridged version of the number, and *That's Entertainment II* showed only the last section (the part danced to 'All of You'). Furthermore, the number itself was shot in segments in an even more discontinuous way than usual, since Charisse wears a different version of her costume (one with culottes rather than a skirt) for two crucial knee spins. For the photographic illustration see Mueller 1985: 397.

9 Both Jerome Delameter and John Mueller, who each comment on Astaire's dancing in great and insightful detail, show how his choreography always resists inserted shots of a spectator, and they both mention this number because of a close-up of Hepburn cut into the middle of the dance (no doubt inserted to ease the transition between actual cuts in the shooting of the sequence). Delameter mentions it to show how Astaire can insert a spectator shot to provide 'an appropriate grounding in the narrative' (112), since the dance is for Hepburn's benefit; whereas Mueller, by contrast, complains that

the number lacks that very narrative ground because 'Hepburn's reaction at the end is not shown,' and it should have been in order to maintain that narrative continuity (Mueller 1985: 382).

10 For a detailed explanation of the studio practice of prerecording sound, see A. Williams 1981, and for discussion of the photographed address of numbers see Feuer 1982: 23–47.

11 Though today one tends to equate the musical with the blockbuster roadshow adaptation of a Broadway hit, the sheer number of ordinary musicals produced during the postwar period, especially at MGM, cannot be underestimated. In its issue of April 14, 1952, *Life* previewed several upcoming musicals in production at the Culver City studio – 'glossy, brassy, cornily plotted, elaborately staged, expensively produced extravaganza' – noting that 'Hollywood, which dearly loves a cycle, is embarked on a congenial one: more producers are making more musicals and expect them to be raking in more and more profits with them.' Two years later, *Variety* reported on June 16, 1954 that 'Metro's leadership in the musical film field continues unabated. At least one third of the company's upcoming releases are slated for the musical treatment and it appears that the number of tuners for 1954 will top the 10 (out of a total of 45) releases issued in 1953.' The musical was primarily bankable for the industry because of its capacity as 'extravaganza' to feature the spectacle of new technologies as the mainstay of its generic identity, which is also what required support from a complex studio system of artisans and technicians, so when that system collapsed, taking with it the economic support of the expensive technology necessary for the genre (like three-strip Technicolor as opposed to the cheaper and muddier Ansco and Eastman color processes), the demise of the integrated musical epitomized by MGM in particular was inevitable, as the highly reduced output of studio-produced musicals at the end of the decade evidences.

12 This is not to say that Gene Kelly is to be excluded from my general remarks about musical stars. Although more conventionally – even relentlessly – 'masculine' than Astaire in his screen persona, Kelly can just as easily be examined in the same terms. For instance, a fear of losing his virility in dance seems to account for the particular inflections of Kelly's screen persona that differentiate him from Astaire: the attention to athleticism in the various set-piece ballets, to cite one characteristic, is a means of compensating for the gaze directed at his body, and yet that gaze is accentuated in some numbers by the recurring wiggle of his buttocks in tights or sailor pants. As a result, all the more conscious of his musical identity as a gender performance, Kelly goes to great extremes to disavow it, producing a more riven and less confident male screen image than Astaire's. A fuller discussion of Kelly in a postwar context will be included in my forthcoming book, *Masked Men: American Masculinity and the Movies During the Fifties*.

13 Mueller 1985 reports that the blocking of all the numbers had already been worked out with Kelly in mind, and that what Astaire primarily changed were the actual steps (p. 277).

14 Though *film noir* tends to be the genre considered most fully representative of Hollywood's postwar treatment of American male urban experience, one shouldn't forget how many musicals were similarly set in cities, or that musicals moved out of the studio to film in the streets of New York City (*On the Town*, 1949) at the same time that *noir* did. The significance of the city to musicals, Astaire's as well as Kelly's, was deeply felt by contemporary audiences, at least if Douglas Newton's appreciation of the genre in *Sight and*

Sound in 1952 is any indication: 'The city is of course one of the great elements of the musical. . . . and as a result the musicals are among the rare poetic works so far to accept big city life without using it simply as decorative detail or a satirical target' (Newton 1952: 36).

BIBLIOGRAPHY

Altman, R. (1987) *The American Film Musical*, Bloomington: Indiana University Press.

Croce, A. (1972) *The Fred Astaire & Ginger Rogers Book*, New York: Galahad Books.

Delameter, J. (1981) *Dance in the Hollywood Musical*, Ann Arbor, MI: UMI Research Press.

Dyer, R. (1986) *Heavenly Bodies: Film Stars and Society*, New York: St Martin's Press.

Feuer, J. (1982) *The Hollywood Musical*, London: Macmillan.

Fischer, L. (1989). *Shot/Countershot: Film Tradition and Women's Cinema*, Princeton, NJ: Princeton University Press.

Johnson, A. (1958) 'Conversation with Roger Edens,' *Sight and Sound* 27: 179–82.

Mast, G. (1987) *Can't Help Singin': the American Musical on Stage and Screen*, Woodstock, NY: Overlook Press.

Mueller, J. (1984) 'Fred Astaire and the Integrated Musical,' *Cinema Journal* 24, 1: 28–40.

—— (1985) *Astaire Dancing: the Musical Films*, New York: Knopf.

Mulvey, L. (1975) 'Visual Pleasure and Narrative Cinema' rpt 1989, in *Visual and Other Pleasures*, Bloomington: Indiana University Press, 14–26.

Neale, S. (1983) 'Masculinity as Spectacle,' *Screen* 24, 6: 2–16.

Newton, D. (1952) 'Poetry in Fast and Musical Motion,' *Sight and Sound* 22: 36–8.

Polan, D. (1986) *Power and Paranoia: History, Narrative, and the American Cinema 1940–1950*, New York: Columbia University Press.

Schatz, T. (1981) *Hollywood Genres: Formulas, Filmmaking, and the Studio System*, New York: Random House.

Williams, A. (1981) 'The Musical Film and Recorded Popular Music' in Rick Altman (ed.) *Genre: the Musical*, New York: Routledge, 147–58.

Williams, L. (1989) *Hard Core: Power, Pleasure, and the 'Frenzy of the Visible'*, Berkeley: University of California Press.

Wood, R. (1975) 'Art and Ideology: Notes on *Silk Stockings*' rpt 1981, in Rick Altman (ed.) *Genre: the Musical*, New York: Routledge, 57–69.

3

MAMA'S BOY

Filial hysteria in *White Heat*

Lucy Fischer

FOREWORD: MAL(E)-AISE

The end of World War II brought millions of men to sudden
consciousness . . . ; they had been away for months or years in the
most masculine endeavor of all, where nothing counted more than
male solidarity, stamina, and 'balls.' Then one day sometime after
the war ended, the American male woke up to find himself . . .
adrift in a world that had no use for his manhood.

(Ehrenreich and English 1978: 214)

During the 1970s, when a gendered perspective first informed the study
of film, criticism tended to define the social world in terms of discrete
oppositions: male and female, surveyor and surveyed, culture and nature,
active and passive, voyeuristic and masochistic. Over the next decade,
however, dichotomies were challenged – especially around static notions
of masculinity. In 1988 *Camera Obscura* entitled an issue 'Male Trouble,'
and in 1989, *differences* published 'Male Subjectivity.' Much of this theoretical work addressed the contemporary scene, a period when gender
boundaries were perceived as fluid. Constance Penley (1989) examined
the histrionic stance of Pee-Wee Herman; Paul Smith (1989) considered
the erotic spectacle of Clint Eastwood; Carole-Anne Tyler (1989) discussed the transsexuality of Renee Richards. But an interrogation of
masculinity is equally valid for eras in which sexual roles were more
fixed.

Such an epoch is 1940s America. While the wartime culture imagined
an ideal of hypermasculinity (of GI Joe), experience lay elsewhere – in
a confluence of (what Dana Polan has termed) 'power and paranoia.'
That phrase might well caption *White Heat* (1949) – a film in which
machismo meets hysteria. The drama's crazed hero, Cody Jarrett (James
Cagney), is a figure who registers myriad cultural fears about masculinity:
suspicions of the discharged soldier, worries about the returning vet,
anxieties about manhood within the American nuclear family.

JUVENILE DELINQUENCY

> We do not know what went wrong with [Cody] Jarrett but we know
> he loved his mother.
>
> (Hurley 1987: 12)

To associate Cody Jarrett with hysteria is to taint him with the specter
of womanhood (tied to the etymological roots of the term).[1] But it is
crucial to trace how the process of 'feminization' marks the text. Clearly,
Cody is portrayed as unbalanced and suffers from 'frequent neurotic fits'
(*Rotarian* 1950: 41). But his dementia takes a particular form – that of
migraine headaches.[2] In the 1940s, psychosomatic medical theories were
popular. As Stanley Cobb states: 'A new word has come into medicine.
It is quite the rage. One must know about "psychosomatics" to be up
with the times' (Cobb 1943: 149). In 1947, Flanders Dunbar quotes P.
S. Graven on the subject of Cody's particular affliction:

> One of the most baffling problems in medical therapeutics is that
> dealing with the treatment of headaches. The main reason for this
> lies in the failure to detect . . . the causal factor, the psychic. . . .
>
> (Dunbar 1947: 74)

Even recently, migraines have been seen as psychologically motivated.
Oliver Sacks compares them to 'dreams, hysterical formations, and neur-
otic symptoms' (Sacks 1985: 207–8). In *White Heat* we are told that
Cody's headaches arose in childhood, as an attempt to garner love. (As
Philip Hartung remarks, they 'were fancied at first and later became real'
(Hartung 1949: 560).) Thus, Cody exhibits the hysteric's 'conversion' of
unconscious tensions into concrete physical symptoms.

If hysteria is tied to women, so are migraines. As Joseph Patrick Perry
notes, 'females are more likely to experience [them] than males' (Perry
1981: 12). That Cody's illness is cephalic feminizes him. With mind linked
to the male, and body to the female – his mental pain (and its translation
into *corporeal* spasms) challenges his masculinity. Cobb argues that a
patient's 'choice' of psychosomatic symptom has semantic overtones.
'The psychological situation through its symbolic meaning, can enter the
pathological functioning upon one or another organ' (Cobb 1943: 158).

Cody bears another mark of hysteria: the tendency to hallucinate.
After his mother's death, he roams the woods just 'talkin' to Ma.' The
fact that Jarrett's delusions are maternal is crucial. For the root of his
hysteria is, clearly, his *uncommon attachment to his mother* – something
that would have interested an audience of the 1940s, witnessing the
ascendancy of psychoanalysis. Polan calls Cody's syndrome a 'perverse
mother fixation' (Polan 1986: 165); Hurley deems it an 'Oedipal complex'
(Hurley 1987: 11); Bosley Crowther (1949: 7) and Dwight C. Smith Jr.
(1975) call Jarrett a 'mama's boy.' Hence, Cody's infantile regression

71

Figure 11 James Cagney and Margaret Wycherly. Film Stills Archive, The Museum of Modern Art, New York

seems the cause of both his neurosis and his criminality, making him a middle-aged 'juvenile' delinquent. With his father dead, and he the only child, Cody has had Ma to himself. Though he is married, his spouse is disloyal, and it is Ma who reveals Verna's treachery. Tom Conley sees Cody as romantically trapped within the 'double bind of subservience to mother and wife' (Conley 1981–2: 144).

Significantly, Cody's hysterical episodes implicate his mother. His first headache occurs in a cabin hideaway, after the gang has pulled a train heist. It is Ma who nurses Cody, retreating with him from the public space of the living room to the private sphere of the boudoir – massaging his temples and cradling him upon her lap. The next seizure (which takes place in the prison machine shop) follows her visit; and the last comes in the mess hall when he learns of Ma's death. Interestingly, research on migraines sought to relate the disease to motherhood. John Pearce describes a 1935 study in which: '[a] psychic mechanism of the migrane attack was tentatively postulated . . . as a conflict between the desire to escape from the mother's influence and a compulsion not to leave her' (Pearce 1975: 52). Thus, patients were seen as caught in a 'maternal attachment' (Pearce 1975: 52).

Cody's final hysterical symptom is his excessive violence, a trait which shocked critics of the time. Crowther (1949: 7) found the film 'cruelly vicious,' while *The Saturday Review* called it 'tough, bloodstained . . . corpse-strewn' and 'callous' (1949: 28). Cody's aggression is encapsulated in the refinery explosion that ends the film and his life. Significantly, it is then that he utters the famous lines: 'Made it Ma! Top of the world!' Some have seen the maternal metaphor imprinted on the segment's very *mise-en-scène*. McGilligan remarks that the 'swirling pipes, retorts, Hortonspheres, coils, and tubes of [the] sprawling oil refinery suggested [to the screenwriters] "mother earth in metal" ' (McGilligan 1984: 18).

If Cody is 'emasculated' through hysteria, traditional gender roles are disrupted at other levels of the text. Though feminine enough to represent malevolent motherhood, Ma Jarrett is also highly 'masculine.' She is an arch-criminal, a leader of the Jarrett gang, the inheritor of her deceased husband's mob mantle. Almost all research on criminality, however, supports its prevalence in males. As Michael R. Gottfredson and Travis Hirschi state: 'Men are always and everywhere more likely than women to commit criminal acts' (Gottfredson and Hirschi 1990: 145). As enacted by Margaret Wycherly (with her broad-shouldered suits and stern, punchy delivery) Ma is rather 'camp' and even 'butch,' a pistol-packin' Mama.

In actuality, the Jarrett story is based on the historic Barker gang – a family of outlaws that terrorized America in the 1930s. It consisted of Ma (Arizona Clark) Barker and her four sons, as well as several cohorts. A controversy reigns about Ma's status as gangster. While legend paints her a hardened criminal, gang member, Alvin Karpis, begs to differ:

She was just an old-fashioned homebody from the Ozarks . . . . Her spare time was spent working jigsaw puzzles and listening to the radio – the way any mother would whose family had grown up.

(Karpis 1971: 81)

A hint of condescension taints Karpis's refusal to see Ma as a mastermind: 'With her personality, brains and style it was impossible' (91). Clearly, Ma Jarrett is modeled on the mythic Barker – a fearsome female who may or may not have existed as such.

In *White Heat*'s scrambling of sex roles, Treasury Department agent Hank Fallon (Edmond O'Brien) also figures. Though he is a he-man T-Man, his undercover operation requires that he assume the female position to win Cody's confidence. Hence, during Jarrett's machine shop migraine, Fallon (Phall-on) protects and nurtures Cody, acting as a 'surrogate Ma' (McGilligan 1984: 30). Gender confusion also dominates the details of Ma's murder. While, at first, Cody believes that the perpetrator is a man (his rival, Big Ed), he later learns that it is Verna.

The polymorphous world of *White Heat* is imbued with no sense of naive abandon; rather it is overlain with perverse control. 'Fair is foul and foul fair' when men act like women and women like men. Extending the reference, it is not hard to envision Ma Jarrett as a *film noir* Lady Macbeth, incestuously manipulating her son – transferring her own infamous hysteria to her child. ('Out, out, damn headache!'). Female 'red' heat (associated with blood) becomes male 'white' heat.

THE CAGNEY PERSONA:
REAL MEN DON'T SING AND DANCE

Made it, Ma! Top of the world!

(Cody Jarrett)

[I]n our mother we always had somebody we could show off for. Whatever impressive things we did, we were saying in effect, 'Look, Ma, I'm dancin,'

(Cagney 1976: 25)

Critics have remarked on how the issue of maternity permeates Cagney's movie image. As Patrick McGilligan notes, 'having a "mother" who roots for him was an essential part of Cagney's screen persona' (McGilligan 1984: 26). Furthermore, Hurley sees in the star the mark of a 'child-within-[a]-man' (Hurley 1987: 11). This filial stance is borne out even in Cagney's autobiography where he finds his mom 'the key' to the Cagney family (Cagney 1976: 2).

The case for *White Heat* is already clear. But the film was preceded by *The Public Enemy* (1931) in which a maternal discourse is central. The drama concerns two brothers: Mike (Donald Cook) and Tom (Cagney) Powers. Growing up in a tough neighborhood, Mike (like the real Cagney) takes the straight and narrow path, gaining an education and succeeding legally. Tom, on the other hand, becomes a criminal. Loving both of them equally is Ma Powers (Beryl Mercer), who (unlike Ma Jarrett) is an Angel In The House. At the end of the drama, Tom (who has been shot, hospitalized, and bandaged) is kidnapped by a rival gang and left on his mother's doorstep, deceased. A virtual 'mummy' comes home to 'mommy' – in a regression synonymous with death.

Although Cagney began his career as a vaudevillian, his movie fame was tied to the gangster genre: not only to *Public Enemy* but to *G-Men* (1935), *Angels with Dirty Faces* (1938), *The Roaring Twenties* (1939). While he had danced in *Footlight Parade* (1933), in the 1940s he more aggressively resisted gangster stereotyping and won an Oscar for his performance in the musical *Yankee Doodle Dandy* (1942). Following that triumph, he left Warner Brothers and formed a production company, seeking less violent roles. He released three films in six years (*Johnny*

Come Lately (1943), *Blood on the Sun* (1935), *The Time of Your Life* (1948), but none was financially remunerative.

Defeated, Cagney returned to Warner's in 1949 reviving his macho stance, and critics embraced him for it. John McCarten finds it 'unfortunate' that in the intervening years 'Mr. Cagney mellowed, became almost lovable, and moved to the side of the angels.' He applauds him for returning to the 'fold' (McCarten 1949: 63). *Life* shouts 'Cagney Kills Again' and assures us that 'The old Jimmy is back' (McCarten 1949: 83). *Time* celebrates his reprise of 'the kind of thug role that made him famous' (McCarten 1949: 100). A film poster brags: 'Jimmy's in action again!' (Halliwell 1977: 122).

For Cagney, however, *White Heat* was just 'another cheapjack job,' a 'formula' picture (Cagney 1976: 125). His preference lay in the more benign role of hoofer:

> In just about every interview, in most conversations, one question emerges unfailingly: what is my favorite picture? Many people assume that one of those knock-down-drag 'em-outs would be my choice. A discerning critic . . . can't understand why I choose *Yankee Doodle Dandy* over *White Heat* and *The Public Enemy*. The answer is simple . . . once a song-and-dance-man, always a song-and-dance-man. In that brief statement you have my life story.
>
> (Cagney 1976: 104)

McGilligan comments on the irony of Cagney's situation, placing it within a biographical frame:

> [He] spent a lifetime resisting his 'tough guy' image by rising above the 'hell's kitchen' of his childhood and later by fighting the gangster typecasting that dogged him . . . A sensitive artist . . . he preferred to think of himself as a song-and-dance man.
>
> (McGilligan 1984: 21)

Veiled in this discussion of opposing roles for Cagney is a discourse on 'masculinity' and 'femininity.' Crime films are linked to the male, while musicals are tied to the female. Although this gender association pertains to the audience, it also relates to the male star. (Steve Neale claims that musicals allow for 'feminization' and are the only mainstream genre 'in which the male body has been unabashedly put on display' (Neale 1983: 15).) While the paradigm gangster (e.g. Edward G. Robinson) is macho, the archetypal dancer (e.g. Fred Astaire) 'risks' effeminacy. Though Astaire remains heterosexually 'viable,' one need only think of the cultural clichés attached to the male ballet dancer to see end point on the continuum. Notice the language used by McCarten to describe Cagney's shift from gangster roles. He regrets that Cagney has 'mellowed,' that he has become 'lovable,' that he has turned into an 'angel' – all 'soft' words associated with the feminine. Similarly, McGilligan refers to Cagney as a 'sensitive artist.' Hence, when Cagney says that he prefers to be 'a song-and-dance-man,' perhaps he seeks to be relieved from monolithic gender dictates: to be a 'male-and-female man.' One is reminded of Tom Powers's line in *The Public Enemy* as he succumbs to a volley of bullets: 'I ain't so tough.' But the audience (another public enemy?) rejected the image of Cagney Power-less.

Even in *White Heat* (that 'cauldron of violent masculine passion' ('Big Shots' 1975: 18)), Cagney is responsible for courting 'effeminacy.' His migraine attacks (the moments of his radical hystericization) are reminiscent of musical production numbers, as Cagney staggers choreographically across the floor.[3] In his autobiography, he also claims authorship for the scene where Cody takes Ma's lap as she nurses his headache:[4]

> I thought we would try something, take a little *gamble* . . . I wondered if we *dare* have him sit in her lap once for comfort. I said to the director, Raoul Walsh, 'Let's see if we can *get away with this*.' He said, 'Let's try it.' We did and it worked.
> (Cagney 1976: 126, italics mine)

Screenwriter, Ben Roberts (who collaborated with Ivan Goff), recalls how excited Cagney was on the day of the shoot:

> Jimmy stopped by the office one day and said, 'I just did something *startling*. I don't know if it will work . . . We said 'What did you do?' He said, 'I sat on Mama's lap.'
> (McGilligan 1984: 26, italics mine)

Goff recalls that when the picture was released, 'The audience was startled but they knew they were looking at something *awfully personal*' (McGilligan 1984: 26, italics mine).

Again, the descriptive phrasing seems revealing. The act of having a grown man sit on his mother's lap is a 'gamble,' 'startling,' 'daring,' something to 'get away with.' (Raoul Walsh also uses the latter term (Walsh 1974: 348), as does the *Time* reviewer ('The New Pictures' 1949).) Thomas Schatz varies the pattern, noting that only Cagney could 'pull [this] off' (Schatz 1981: 108). Clearly, it is not only the regression of this act that is shocking, but its *femininity*. While most grown-ups do not sit on other adults' laps, women can – but men cannot.

Significantly, Goff sensed in Cagney's gesture 'something *awfully* personal.' Given the song-and-dance man who loved his mother, this might well have been true. But why is it the *awful* truth?

WHITE HEAT AND COLD SWEATS

Certain illnesses seem so closely related to the culture of an era that it's as though they sprang from the dark side of the collective imagination.

(Miller 1991: 1)

Having uncovered both maternal and hysterical discourses in *White Heat*, we might ask how the film is a product of its times. (Conley calls it a 'scenario' for the 'unconscious of the post-war years' (Conley 1981–2: 138).) What cultural trends in 1940s America help us to decode the film's aberrant, yet powerful address?

Clearly we must examine the impact of World War II, over barely four years when the movie premièred. Some critics have mentioned *White Heat*'s apocalyptic ending, citing parallels between the refinery explosion and the atomic bomb.[5] Similarly, McCarten compares the film's high-tech police pursuit to 'the invasion of Normandy' (McCarten 1949: 127–8). Other writers have noted the rampant cynicism of the movie, seen as indicative of the era's disillusionment. McGilligan claims that the screenwriters intended the film to symbolize 'everything that had gone wrong with the world. . . . the United States had emerged a victor . . . but crippled veterans returning home found a changed spirit in the land' (McGilligan 1984: 9). While the postwar angst of *White Heat* is noted, no one draws a specific parallel between Cody Jarrett and the returning GI – this, despite McGilligan's reference to 'crippled veterans.' Yet once we imagine the comparison, it becomes unavoidable.

Weighing upon the American mind were the myriad men declared 'psychoneurotic' during enlistment or in the war itself. Speaking of the draft, Benjamin C. Bowker states that 'approximately 14 per cent of all men examined for service were rejected for psychoneurotic reasons' (Bowker 1946: 33). Commenting on shell-shock, Willard Waller remarks that 'the armed services were discharging psychoneurotic veterans at the rate of 10,000 cases a month in late 1943 and in early 1944' (Waller 1944: 155). Hence, the topic of male hysteria was in the air; and it is understandable that it should drift into *White Heat*. But why, specifically, might we compare Cody Jarrett to a psychoneurotic vet?

Primary among the concerns for the returning soldier was his potential *violence*. It was understood that he had been trained as a murder machine and that he might fail to override his 'education' in a civilian context. Waller calls the vet a 'threat to society' (13) and a 'connoisseur of death' (Waller 1944: 247):

The soldier's business . . . is killing, and the army does a good job of conditioning him for it. The soldier learns to kill in a cold-blooded, professional way . . . On occasion, however, the sadistic-aggressive tendencies of men in uniform get out of control.

(Waller 1944: 45–6)

It is not a great leap to apply this description to Cody Jarrett a 'cold-blooded,' 'professional,' 'connoisseur of death,' who shoots a cohort in the trunk of a car. Waller also links the term 'explosive' to the returning GI (Waller 1944: 167) and Bowker tells us that society is consequently 'sitting on an atomic bomb' (Bowker 1946: 30). Again, one is reminded of the dénouement of *White Heat*, with Jarrett straddling a detonating gas storage tank.

But there are even stronger parallels between Cody and the returned vet: their mutual association with crime. Bowker catalogs the menacing headlines that inundate the American public:

VETERAN BEHEADS WIFE WITH JUNGLE MACHETE
EX-MARINE HELD IN RAPE MURDER
FATHER SHOT TO DEATH BY YEOMAN SON
TWO VETERANS HELD AS HOLDUP SUSPECTS

(Bowker 1946: 25–6)

And Waller claims that 'the veteran has been so completely alienated from the attitudes and controls of civilian life that he becomes a criminal' (Waller 1944: 124). Elsewhere, Waller describes the military in a manner reminiscent of a gang. He talks of the soldier following the 'will of the leader' (Waller 1944: 19), and of the institution 'crushing out every resurgence of . . . private will against it' (Waller 1944: 21). He also compares the returned vet to a released prisoner: 'Like the orphan and the prisoner, the soldier has been institutionalized and thereby to some extent incapacitated for any life but the soldier's' (Waller 1944: 119). (Jarrett is, of course, both orphaned and imprisoned.) Finally, Waller cites statistics that link war and sociopathology. Based on the experience of World War I: 'we should expect at least 60,000 of the mobilized men to be sent to prison for serious crimes' (Waller 1944: 127). According to Bowker, in 'San Quentin alone, 25% of convicts consist of veterans of World War II' (Bowker 1946: 28).[6]

While one fear of the returning GI involved inordinate violence, another expressed the inverse: *weakness* and *nervousness*. While the first problem might be culturally imagined as an excess of masculinity, the other might be conceived as its paucity. As Waller notes: 'Where men of previously stable personality break under the strain of combat, their condition may be diagnosed as traumatic war neurosis' (Waller 1944: 167). Erik Erikson describes a soldier who (like Cody Jarrett) suffered 'incapacitating headaches' (Erikson 1950: 38). Intriguingly, they first occurred in a mess hall, the site of one of Cody's monumental attacks:

The metallic noise of the mess utensils went through his head like a salvo of shots. It was as if he had no defense whatsoever against these noises, which were so unbearable that he crawled under a cover while the others ate. From then on his life was made miserable by raging headaches . . . his headaches and jumpiness made it necessary for him to be returned to the States and to be discharged.

(Erikson 1950: 40)

Similarly, Dixon Wecter speaks of a soldier whose 'association of terror with the sound of planes [made] even the noise of a passing truck intolerable' (Wecter 1944: 546). Here, we are reminded of the scene of Cody, Ma, and Verna at a drive-in movie which is playing a war film, *Task Force* (1949). As the noise of battle echoes, it annoys Cody, who shuts the soundtrack off.

Let There Be Light (1946), directed by John Huston, is an extraordinarily interesting artifact to examine intertextually with *White Heat*. For, in this documentary, rather than see the soldier as conquering hero, we view him as patient, wreck, 'human salvage,' as 'casualty of the spirit' (Bowker 1946: 28). In vignettes represented as unstaged, we witness physicians treating men for a variety of war-related nervous disorders: amnesia, hysterical paralysis, stuttering, depression, insomnia, tics, and headaches. Submitting themselves to hypnosis, truth serum, art therapy, and psychoanalysis, they are subject to the 'medical gaze' which normally attends the female (Doane 1987: 38–69). The film's narrative proposes a series of optimistic cures, moving the GIs from illness to health, from hospitalization to release.

Recalling one of the privileged histrionic moments of *White Heat* (when Cody sits on Ma's lap), we recollect that Hurley calls it 'dis-arming' (Hurley 1987: 11). Given the de-militarization of the era, this term has a resonant double meaning: highlighting the linkage of war, shock, and hysteria.

'THEIR MOTHERS' SONS'

The first thing I remember hearing about mothers and sons . . . was the story of the 'brave Spartan mothers' who sent their sons forth to battle with the adjuration: *with your shield or on it*, meaning that the young man was to return victorious or dead. Over and over a picture played in my mind: the young man, wounded, without his shield, finds his way back to his mother's door. Would she really refuse to open it?

Vous travaillez pour l'armée, madame?

(Rich 1982: 192)

With mounting concern for the mental health of the American male came a search of causal agents – and it landed at mother's doorstep (much as Tom Powers does in *The Public Enemy*). When he falls to the ground (bound, bandaged, and wrapped in a blanket), he looks more like an overgrown papoose, or a babe in swaddling, than he does a mature criminal. At the end of the film a title reads: ' "The Public Enemy" is not a man, nor is it a character – it is a problem that sooner or later WE . . . must solve.' The homily correctly predicts that the public enemy is 'not a man' – for (by the 1940s) it is Mother, reconfigured as heinous 'Mom.' As Edward Strecker states: 'No nation is in greater danger of failing to solve the mother–child dilemma than our own' (Strecker 1946: 24).

The charge that American culture was warped by 'Momism' reverberated everywhere. One of the first to register alarm was Philip Wylie in *Generation of Vipers*, a text which reveals its milieu: 'I cannot think offhand, of any civilization except ours in which an entire division of men has been used, during wartime . . . to spell out the word 'mom' on a drill field' (Wylie 1942: 184). On one level, Wylie seems to find Mom the driving force behind *all* combat: 'Mom . . . has patriotism. If a war comes, . . . the departure of her son may be her means to grace in old age. Often, however, the going of her son is . . . an occasion for more show . . . She does not miss him' (Wylie 1942: 192). Elsewhere, he likens her to a 'Hitler' who masters 'a new slave population continually go[ing] to work at making more munitions for momism' (Wylie 1942: 193).

But Mom's major link to the military comes through her ruination of the American child. Strecker describes her progeny 'paddling about in a kind of psychological amniotic fluid' (Strecker 1946: 31). Wylie sees her as a 'female devouring her young' (Wylie 1942: 185), keeping them close at the expense of their normal development. 'Our land, subjectively mapped, would have more silver cords and apron strings crisscrossing it than railroads and telephone wires' (Wylie 1942: 185). Though Moms have children of both sexes, it is clearly the *male* to which these writers attend. Without openly acknowledging their bias, they slip into references to mothers and sons. Even in 1976, Hans Sebald resurrects momism and talks of the special 'vulnerability of the boy' (Sebald 1976: 105).

In *Their Mothers' Sons*, Strecker argues that rampant Momism caused the rejection or discharge of men from the armed services. He concludes that while not all traumatized soldiers had Moms, many did: 'A psychoneurosis serves the same purpose mom served' (Strecker 1946: 108). Hence, Mom is not only a social problem but a psychiatric disease.

Significantly, in *Let There Be Light*, when doctors examine patients, they raise questions about their mothers, even when the men have not mentioned them. When one soldier says he felt uncomfortable as a youngster being restricted to playing with select children, the physician tells him that his mother must have felt inferior to people. When another fails to confide problems to his parents, a doctor remarks how his mother must have hidden family troubles. When a veteran (under sodium pentothal) mentions arguing with his mother, the doctor queries leadingly: 'Have you *always* tried to please her?'

In *Modern Woman: the Lost Sex*, Ferdinand Lundberg and Marynia Farnham state that the central thesis of their book is that 'contemporary women . . . are psychologically disordered and that their disorder is having terrible social and personal effects involving men in all departments' (Lundberg and Farnham 1947: v). In particular, the authors blame the feminists for 'turning their backs' on a traditional life, and for expressing 'penis-envy' (303–4). Thus, Moms are overly masculine women who 'castrate' their sons, 'stripp[ing] them of their male powers,' turning them into 'passive echoes' (317–19). Through a taxonomy of malign maternal paradigms, they attack 'rejecting,' 'oversolicitous,' and 'dominating' mothers – all of whom 'slaughter the innocents' (298). Here is how they describe the latter parental type: 'The dominating mother . . . obtains release for her misdirected ego drives at the expense of the child . . . she makes her children her pawns, usually requires of them stellar performances in all their undertakings' (304).

All three Moms are blamed for the rise of crime. They 'produce delinquents' and 'some substantial percentage of criminals' (Lundberg and Farnham 1947: 305). Erik Erikson is a lone voice in defense of maternity, wondering if such mass condemnation masks some 'revengeful triumph':

> Who is this 'Mom'? How did she lose her good, her simple name? How could she become an excuse for all that is rotten in the state of the nation and a subject of literary temper and tantrums? *Is* Mom really to blame?
>
> (Erikson 1950: 289)

It is intriguing to read *White Heat* against these contemporaneous debates on Momism. Of all the critics who covered the film only one made this connection. The writer for *Saturday Review* comments on how Cody feels 'an affection [for Ma] which would startle Philip Wylie. Momism has seldom found a less likely victim or produced a more incredible mother's boy' (*Saturday Review* 1949: 28).

Like the male child mourned in the literature, Cody is neurotic and tied to his [aging] mother's 'silver' apron strings. (Hence the furor around his sitting on her lap – the site at which this 'psychic umbilicus' is most clear (Wylie 1942: 195).) Though Cody is hardly passive, he can be seen as sexually 'castrated,' loving Ma more than Verna. As Wylie warned us: 'Mom steals from the generation of women behind her . . . that part of her boy's personality which should have become the love of a female contemporary' (Wylie 1942: 196).

Ma Jarrett is portrayed as a masculine woman (a godmother in the land of godfathers) – confirming Lundberg and Farnham's worst fears. We might even imagine her as a cartoon 'feminist' – an 'ego-driven' career woman who runs the family business while her son is in jail. In many respects, her perverse representation smacks not only of Momism but of the hostility felt by the discharged soldier for the working woman who took his job. As Strecker notes: 'The returning veteran feels perhaps that his wife has gained entirely too much independence during his absence' (Strecker 1946: 144).

Ma fits clearly into Farnham and Lundberg's 'dominating' category, requiring of her son 'stellar' feats. Hence, the taunt in Cody's self-destructive cheer: 'Made it Ma! Top of the World!' (As Wylie tells us: 'Men live for [Mom] and die for her . . . and whisper her name as they pass away' (Wylie 1942: 185–6).) Like the son of all Moms, Cody comes to an ignominious end: here, criminality and suicide.

GENDER TROUBLE: MIMESIS AND MOM-ESIS

Acting as a woman . . . is not necessarily a tribute to the feminine.
(Showalter 1983: 138)

When Cody utters 'Made it Ma! Top of the World!' there is a double sense to his use of the verb. On the one hand, 'making it' mocks his aspiration to please his gangland matriarch: his grandest heist is also his spectacular death. On the other hand, this phrase is voiced at the moment when he is most hystericized, most feminized – when he has symbolically 'made it' to his mother's gendered stance. According to this reading, Cody has made it not only *for* Ma, but in order to *be* Ma.

It is interesting to place this view within the context of Sebald's theories of Momism and its relation to sexual difference. For Sebald, 'if a girl is exposed to a Mom, she will rarely suffer the harm that befalls her brother because she can escape from being a stifled personality by *imitating* the mother's ways' (Sebald 1976: 105, italics mine). A boy, on the other hand, '*may not imitate* [his] mother. Not being allowed to identify with his mother renders the boy helpless against her guiding powers' (Sebald 1976: 105, italics mine).

A paradox emerges whereby man is damned if he does and if he doesn't. On the one hand, boys suffer from a *lapse* of mimesis, being prohibited from imitating their potent Moms. On the other hand, they evince an *excess* of mimesis in becoming feminized by their awesome mothers. This paradox invokes another that entraps the female sex. While imitation may, conventionally, be seen as 'the sincerest form of flattery,' *White Heat* belies that common wisdom. For, rather than dismantle patriarchy, Cody's feminization secures it. While he (and not a woman) is the hysterical *subject* of the film (and, in this regard, marks his posture as 'transgressive'), woman re-enters as insanity's *cause* – embodied in the familiar figure of Mother. Hence male hysteria evacuates the uterus, only to return there with a vengeance – assigning guilt to the maternal womb.

NOTES

1 The word 'hysteria' derives from the Greek word 'husterikos' which means 'a suffering in the womb.'
2 In my discussion of Cody Jarrett's migraine headaches and of the medical research on the subject, I am not arguing for the accuracy of those portrayals. I am simply reporting their depiction, allowing for the possibility that they are shaped by ideological factors.
3 William Simon once made this comparison years ago in a class on the film at New York University.
4 Raoul Walsh also claims authorship for the idea of having Cagney sit on Wycherly's lap, but McGilligan favors Cagney's claim (McGilligan 1984: 26).
5 Thomas Clark (1976: 62) compares the end of the film to the destruction of Germany and Japan.
6 Bowker is quoting a July 1945 issue of *The Technocrat*.

BIBLIOGRAPHY

'Big Shots' (1975) *Movietone News* 45, 11: 14–21.

Bowker, B. C. (1946) *Out of Uniform*, New York: Norton.

Cagney, J. (1976) *Cagney by Cagney*, Garden City, NY: Doubleday.

'Cagney Kills Again' (1949) *Life* 27, September 24: 83–4.

Clark, T. (1976) '*White Heat*: the Old and the New,' *Wide Angle* 1, 1: 60–5.

Cobb, S. (1943) *Borderlands of Psychiatry*, Cambridge, MA: Harvard University Press.

Conley, T. (1981–2) 'Apocalypse Yesterday,' *Enclitic* 5/6, 1–2: 137–46.

Crowther, B. (1949) 'James Cagney Back as Gangster in *White Heat*, Thriller New at the Strand,' *New York Times* 3 September: 7.

Doane, M. A. (1987) *The Desire to Desire: the Woman's Film of the 1940s*, Bloomington: Indiana University Press.

Dunbar, F. (1947) *Emotions and Bodily Changes: a Survey of Literature on Psychosomatic Interrelationship 1910–45*, 3rd edn, New York: Columbia University Press.

Ehrenreich, B. and English, D. (1978) *For Her Own Good: 150 Years of the Experts' Advice to Women*, Garden City, NY: Anchor–Doubleday.

Erikson, E. H. (1950) *Childhood and Society*, 2nd edn 1963, New York: Norton.

Fischer, L. (1989) *Shot/Countershot: Film Tradition and Women's Cinema*, Princeton, NJ: Princeton University Press.

Gottfredson, M. R. and Hirschi, T. (1990) *A General Theory of Crime*, Stanford, CA: Stanford University Press.

Halliwell, L. (1977) *The Filmgoer's Companion* 6th edn, New York: Hill and Wang.

Hartung, P. T. (1949) 'The Screen,' *Commonweal* 50: 560.

Hurley, N. (1987) 'James Cagney: the Quintessential Rebel,' *New Orleans Review* 14, 2: 5–15.

Karpis, A. (1971) (with B. Trent) *The Alvin Karpis Story*, New York: Coward, McCann and Geoghan.

Lundberg, F. and Farnham, M. (1947) *Modern Woman: the Lost Sex*, New York and London: Harper.

McCarten, J. (1949) 'The Current Cinema,' *The New Yorker* 25: 62–3.

McGilligan, P., ed. (1984) *White Heat*, Madison: University of Wisconsin Press.

'Male Trouble' (1988) *Camera Obscura* 18: entire issue.

Miller, M. V. (1991) 'Anybody Who Was Anybody Was Neuroasthenic,' *New York Times Book Review*, 1, July 7: 24–5.

Neale, S. (1983) 'Masculinity as Spectacle: Reflections on Men and Mainstream Cinema,' *Screen* 24, 6: 2–16.

'The New Pictures' (1940) *Time* 54: 100.

Pearce, J. (1975) *Modern Topics in Migraine*, London: William Heinemann Medical Books.

Penley, C. (1989) 'The Cabinet of Dr. Pee-wee: Consumerism and Sexual Terror,' in *The Future of an Illusion: Film, Feminism and Psychoanalysis*, Minneapolis: University of Minnesota Press.

Perry, J. P. (1981) 'A Descriptive Study of the Subjective Experience of Migraine Headache,' unpublished Ph.D. Dissertation, University of Pittsburgh.

Polan, D. (1986) *Power and Paranoia: History, Narrative and the American Cinema, 1940–1950*, New York: Columbia University Press.

[Review] (1950) *Rotarian* 76: 41.

Rich, A. (1986) *Of Woman Born: Motherhood as Experience and Institution*, 10th edn, New York and London: Norton.

Sacks, O. (1985) *Migraine: Understanding a Common Disorder*, Berkeley: University of California Press.

Saturday Review (1949) 32: 28–9.

Schatz, T. (1981) *Hollywood Genres: Formulas, Filmmaking, and the Studio System*, New York: Random House.

Sebald, H. (1976) *Momism: the Silent Disease of America*, Chicago: Nelson Hall.

Showalter, E. (1983) 'Critical Cross-Dressing and the Woman of the Year,' *Raritan* Fall: 130–49.

Smith, D. C. Jr. (1975) *The Mafia Mystique*, New York: Basic Books.

Smith, P. (1989) 'Action Movie Hysteria, or Eastwood Bound,' *differences* 1, 3: 88–107.

Strecker, E. (1946) *Their Mothers' Sons: the Psychiatrist Examines an American Problem*, Philadelphia and New York: Lippincott.

Tyler, C. (1989) 'The Supreme Sacrifice? TV, "TV", and the Renee Richards Story,' *differences* 1, 3: 160–86.

Waller, W. (1944) *The Veteran Comes Back*, New York: Dryden Press.

Walsh, R. (1974) *Each Man in His Time: the Life Story of a Director*, New York: Farrar, Straus and Giroux.

Wecter, D. (1944) *When Johnny Comes Marching Home*, Cambridge, MA: Houghton Mifflin.

Wylie, P. (1942) *Generation of Vipers*, New York and Toronto: Rinehart.

Part II

MEN IN WOMEN'S PLACES

Figure 12 Michael Caine and Angie Dickinson in *Dressed to Kill*

4

THE DIALECTIC OF FEMALE POWER AND MALE HYSTERIA IN *PLAY MISTY FOR ME*

Adam Knee

This essay will attempt to examine the dynamics of Hollywood conceptualizations of the masculine through an analysis of a film which appeared concurrently with the cresting of a wave of progressive social movements, many of which questioned such conceptualizations: Clint Eastwood's *Play Misty for Me* (1971). The film appeared at a time when American discourses regarding the masculine were being destabilized – though admittedly perhaps temporarily and superficially – and this destabilization is manifested within the film in the form of tensions and contradictions in the representation of the Eastwood character: It appears that Eastwood runs into difficulty here, both as first-time director and star persona, in negotiating contemporary discourses about masculinity, in dealing with a changing (and loosening) sense of the way maleness is constructed in social terms. This discussion will examine Eastwood's figuration as a site of contradiction, both within *Play Misty for Me* and in contemporary discourses surrounding the text, as a means of locating historically specific tensions on the 'tough guy' persona and Eastwood's troubled response to them.

In recent years a number of scholars have also characterized the construction of masculinity in Eastwood's later films in particular as 'troubled' and/or ambiguous – as offering the tools for its own deconstruction. Christine Holmlund (1986), for example, argues that despite *Tightrope*'s (1984) ideological equivocations, that film allows us to see 'the underside of Clint Eastwood's tough guy persona' and directly raises questions about the interrelationships among gender, sexuality, and power. Judith Mayne (1987) suggests that in this reflexive problematizing of links between different kinds of desire and between sexuality and violence, *Tightrope* becomes the theory for the practice exemplified by Dirty Harry. Paul Smith (1989) argues that, in fact, questions of representation and sexual politics are raised across the body of Eastwood's work, although these questions surface more clearly in the most recent films. While this essay will not be arguing with the substance of any of these positions, I do feel that the political ambiguities of some of Eastwood's earlier work have been underexamined, owing in large measure to Eastwood's stronger association with the Dirty Harry and Western 'Man With No Name' personas into the early 1970s. I want to stress therefore the emphatic nature as well as the historical specificity of the 'male trouble' evoked by *Play Misty for Me*, a text which strongly and repeatedly anchors itself in terms of time and geography. *Tightrope* may be the source for a unified 'theory' of Eastwood, especially in psychoanalytic terms, but the historical gendered subject of *Play Misty* has its own very particular problems.

The narrative of the 1971 film entails a literal attack upon the masculine; the plot concerns the stalking of disc jockey David Garver (Eastwood) by an enamored and neurotic fan, Evelyn (Jessica Walter). Even aside from the fact that he is seriously threatened by a female character, the masculinity of the Eastwood persona is already called into question here in that he possesses a number of evidently contradictory characteristics. David does refer us to the machismo of many earlier Eastwood characters in his tendency toward violence, his trademark stony stare, etc., but at the same time director Eastwood offers an implicit acknowledgement that such a traditional figuration of the masculine may be (for the time being) somewhat outmoded: strong efforts are made to imbue David with signifiers of 'sensitivity' and 'hipness,' to suggest at least a tacit assent to the social aims of contemporary progressive political movements – in short, to make him a man in tune with the 1970s.

Thus, while he disdains drug use, he at the same time uses hip lingo, wears mod print shirts and pants, and has a number of relatively close black acquaintances. He takes an utterly antagonistic, machismo posture with a gay acquaintance of his girl friend, but at the same time he enjoys the traditionally non-macho activity of reading poetry on his jazz radio show. And while he occasionally likes to sleep around (a characteristic the film links with traditional male sexual aggression rather than 1960s sexual liberation), he now wants to bring his promiscuity under control and re-establish a more serious relationship with his estranged girl friend, Tobie (Donna Mills).

Although the film registers such changes, it does not appear fully prepared to negotiate them coherently; as suggested, David's own characteristics seem self-contradictory. Although the only male friend of David's we see is his black colleague Al Monte, his comportment toward his fellow DJ is generally so sarcastic and sullen as to appear downright hostile. He refuses all offers of social activities with Al, and when we do see the two together at the Monterey jazz festival, it turns out they are there at least in part on business – to record the music. Director Eastwood appears to share David's equivocal position, filming black spectators at the festival in such a way as to suggest they exist in a general state of exaggerated dancing, grimacing, and buffoonery.[1] Both Al and David's black cleaning woman are themselves generally presented in a stereotypically comic light. In a similar fashion, while this post-Stonewall text can accommodate Tobie's having a close gay friend (JJ), it does so with an exceptionally unsympathetic portrayal. Most of JJ's lines are misogynistic comments delivered with an extremely heavy lisp, and David's final advice to him is to 'go pick up some sailors.' It is strongly suggestive of a crisis in the representation of white masculinity here that the text elicits such hostility toward these characters while retaining formal connections between them and David: aside from having social attachments to blacks and gays, David actively pursues a career in promoting a black musical idiom and is the only character to share JJ's predilection for clothing with wild patterned prints, much in fashion at the end of the 1960s. David sports not only these, but formerly non-macho flower prints as well; he's a veritable wolf in chic clothing.

THE POLITICS OF NORTHERN CALIFORNIA

In the film's terms, then, the refiguration of white masculinity involves new levels of interactivity with members of groups whose social and political rights were being championed by various liberation movements that had gained momentum in the 1960s. *Play Misty for Me* thus becomes, on one level, a drama of relinquishing certain heterosexual white male prerogatives, a film about a male protagonist attempting, with varying degrees of success, to defer to blacks, gays, and, most centrally, women. The film's being set within striking distance of the San Francisco–Oakland–Berkeley area – a seat of student protest and black and gay liberation movements of the previous decade, as well as of heterosexual experimentation with alternatives to monogamy – indeed establishes the political backdrop for this drama. As suggested earlier, the film moreover continually stresses the distinctiveness and specificity of its setting, in, for example, numerous sweeping helicopter shots of the rocky northern California coast and David's oft repeated on-air identification of a station whose call letters even refer to the locale, 'KRML, Carmel.' A contemporary review in *Variety* goes so far as to complain repeatedly about the film's 'frequent disgressions into land-scape' (Review 1971: 6). Historical context is foregrounded by the very fact that the film offers Eastwood's first major lead role in a contemporary setting – excepting his lead in *Coogan's Bluff* (1968), where his character is posited as an anachronism, an old-West cowboy dropped into modern-day New York City. Eastwood's appearance as an average resident of 1970s northern California, then, would have come as a jolt for most contemporary spectators and strongly implied tensions being exerted on the Old-World Eastwood persona.

89

Of course, while *Play Misty*'s setting is *near* the politically weighted San Francisco Bay area of the early 1970s, it is also distinctly *removed* from that area, an exclusive, non-urban, monied enclave. This sense of simultaneous social/economic/geographic proximity and removal reverberates with David's trouble in relating to many of the individuals he regularly encounters and the social trends they represent. The desire for escape is inscribed again in the location and architecture of David's own particular abode, a quiet house by the ocean, well removed from downtown Carmel, and set back from the road by a garden. The desire is also suggested in David's choice of a highly solitary profession and even, arguably, in the type of music he plays: soft, unobtrusive jazz, nearly in the 'easy listening' category, rather than jazz with a harsh or aggressive edge. It is music designed for the Carmel lifestyle, and David's occupation thus centers on promoting such an existence of escape and leisure.

Carmel resonates in this text not only because of its political associations and because of its engendering of a trope of simultaneous proximity and removal – but also because of its associations with Eastwood in extratextual discourses, this being the actor–director's own real-life place of residence at the time of the film. The aforementioned *Variety* review makes such an association when it complains about parts of the film which serve 'as an overdone travelog for the Monterey Peninsula–Carmel home environment of star, producer, and debuting director Clint Eastwood' (Review 1971: 6). Indeed, such discourses invite a number of comparisons between the textual construction of David Garver and the extratextual construction of actor–director Eastwood. In one mid-1970s interview, for example, Eastwood allows that there are similarities between him and David (and some of his other characters) in that they are all loners, 'individuals,' and he also suggests that he himself was in a situation like David's in his own life (Knight 1974: 60, 70).[2] One could add that both figures are bashful media stars, both are jazz enthusiasts, and both worked to promote Carmel leisure culture in the 1970s – Eastwood being part-owner of a chic Carmel health food restaurant.[3]

Perhaps more pertinent to the arguments in this essay is that the sense of the Eastwood persona as a site of contradictions also extends into extratextual discourses. The dust-jacket blurb for a 1974 fan-oriented biography tells us that Eastwood 'is a man of many – often seemingly contradictory – parts' (Douglas 1974). It goes on to enumerate some of these: 'A painfully shy youth who had to make a conscious effort to overcome his social backwardness, he is adored by millions of women and admired by nearly as many men. An actor whose trademark is violence, he abhors violence in real life, especially cruelty to animals . . . A man whose body is constantly mistreated in the movies, he is a health and organic food addict' (Douglas 1974). Arthur Knight's introduction to his interview with Eastwood in *Playboy* (1974), a journal which had

itself been long concerned with synthesizing traditional and more progressive concepts of masculinity, immediately foregrounds similar
notions:

> Though Eastwood is the world's hottest star, it's hard to believe he
> believes it. And it's difficult to reconcile the real Clint Eastwood –
> gentle, soft-spoken, self-effacing – with the violent men he's played
> onscreen, men who were ready to shoot first and talk later if at all.
> There are other contradicitons; he's a physical-fitness buff but a
> chain beer drinker; he enjoys shooting but refuses to hunt; hates
> giving out autographs, but the fans who besiege him whenever he
> makes a rare personal appearance are unlikely to discover this unless
> they become unbearably persistent.
>
> (Knight 1974: 58)

The interview which follows reiterates most of Knight's asserted contradictions, with Eastwood stressing that, despite the action-oriented, macho
roles he has played, he detests violence and concurs with the premises
behind the contemporary women's liberation movement. The political
positionality Eastwood traces out also hearkens back to that of David
Garver: 'I'm a political nothing. I mean, I hate to be categorized . . . I
suppose I'm a moderate, but I could be called a lot of things. On certain
things I could be called very liberal; on others, very conservative' (ibid.:
170). In an interview with Patrick McGilligan (himself surprised by Eastwood's 'soft and composed voice' (McGilligan 1976: 12)), Eastwood
concordantly claims, 'The only time I've been associated with anything
political is by innuendo or by people's assumptions that I have certain
political aspects' (12). This extratextual Eastwood, like Garver, appears
to fear the intrusion of others into his insular political discourse and to
desire the leeway for political contradictions.

GENDER TROUBLES

Evelyn functions in one sense as just such an intrusion, as an overt
manifestation of the threat posed by the flourishing of the women's
liberation movement. David's trepidation over the new deference to
women required of him as a man of the 1970s – his fear of women with
newly won social power – surfaces in the form of an ultimately violent,
sexually desirous female aggressor. Ironically, Evelyn appears as a threat
precisely because she has taken on traditional masculine characteristics,
of the very type David is being forced to give up, and in this way she
is simultaneously a return of the masculine repressed. The narrative logic
of the film suggests this in part because David becomes entangled with
her when he indulges in his former macho habits; she is an intended
one-night stand gone awry, a clear model for the Glenn Close character

in *Fatal Attraction*. Evelyn thus stands as a constant reminder of David's macho past, impeding his efforts to reconnect with Tobie, to become a man of the 1970s. This notion is underscored in a scene in which Evelyn prevents David from getting a new job by interrupting the lunch date with his would-be employer in a fit of jealous fury. The employer describes the job as an 'unstructured, loosey-goosey, Monterey Pop, Woodstock type of thing' in which he would be 'working with kids'; and Evelyn's ruining the interview thus prevents him again from hooking up with the 'now generation.'

The reversal of traditionally gendered characteristics between David and Evelyn, in tandem with a subtle paralleling of their emotional proclivities, in fact becomes a central structuring element in the film, evoking a strong sense of doubling or identity between the two characters. Evelyn manages to wear the pants in this film, while still sporting miniskirts, by occupying a masculine position in terms of Hollywood codes (and broader cultural conventions) of action, of the gaze, and of voice. While David is at pains to repress physical impulses of various sorts, his performance suggesting a violence seething beneath the surface (and largely stuck there), Evelyn controls a substantial portion of the physical action of the film. By acting on violent and sexual desires in ways no longer open to the Eastwood character – in being sexually aggressive and ultimately homicidal – it is Evelyn rather than David who is crucial to forwarding the narrative; for the most part, she acts, while he reacts. In conjunction with this, Evelyn's presence undermines traditional Hollywood conventions of the male orientation of the gaze.

POWER REVERSALS

The initial 'pick-up' scenes between Evelyn and David are instructive in the way they exemplify the play on reversals of ocular and sexual power this text is fraught with. After his show one evening, David heads over to his usual watering hole, where the bartender (played by Eastwood's friend and sometime director Don Siegel) thanks him for having plugged the establishment – for fulfilling his role as a promoter of Carmel leisure industries. The discussion between the two men is suddenly interrupted when a miniskirted Evelyn, whom we have glimpsed in the background and also reflected in the mirror behind the bar, calls for the bartender; even aside from this interruption, Evelyn's appearance at the bar, in and of itself, already signifies an intrusion into a traditionally male realm. The first shot focused directly on her, in which her bare legs figure prominently, is followed by a reaction shot of David appraising her; the filmic syntax has clearly positioned the spectator as sharing the desiring gaze of the DJ. The shot of this gaze is then itself interrupted by a very prohibitive 'uh-uh' from off-screen; the bartender explains to David that the woman has been turning down men all evening. The two men proceed to play an arcane game with old corks and bottle stoppers on top of the bar, and we thus have a dramatization of the Oedipal competition which has been suggested; a shot/reverse shot sequence opposes David to the bartender – a father figure both in his age and in his being played by Eastwood's directorial mentor – and the bartender/father 'possesses' Evelyn in this series of shots by sharing his frame with her, as she can be seen reflected in the mirror behind him.

A cut to a one-shot of Evelyn sucking her drink through a straw and watching the two men intently suggests that there has been a shift in who is gazing upon whom, that perhaps the bartender's prohibition has been successful. This shot is replaced by one with the camera at the same angle but placed further back, so that the two men, still facing each other, are now in the foreground, their shared line of vision perpendicular to that of Evelyn, who is positioned directly between them; we thus have reiterated the sense that the men have become the object of the gaze, that their vision is less comprehensive than Evelyn's, whose view is the reverse field of our own. At the same time, however, our identification remains with David to a large degree – both because he has been the key focal character up until now and because, in this specific shot, he is far closer to us.

We return to this three-shot moments later, as Evelyn decides to get up and walk toward the men, remaining in the position of observer and aggressor; as she does so, we hear David say, 'Be careful now, really careful,' but his remarks appear directed toward his overt opponent, the bartender. Evelyn accepts an offer of a drink from David, and the two men admit that the 'game' they had been playing was a ruse, set up as part of a bet on whether David would indeed be able to buy the woman a drink. Thus, in a re-reversal of power and looking relations, it is revealed that Evelyn had been the object of observation and pursuit all along – and that the men had played the game, in a sense, over possession of the woman.

This return to the *status quo* itself proves temporary, however. The dialogue immediately suggests that Evelyn may still be a potential threat, as she quips, 'I ought to be mad.' David responds, 'But you're not,' and she adds 'Not really,' in a barely audible whisper. A cut a moment later to Evelyn wielding an ice pick – at her freezer, it turns out – suggests that she may indeed be mad in both senses of the term and repositions her as an aggressor. We learn that David has given her a lift to her house, and as the sequence of his visit with her unfolds, Evelyn remains in a largely dominant position both visually and dramatically. She refuses David's offer of assistance with the ice and instructs him to start a fire. She enters a high-angle shot of David kneeling by the fireplace, her head remaining out of the frame, and there is a cut to a low-angle close-up

Figure 13 Clint Eastwood and Jessica Walter

of her face as she admits that her appearance at the bar had been with the express intent of meeting the DJ; we thus see David in a diminutive and servile position, being looked down upon by an initially faceless predator – one who dominates but whose motives are kept at a disquieting remove.

The low-angle close-up of Evelyn, whose face is framed with a candle and a bunch of white flowers on the mantel, is replaced by a complementary reaction shot of David looking upward. The traditional male position is undermined in numerous ways through this juxtaposition. The white flowers on David's shirt both feminize him and yoke him to the flowers in Evelyn's frame; David's flowers are, moreover, an inadequate reflection of Evelyn's, lacking the presence of their three-dimensionality. The skinny illuminated fireplace match he holds is compositionally angled toward the woman's crotch, yet this woman formally overwhelms him, her bare leg dominating the foreground of his frame. Despite the obvious phallic symbolism of the object, it is no match for the much thicker wax phallus in Evelyn's frame, which only lacks its fire. Thus, while David does gaze upon Evelyn, he is simultaneously dominated by this object of desire, and while the image objectifies and eroticizes Evelyn through nudity and fragmentation, we simultaneously share the woman's position in casting an off-screen gaze at David. David attempts to regain his male positioning by standing up into Evelyn's frame, but in the resultant two-shot, it is she who dominates the conversation and who suggests they sleep together. Two ensuing shots reveal that her suggestion has been followed, and their darkness and brevity de-emphasize the fact that David is on top as the couple have sex.

The sequence at Evelyn's ends with a shot of David walking toward his car in the morning – from a perspective which is retroactively revealed to be motivated by Evelyn's presence, as she enters the frame and gazes quietly at David, then stares off, contemplatively. Just as the foregoing sequence sets up a pattern of pursuit and of threat to male dominion, so does this unexpected play on point of view establish a pattern of similar revelations about perspective throughout the film. In a number of instances, long shots of David, or of David and Tobie, are retroactively revealed to be from a vantage point shared by Evelyn, who has a habit of spying on them. Such revelations unsettle and problematize spectator feelings of identification with David, while also suggesting, again, a transfer of narrative power from him to Evelyn.

UN/SOUND POLITICS

Perhaps one of the most intriguing and significant of gendered power reversals in the film involves the soundtrack. A further oxymoronic characteristic of David's already problematic persona is that he is an *inarticulate* DJ; David's incohcrence of character manifests itself in a literal inability to express himself in scene after scene, even where such self-expression would appear crucial to his well-being. The situation with Evelyn gets out of hand in part because he is unable to speak to her at length about anything – especially because he is extremely slow to make explicit his position on their relationship; he himself tells her, 'I don't know what to say to you.' Even with sane characters David appears oddly speechless. Both Al Monte and McCallum, the police sergeant who investigates when Evelyn runs amok, must constantly prod David to get any kind of verbal response, and even then, his statements are generally lacking in crucial information. David is also quite slow to tell Tobie about his predicament, and far too slow to explain Evelyn's tirade to his would-be employer. When David does speak, his words are regularly ignored by the other characters, who prattle on as though there has been no verbal input; even the cleaning woman brushes off his request that she leave in one scene and continues to prod him with questions about the state of his home.

The largely jazz musical score itself originates from outside David's white male realm, and an extended love scene with Tobie is accompanied by Roberta Flack singing 'The First Time Ever I Saw Your Face,' a black female expression of sexual desire and voyeuristic control. Significantly, while David's girl friend Tobie is positioned on her back and below him in this scene, the clear suggestion, through conventional cinematic coding, is that he is nonetheless in the passive role of orally servicing and pleasuring her. This is, of course, structured as another indicator of 1970s male sensitivity, of David's move into a new age; indeed, the very act of representing this form of sexual activity foregrounds its *historical* importance, as the institutional context of commercial feature film-making is one which had only recently come to allow such representations. The distinct unfamiliarity of Eastwood performing oral sex on screen, even in such highly codified form, likewise underscores again tensions on his own constructed image. Within the context of *Play Misty for Me*, David's act of cunnilingus is opposed to the male-dominated sexual intercourse we briefly see him engaged in with Evelyn and which Evelyn refers to as male-dominated in later dialogue. In terms of the film's acoustic dynamics, the act is significant because it once more hinders verbal articulations on the part of the male protagonist.

It is pertinent here that David's position of powerlessness on the soundtrack is a traditionally feminine one in the Hollywood film, where men have generally (though by no means always) controlled voice-over narrations and dominated speech acts. Certainly there is a tradition of laconic macho heroes, Eastwood's Westerner being one of the most obvious examples, but the speechlessness of these men is not figured in the way David's is here. To the extent that David *is* linked to these previous heroes, the film's suggestion is that such laconism no longer functions effectively in a changed social landscape. Evelyn, in opposition, gains power precisely through her (masculine) control of sound, through her constant, manipulating articulations. Her requests and declarations come too fast and furious for David to fend them off; even when she is out of earshot, she wields control through phone calls, a motif underscored in a number of phone-ring-sound bridges. One of Evelyn's most oft-repeated verbal requests, and thus a crucial signifier of a potentially dangerous female desire, in fact constitutes the title of the film.

A scene which strongly suggests that Evelyn is indeed taking on a degree of masculine power in the vocal scheme of things occurs when she accosts David outside the bar one day. As she and David struggle over his car keys, two passers-by ask if she needs help. David shouts, 'Get lost,' and Evelyn immediately emulates and expands upon this verbal action, shouting in guttural tones reminiscent of David's, 'Yeah, get lost, assholes.' She then turns to David, positively beaming, as though expecting praise for learning a lesson in machismo. Evelyn's various knife and scissor attacks later in the film are themselves accompanied by guttural grunts and shouts rather than shrill screams.

96

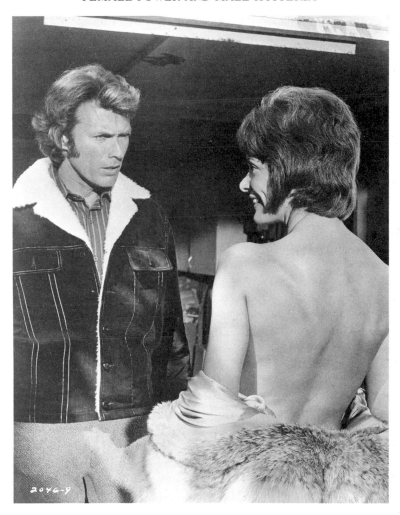

Figure 14 Clint Eastwood and Jessica Walter

In another scene, David even appears to be driven to a state of hysteria by his powerlessness in the face of the quantity of verbiage Evelyn thrusts upon him. He has visited her with the intent of fully ending their involvement and finds her posing in new pajamas, serving him sand-wiches, and talking incessantly. Believing himself unable to get a word in edgewise, he suddenly breaks into a sputtering, trembling rage, on the verge of exploding into unthinking violence, and manages to growl 'I'm just trying to be straight with you,' before departing. We get the sense here that just as Evelyn has taken on masculine power, David, in the face of forces and changes he cannot handle, takes on some of the loss of rationality associated with Evelyn and traditionally with the feminine. And just as David starts to show hysterical symptoms – the inability to speak or to act in a rational or effective manner – as a result of being forced to repress traditional masculine tendencies and to live with contradictions, so can we read the closely linked implied figure of Eastwood as starting to become hysterical and unable to direct a fully coherent text.[4] In its wavering between misogyny and women's liberation, racism and the acceptance of black culture, puritanism and sexual liberation, and violence and romance, *Play Misty for Me* becomes an historically relevant symptom in itself.

DIFFICULTIES OF DOUBLING

The contradictions embodied in both the textual David and the extratextual Eastwood appear to dialectically explode into the violent final sequences of the film, in which Evelyn, as a kind of stand-in for both men, goes on a murderous rampage. In these terms, Evelyn's earlier narratively unmotivated knife attack on David's black cleaning woman (the source of some of his 'male trouble') makes perfect sense; even as a victim, the cleaning woman is the subject of the film's ridicule, telling David from a stretcher that he will have to pay double for the mess Evelyn has left at his house. Evelyn is caught and sent away, but comes back to wreak more havoc when she gets paroled (a twist which portends the critique of legal procedure central to some of the Dirty Harry films). As the return of David's repressed, she now moves in with his girl friend Tobie (who has been looking for a roommate) and, once her real identity is revealed, ties Tobie up and runs her fingers through her hair, asking if David does the same.

If we understand Evelyn as David's double here, it is certainly significant that Sgt McCallum, who has come to the house to look in on Tobie, is the only character she kills. McCallum has irritated David throughout the film with his efforts to develop a machismo rapport, largely through jokingly flirtatious gestures like winking or declaring that the DJ is not his 'idea of a swinging date.' In the film's logic, it would seem that the prospect of homosexuality is so horrifying (presumably because also fascinating) that even McCallum is a threat – whom Evelyn offs in the film's only explicitly depicted act of bodily penetration, by plunging scissors into his chest. The attack can be read not only as a displaced act of predatory, violent male homosexual intercourse, but also as Evelyn's own expression of jealousy over McCallum's flirtatious relationship with David and as a displacement of her homicidal feelings towards David. The homosexual/homophobic subtext is also present here in Evelyn's masculinizing of David's androgynously-named girl friend by cutting off her hair – which draws attention to the fact that Evelyn's hair is short itself.[5]

The extent of the character displacement evident in this scene of Evelyn's final rampage is in itself significant: it is at the narrative's crisis point that the text's unstable nature in this regard threatens to surface. Character displacements have indeed been suggested throughout the film. At one point, David follows a woman he believes to be Tobie, only to discover that she is a roommate wearing Tobie's sweater, while in another instance he comments on the constant turnover of Tobie's roommates. By implication, it would appear that not only are Tobie and her roommates interchangeable, but so are Tobie and Evelyn – and indeed all women. As this essay has shown, however, Evelyn and David are themselves interchangeable on some levels – as are, in the rampage scene, McCallum and David and even Tobie (as recipient of Evelyn's caresses) and David. Character displacement thus becomes gender displacement on a large scale, and the stability of masculine identity is again thrown into question owing largely to Evelyn's actions.

It is therefore appropriate that Evelyn's final attack on David is figured as an attack on his gaze, on the traditional locus of masculine cinematic power. As she waits for David to arrive at Tobie's house, Evelyn slits the eyes in a portrait of him and indicates that her cutting of Tobie's hair has the purpose of reducing David's pleasure in looking. When David does arrive, he finds that the lights have been put out of commission, and Evelyn becomes a major threat because of his resultant loss of vision. David finally dispatches Evelyn by reclaiming his machismo power, landing an Old-World punch that sends her flying through a picture window.[6]

Christine Holmlund's analysis of Eastwood's more recent film *Tightrope* suggests that there again historically specific received notions of masculinity are being questioned, in large part through the doubling of Eastwood's detective character with a misogynistic killer, and that the presence of feminist discourses in the text 'testifies to the magnitude of public concern for issues of sexuality and power in 1984' (Holmlund 1986: 38). The differences between these two very similar texts, thirteen years apart, are instructive. Holmlund notes that *Tightrope* is fraught with ambiguity, that 'in it feminism and misogyny vie for first place' (39); and yet, compared with David Garver, Detective Wes Block is a relatively stable character. His underside is thrown into question, yet he is nowhere near as fragmented and self-contradictory a figure as David. While *Tightrope* is indeed ambiguous, it is able to accommodate its ambiguity, to negotiate the presence of certain politically progressive discourses in a relatively coherent fashion. In contrast, *Play Misty for Me* is not nearly as comfortable in dealing with such discourses, which are still comparatively new in 1971. This is evident in part in the differences between the two films' structures of doubling. *Tightrope*'s doubling is relatively overt, the *doppelgänger* being a male with strong visual and narrative parallels to the protagonist – a male whose destruction signals a need to come to terms with aspects of Wes's masculinity. In *Play Misty for Me*, on the other hand, the doubling is relatively submerged and the *doppelgänger* is a woman, so that David's killing of her at the film's conclusion finally serves not to question his masculinity so much as to violently attack the feminine forces which insist upon such questioning.

Such ideological equivocation at the film's close signals a crisis in efforts towards a viable figuration of a 1970s masculinity. David is supposed to relinquish a machismo past and become more sensitive to women, yet in a textual sleight of hand this is achieved by his killing of the woman he interacts with through most of the film. The film, moreover, has insidiously aligned promiscuity with the past, thus allowing David's move into a new social realm to be compatible with embracing an older sexual *status quo* (that of heterosexual monogamy); the politics of sexual liberation are thereby nimbly elided, and David can walk off into the sunset with his one and only. No matter how hip this 1971 manifestation of the Eastwood persona may appear, he's still got one foot firmly planted in the old West.

What is ultimately most provocative about *Play Misty for Me*, however, is the extent to which Eastwood's tough guy persona is forced into a contemporary context and is cast into doubt, despite the film's hardly progressive conclusion. Indeed, the film has much in common with what Thomas Elsaesser, writing in 1975, delineates as a new liberal American cinema of the early 1970s: a group of commercial features which question conventional Hollywood narrative form, and by implication mainstream American ideologies, in their utilization of unmotivated or uncommitted heroes and a non-goal-oriented journey structure (Elsaesser 1975: see especially 13–14). In *Play Misty*, David does indeed seem to lack strong motivations, and much of the narrative is instead driven by Evelyn's actions with respect to him; David appears quite ready to endanger his professed main goals – of returning to Tobie and moving up in his disc jockeying career – by getting involved with Evelyn in the first place. The opening of the film concordantly implies a search for identity and in fact engages some conventions of the contemporary alienated road movie Elsaesser discusses: David looks out at the ocean behind his house, then regards a portrait of himself – as though questioning his image, his constructed identity – before hopping into his car and zooming down the coastal highway, with no destination as yet articulated to us.

As it turns out, David's journey, like his self-examination, indeed goes nowhere; throughout the film he merely drives between the same old locations – his home, the radio station, the bar, his girl friends' homes. The questioning and tempering of David/Eastwood's macho image is ultimately overtaken by a resurgence of male violence in the form of a reaction to Evelyn, and David starts to behave more like the protagonist of Eastwood's next film, *Dirty Harry* (1971) – a film Elsaesser (like many others) links to conservative trends of the decade. As Elsaesser describes it, 'the Clint Eastwood or Charles Bronson characters (*Dirty Harry*, *Death Wish*), who are so purposive and determined, so firm and single-minded, appear powered by the purely negative energy of resentment, frustration, and a petit-bourgeois spite seeking to vent its destructive rage under the guise of a law-and-order morality' (Elsaesser 1975: 15). In these terms, we can perhaps see Eastwood's first directorial effort as indicative of a passing moment of progressive questioning of traditional constructions of male identity prior to the conservative reaction which launched him to greater macho stardom.

NOTES

I would like to acknowledge Jeanne Hall's helpful suggestions in revising this essay.

1 This portrayal arguably brings to mind the supposedly sympathetic, happy-go-lucky blacks who people southern streets in D. W. Griffith's *Birth of a Nation* (1915).

2 Such comparisions might call for a qualification of Dennis Bingham's recent assertion that 'It was only in the early 1980s, when Eastwood began to revise and "humanize" his screen image, that his private life took on resonance in his films' (Bingham 1990: 33).

3 Eastwood's cultivation of this Carmel culture culminated in his being elected mayor of the town in 1986.

4 Paul Smith indeed finds a 'residual, barely avowed male hysteria' in many of Eastwood's action and western films. Smith argues that this hysteria 'is often expressed narratively as the sensation of the dangers inherent in identification with women or with homosexuals (of either gender). Or else it is an hysterical formation that can be glimpsed in moments of incoherence or powerlessness in the male body and in the male presence' (1989: 103). In these terms, we can see David's being given over to contemporary dress trends in *Play Misty for Me* as yet another manifestation of his hysteria.

5 Smith (1989), Mayne (1987), and Holmlund (1986) all refer, to varying degrees, to a homophobic subtext within Eastwood's films.

6 In Lacanian terms, this punch can arguably be read as marking a shift from the 'mirror stage' to the symbolic order. The picture window is aligned with a mirror at the film's opening, when David looks at the portrait of himself through the window. Evelyn reveals the absence of the object in this image, and also underscores her own anxiety-inducing difference, in her piercing of the eyes in the portrait. David soon afterwards destroys the window/mirror in the act of killing the woman who has hindered his control of language throughout the film. The result of the act (itself predicated upon a reclaiming of neglected motor skills) is thus a (re)acquisition of language as well as a shift from an 'infantile' polymorphous sexuality (figured here as heterosexual promiscuity) to a socially orthodox monogamy with Tobie.

101

BIBLIOGRAPHY

Bingham, D. (1990) 'Men With No Names: Clint Eastwood's "The Stranger" Persona, Identification, and the Impenetrable Gaze,' *Journal of Film and Video* 42, 4: 33–48.

Douglas, P. (1974) *Clint Eastwood: Movin' On*, Chicago: Henry Regnery.

Elsaesser, T. (1975) 'The Pathos of Failure: American Films in the 70's,' *Monogram* 6: 13–19.

Holmlund, C. (1986) 'Sexuality and Power in Male Doppelgänger Cinema: the Case of Clint Eastwood's *Tightrope*,' *Cinema Journal* 26, 1: 31–42.

Knight, A. (1974) 'Playboy Interview: Clint Eastwood,' *Playboy* 21, 2: 57–.

McGilligan, P. (1976) 'Clint Eastwood,' *Focus on Film* 25: 12–20.

Mayne, J. (1987) 'Walking the *Tightrope* of Feminism and Male Desire,' in A. Jardine and P. Smith (eds) *Men in Feminism*, New York: Methuen.

Review of *Play Misty for Me* (1971) *Variety* 264, Sept 15: 6–.

Smith, P. (1989) 'Action Movie Hysteria, or Eastwood Bound,' *differences* 1, 3: 88–107.

5

'DON'T BLAME THIS ON A GIRL'
Female rape-revenge films
Peter Lehman

During the 1970s and 1980s a new sub-genre of female rape-revenge films appeared in the US. In these films, a beautiful woman hunts down the men who raped her and kills them one by one, frequently reveling in the pleasure of the man's agony when he realizes who she is and what she is about to do. Although these films have appeared in a number of genres, several B movie cult classics such as *I Spit on Your Grave* (1978), *Ms. 45* (1981), and *Alley Cat* (1982) are the quintessential examples. This structure has, however, entered the mainstream Hollywood cinema. In fact, *Hannie Caulder* (1972), a Western starring Raquel Welch and directed by Burt Kennedy, is the earliest such film I have identified. Clint Eastwood's *Sudden Impact* (1983), starring Sondra Locke, is a more recent example of a major Hollywood genre film which conforms to the pattern. Even such seemingly serious films as *Extremities* (1986), an adaptation of William Mastrosimone's play starring Farrah Fawcett, are related.

Of all the films in the genre, *I Spit on Your Grave* is by far the most controversial. Indeed, it may be one of the most reviled films of all time, not I would argue because it is bad but because it is graphically uncompromising. Some of the critical comments made about the film are revealing. Roger Ebert begins his review by noting:

> *I Spit on Your Grave* is a vile bag of garbage that is so sick, reprehensible, and contemptible that I can hardly believe it played in respectable theaters. But it did. Attending it was one of the most depressing experiences of my life.
>
> (Ebert 1989: 359)

Near the conclusion of his review, Ebert returns to the same type of language with which he began it: 'at the film's end I walked out of the theater quickly, feeling unclean, ashamed, and depressed. This movie is an expression of the most diseased and perverted darker human natures' (Ebert 1989: 360).[1]

Much of the review centers on what Ebert interprets as an extremely disturbing audience response. In his estimation, the rape brings out the worst elements of the men in the audience and the avenging woman's attacks the worst elements of the women. He thus presumes, in a manner which I will argue is mistaken, that the pleasure of watching these films for men lies in identification with the rapists and their assault on the woman. Indeed, the unusually long, graphic, and ugly nature of the two rapes in the film are free of conventional ways of eroticizing such scenes. Much of the outdoor rape scene, for example, is in extreme long shot, and the woman's body is covered with dirt. Neither of the rapes contains fetishized close-ups of the woman's face or of fragmented body parts. Her dirty, bruised, bloody body is never lit or in any way represented as part of an erotic spectacle. The protracted nature of the scenes, far from extending pleasurable eroticism, work to make the rapes painfully difficult to watch, though not for the reprehensible reasons Ebert suggests. The reverse is closer to the truth. Watching these despicable men engage in this atavistic brutality allows the audience to feel that what follows is justified. Male spectators are positioned to be disgusted by the rape and to identify with the avenging woman. Although Ebert concludes the pleasures of the film are sadistic in a simple manner, whereby men enjoy watching women getting raped and women enjoy watching men get blown away, I argue that the sadistic elements function quite differently and that they are complicated by male masochistic pleasures.

Finally, it is worth noting Ebert's observation that 'The movie is nothing more or less than a series of attacks on the girl and then her attacks on the men' (Ebert 1989: 360). This description is accurate as far as it goes, but it does not go far enough. It is perhaps no coincidence that Ebert's language recalls common ways of talking about pornography as nothing more or less than an excuse to have a series of sex scenes. In her superb analysis of hard-core porno films, Linda Williams has shown that such a description misses much of what characterizes the genre. This is not to deny that hard-core porno films contain flimsy narratives that motivate a series of sex scenes, but rather to suggest that the meanings and pleasures offered by the genre are much more complex than such a description implies. In this regard, Ebert's being appalled that the film played in 'respectable' theaters is revealing. Like hard-core porno, presumably it is nothing but trash that should be relegated to other sites where respectability will not be contaminated. I agree that *I Spit on Your Grave* is an extremely disturbing movie, but like many disturbing films in disreputable genres (e.g., *The Texas Chainsaw Massacre*, 1974) it is so because of the manner in which it foregrounds and intensifies many of the elements that these same reviewers find acceptable in more muted versions of other films in the genre. Martin and Porter, for example, give *Ms. 45* four stars and have no reservations about the film. Similarly Leonard Maltin calls the film 'well-made' and notes that 'it won some strong reviews' (Maltin 1990: 780). Although *Ms. 45* obviously has a respectability which *I Spit on Your Grave* lacks, they are closely related both generically and in terms of the pleasures they afford male spectators.[2] This essay is an inquiry into the nature of those pleasures which, I will argue, are complex, multiple, and fluid and address a male subjectivity which is both heterosexually masochistic and homosexually sadistic.

In order to identify the defining features of this sub-genre, it is necessary to briefly synopsize a few of these films, starting with the core B features. They nearly all begin with a rape or rapes involving several men. In *I Spit on Your Grave*, an author goes to the country in order to write. Immediately upon her arrival, she is brutally gang raped first outside her home and then once again when she seeks refuge inside. In *Ms. 45*, a mute woman works as a seamstress in the garment district. She is raped on her way home from work, and then when she gets home, she is raped by a burglar. In *Alley Cat*, a woman discovers some men stealing the tires on her car. Using karate, she fights them off but shortly afterwards the men and some of their gang rob a liquor store and brutally attack the girl's grandparents, mortally wounding the grandmother. As the girl jogs in the park, she encounters two men raping a woman. On a later jog in the park, a man attempts to rape her. When the police and the courts fail to see that justice is done, the woman goes berserk in the courtroom and is jailed for contempt of court. When she gets out and resumes jogging, she is once again the target of an attempted rape.

After the opening attacks, much of the remaining narrative of these films is structured around the way in which the wronged women enact their vengeance. During the remainder of *I Spit on Your Grave*, we watch the rape victim methodically revenge herself on each of the rapists. She hangs one, castrates another, and runs over one with a motorboat. The film ends when she has killed them all. In *Ms. 45*, the raped woman kills her second attacker and cuts up his body so that she can slowly dispose of it in pieces. In the course of the film, however, she kills other men, including a fashion photographer, a pimp, a rich oil sheik, and members of a street gang, who harass her or other women on the street. At one point, she even tries to kill a man whom she has seen making out with his girl friend on the street. Although she is foiled in her attempt, her only motivation appears to be disgust at the display of male sexuality. At the end of the film, she attends a costume party where she first kills her date as he prepares to make love to her and then starts to shoot all the men at the party. Finally, she is stabbed from behind by another woman. By the end of *Alley Cat*, the woman hunts down the gang who victimized her and her grandparents at the beginning of the film and kills them all. The film concludes with her united with a kindly police officer with whom she has fallen in love.

Although *Sudden Impact* is one of Clint Eastwood's Dirty Harry films and a major Hollywood production, its central narrative line closely relates to those outlined above. The film begins with what appears to be a love-making scene in a parked car. The woman, however, pulls out a gun, shoots the man in the groin and then kills him with another shot. We learn through flashbacks that the woman and her sister, who is now institutionalized in a near-comatose state, were gang raped years earlier. The woman from the opening scene hunts down the rapists one by one, and, after forcing them to recognize her and realize what she is about to do, she shoots them first in the groin and then in the head. The film concludes when Harry rescues her from the last remaining rapist, who is about to rape her again. He then pins all the murders on the last rapist, whom he kills, and in the final image we see Harry and the avenging woman alone together.

By contrast *Thelma and Louise* (1991) has elements obviously related to rape-revenge films, but it does not fall into the genre as I have defined it. Indeed, the identification that many women have with the central characters in the film may result from the way in which it avoids male fantasies of eroticizing female violence against the male body. The moments of deadly violence or threats to men are extremely brief. Louise's decision to shoot Thelma's attacker occurs in a split second due to her rage at his arrogant, unrepentant attitude. She expresses nothing but genuine anger on her face when she shoots him. Similarly, near the end of the film, when they blow up the truck of the crude driver who has harassed them repeatedly on the highway, they do so quickly and without erotic enticement. The trucker pulls over clearly expecting sex, but Thelma and Louise do not playfully delude him before revealing their true motives. There is absolutely no structure of anticipation in these scenes. They are brief eruptions showing angry rather than flirtatious women. There is no overt sexualization of the actions. The rapist is not shot in the genitals as in *Sudden Impact* and the trucker is not forced to strip. Since there is no gang rape, the overall narrative structure of the film also avoids any structure of anticipation as to when and how we will see the guilty men get what they have coming. Such large and small structures of erotic anticipation are defining features of the genre and it is not coincidental that the primary structure of *Thelma and Louise* has the women being hunted by men rather than them being the avenging hunters.[3]

The rape-revenge sub-genre raises a number of interesting questions in relationship to current theoretical work on masculinity and the male body. Men in these films are positioned in places traditionally reserved for women. Second, the punishment of the male is highly spectacularized. These films, which are nearly always made by men and for men, revel in the spectacle of a woman killing men in a gruesome and protracted fashion. Sometimes the contexts are even overtly erotic as in *I Spit on Your Grave* when the revenging woman leads a victim to believe that she is about to make love to him, but instead slips a noose around his neck and hangs him, or, in another similar scene, when she cuts off her victim's penis. Both scenes are followed by shockingly graphic images of, respectively, the partially naked body swinging at the end of a rope and the naked man hysterically screaming as blood gushes from the wound. The opening scene of *Sudden Impact* fully conforms to this erotic pattern. First we see the couple hotly making love as the woman's hand caressingly moves down the man's body and unzips his pants. Then we see her take her gun out of her purse and aim it at his crotch. The noise of her cocking the pistol elicits a look of pure terror in his eyes as he realizes what is about to happen, and the film cuts to an exterior long shot of the car as we hear the shots. We then see a close-up of the woman's beautiful legs and high-heel shoes as she gets out of the car and walks away. Later when the body is found, we see the victim's hand clutching his bloody groin in death. In light of the explicitly sexual nature of these scenes, it is not surprising that there are even hard-core pornography rape-revenge films such as *Naked Vengeance* (1985).

Of particular interest to me here is the nature of the appeal of these films for men. Most of the films are either so overtly exploitational or so clearly within entertainment genre traditions that they do not even masquerade as seriously concerned with women and rape. The women in these films are nearly always beautiful (e.g., Locke and Welch), which suggests that their sexual attractiveness is crucial to the pleasure that men get from watching them exact retribution. But it is not just the women who are watched – it is also the men in their horror and pain. These films position their target male audience to enjoy the gruesome spectacle of a woman wreaking havoc on the male body. Her rape is merely a narrative pretext for setting this bizarrely pleasurable pattern in motion. These films, which are made by and frequently marketed for men, make male characters victims and spectacularize their punishment for the pleasure of the male viewers.

The above synopses show a number of elements common to each film in addition to the beauty of the avenging woman. The rapes nearly always involve a group of men who are identified as being friends or gang members. This serves two functions. At the simplest level, the gang rape lends itself well to the narrative demands of the feature film since the avenging woman hunts down the men one by one. Rather than wait ninety minutes for a single pay-off, in other words, there is a pattern of repetition and variation which builds to a climax. The gang rape structure, however, also points to male homoerotic bonding. The friends 'share' the woman in a manner which unites them. This element is foregrounded in *I Spit on Your Grave* where we first see the friends hanging out at a gas station where one of them works. As the soon-to-be victim pulls into the station, we see two of them playing together with a knife. After she leaves the station and immediately before the rape, we see them fishing together. Thus, they go directly from the quintessential male tradition of being together in nature without women to raping a woman. Both activities share a common bonding. Similarly, the flashbacks to the rape in *Sudden Impact* stress the party aspect of a group of young men who sit around a campfire near an amusement park laughing and having a good time before they 'share' the two women. Later we learn that they are all close friends, and we even see a photograph of the friends gathered together.

The rapists in these films are typically characterized as extremely repulsive, a characterization which frequently employs stereotypes of class and ethnicity. In *I Spit on Your Grave*, the working-class nature of the men is established in the gas station scene, and throughout the film they are represented as poor white trash. One of them is even mentally retarded. Their depravity is further highlighted by the brutal way in which they twice rape the same victim, once outside and then again after she has sought shelter in her home. In *Alley Cat*, the rapists are similarly characterized, but this time as urban rather than country trash which includes Latinos. They drink and constantly behave in a vulgar fashion which is strongly coded as lower class. They even have an unhealthy, unkempt appearance. In *Ms. 45*, the rapists and would-be rapists include street people, criminals, an Arab, and a gang of blacks.

This excessive characterization of the rapists points to other excesses within the genre. These films are wildly 'unrealistic' by current standards of what constitutes plausible narrative development. At the beginning of *Ms. 45*, for example, the same woman is raped twice by two different men as she returns home from work. After the first rapist finishes and flees, she stumbles into her apartment only to discover a burglary in progress and then become the intended victim of another rape by the burglar. In *I Spit on Your Grave*, the very first people that the woman meets upon arriving in the country are the gang of rapists. In *Alley Cat*, it is no exaggeration to say that virtually every time the woman steps out of the house, either someone attempts to rape her or she comes across someone who is being raped. As if this were not enough, many of the crimes committed against her, her family, and unknown victims she encounters are committed coincidentally by the same gang of depraved friends. At the same time she is out jogging in the park and encounters a rape in progress, her grandparents become victims in a liquor store robbery committed by the very men who tried to steal her tires and some of whom will later rape a woman in the park when she once again jogs to the rescue. These films present a world where there is a rapist waiting behind every tree and on every street corner. Thus, the rapists are not only excessively characterized as evil and depraved, but the number of rapes and at times the reliance on extreme coincidence are equally excessive.

Perhaps not surprisingly, in some of these films nearly all men are presented as sexually repulsive. *Ms. 45* and *I Spit on Your Grave* are perhaps the most extreme in this regard. In the former, everyone from the central character's boss to the men she encounters on the streets are offensive. In one scene, for example, she eats lunch with her fellow workers in a restaurant where a man makes out with his girl friend. The girl friend leaves, and the man immediately tries to move in on the women. After the others return to work, the man follows the main character out of the restaurant and, after identifying himself as a photographer, sleazily invites her to his studio where he plans to have sex with her. There are no positive images of men anywhere in the film, not even in the form of a kindly or attractive investigating officer. In fact, until she is stabbed by a woman at the end of the film, the central character acts totally outside the control of any romantic figures or representatives of the law. *I Spit on Your Grave* is even more extreme in this regard. Once again, there are no decent men to be seen anywhere in the film. There is no romantic subplot, and there are no police who investigate the crimes. Quite remarkably, at the end of the film, the avenging woman goes off by herself with no indication that she will ever be punished for the murders.

The other films are somewhat more conventional in the way in which they bring the avenging woman under the control of a man or the law. *Alley Cat* and *Sudden Impact* combine both methods of control in the figure of one man. In both films the avenging woman falls in love with a police officer, makes love with him during the course of the film, and is united with him at the end. In these films the police officer supplies a more attractive and 'normal' image of masculinity than any found in the other films but, in a manner typical of some of Clint Eastwood's most interesting police films, *Sudden Impact* draws a connection between Harry and the guilty woman – both have a need to take the law into their own hands since justice is not served by the powers that be.

The question, however, remains as to just what pleasures these films afford their target male audience. A recent film, *Steel and Lace* (1990), foregrounds the role of the male spectator in a manner unique for the sub-genre. Although it is not as complex or sophisticated as *Peeping Tom* (1960), it in some ways parallels the manner in which that film foregrounded the disturbing nature of male spectatorial pleasure within what would become known as the slasher genre. *Steel and Lace* makes clear that it is really a man rather than a woman behind its revenge murders, and it represents that man as one who derives spectatorial pleasure from watching gruesome videos of the killings.

Steel and Lace might best be described as a cyborg rape-revenge film. Set in the present, it tells the story of a scientist who creates a cyborg in the image of his sister in order to avenge her rape since, after the courts fail to convict the rapist, the sister commits suicide. The film starts with the trial scene intercut with the rape scene and the eventual suicide. A title then announces 'Five Years Later', and the revenge killings begin. We soon learn that a cyborg who looks like the sister but usually disguises her appearance is killing the four men who witnessed the rape and then falsified their testimony so that the rapist, their friend and criminal business leader, is not convicted. The emphasis on the way in which the buddies witness the crime and then cover up for their friend conforms to the gang rape and male bonding pattern I outlined earlier.

The first killing typifies the genre's emphasis on the spectacle of a beautiful, erotic woman gruesomely mutilating the male body. One of the four friends who lied at the trial experiences car trouble. A beautiful woman appears, behaves in a torridly seductive manner, and offers him a ride. She takes him to a 'no-tell motel' and, just as he thinks they are about to make love, she kills him. As they embrace, a phallic drill emerges from her body and penetrates him, graphically splattering his blood in the process. All five killings continue this graphic pattern of extreme violence against the male body. The next victim is decapitated when, in a single take, the cyborg pulls his head off his body. The third perjurer is castrated as he penetrates the cyborg, who has taken the disguise of an attractive temporary office worker. She in turn drills him to death through his groin. The cyborg lifts the last witness in the air next to a helicopter, and we once again see a single shot of a decapitation; this time the severed head sails off after the blades cut it. Finally, she confronts the rapist himself on a rooftop where she strikes him with a laser beam which sets his entire body ablaze. The fiery ball then falls from the roof in a manner which recalls the sister's earlier suicide.

What is unique about this film is the way in which the cyborg element brings up the issue of male pleasure and control, for in this film it only *seems* to be a woman acting out her desire for revenge. We learn after the second killing that the brother has constructed a cyborg to act out his desire for revenge in her name. He has programmed the cyborg in such a way that he controls everything she thinks, says, and does. And although his control breaks down near the end of the film, the narrative structure makes clear that the seeming female revenge takes place entirely in the service of male desire. But the cyborg element allows something even more remarkable to occur – it enables the brother to watch videotape playbacks of the murders, and the manner in which he does so brings the most repressed element of the genre directly to the surface by showing us a male spectator within the film who finds pleasure watching the gruesome deaths of the men.

We first see the brother watching the tapes after the first decapitation. We see the victim dying from the cyborg point of view, and the brother freeze-frames the action at a particularly horrifying moment. He re-watches the tape a couple of times, including in slow motion before leaving it frozen on a terrified close-up of the victim's face. On an adjacent monitor, he similarly freeze-frames the previous victim's face.

A similar scene occurs after the office castration scene, and now there are three images of monitors of terrified men about to die horrible deaths. The multiplication of horrors for the male victims intensifies the brother's pleasure. After the second decapitation, a remarkable conversation takes place between the brother and a female courtroom sketch artist who has become re-involved in the case and who has investigated and discovered the truth. Predictably, the brother explains, 'Now they're paying, and she's getting her revenge.' But another thread of the conversation calls this easy explanation into question. 'Don't blame this on a dead girl,' the woman replies, 'Your sister couldn't kill anybody.' 'She was dead, they were alive,' he responds. The standard female rape-revenge film does in fact blame everything on a 'raped girl' rather than a 'dead girl,' and then enlists her in the service of the male desire for an eroticized form of revenge like that in which the brother revels in *Steel and Lace*. Rather than pointing out that such revenge is for male pleasure, there the women seem to want it as well as enact it. This may account for the bizarre impact of the second revenge killing in *Steel and Lace* when, much to our surprise, the cyborg is not disguised as the beautiful woman we think she is but as a man. Before the murder, she opens her suit jacket, unbuttons her blouse, sprouts breasts, and metamorphosizes into a woman in front of our eyes. The moment eerily suggests that these avenging women are really men. Indeed, when the brother encounters the courtroom sketch artist after she has discovered the truth, he asks her, 'Now what possible interest could you have in the deaths of these men?' The line has an uncanny reverberation within the genre, for in fact such eroticized deaths are male fantasies which are unlikely to be of 'interest' to women.

But why should they be of interest to men? If, on the one hand, *Steel and Lace* provocatively raises that question, on the other hand, it covers its tracks and obscures the real reasons. The brother appears driven by a nearly incestuous love of his sister which seemingly explains the bizarre lengths to which he has gone in order to exact revenge for her death. Yet the images of him watching and re-watching and freeze-framing the brutal deaths clearly indicates that he has something more invested in all of this. I would similarly suggest that the heterosexual male spectator of these rape-revenge films has more invested in them than a simple desire to see justice done.

It has been suggested to me that since the sexual desirability of the avenging woman is central to these films, the pleasure men get from seeing the rapists killed may come from being rid of other men who also desire her and who in a sense are competitors for her. I think, however, that a second hypothesis which can be linked to this is closer to the truth. Many male action films present a hero and a villain who seem to be opposites but are, in reality, very much like each other. *The Man who Shot Liberty Valance* (1962) is a classic instance. The evil Liberty Valance (Lee Marvin) becomes the bad object, and spectators are likely to identify with Tom Doniphon (John Wayne) as the hero gets rid of Valance.[4] Never mind that he is the other side of the same coin. Now, the heterosexual male spectators of female rape-revenge films have the same desire for the erotic woman as the rapists do but they cannot, of course, acknowledge any similarity between themselves and the rapists. Much as Ethan Edwards (John Wayne) in *The Searchers* (1956) turns Chief Scar into the external, evil embodiment of desires that are within himself, male spectators of rape-revenge films turn the rapists into the same type of embodiment. In other words, they project on to these characters internal desires of their own. It is for this reason, I would argue, that the rapists are always characterized in the sleazy, unappealing ways described above. The male spectator can hate rather than simply identify with these men who embody desires similar to his own.

Steel and Lace fully conforms to the genre in this regard, although it does have an interesting variation on the class issue. The gang are yuppie corporate executives rather than lower-class or working-class men. The film, however, characterizes this lifestyle as repulsive. After the trial, they celebrate their victory by drinking champagne in a limousine. Shortly after that, we see them brutally threaten a kindly old man into selling his house at an unfair price so that they may acquire the property for a business venture. Although rich and successful, they are as unsavory as any of the thugs who typify rapists in many of the other films in the genre. And this certainly also holds true for the way in which they are characterized sexually. For example, a secretary comes into the executive office to take up a collection for the family of the first victim. One of the surviving friends leers at her and as soon as she leaves he inquires about her. When one of the other friends remarks that she is a temporary from the 'pool,' the leering man asks, 'And have you taken a dip in the pool yet?' He is the man who will later be drilled through the groin. The sexual desire these men have for the women must, in other words, be made to seem as far removed as possible from the male viewer's similar desire for her. In this sense, the rapist and his cohorts in this film and others like it are the rape-revenge genre equivalents of Liberty Valance and his cohorts in Westerns. In *The Man who Shot Liberty Valance*, when Doniphon brutally kicks one of Valance's side-kicks in the face, the usual audience response is one of pure pleasure. The deaths of the four friends in *Steel and Lace* are similar. And the rapist's death bears comparison with Valance's death and with Scar's death in *The Searchers* insofar as all three films narratively build towards the death of these individuals who most embody this detested, evil 'otherness.'

While I believe that such a desire for heterosexual male spectators to displace something within themselves may explain some of the appeal of the rape-revenge genre, there is yet another compelling hypothesis, namely masochism. From this perspective, the evil rapists supply a smokescreen which justifies the woman's revenge. She must be beautiful and the deaths eroticized precisely because the genre plays out a male masochistic fantasy so extreme that even brutal death can be part of the scenario. The traditional masochistic image of the cold woman in furs with a whip developed by Leopold von Sacher-Masoch in *Venus in Furs* and analyzed so incisively by Gaylyn Studlar (Studlar 1988) as a major component of the films of Josef Von Sternberg seems far removed from these 'hot babes' in miniskirts with guns, but I suspect there is a connection, and one which relates to other films seemingly far removed from this genre.

When the cyborg finally confronts the rapist at the end of *Steel and Lace*, she says to him, 'You're so much smaller than I thought you'd be. I thought you'd be terrible, a monster, but you're so small, so weak.' In a previous essay on penis-size jokes in Hollywood films (Lehman 1991), I suggested that the prevalence of such jokes, many of which are uttered by beautiful women, may be related to the rape-revenge genre in that the former structure makes the male body the butt of the joke for male masochistic pleasure while the latter structure plays it out in a brutally painful fashion. In *Steel and Lace*, the cyborg is not literally talking about the penis, though the metaphoric implications are clear. The rape-revenge films as a sub-genre historically coincide almost exactly with the proliferation of penis-size jokes in films, something which may suggest a deep desire to sexually assault the male body either comically and psychologically or brutally and physically for the pleasure of the male spectator. Furthermore, both of these trends coincide with the development of the women's movement and feminism. Indeed, one rape-revenge film, *Act of Vengeance* (1974), contains several such jokes and remarks which are uttered by socially aware, organized women who have decided to take the punishment of rapists into their own hands. After catching a rapist, a group of women tie him to his bed and take his pants off. One of the women says, while looking at his penis, 'For a big guy, you're not too terrific.' 'No, and I'm afraid this isn't going to help much,' another woman adds as she pours dye on his genitals. Later, the leader of the revenging women says to her former boy friend when he tries to talk her into giving up the vengeance, 'All you're concerned about is your tiny sense of manhood,' glancing at his groin while she

113

speaks. Later when they catch a man who has harassed a woman on the phone, they tell him, 'Pussycat, we listened to a lot of your performances on tape. What's the story? Are you all talk or have you got something to back it up with?' 'Why don't you show it to us?' a different woman says. 'Clothes off,' one demands and another adds, 'Yeah, let's see your wang, you got a big wang?' They then make fun of his body when they take off his shirt.

When analyzing the penis-size jokes, I suggested that the women who tell such jokes in the films may mask the presence of homosexual desire. Although I did not expand upon it at the time, I find it imperative to do so now since what functions as masochism at one level in the rape-revenge films suggests repressed homosexuality and, in the extreme, homophobia at another since, as Robin Wood so perceptively phrases it, 'the homophobe hates the precariously repressed homosexual side of himself' (Wood 1986: 250). Using Freud's work on paranoia and repressed homosexuality, Wood discusses violence by men against men in his brilliant analysis of *Raging Bull*:

> I refer to the cultural significance of boxing itself as licensed and ritualized violence in which one man attempts to smash the near-naked body of another for the satisfaction (surely fundamentally erotic) of a predominantly male mass audience. It would be interesting to discover whether there is any significant correlation between an enthusiasm for boxing and homophobia.
>
> (Wood 1986: 254)

Since in my analysis female rape-revenge films are a licensed form of violence in which a woman acts out male desires for the erotic satisfaction of a predominantly male mass audience, it would be equally interesting to see whether there is any correlation between an enthusiasm for such films and repressed homosexuality and also between such films and related male rape-revenge films such as *Death Wish* (1974). The latter films, of course, do not have the sexual veneer of the female rape-revenge films. Nevertheless, as *Cat Chaser* (1988) shows, there may be a connection. The film, directed by Abel Ferrara, who also made *Ms. 45*, contains an extraordinary scene in which a male character orders two other men to strip and then sadistically prolongs their agony before shooting them. The sexual element raised by making the men strip is heightened by the unusual frontal nudity of both victims. Although the film attempts to naturalize this scene by characterizing it as a reversal of the manner in which the villain has treated others including his wife, it nevertheless implicates seemingly justified, non-sexual male violence against males as containing an erotic component. That such an unusual scene should surface within the oeuvre of a film-maker who years earlier helped define the female rape-revenge genre suggests a connection between the two forms of violence. Wood's assumption derives from his application of Freud's work on paranoia and homosexuality whereby a man can transform the initial proposition 'I love him' into four different variations: 'I do not love him – I hate him'; 'I don't love men – I love women'; 'I don't love at all – I love only myself'; and 'It is not I who love the man – she loves him.' These variations, in other words, deny and repress the original love for the man and end up replacing it with respectively hatred for the man, womanizing, self love, or jealousy. All those forms of behavior repress homosexual love and, if Freud was right, all heterosexual men have repressed such love. This results from the passage through the stage of auto-eroticism to object love which includes a period of narcissism 'which may be indispensable to the normal course of life' (Freud 1909–18: 163). This stage places particular emphasis on the penis:

> The point of central interest in the self which is thus chosen as a love-object may already be the genitals. The line of development then leads on to the choice of an outer object with similar genitals – that is, to homosexual object choice – and thence to heterosexuality.
>
> (Freud 1909–18: 163)

If, as in *Steel and Lace*, the woman in female rape-revenge films is actually a surrogate for male desire, the genre may be closely linked to the dynamics Wood discerns in *Raging Bull* and in boxing. Freud's analysis of paranoia may also help explain one of the constitutive features of the female rape-revenge genre. In paranoia a man transforms his original love for another man into hatred through the delusion of persecution:

> The mechanism of symptom formation in paranoia requires that internal perceptions, or feelings, shall be replaced by external perceptions. Consequently the proposition 'I hate him' becomes transformed by *projection* into another one: 'He *hates* (persecutes) *me*, which will justify me in hating him.'
>
> (Freud 1909–18: 166)

I have emphasized the extremes to which the genre goes to characterize the rapists as excessively repulsive. Without exception, all the films discussed in this essay conform to that pattern, one function of which may be, as previously noted, to project outward on to the rapists something which is internal, i.e., a similar desire for the beautiful woman. But such characterization could also function analogously to the paranoid's delusions of persecution. As the paranoid justifies his hatred of the other man by believing that the other man hates him, the heterosexual male spectator of rape-revenge films hates the rapists for their repulsive behavior which in turn 'justifies' anything that is done to them. That

115

what is done to them at times involves the genitals may be expected within the Freudian framework since it is the genitals that were the focus of the repressed homosexuality during the narcissistic transition from auto-eroticism to object choice. It may be the unique function of the female rape-revenge genre to disguise the homosexuality by having a beautiful woman brutally attack the male body in general and the genitals in specific.

Given the multi-layered, disturbing nature of the psychodynamics of the genre, it is not surprising that it is first and foremost a B genre. Nor is the critical reaction to *I Spit on Your Grave* such a surprise. That film more than any of the others graphically intensifies both the repulsive nature of the rapists and the erotic nature of their punishment. Similarly, more than any other films in the genre, *Steel and Lace* raises the bizarre question, what do heterosexual male spectators find so pleasurable about all this? Not surprisingly, it cannot bring itself to fully and honestly address the very issue it raises.

NOTES

I would like to thank Chris Staayer, Chris Holmlund, Patricia Erens, and Ed O'Neill for their comments on an earlier version of this essay and Melanie Magisos for her help in revising it.

1 In a similar manner, Mick Martin and Marsha Porter remark of the film, 'This is, beyond a doubt, one of the most tasteless, irresponsible, and disturbing movies ever made' (Martin and Porter 1990: 742).

2 *Ms. 45* is in fact an extremely interesting film, partly because of the way it positions the mute woman and, symbolically, women in general in relationship to male dominated language; she is not only raped and harassed by men but, also, oppressed by her exclusion from the powerful realm of speech.

3 I do not intend these distinctions to be praise for nor a defense of *Thelma and Louise*; they are, however, significant in understanding the reception of the film.

4 I have discussed this aspect of *The Man who Shot Liberty Valance* and the related following reference to *The Searchers* in greater detail in Luhr and Lehman 1977.

BIBLIOGRAPHY

Ebert, R. (1989) *Movie Home Companion*, New York: Andrews and McMeel.

Freud, S. (1909–18) *Three Case Histories*, P. Rieff, ed., 1963, New York: Collier Books.

Lehman, P. (1991) 'Penis-size Jokes and Their Relation to the Unconscious,' in A. Horton (ed.) *Comedy/Cinema/Theory*, Berkeley: University of California Press.

Luhr, W. and Lehman, P. (1977) *Authorship and Narrative in the Cinema: Issues in Contemporary Aesthetics and Criticism*, New York: Putnam.

Maltin, L. (1990) *TV Movies and Video Guide*, New York: Penguin.

Martin, M. and Porter, M. (1990) *Video Movie Guide 1991*, New York: Ballantine.

Sacher-Masoch, L. v. (1870) *Venus in Furs*, trans. G. Deleuze, 1989, New York: Zone Books.

Studlar, G. (1988) *In the Realm of Pleasure: Von Sternberg, Dietrich, and the Masochistic Aesthetic*, Urbana: University of Illinois Press.

Williams, L. (1989) *Hard Core: Power, Pleasure, and the 'Frenzy of the Visible'*, Berkeley: University of California Press.

Wood, R. (1986) *Hollywood from Vietnam to Reagan*, New York: Columbia University Press.

6

DARK DESIRES

Male masochism in the horror film

Barbara Creed

> The body must bear no trace of its debt to nature: it must be clean
> and proper in order to be fully symbolic
>
> (Kristeva 1982)

Whenever male bodies are represented as monstrous in the horror film
they assume characteristics usually associated with the female body: they
experience a blood cycle, change shape, bleed, give birth, become penetrable, are castrated. Traditionally, the male body has been viewed as
norm; the female body a deviation. One of the more popular medieval
ideas of the difference between the sexes was that women were men
turned inside out. Galen explains in careful detail how this reversal
works. His discussion is part of a wider treatise justifying woman's inferiority.

> A second reason is one that appears in dissecting . . . think first,
> please, of the man's [sexual organs] turned in and extending inward
> between the rectum and the bladder. If this should happen, the
> scrotum would necessarily take the place of the uteri [*sic*], with the
> testes lying outside, next to it on either side; the penis of the male
> would become the neck of the cavity that had been formed; and the
> skin at the end of the penis, now called prepuce, would become the
> female pudendum itself . . . In fact, you could not find a single male
> part left over that had not simply changed its position; for the parts
> that are inside in woman are outside in man.
>
> (quoted in Bullough 1973: 492)

The reason Galen gives for this unusual state of affairs is body tempera-
ture. Because woman is colder than man, her bodily parts, formed when
she was still a fetus, 'could not because of the defect in the heat emerge
and project on the outside.' The view that women's internal organs were
the reverse of man's external ones dominated medical thinking until the
late eighteenth century; it even included the naming of the ovaries as
female testes. One of the more novel superstitions, which sprang from

this view, was that if women stood or sat with their legs spread apart their internal organs would fall out – the vagina would drop through as a penis – and women would become men! Young girls who wanted to be 'lady-like' should keep their legs crossed at all times. At the heart of this medieval view, influenced no doubt by the Platonic theory of ideal forms, is a belief that there is only one sex and that men represent its more perfect expression.

In the 1980 horror film *Dressed to Kill*, we find an unusual re-working of this ancient theme, although an interesting reversal has taken place – woman is now the prototype. Brian De Palma's *Dressed to Kill* tells the story of Dr Elliott (Michael Caine) a man who masquerades as a woman, Bobbi, and who wants to have a sex-change operation. *Dressed to Kill* belongs to a group of horror films (*Psycho*, 1960, *Homicidal*, 1961, *A Reflection of Fear*, 1973) in which the monster is seen as monstrous precisely because she or he does not have a clear gender identity. Dr Elliott/Bobbi is monstrous because of his cross-dressing/transsexuality. Towards the end of *Dressed to Kill*, two of the main characters, Liz (Nancy Allen) and Peter (Keith Gordon), sit in a restaurant discussing transsexualism. Liz, a prostitute, begins to tell Peter, who is younger and relatively naive, about the procedure for changing sex. She explains that if a man wishes to become a woman he takes female hormones which will soften his skin, cause breasts to grow and stop him from having erections. Peter, who never shows any sexual interest towards Liz, is extremely interested in this proposition. 'Instead of building a computer, I could build a woman,' he says with great delight. Liz, who loves to shock, gives Peter all the details. A lot more is involved than simply letting it all 'hang out.'

> Liz: 'The next step is . . . penectomy.'
> Peter: 'What's that?'
> Liz: 'Well, you know. They take your penis and slice it down the middle.'
> Peter: 'Yeh, yeh. That's what I thought it was.'
> Liz: 'Then castration. Plastic reconstruction and the formation of an artificial vagina of vaginal plastics – for those in the know.'
> Peter: 'I thought Elliott just put on a dress.'
> Liz: 'Oh, he did and a wig too. But that's not good enough in bed when you've got to take everything off.'
> Peter: 'Well, I think I'm going to stick with my computer.'

In *Dressed to Kill*, woman's body is represented as the ideal body desired by man – and voyeuristically by the camera. On the one hand, it might be argued that we cannot accept Bobbi's desires as true for other men; Bobbi is psychotic, a monster whose desires are sick and perverted. On the other hand, the monster of the horror film is, in a

Figure 15 Michael Caine in women's clothes as 'Bobbi' attacks Angie Dickinson in *Dressed to Kill*

sense, monstrous because he/she dares to speak the truth of repressed desire. Whether male or female, the monster speaks the unspeakable, defies order and system, flaunts morality and the law. By drawing a number of parallels between Bobbi and Peter, De Palma, in fact, makes it clear that Bobbi's desire to become a woman should not be seen simply as the desire of an insane mind. The problem with *Dressed to Kill*, and other films about the sexually ambiguous monster, is that, while they might present a critique of a culture fearful of changes in traditional sex roles, they also equate cross-dressing and transsexuality with monstrousness.

In 'The Economic Problem of Masochism,' Freud described three forms of masochism: erotogenic, moral, and feminine. Erotogenic refers to the primary experience of 'pleasure in pain' and moral masochism to the ego's need for punishment either from the super-ego or from outside powers. By 'feminine,' Freud did not mean 'masochism in women,' but rather the *feminine position* adopted by the subject in relation to masochistic desire. He proposed that what constitutes the essence of a masochistic phantasy in men is that they place the male in a 'characteristically female situation'.

> But if one has an opportunity of studying cases in which the masochistic phantasies have been especially richly elaborated, one quickly

discovers that they place the subject in a characteristically female situation; they signify, that is, being castrated, or copulated with, or giving birth to a baby.

(Freud 1924: 162)

Freud also linked masochism to the infant's developmental phases: fear of being eaten by the totem animal (the father) originates in the primitive oral phase; the wish to be beaten by the father relates to the sadistic-anal phase; and castration is a precipitate of the phallic stage. Here Freud specifies two other forms of masochism in addition to those associated with the specifically feminine position: a desire to be eaten and a desire to be beaten. Phantasies of man's masochistic desire to take up a feminine position are one of the central topics that the horror film exists to explore.

Almost all articles (Lenne 1979, Neale 1980) written on the horror film define the majority of monsters as male, the victims female. Very few writers (Williams 1984, Hollinger 1989) have attempted to qualify this opposition in any way. Yet, it seems clear that in the process of being constructed as monstrous the male is 'feminized.' This process is not simply a consequence of placing the male in a masochistic position – although this is crucial to many texts – but rather it stems from the very nature of horror as an encounter with the feminine. Julia Kristeva's theory of the abject provides us with a preliminary hypothesis for understanding the maternal bases of horror.[1] Kristeva, like Freud, also defines the 'feminine' as essential to her project.

In *Powers of Horror*, Kristeva argues that the constitution of acceptable forms of subjectivity and sociality demands the expulsion of those things defined as improper and unclean. Whatever is expelled is constituted as an abject, that which 'disturbs identity, system, order' (Kristeva 1982: 4). A crucial aspect of the abject is, however, that it can never be fully removed or set apart from the subject or society; the abject both threatens and beckons. The abject constitutes the other side of seemingly stable subjectivity. 'It beseeches, worries, and fascinates desire' (ibid.: 1). The abject constitutes the gap or hole at the border of subjectivity which threatens to engulf the individual when its identity is threatened. The place of the abject is 'the place where meaning collapses' (ibid.: 2), the place where 'I' am not. Kristeva distinguishes between three main forms of abjection; these are constituted in relation to food, bodily wastes, and sexual difference. The ultimate in abjection is the corpse. The body expels its wastes so that it might continue to live. But the corpse is a body which can no longer expel its wastes. The corpse is 'the most sickening of wastes, is a border that has encroached upon everything. It is no longer I who expel, "I" is expelled' (ibid.: 3–4).

The notion of the border is crucial to our understanding of the abject and the way it is represented in the horror film. The abject exists on the other side of a border which separates out the subject from all that threatens its existence. 'We may call it a border; abjection is above all ambiguity' (Kristeva 1982: 9–10). It is the ambiguous side of abjection that the horror film explores, particularly in relation to the monster. The border is defined in a number of crucial ways – between human and beast (the werewolf, ape man); good and evil (*The Omen*, 1976, *The Boys From Brazil*, 1978); male and female (*Dressed to Kill*, 1980, *A Reflection of Fear*, 1973); or between the body which is clean and proper and the body which is aligned with nature and abject wastes (*The Exorcist*, 1973, *The Brood*, 1979).

The body which is most closely aligned with the abject is the feminine, maternal body. All experiences of bodily horror, as well as those which involve a loss of subject boundaries, can be traced back to the infant's experience with the maternal entity. In her discussion of the 'clean and proper body' as defined within religious discourse, Kristeva distinguishes between the symbolic and non-symbolic body.

> The body must bear no trace of its debt to nature . . . it should endure no gash other than that of circumcision, equivalent to sexual separation and/or separation from the mother. Any other mark would be the sign of belonging to the impure, the non-separate, the non-symbolic, the non-holy.
>
> (Kristeva 1982: 102)

The abject is placed on the side of the feminine and the maternal in opposition to the paternal symbolic, the domain of law and language. The prototype of the abject body is the maternal body because of its link with the natural world signified in its lack of 'corporeal integrity': it secretes (blood, milk); it changes size, grows, and swells; it gives birth in 'a violent act of expulsion through which the nascent body tears itself away from the matter of maternal insides' (Kristeva 1982: 101). Such actions violate the boundary of the skin which should remain smooth, taut, unblemished. As mentioned above, however, the abject does not simply repel; it also 'fascinates desire,' lures the subject to its side. The horror film explores the attraction of the abject feminized body through its graphic representation of the body-monstrous.

We can see the feminization of the monstrous male body at work in the representation of a number of archetypal figures of male monstrosity, in particular the vampire and werewolf. In the cinema, the archetypal vampire is represented by Count Dracula. He is usually depicted as a sinister but seductive heterosexual male who dwells in a Gothic castle characterized by long winding stairs, dark corridors, cobwebs, and a crypt or cellar containing his coffin. These features of the vampire film are clearly evident in John Badham's *Dracula*, a 1979 version of the classic myth. Dracula (Frank Langella) is a sleek, elegant, aristocratic figure who wears a flowing black cloak, with red lining, speaks in softly modulated tones and glides silently through the dark on his nocturnal journeys. He is linked with images of bats, spiders, rats, and the deadly *vagina dentata* – symbols usually associated with female monsters. Compared to the more rugged, masculine Van Helsing (Laurence Olivier), Dracula's arch-enemy, and a pillar of patriarchal Christian society, Dracula is a sexually ambiguous figure. In their description of the stereotypical features of the Dracula figure, Alain Silver and James Ursini draw attention to his 'dark clothes and full-flowing red-lined cape, the hair brushed back straight and flat from the forehead, the lips extraordinarily crimson and distended . . .' (Silver and Ursini 1975: 61).

Not only is his appearance and behavior feminized, Dracula's need to replace his blood at periodic intervals suggests he experiences a form of menstrual cycle. In *Idols of Perversity* (1986), Bram Dijkstra points out that it was popularly believed that woman became a vampire in order to replenish the blood she lost during menstruation and pregnancy. In their study of menstruation, Penelope Shuttle and Peter Redgrove argue that Count Dracula symbolizes two figures: the 'other' husband, the one who understands woman's bodies; and woman herself, 'expressed in masculine disguise' (Shuttle and Redgrove 1978: 269). They see the vampire myth as a rite of passage story used to explain the onset of menstruation in girls. Before the vampire approaches, his victims – almost always young virgins – lie in bed, pale and wan. Andrew Tudor emphasizes this feature of Tod Browning's *Dracula* (1931) in which the female victims lie languidly in their beds 'unable and unwilling to resist' (Tudor 1989: 164). Once bitten, their blood flows freely, and in almost all vampire films, Dracula's victims rise from their beds filled with a new energy which is both predatory and sexual. In Badham's *Dracula*, Lucy's frustration with her passive feminine role as a 'chattel' in her father's world is replaced with new energy and purpose once she joins Dracula's world. 'I despise women with no life in them, no blood,' says Dracula. The vampire always bites the neck of his victims, which Shuttle and Redgrove argue symbolizes the neck of the uterus through which menstrual blood flows.

A number of myths from ancient cultures associate woman's monthly bleeding with the full moon and the snake because all move through stages in which the old is shed and the new is born. Various myths state that a young girl begins to bleed when she is bitten by a snake – or similar creature – that lives either in the moon or on her womb. Robert Briffault refers to Rabbinical teachings which stated that the onset of menstruation was caused by copulation with a snake (Briffault 1927: 666). Lévi-Strauss points out that the Aztecs and Colombians believed menstruation was brought about by the bite of vampire bats (Lévi-Strauss

1973: 382). In his essay on the virginity taboo, Freud states that some primitive people believed menstruation was caused by 'the bite of some spirit animal' (Freud 1918: 197). In the light of these myths and beliefs, it is relevant to note that Dracula's teeth are like the fangs of a snake and that his bite resembles the two round puncture marks of the snake. Dracula himself is very much like a snake: in his black clothes he glides silently through the night, his fangs bared in his white moon-like face. Dracula's feminization then relates to his appearance as well as his symbolic association with the need of woman's body to release and replenish its blood at regular intervals. For just as Dracula ushers in the blood-flow, he also takes this blood into his own body. Like the menstrual cycle, Dracula's 'life' depends on this exchange.

The werewolf is another cinematic monster who, like Dracula, is a feminized figure associated with woman's menstrual cycle. According to Walter Evans, 'the werewolf's bloody attacks – which occur regularly every month – are certainly related to the menstrual cycle which suddenly and mysteriously commands the body of every adolescent girl' (Evans 1973: 357). The legend of the werewolf (Douglas 1966, Twitchell 1985) is probably as old as that of Dracula and is known throughout the world; it is most common in Europe where the wolf is one of the most savage of carnivorous animals. The most heinous crime the werewolf commits is cannibalism, and in those countries where the wolf was not common, the human animal would transform into a different carnivorous beast – usually a tiger, bear, or leopard. Jacques Tourneur's classic horror film, *Cat People* (1942) deals with the transformation of a young woman into a man-eating cat.

The werewolf is recognized in a number of ways: hair growing on his palms; an index finger which is longer than any of his others; and the mark of the mystical pentagram on some part of the body. The pentagram, a five-pointed star, is an interesting symbol which appears to have been closely related to paganism. It was once worshipped by Pythagorean mystics as the birth letter interlaced five times (Hornung 1959: 212). In Egypt the pentagram represented the underground womb (Walker 1983: 782). It is during the full moon that the werewolf's blood undergoes chemical changes which force him to seek the blood and flesh of humans. Whereas the vampire can roam abroad on any night (although the full moon is particularly propitious) the werewolf strikes *only* on the night of the full moon, particularly if the wolfbane is in blossom. The only reliable way of killing a werewolf is with a bullet or weapon of silver. When the werewolf is slain, he always returns to his human form. As with the vampire myth, the werewolf story also has its own symbols and motifs: the full moon, wolfbane, wounds, transformation, the pentagram, cannibalism, silver bullets, death.

Walter Evans argues that the 'horrible alterations' which afflict the transformation monster, such as the Wolfman, Frankenstein's monster, and Dracula, are associated with the changes which mark the body of the adolescent. The most significant of these is 'the monstrous transformation which is directly associated with secondary sexual characteristics and with the onset of aggressive erotic behaviour' (Evans 1973: 354). In particular he associates the werewolf's sudden growth of body hair and his aggressive behavior with these changes. Evans's interpretation is interesting, but it ignores the crucial themes of menstruation, totemism, and self-rebirth in the werewolf films.

The theme of rebirth is particularly relevant to the filmic representation of the werewolf and helps to explain its feminization. In most narratives (*The Wolf Man*, 1941, *An American Werewolf in London*, 1981, *The Howling*, 1981), the victim is savagely mauled and his body covered in bloody wounds prior to his transformation into the beast. In all werewolf films, the transformation involves a series of terrifying bodily changes which signify his abject status. As he metamorphoses into a wolf, his human form remains somehow encased inside his animal exterior. When he changes back into human form, the animal remains inside. In other words the werewolf is able to give birth to himself, in either animal or human form, at the time of the full moon or once a month. Once transformed he feeds on the blood and flesh of others – presumably to replace his own blood which is at a low ebb. Like the woman with her menstrual cycle, the werewolf replenishes his blood monthly and is reborn monthly. Like the female body in the act of birth, his transformation is accompanied by a series of dramatic bodily changes.

With the revolution in special effects technology, the contemporary werewolf film is able to represent these bodily alterations in minute detail. *An American Werewolf in London* illustrates the power of this technology to challenge our disbelief. We see body and legs sprout hair, a nose extend into a snout, nostrils broaden, teeth extend into fangs, muscles bulge, hands change into paws with long pointed nails, and eyes become blood red. Insofar as man gives birth to himself in another form, he takes on the characteristics usually associated with woman when she gives birth. His body shape changes, his eyes bulge, his muscles stretch and pull. In a sense, the werewolf gives birth to himself by turning himself inside out. In his description of the transformation scene in *An American Werewolf in London*, Twitchell writes: 'And this seamless metamorphosis happens with no break-away before our unbelieving eyes, almost as if the wolf is unfolding outward *through* the skin of a man' (Twitchell 1985: 217). What is most interesting about this transformation is that the inside of the human body is represented in terms of the animal. When man gives birth to himself – and hence takes up a feminine position – he is represented as an integral part of the animal world. His new body is distinguished by coarse hair, a fanged gaping mouth, and a need for blood. The border separating human from animal, the symbolic from all that threatens its integrity, is literally only skin-deep.

In some films, the world of the werewolf is clearly associated with the mother. In *The Wolf Man*, directed by George Waggner, the werewolf/son (Lon Chaney Jr.) rejects the father's world, represented by his own father, Sir Larry Talbot (Claude Rains), and returns to the world of the mother, represented by the Gypsy Queen, Malvena (Maria Ouspenskaya). The narrative establishes a series of oppositions which separate these two domains. The father's world is associated with civilization, rationality, the law, church, authority, tradition: the mother's world with nature, superstition, fate. Insofar as Malvena is the mother of the two werewolves in the film (her son is a werewolf and she calls Larry 'my son') she is also associated with orality, totemism, and taboo. Throughout the narrative the son is ill at ease in his father's world, yet is inexplicably attracted to the gypsy camp located in the forest. The carnivalesque atmosphere of the gypsy life stands in marked contrast with the sober propriety of life at Talbot castle. In the end, the father murders the son/wolf by beating him to death with a silver-headed cane. In an earlier scene, the father ties his son to a chair to prevent him from transforming. The binding and beating episodes suggest a sadistic/masochistic scenario of punishment in which the father reinforces paternal law. Through his transformation, the son transgresses against the symbolic order, retreating into a world of totemism and taboo presided over by Malvena, the mother. A murderous father–son relationship is also important to *Werewolf of London* (1935) and *Curse of the Werewolf* (1961).

A recent horror film which explores the male subject's relationship to the feminized totem animal is *The Silence of the Lambs* (Jonathan Demme, 1991). The psychotic killer, known as Buffalo Bill (Ted Levine), hunts, kills, and flays his female victims in order to make for himself a lifesize female suit from their skins. The totem animal associated with the original Buffalo Bill was the buffalo; in *The Silence of the Lambs* it is woman herself. Buffalo Bill wants to become a woman – presumably because he sees femininity as a more desirable state, possibly a superior one. In primitive cultures (Freud 1913) the totem animal was a revered creature who protected the whole group; in return human beings showed their respect by not killing the totem if it were an animal or cutting it if it were a plant. If it were necessary to kill the totem animal, various practices had to be strictly observed. To emphasize kinship with the totem, special ceremonies would be held in which people of the clan would dress up in the skin of the totem animal and imitate its behavior.

The Silence of the Lambs draws on these ancient practices in which woman is represented as a kind of totemic animal. Buffalo Bill not only wants to wear woman's skin, he also wants to be a woman. This is clearly brought out in the scene where we watch the killer preparing for his transformation; as he dances in his dark shadowy room, dressed in woman's clothes, we watch him tuck his penis up behind his legs in order to create the impression he is without a penis – 'castrated' like a woman. Woman is the object of his hunt and his perverse desires. After murdering his victims, Buffalo Bill places the larvae of a rare caterpillar inside their mouths. Reborn as a beautiful butterfly, the caterpillar symbolizes the killer's own desire for rebirth. But, in order to experience a rebirth as woman, Buffalo Bill must wear the skin of woman not just to experience a physical transformation but also to acquire the *power of transformation* associated with woman's ability to give birth. As in the rituals associated with the wolf cults, the skin of the totem animal must be worn if the individual is to assume the power of the divine animal.

The other killer of *The Silence of the Lambs* is Dr Hannibal Lecter (Anthony Hopkins). Although a very different character, Lecter is represented, in a sense, as Buffalo Bill's alter ego, his other self. Lecter doesn't skin his victims; he eats their internal organs. Totemism also permitted the eating of certain parts of the sacred animal. Both men are thus engaged in totemic actions: one eats special parts of the human animal, the other wears its skin. Taken together the actions of the two men constitute a debased version of a primitive ritual in which the totem animal is human and female. Although the actions of both men are monstrous, it is Buffalo Bill who is constructed as the central or 'true' monster of the film. Lecter almost assumes the status of hero, and his relationship with the heroine, Clarice Starling (Jodie Foster), borders on a romance. Like Dracula, Lecter is an orally sadistic monster with a mesmerizing stare. He is also articulate, cultivated, and well-mannered. 'Discourtesy is unspeakably ugly to me,' says Lecter.

Part of Buffalo Bill's construction as monster involves his feminization, his desire to become a woman and his wearing of women's skins. Lecter is also associated with totemism in that when he is near people he is made to wear a mask to stop him from eating them. It transforms him into a horrifying animal-like creature. Throughout the narrative, woman is associated with the animal world (the flayed totem creature, the larvae, the lamb); even the heroine's surname, 'Starling,' locates her in the world of nature. For different reasons both killers are drawn to this world, Buffalo Bill to the possibility of becoming woman, Lecter to the possibility of devouring/incorporating Clarice. When she tells Lecter about her dream of saving the lambs from slaughter, he orders lamb chops for his next meal. The incident is intended as a joke but nevertheless it points to Lecter's ambivalent attitude to Clarice.

Lecter's cannibalism also underlines a desire to devour in order to avoid being devoured. His amazing skill with words, his superior command of language also points to an obsession with the oral. In terms of abjection, Kristeva – drawing on Freud – argues that one of the infant's

Figure 16 Ted Levine as Buffalo Bill at his sewing machine in *The Silence of the Lambs*

earlier fears is of the incorporating mother. 'Fear of the uncontrollable generative mother repels me from the body; I give up cannibalism because abjection (of the mother) leads me toward respect for the body of the other, my fellow man, my brother' (Kristeva 1982: 78–9). The symbolic body, the clean and proper body, is 'non-assimilable, uneatable' (78). The subject who breaks the taboo of cannibalism signifies his alliance with the abject, his continuing identification with the devouring maternal body as well as his fear of that figure.

Dr Lecter uses his mastery of language and his ability to read human behavior to get inside the skins of his victims psychically – even driving one to commit suicide rather than listen any longer to Lecter's sadistic verbal attack. He dies by swallowing his own tongue. As Lecter's 'other self,' Buffalo Bill confronts this fear by incorporating woman literally – he physically gets 'inside woman's skin'. Both men also inhabit an under-world associated with darkness, the earth, womb-like enclosures, death: Lecter is confined underground in a cell, Buffalo Bill lives in a darkly-lit house built over a deep earthen pit in which he imprisons his victims. *The Silence of the Lambs* creates a world of horror in which the composite male monster confronts his greatest fear, woman, but in so doing is made monstrous through the processes of feminization.

In some horror films a male scientist attempts to create a new life form (*Frankenstein*, 1931) or tamper in some way with the natural order (*Altered States*, 1980, *The Fly*, 1986). Practices of couvade, a term which refers to man's desire to give birth, have been documented in the rituals of a number of peoples. The couvade is a custom in which the father, during the period when his wife is giving birth, also lies in bed where he enacts the motions of childbirth (Walker 1983: 106). Myths and legends from many cultures attest to the desire of the male to give birth. Zeus gave birth to Athena from his head. In the Christian myth, Adam gives birth to Eve from his ribs. The horror film also explores the notion of the male mother/scientist, who attempts to create new life forms in his laboratory, and whose *mise-en-scène* is coded to suggest an intra-uterine world. But in his bizarre attempt to usurp female reproductive powers, the male monster of science can only create monsters. Male interest in, and obsession with, birth is explored from a number of perspectives. As the scientist of *The Fly* is re-created as a Brundle fly, coded as female in the text, his genitals drop off. In *Alien* (1979), a male astronaut gives birth from his stomach whereas in *Total Recall* (1990) the baby leader of the mutant rebels lives permanently in a man's stomach. *Dead Ringers* (1988) explores male womb envy in relation to a woman who possesses a triple uterus which is described as 'fabulously rare.' In *Videodrome* (1983), the male protagonist inserts a gun into a vagina-like opening in his stomach as if impregnating himself.

While some horror films explore man's desire for castration in order to become a woman, others explore castration as part of a male death wish. We see this in rape-revenge films such as *I Spit on Your Grave* (1978) and *Naked Vengeance* (1984). In this sub-genre of the horror film, woman enacts a deadly revenge on the men who have raped her; she hunts them down and kills them in scenes of gruesome horror. In both these films, a male rapist is castrated at the very moment when he is experiencing intense sexual pleasure. In *I Spit on Your Grave*, the heroine caresses then castrates the male as he lies in a hot bath. In *Naked Vengeance*, she castrates him as they embrace in a river. In both films, the castration scenes place the male in the position of victim, and there is no doubt that the audience is intended to enjoy his savage punishment as he has earlier been portrayed as a vicious, brutal rapist.

The difference in the representation of the rape and castration scenes, however, is crucial. The rapes are represented in a more confronting manner and are depicted as violent, sadistic, and horrifying whereas the castration scenes are represented within a seduction scenario in which the atmosphere is initially romanticized. On the one hand, these scenes are romanticized because the heroine lures her victim to his doom with a promise of sexual bliss. On the other hand, the effect of this is to link man's sexual desire with a desire for death. He willingly surrenders to the woman he has previously brutalized and who has good reason to wish him dead. Dressed in a long white robe, her hair tied regally in a bun, the female avenger of *I Spit on Your Grave* looks like a pagan goddess officiating over an ancient ritual. After she castrates the male, she locks him in the bathroom and listens to his death cries rise up against a background of classical music.

Man's desire for sex and death is clearly brought out in Brian De Palma's *Sisters* (1973). Margot Kidder plays Siamese twins, Danielle and Dominique; the former is sweet and gentle, the latter dangerous, aggressive. During an operation to separate the twins, Dominique dies. Unable to come to terms with her sister's death, Danielle takes on her sister's identity. Emile (William Finley), the doctor who performed the operation, is also Danielle's husband. He knows that Danielle has become a divided personality but is able to control 'Dominique' by keeping Danielle sedated. This is only partly effective. Emile says to Danielle that he knows whenever he makes love to her that Dominique is present. Yet Emile chooses to arouse Danielle sexually even though she has just castrated the last man with whom she made love. Predictably, Danielle/Dominique also slashes Emile's genitals, and as he dies he clasps her hand over his bleeding wound. Emile's wound parallels the one which runs down Danielle's side, a hideous reminder of her separation/castration from her sister. The image of their two hands clasped together and covered in Emile's blood reminds us of the abject nature of desire. *Sisters* presents an interesting study of male and female castration fears as well as exploring a male sexual death wish. In her interesting discussion of the male dread of woman, Karen Horney argues that perhaps the death wish for man is more closely aligned with sex.

> Is any light shed upon it by the state of lethargy – even the death – after mating, which occurs frequently in male animals? Are love and death more closely bound up with one another for the male than the female, in whom sexual union potentially produces a new life? Does man feel, side by side with his desire to conquer, a secret longing for extinction in the act of reunion with the woman (mother)? Is it perhaps this longing that underlies the 'death-instinct'?
>
> (Horney 1967: 138–9)

The conventional interpretation is to argue that the male monster of the classic horror film (ape, werewolf, vampire) represents the repressed bestial desires of civilized man and that woman is almost always the object of this aggression.[2] 'Women are invariably the victims of the acts of terror unleashed by the werewolf/vampire/alien/'thing' (Mercer 1986: 39). What this interpretation ignores is the extent to which the beast is also feminized through the processes of transformation. It is this aspect of male monstrousness that Linda Williams addresses in 'When the Woman Looks' (1984). Here she discusses the relationship between the classic monster (werewolf, ape, vampire) and the heroine. Williams argues that there is 'a surprising (and at times subversive) affinity' (85) between monster and woman in that, like woman, he is represented as 'a biological freak with impossible and threatening appetites' (87). Whereas Williams ties the monster's freakishness to its phallic status (either symbolically castrated or overly endowed), I would argue that the affinity between the monster and woman resides in the way in which all monstrous figures are constructed in terms of Kristeva's 'non-symbolic' body: the body that gives birth, secretes, changes shape, or is marked in some way. This is also Freud's masochistic, feminized body.

Williams argues that while the male spectator's look at the monster 'expresses conventional fear' (Williams 1984: 87) because the monster is different, the female spectator is punished for looking because she recognizes the monster's freakishness as similar to her own. 'The woman's gaze is punished, in other words, by narrative processes that transform curiosity and desire into masochistic fantasy' (85). In my view, the gaze of *both* male and female spectators is constructed as masochistic by the signifying practices of the horror text. Although the male monster is placed in a feminine position in terms of the workings of abjection and masochistic desire, he is still male and as such elicits identification from male spectators. Furthermore, the monster is frequently represented as a sympathetic figure with whom all spectators are encouraged to identify (*King Kong*, 1933, *The Creature from the Black Lagoon*, 1954, *Psycho*, 1960, *An American Werewolf in London*). For similar reasons I would argue that female monsters (*Carrie*, 1976, *The Exorcist*, 1973, *The Hunger*, 1983, *Repulsion*, 1965) also elicit identification from both male and female spectators.

In my view, a crucial reason why the monster – regardless of its gender – draws on the masochistic aspects of looking lies with the origins of monstrosity as a form of abjection. Abjection constitutes a process by which we define the 'clean and proper body' as well as the rational, coherent, unified subject. Insofar as abjection speaks to the perverse and irrational aspects of desire it speaks to all spectators regardless of gender. It also addresses most clearly the masochistic desires of the spectator. As a consequence, the male spectator is punished, as he looks at the abject body of the other – his monstrous, feminized gender counterpart. In this way, the horror film makes a feminine position available to the male spectator – although this position is not necessarily identical to that offered to the female spectator. The problem does not lie with the horror film's appeal to the spectator's masochistic desires but rather with the fact that the abject body is identified with the feminine, which is socially denigrated, and the symbolic body with the masculine, which is socially valorized. If the horror film exists to explore our darker desires, it does so at the expense of woman's abjected body. But insofar as horror represents an encounter with the feminine body, it also points to the perversity of masculine desire and of the male imagination.

NOTES

1 For a fuller discussion of Kristeva's *Powers of Horror* in relation to the horror film see my earlier article, 'Horror and the Monstrous-Feminine: an Imaginary Abjection', *Screen* 27, 1 (1986): 44–70. Also included in *Fantasy and the Cinema*, ed. James Donald, London: BFI Publishing, 1989, 63–90.
2 I am not arguing that women do not constitute the majority of victims in the horror film. Rather, I am arguing that the nature of male monstrosity is itself problematic and should be given more consideration than is usually the case. The formula monster/male and victim/female is too simplistic.

BIBLIOGRAPHY

Briffault, R. (1927) *The Mothers*, vol. 2, New York: Macmillan.
Bullough, V. L. (1973) 'Medieval Medical and Scientific Views of Women,' *Viator: Medieval and Renaissance Studies* 4: 485–501.
Dijkstra, B. (1986) *Idols of Perversity: Fantasies of Feminine Evil in Fin-de-Siècle Culture*, New York: Oxford University Press.
Douglas, D. (1966) *Horrors*, London: John Baker.
Evans, W. (1973) 'Monster Movies: a Sexual Theory,' *Journal of Popular Film* 2: 353–65.
Freud, S. (1924) 'The Economic Problem of Masochism,' vol. 19 of *The Standard Edition of the Complete Psychological Works of Sigmund Freud*, trans. J. Strachey, London: Hogarth.
—— (1918) 'The Taboo of Virginity,' *Standard Edition*, vol. 11.
—— (1913) 'Totem and Taboo,' *Standard Edition*, vol. 13.
Hollinger, K. (1989) 'The Monster as Woman: Two Generations of Cat People,' *Film Criticism* 13, 2: 36–46.
Horney, K. (1967) *Feminine Psychology*, New York: Norton.
Hornung, C. P. (1959) *Hornung's Handbook of Designs and Devices*, New York: Dover.
Kristeva, J. (1982) *Powers of Horror: an Essay on Abjection*, trans. L. S. Roudiez, New York: Columbia University Press.
Lenne, G. (1979) 'Monster and Victim: Women in the Horror Film' in P. Erens (ed.) *Sexual Stratagems: the World of Women in Film*, New York: Horizon.
Lévi-Strauss, C. (1973) *From Honey to Ashes*, London: Jonathan Cape.
Mercer, K. (1986) 'Monster Metaphors – Notes on Michael Jackson's "Thriller," ' *Screen* 1, 27: 26–43.
Neale, S. (1980) *Genre*, London: British Film Institute.
Shuttle, P. and Redgrove, P. (1978) *The Wise Wound*, New York: Richard Marek.
Silver, A. and Ursini, J. (1975) *The Vampire Film*, Cranbury, NJ: A. S. Barnes.
Tudor, A. (1989) *Monsters and Mad Scientists: a Cultural History of the Horror Movie*, Oxford: Basil Blackwell.
Twitchell, J. B. (1985) *Dreadful Pleasures: an Anatomy of Modern Horror*, New York: Oxford University Press.
Walker, B. G. (1983) *The Women's Encyclopedia of Myths and Secrets*, San Francisco: Harper and Row.

Williams, L. (1984) 'When the Woman Looks' in M. A. Doane, P. Mellencamp and L. Williams (eds) *Re-Vision*, Los Angeles: American Film Institute.

7

'MORE HUMAN THAN I AM ALONE'

Womb envy in David Cronenberg's *The Fly* and *Dead Ringers*

Helen W. Robbins

In a spectacularly composed shot from David Cronenberg's *Dead Ringers* (1988), Beverly Mantle (Jeremy Irons), one of the twin gynecologists whose rise and fall the film chronicles, prepares to enter the surgical theater to operate. Completely shrouded in a blood-red surgical gown and hood, his arms raised and out-stretched and his palms upward as a nurse makes final adjustments to his costume, he looks more like a cultic high priest than a modern man of science. Cronenberg has staged the *mise-en-scène* so that the woman on the surgical table, whose anesthetized body awaits the doctor's ministrations, is visible, too. The camera, apparently located in the operating room itself, shoots Dr Mantle through the window of the antechamber where he dresses. As he stands there in his posture of medical omnipotence, a shadowy, transparent image of the patient – formed by a reflection in the glass of the window in front of him – is superimposed upon his clearly outlined, opaque figure, the 'V' of her parted legs pointing at his loins.

Simultaneously figuring two antithetical drives – both the sadistic ascension to godhead, vision, and patriarchal control and the masochistic regression to nature, unconsciousness, and fusion with the maternal body – the image of the doctor–god with the spectre of the womb over which he will preside floating mid-belly neatly summarizes the common theme of Cronenberg's last two films of the 1980s. Both *The Fly* (1986) and *Dead Ringers* prominently feature men of science whose hubristic control over advanced technologies epitomizes what might be called 'phallic' power – the power that in the familiar Lacanian scheme belongs to the phallus because it operates within the symbolic order of signification, discourse, and progressive detachment from the real.[1] Phallic power relegates nature, matter, and the female to a position of inferiority, otherness, and objecthood that is nevertheless potentially dangerous and therefore must be controlled through complex institutions of dominion.

134

Bev Mantle's exaggerated vertical posture and hieratic raiment, connoting the two male-dominated institutions of medicine and priesthood, are strong visual signs of the phallic drive to detach himself from and wield power over the passive female Other. The 'Gynaecological Instruments for Working on Mutant Women,' invented by Beverly Mantle to accommodate women whose insides he fantasizes are 'deformed,' are ready for use in this scene; these nightmarishly misshapen probes and specula symbolize the furthest extreme of this phallic tendency, and attest that sadism erupts when nature is imagined to elude institutional control. However, the reflected trace of the anesthetized woman, her raised, parted *legs* and supine position inverting the doctor's magisterial stance, tells a different story. The precise situation of her image at his midsection suggests Bev Mantle's seemingly contradictory desire to incorporate her womb, to *be* the woman (a desire also encoded in Bev's feminine name) rather than to distance himself from and dominate her.

The protagonists of *Dead Ringers* and *The Fly* suffer from *womb envy*, a feeling of impotence clearly stemming from their jealousy of female reproductive power. In an essay that provides a remarkably accurate profile of Cronenberg's 'heroes,' Eva F. Kittay explains that the clearest symptoms of womb envy are the defenses men mount against it, the most prevalent being what she labels 'appropriation.' Womb appropriation involves the invention and exaltation of male activities that mimic natural female functions. In pre-literate, agricultural societies these simulacra may include rituals of 'male menstruation,' the practice of couvade, and circumcision rites which reclassify male adolescence as a 'birth' into manhood replete with displaced 'umbilical' cutting presided over entirely by men (Kittay 1984: 109–10). In modern industrial society,

> appropriations are no longer of this symbolic or imitative sort. Instead of ritualized symbolic births and symbolic menstruation, we find men employing birth as a metaphor for more valued activities. Instead of men mimicking the behavior of the laboring mother to aid, to upstage, or to displace her altogether, we find the actual intervention of men into the childbearing process. Instead of symbolic appropriations which are clearly at the center of social organization, we find scattered evidence of men conceptualizing their work or creating roles so as to give them access to the good they attribute to women's powers.
>
> (Kittay 1984: 111–12)

The modern men of Cronenberg's films exhibit womb envy in both its interventional and metaphoric forms: they devote themselves to compensatory phallic behaviors involving either the attempt to usurp control over the womb itself, as in the case of the Mantles, whose institutionalized gynecological expertise gives them power over human fertility

135

exceeding that of the women patients who will actually give birth, or the construction and control of enterprises that substitute for and may even mimic the female role in reproduction, as in the case of Seth Brundle (Jeff Goldblum)'s womb-shaped teleportation pods or Stathis Borans (John Getz)'s editorship of *Particle* magazine. *The Fly* and *Dead Ringers* resonate intertextually (Cronenberg had begun the *Dead Ringers* project in the late 1970s, well before he decided to make his cameo appearance as a gynecologist in *The Fly*'s delivery room dream sequence) to offer an anatomy of modern male womb envy,[2] laying bare its origins in men's anxieties about creativity, and especially about controlling, keeping, and getting credit for their productions.

These anxieties are at work in a scene where Beverly chastises a patient he is examining (with the wrong instrument): '*This* hurts? Mrs Bookman, this is a solid gold Mantle retractor. . . . *solid gold* . . . ! It's the best there is! It couldn't possibly hurt.' The authority of the doctor's name coalesces with his technology to silence the woman and the truth of her body; later, he will explain to his twin brother, Elliot: 'There's nothing the matter with the instrument . . . it's the body; the woman's body was all wrong!' However, not only is the instrument he uses on Mrs Bookman the wrong one for the procedure (the Mantle retractor is for surgery rather than pelvic exams), it is not even a functional instrument, but rather a trophy – a gold replica awarded to the Mantles to honor their invention of its working prototype. The clash of a mere symbol for personal accomplishment in medicine with a live human body, and particularly Mantle's insistence that the symbol prevail, amounts to the envious promotion of *his* creativity over his patient's: his technological 'offspring' and its capacity to proliferate the *Mantle* name have ironically eclipsed the female fertility the technology was devised to serve.

Cronenberg typically undercuts such episodes of male mastery and self-assertion, exposing the womb envy that motivates them. Simultaneously examining and interviewing this patient, Bev Mantle becomes disoriented and has to ask, 'Where was I?' Mrs Bookman reminds him: 'You asked me whether or not it hurt when I have intercourse,' interpreting Dr Mantle's question in its customary, figurative sense to mean 'What was I *saying*?' But because Dr Mantle's hand with the Mantle retractor, though hidden from the camera, is unmistakably imbedded in Mrs Bookman's vagina during the exchange, the question's literal meaning is impossible to fend off. It is as if looking too closely and reaching too far into the womb have endangered Beverly's 'I,' threatening the position of privilege from which he asserts not just his control over but more importantly his *difference from* the female, tempting him too irresistibly with the surrender of his male subjecthood to the maternal body.

Phallic technology inexorably reveals the womb envy that motivates it in Cronenberg's updated version of *The Fly*. In Kurt Neumann's original

(1958) sci-fi classic, the scientist who accidentally splices himself with an insect is married and has a son, who after his father's death declares that he will become an 'explorer like *him*.' One of Cronenberg's modifications, centering the story on an unstable sexual triangle between unmarried participants, pointedly denies the consolation of unbroken paternal legacy that the original film promises. Close to the surface of the new *Fly*'s narrative are old anxieties about paternity that modern reproductive technology and especially the social and sexual liberation of women have exacerbated. In Cronenberg's *Fly*, Veronica ('Ronnie') Quaife, played by Geena Davis, is the sexually liberated heroine who has rejected a former lover and taken on another. Her behavior motivates the male characters' excessive disturbance at the site of reproductive certitude, exposing their failure to accept the biological reality of the brief, merely speculative role of the male individual in procreation.

Significantly, Seth Brundle's precipitous first attempt at self-teleportation, resulting in his genetic fusion with a fly and the narrative's tragic reversal, originates in a bout of drunken self-pity over Ronnie's purely *imagined* infidelity. That in *Dead Ringers* Bev Mantle's irreversible decline into drug addiction results from another case of misconstrued infidelity – from Bev's mistakenly assuming that the voice of Claire Niveau (Geneviève Bujold)'s manager on her hotel room phone is that of her lover – confirms the importance of dissemination anxiety in Cronenberg's characterizations of male protagonists. In both films the source of disaster is not female inconstancy, but the inevitable failure of patriarchy – the law binding the female Other – to live up to the impossible task for which it was instituted: maintaining the illusion of fixed paternity. And jeopardized paternity breeds womb envy. Seth's teleportation pods, with their frankly uterine shape and vulviform glass doors, are clear womb simulacra; the lingering shots of his naked fetal crouch in the transmitter pod and his triumphant naked emergence from the receiver pod figure his teleportation project as an attempt to give birth to himself. Stathis Borans, Veronica's rejected lover, represents a more 'phallic' response to male progenitive anxiety. His womb-appropriative activity, involving the production of the printed word, is far more abstracted from its prototype than Seth's construction of a physical womb-substitute and far less conscious of its own origin. He controls with iron hand the dissemination of scientific news from an upper-storey office in the high-tech 'MONOLITH PUBLISHING' building, a skyscraping edifice whose name and whose phallic perpendicularity, emphasized by insistent extremely low-angle shots, make it a kind of monument to the hegemony of patriarchal discourse. Stathis's unusual name, combining 'stat' – the Greek for 'standing' or 'stationary' – with 'his,' identifies him with this building and subtly links his zeal for strong editorial management, a highly advanced version of the phallic control of the world

Figure 17 Jeff Goldblum in *The Fly*

through control of signification, with the repressed desire for immortality, with his longing to leave behind a permanent legacy. Stathis Borans's grip on *Particle* magazine thus can be seen as a figuration of the problematics of biological paternity and its relationship to patriarchy.

Even Stathis's most exaggeratedly phallic behavior contains subtle traces of unsatisfiable paternal yearnings – unsatisfiable because of paternity's merely symbolic authenticity. When Stathis casually tells Veronica: 'I have to put this issue to bed,' the standard journalistic slang for completing an issue ('putting the paper to bed') becomes a patent example of what Kittay describes as 'men conceptualizing their work or creating roles so as to give them access to the good they attribute to women's power.' The unintentional pun on 'issue,' together with the metaphorical transformation of his magazine into a completely gestated and delivered child to be put to bed, betrays a fantasy of triumphing over dissemination, presiding over the fruition of his seed from conception to birth. Clearly his responsibilities as chief *Particle* editor have for him this significance. When Veronica protests his theft of her story about Seth's teleporter, Stathis proclaims: 'Your discovery is my discovery.' But, later, when Ronnie announces her pregnancy, Stathis is forced to acknowledge that what is *hers* is not necessarily *his*. We witness the studied transformation of John Getz's facial expression from a brief look of undisguised pride to one of horror as he realizes that the baby is Brundlefly's and not his own. Erecting patriarchy on the ruins of paternity, Stathis usurps the rights to Ronnie's verbal production in order to compensate for his inability to regulate her sexuality, to successfully colonize her womb.

Stathis Borans's counterpart in *Dead Ringers* is Bev Mantle's twin, Elliot (Jeremy Irons): he wields power through discourse by publishing papers and going on lecture tours to deliver official medical truths about women's bodies. However, not once in *Dead Ringers* do we actually witness one of the Mantles' vaunted successes in making women fertile; between award ceremonies and scenes from Elliot's lecture tour we instead see manifold evidence of failure: a patient sobbing in the Mantle Clinic, a patient being dismissed with the recommendation that her husband is 'the problem,' and the 'trifurcate' uterus of actress Claire Niveau precluding surgical reparation. Even though Elliot Mantle is almost always able to turn a clinical defeat into a publication victory, it is clear that his discursive command over the Other only partially masks the futility of more direct womb appropriations.

If phallic, discursive potency is revealed as an inadequate substitute for the female reproductive power it must attempt to master, it seems that Cronenberg's male subject may possess all the privileges associated with owning a penis and still be, in a sense, *castrated*. The womb envy of Cronenberg's protagonists actually amounts to the prioritization of the female, maternal body in a patent reversal of Freud's phallocentric idea of the castration complex. *Dead Ringers* opens with a scene in which the pre-adolescent Elliot Mantle explains to his twin brother that heterosexual intercourse is an unfortunate necessity because 'humans don't live under water' and therefore cannot, like fish, deposit and fertilize eggs without touching each other – a prospect Beverly claims he would prefer. Humans, Ellie solemnly notes, 'have to internalize the water.' When this discussion of heterosexual reproduction is immediately followed by a squabble with a neighbor girl, Elliot's philosophic conclusion, 'They're so different from us, and all because we don't live under water,' suggests a desire to return to the evolutionary past as a way of forestalling the difficulties of sexual difference. But the nostalgia for the phylogenetic past of life underwater conceals a nostalgia for the ontogenetic past of life in the womb, for it is the female body that 'internalizes the water' through the amniotic fluid that supports prenatal, or what Freud calls – in a metaphor condensing the 'ontogeny repeats phylogeny' formula – 'oceanic' existence (Freud 1961: XXI, 64–5). Elliot's phantasy of life before sexual reproduction is a fantasy of life in the womb. The female body is the original condition lost through the emergence of sexual difference; thus the womb envy of Cronenberg's men is often indistinguishable from their masochistic, regressive desire to return to the pre-symbolic connection with the maternal real.[3]

The Fly contains a scene that makes this inversion of Freud's castration complex even more explicit. Early in the film, Ronnie Quaife is surprised to return home one afternoon and find her ex-lover Stathis Borans in her shower, having admitted himself with the key she had once given him. The return via the key can be read in terms of Lacan's version of the Oedipus complex (Lacan 1977: 284–91): beginning to suspect Ronnie of turning to another lover, Stathis uses whatever phallic item he can marshal to recover his relationship with the womb. Stathis's specific appropriation of Ronnie's *shower* for his return emphasizes the immersion in water and recalls both Freud's oceanic existence and the internalized water of the Mantles' childish speculations. But when Ronnie scalds Stathis by deliberately flushing the toilet and then throws him out of her apartment, retained key and all, she destroys his fantasy of reunion with the maternal. The penis has become secondary: Stathis Borans has retained his phallic key, but as long as that key cannot access the womb, he remains in a state of lack.

In refiguring the male condition as inherently castrated or incomplete, Cronenberg protagonists also experience notable losses that correspond to the 'splittings' from the subject of the Lacanian *objets a* (Lacan 1981: 17–18; 103–5; 198). These losses of substance reactivate the trauma of individuation from the mother and activate womb envy. In *The Fly*, shortly after Seth Brundle has fused with the housefly but is still unaware of his condition, he stands before the bathroom mirror examining his strangely blemished face and biting a fingernail. Unexpectedly, the entire nail sloughs off against his teeth. When, in his horrified fascination, Seth examines, probes, and finally squeezes the naked pad of his finger, it disgorges a thick whitish fluid against the mirror. The image is overloaded with visual *double entendre*, suggesting simultaneously the two furtive adolescent rites of masturbation (the finger's phallic shape) and pimple squeezing (the splat of goo that Brundle wipes off the mirror with a tissue). Here the unsettling visceral effects for which Cronenberg is famous are wrapped in a familiar context, substantiating theories that much of the horror genre's chilling impact derives from its allowing its audience to experience the return of the repressed in disguised forms (Wood 1978: 25–32). What is repressed and what returns in this scene is not so much the shame attached to these adolescent activities as the

140

deep content for which they act as screen memories: both pimple-squeez-
ing and ejaculation involve losses of parts of the self, losses that may
reactivate primary castration anxieties.

In his article 'Vas' Paul Smith has argued that ejaculation itself can
provoke castration anxiety, that the ejaculatory sensation is potentially
a point of vulnerability, loss, and lack (Smith 1988: 98–9). In *The Fly*
and *Dead Ringers*, male effeminization, or reappropriation of the womb,
confirms Smith's point by explicitly carrying out the function of recovering the losses ejaculation entails. Significantly, Seth Brundle's doomed
scientific project is motivated by the fact that he suffers motion sickness:
his personal stake in teleportation is the desire to find a method of travel
that will not make him nauseous. The malady Seth suffers does not
appear in Kurt Neumann's original *Fly*, and is itself a mark of the
Cronenberg scientist's castrated condition, representing a conspicuous
deviation from the coding of gender in several recent popular films. The
supermasculine cultural ideal represented in the heroes of *Top Gun*
(1986), *An Officer and a Gentleman* (1982), and *The Right Stuff* (1983),
for example, depends in part on their ability to tolerate radical motion
in customarily phallic-shaped vehicles. (The training vehicles and motion-
simulator machines of NASA and the military reputedly have such colorful nicknames as 'the Vomit-Maker.') In the light of this association of
motion sickness with inadequate masculinity, Seth's confession in Ronnie's car that when he was a kid he 'puked on his tricycle' is a patent
signal of his effeminization. And Brundle's willingness to go to great
lengths, to deconstruct and reassemble the human body in order to
circumvent motion sickness, suggests that the manly ideal of withholding
one's substance is simply another defense against castration, the proscrip-
tion against vomiting a displaced defense against the other, inevitable
ejaculatory loss. For Seth Brundle, the danger represented by this symbolic dissemination can be 'contained' by appropriating the womb where
male substance falls, by his invention of the wombic pods that will
prevent his motion sickness from causing the loss of the *objet a*.

The association between vomiting and ejaculation as similar splittings
off of the subject is the manifest subtext of a scene depicting one of the
later developments of Brundle's metamorphosis into Brundlefly. Upon a
visit to her now barely recognizable ex-lover, Ronnie watches appalled
as Brundle raises a donut to his mouth and then involuntarily and copi-
ously vomits a thick white liquid on to the food. Suggesting nothing so
much as a parody of the pornographer's 'money shot,' the moment is
shocking not only to Ronnie but to the film's audience, for only later
does Brundlefly explain that the fly he has become must eat by vomiting
a corrosive substance on to its food before taking it in. This linkage of
ejaculatory vomiting and eating significantly invokes childish theories of
impregnation through ingestion (Freud 1961: XI, 78–9), and functions

iconographically as a means of protecting the male against the loss of bodily intactness incurred through his normal role in human reproduction. Brundlefly's new ability to figuratively ejaculate, but to subsequently re-incorporate that lost fluid in digestion, a process that actually *adds* to his bodily substance, symbolically locates both male and female contributions to reproduction in Brundlefly's own body. In this way, Brundlefly's recycled 'ejaculate' anticipates his final project of genetically splicing his own body with that of a pregnant female. Brundlefly's final words in the film are a plea to his former lover to enter one of his pods and fuse with him so that, by incorporating the bodies of both Veronica Quaife and the child she is carrying, he can become 'more human than I am alone.' The incorporation of the female signifies the possibility for being whole, and for recovering the losses suffered through the dubious achievement of male subjecthood.

Eating appears as a repetitive trope in both *The Fly* and *Dead Ringers* and underscores the characters' womb envy through suggesting infantile theories of both oral impregnation and incorporation of the mother's body (Freud 1961: VII, 196). A striking feature of *Dead Ringers'* setting is that, with few exceptions, almost the entire film takes place at one of two kinds of tables: the narrative advances either over meals or over gynecological procedures. The *mise-en-scène* of the operating room is composed to echo that of the Mantles' dining room: both feature a cold, high-tech schematization and are often introduced by a trademark head-on shot that reduces the visual geometry to a central rectangular table beneath a central circular light. In addition, Cronenberg's editing often underscores the subtle analogy being proposed between the medical establishment's intervention into women's bodies and eating: for example, he cuts immediately from a scene involving hastily dispatched patients at the clinic to a close-up shot of a pizza box on the Mantles' dining room table. The Mantles ply their gynecological trade; they eat. Through the film's insistent rhythm, food consumption becomes associated with the physical incorporation of the female already noted in the image of Beverly entangled with his patient's reflection, the gynecology/eating trope a vehicle for the fantasy of appropriating the womb and its powers through engulfment.

This ingestion of the female with her feared and desired powers is the sly subtext of a scene in which Ellie joins Claire and her manager, Leo, for dinner at a restaurant directly following Claire's examination that afternoon at the Mantle clinic. The immediate cut from Claire on the exam table to the three at the dinner table activates the consumption-of-the-mother's-body metaphor: to reinforce the analogy, when Claire demands that Elliot tell her about her uterus, the camera cuts to Leo's ostentatious choking on a mouthful of food. When Elliot next asks Claire about her periods, the camera again shifts to Leo, who at this last straw awkwardly excuses himself from the table. As Leo – who has had little purpose in the scene but to register the 'normal' male reaction to gyneco-logical shop-talk – leaves the restaurant, Elliot can be seen in the extreme foreground sipping serenely from his glass of red wine. Leo's loss of appetite in the atmosphere of female organs and blood – in fact, in the presence of specific images of the original nurturing environment – recalls the young male's achievement of subjecthood through alienation from the feminine in the Lacanian passage through the Oedipus complex. His disgust reflects what E. Ann Kaplan has hypothesized as the male child's customary inability to 'recover from the fact of having been mothered [by] and totally dependent on a figure who . . . possesses a genital organ . . . that seems sinister to him (Kaplan 1983: 200). In contrast, Ellie, almost caressing his glass of red wine, eagerly ingests what clearly has become, like the pizza, a symbol for the uterine medium. This scene and others in which Ellie presides over dining table encounters with the feminine foreshadow through the trope of incorporation his final exchange of roles with his female patients. Ellie's death is brought about through his submission to being effeminized: after an orgy of food con-sumption, *he* is put on the table, rendered unconscious, and penetrated with the instruments that his brother has designed for the mutant woman he is finally revealed to be.

Elliot Mantle is not alone: what makes *Dead Ringers* remarkable is its relentless inclusion of the male viewer in its redefinition of masculinity as mutant womanhood. The restaurant scene is notable for its deliberately disruptive encoding of gender, although at first this would not seem to be the case. A configuration of a woman actress, her male manager, and particularly her male gynecologist contains the potential for maximizing female objectification before male power and vision, according to Laura Mulvey's now-famous analysis of how cinema uses representations of women to activate and then allay castration anxiety in its male viewers. Leaning on Freud's versions of the castration complex and the fetish, Mulvey posits that the male spectator looking at the woman's image on screen overcomes the threat of castration that she represents either through sadistic voyeurism, through identifying with a powerful male character whose look penetrates the woman in order to know, devalue, and efface her, or through fetishization, through investing her body with an often fragmentary perfection (her legs, her face, her breasts) that substitutes for the absent penis (Mulvey 1975: 6–18). Thus the male viewer's pleasure in watching film derives from his repeatedly triumphing over the threatened loss of his own potency, vicariously fortifying his position of power via vision.

This is clearly *not* what happens in the *Dead Ringers* scene. If fetishism requires the idealization of a non-genital aspect of the female body in order to disguise its 'wounded' condition, then Claire's frank report of her uterus and her periods amounts to a kind of inversion of fetishism. More broadly, as a film *about* gynecology, *Dead Ringers* can be said to represent a thorough, iconoclastic refusal to solidify the male spectator's subjectivity against castration by deflecting attention *away* from the female 'wound.' In fact, it is tempting to read into Cronenberg's own report of a talk-show host – who, in the middle of an interview, 'freaked out on his own TV show and walked off the set,' saying over and over ' "My God, gynecology, why gynecology?" ' (Hickenlooper 1989: 6) – that *Dead Ringers* has the quite opposite effect of 'dismantling' traditional phallic subjectivity. The talk-show host's reaction against 'gynecology' remarkably duplicates Leo's intradiegetic retreat from the dinner table, and thus suggests why voyeurism is no more an option than fetishism for protecting Cronenberg's male spectator. The dinner conversation centering on Claire's irregular reproductive physiology admittedly entails her being penetrated, known, and devalued, but the scene provides no safe ego-ideal with whom the male viewer can identify so as to be empowered by this knowledge. Voyeuristic investigation is supposed to work by revealing that the woman thus devalued never had a penis anyway (or that she *deserved* to have it taken away) and is therefore neither castrated nor fearsome; however, Leo's hasty departure from the table suggests that even the woman who never had a penis possesses something powerful enough to evoke fear in him and thus disqualifies him as a sadistic masculine ego-ideal. If the real-life talk-show host's displeasure is in any measure a typical male reaction to the film's gynecological theme (and Cronenberg's ten-year struggle to find financial backing for the *Dead Ringers* project suggests that it is (Hickenlooper 1989: 4)), then the male spectator of this scene will have to struggle against the tendency to identify with Leo's discomfiture in order to forestall recognizing his own powerlessness before the female.

The option remaining to the male spectator is of course to adopt Ellie's subjective position, and *Dead Ringers* tentatively invites this identification: after all, Ellie is the twin who personifies both seductive charm and the detached control over the Other through medical discourse. However, identification with Elliot's ultra-phallicism is fraught with its own set of dangers for the male viewer. For one thing, the same question that discommodes Leo – Elliot's cool inquiry into Claire's menstrual history – is figuratively a red flag that decodes Elliot's exemplary malehood by implying the instability of his omniscient distance from the female. His deep involvement, familiarity, and comfortable habitation with female mysteries suggest that his redundantly propped phallicism is always in danger of collapsing into its opposite: identification with femininity. In addition, and to a similar effect, throughout *Dead Ringers* Elliot's voyeuristic assumption of discursive power over women actually undermines his masculine subjectivity through its exaggeration to the point of obvious parody: for example, in one scene, Elliot struts in his neat suit and tie before two video monitors in a glass-enclosed surgical observation room, lecturing to a captive audience on a procedure that Bev, in the adjacent surgery, is simultaneously performing. Doubly protected by two glass screens, that of the window and that of the monitor, Elliot fastidiously maintains his distance from the physical body of the woman. His exaggeratedly voyeuristic subjectivity is manifested in the fact that the woman, for him, has been so far abstracted that she exists only in an obliquely pornographic video image of magnified reproductive organs which he then – wielding his unmistakably phallic microphone – masters through language. Elliot Mantle fails as an ego-ideal because his voyeurism is too clearly labelled. And, because Ellie's insulated processing of the woman as video image too nearly reproduces the viewer's own cinematic experience, the male spectator who identifies with Ellie will eventually be forced into an unpleasant and unresolved confrontation with his own voyeurism and the castration anxiety that motivates it.

The traditional Hollywood cinema that Mulvey describes cannot afford to risk this kind of self reflexivity; as Kaja Silverman has pointed out: 'classic cinema organizes its flow of images so as to protect the male subject against precisely this sort of unpleasurable self-encounter' (Silverman 1988: 38). Cronenberg's refusal to grant his male viewer the asylum of untroubled identification with a powerful male subject is reinforced by the later revelation that the surgical procedure verbally superintended by Elliot has been a failure. In a scene shortly after the Fallopian tube transplant, Ellie asks Bev for his 'tissue rejection data' so that he can write yet another paper.

Of course the Mantles' use of video monitors in surgery involves their production as well as consumption of the video image; in fact, both *Dead Ringers* and *The Fly* are highly self-reflexive in that they refer repeatedly to this analogue of the film-maker's art.[4] In *Dead Ringers* the surgical camera that penetrates to reveal the hidden interiors of women's bodies emblematically equates the Mantles' enterprise with Cronenberg's own, and Cronenberg's cameo acting role as an obstetrician in *The Fly* anticipates and reinforces this linkage of gynecology with film-making. In *The Fly*, cinematic production is represented by the video camera with which Ronnie tapes all phases of Seth Brundle's project. Particularly emphasized are Ronnie's sweeping shots from the sender teleporter pod to the receiver pod as she records the miraculous movement of objects from one location to the other. The way her camera follows the teleporter's route reminds us how like a teleportation device is the cinematic apparatus that can move images through space, from the site of the film-maker's production to that of the audience's consumption.

Through this reflexivity both films identify Cronenberg's art with the enterprises of his womb-envious mad scientists, as if Cronenberg were revealing the motive for film-making to be a literalization of the 'natal metaphor' Kaja Silverman quotes from the writings of the early film theorist Siegfried Kracauer, who tells how the camera extracts objects ' "from the womb of physical existence" ' and presents them ' "as if the umbilical cord between image and actuality" ' were intact (Silverman 1988: 8). Certainly the cables connecting Seth Brundle's teleportation pods are deliberately suggestive of umbilici. Cronenberg's willingness to identify himself with his protagonists and thereby indict his own cinematic enterprise as a metaphorical womb-appropriation should make those eager to label his films misogynistic pause; and his position as a maker of misogynistic images is probably most accurately illustrated by yet another self-reflexive gesture.

Near the end of *Dead Ringers*, Beverly Mantle, stumbling down the sidewalks of downtown Toronto, gazes into the display window of a gallery hosting artist Anders Wolleck's show, where he discovers copies of the instruments he had himself designed and commissioned Wolleck to produce. A placard bears the caption 'Gynaecological instruments for operating on mutant women – by Anders Wolleck.' Dr Mantle's immediate, outraged seizure of his pirated invention underscores Cronenberg's preoccupation with exposing men's anxieties about dissemination; however, Wolleck's use of the 'mutant instruments' as *objets d'art* has another function, and suggests that Wolleck is but another figure for Cronenberg himself. The 'Gynaecological Instruments for Working on Mutant Women' which Beverly Mantle designs for use on his patients are patent embodiments of his misogyny, of what has become his sadistic fear and envy of the womb. But when Wolleck turns the same instruments into art objects, his purpose is clearly the detached objectification of womb envy; they become objects for contemplation in a show whose *theme* is misogyny. The presentation of these devices in two forms should remind us that Cronenberg's cinema is ultimately not Bev Mantle's surgery, but Wolleck's gallery: where images of womb envy are carefully labelled and exposed to the eye of the self-conscious viewer.

NOTES

1 I am relying upon both Lacan's explanation of 'The Signification of the Phallus' (Lacan 1977: 281–91) and Margaret Homans's Lacan-based account of phallocentric culture (Homans 1986: 5–10).
2 Two recent publications refer briefly to womb envy in *Dead Ringers*. Marcie Frank writes that 'the film reflects a powerful male fantasy and its impossibility: the ability for a man to give birth to himself without the mediation of the maternal body' (Frank 1991: 468). Frank's use of the verb 'reflects' betrays her feminist uneasiness about Cronenberg's representation of male fear and envy of the womb: indeed, Cronenberg has been accused of making misogynist films that sanction – through encouraging male viewers to identify with –

his protagonists' dread of the female body. My view is the opposite; I agree with Elaine Showalter, who sees in Cronenberg's work the deliberate and critical exposure of misogyny, as well as the keen analysis of its origin in male castration anxieties (Showalter 1990: 140–3).

3 Nancy Chodorow argues convincingly that a woman's capacity to bear children allows her symbolically to recuperate her relationship with the maternal real; thus the man's womb envy can betray his desire to re-experience infantile dependence on *his* mother (Chodorow 1978: 199–207).

4 Cronenberg's thematic use of video technology recalls his earlier film *Videodrome* (1982), in which a cable-television operator's mind is 'programmed' by a sinister organization that employs impulses transmitted over cable TV and videocassettes in its scheme to overtake the world.

BIBLIOGRAPHY

Chodorow, N. (1978) *The Reproduction of Mothering: Psychoanalysis and the Sociology of Gender*, Berkeley: University of California Press.

Frank, M. (1991) 'The Camera and the Speculum: David Cronenberg's *Dead Ringers*,' PMLA 106: 459–70.

Freud, S. (1961) *The Standard Edition of the Complete Psychological Works of Sigmund Freud*, ed. and trans. J. Strachey, 24 vols, London: Hogarth Press.

Hickenlooper, G. (1989) 'The Primal Energies of the Horror Film: an Interview with David Cronenberg,' *Cineaste* 17, 2: 4–7.

Homans, M. (1986) *Bearing the Word: Language and Female Experience in Nineteenth-Century Women's Writing*, Chicago, IL: University of Chicago Press.

Kaplan, E. A. (1983) *Women and Film: Both Sides of the Camera*, New York: Methuen.

Kittay, E. F. (1984) 'Womb Envy: an Explanatory Concept' in Joyce Trebilcot (ed.) *Mothering: Essays in Feminist Theory*, Totowa, NJ: Rowman and Allanheld.

Lacan, J. (1977) *Ecrits*, trans. A. Sheridan, New York: Norton.

_____ (1981) *The Four Fundamental Concepts of Psychoanalysis*, ed. J. A. Miller, trans. A. Sheridan, New York: Norton.

Mulvey, L. (1975) 'Visual Pleasure and Narrative Cinema,' *Screen* 16, 3: 6–18.

Showalter, E. (1990) *Sexual Anarchy: Gender and Culture at the Fin de Siècle*, New York: Penguin.

Silverman, K. (1988) *The Acoustic Mirror: the Female Voice in Psychoanalysis and Cinema*, Bloomington: Indiana University Press.

Smith, P. (1988) 'Vas,' *Camera Obscura* 17: 89–111.

Wood, R. (1978) 'The Return of the Repressed,' *Film Comment* 14, 4: 25–32.

Part III

MAN TO MAN

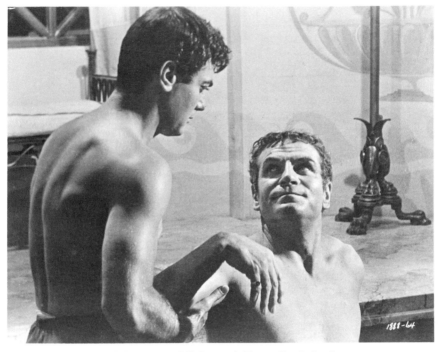

Figure 18 Laurence Olivier and Tony Curtis in *Spartacus*

8

ANIMALS OR ROMANS
Looking at masculinity in *Spartacus*
Ina Rae Hark

When Laura Mulvey's 'Visual Pleasure and Narrative Cinema' detailed how the cinematic apparatus and the conditions of cinema spectatorship invariably place woman as an object of the desiring male gaze, required to present herself as spectacle, its argument did not necessarily exclude the possibility that the apparatus could similarly objectify men who symbolically if not biologically lacked the signifying phallus. Although those who have built upon Mulvey's landmark work have overwhelmingly concentrated on the construction of the male viewing subject and the female spectacle, male spectacles, as the essays in this book demonstrate, abound in films. They surface especially in narratives and genres that feature power struggles between men.

If the structures of gender difference underwrite the economics of spectacularization, these practices nevertheless replicate themselves in many systems that operate through the empowerment of one group by the subjection of another. As Susanne Kappeler notes: 'Gender . . . lends a powerful cultural metaphor to oppression, as the working class becomes the object to the economic subject, becomes objectified, "feminized," animalized, commodified' (Kappeler 1986: 70). Looking at bodies, regardless of their gender, marks a principal form of control exercised in the discourses of institutional power that Michel Foucault has traced. In these systems where political control or subjugation intersect psychoanalytic models of subjectivity or lack, a male may very well find himself situated in positions analogous to those of the fetish or object of punishing voyeurism Mulvey describes as woman's in cinema's classic scopic regime.

The numerous film genres that focus on men in conflict with other men – Westerns, epics, swashbucklers, science fiction, sword and sorcery, war dramas, gangster and cop movies – often contain episodes in which a male protagonist's enemies make a spectacle of him. Extreme forms of this display occur in the appropriately named spectacular, where the genre's cultural settings (biblical, Greco-Roman) allow for both male and female fashions that reveal considerable flesh; moreover, in these cultures

151

homoerotic practices are widely acknowledged and the punishment of criminals or conquered foes is a highly elaborated public show, allowing for the ample spectacularization of male characters. Most frequently this spectacle is sado-masochistic, enacted through beating or torture, during which the male body, marked by the punishment, is eroticized through stripping or binding.

This is not to say that such films present the spectacularized male as transparently as the female. By contrast, they frequently code such spectacles as unnatural, in contrast to those of women, which transpire unremarked within the diegesis. Males played by movie stars become spectacularized or commodified, these narratives assert, only because the rightful exercise of masculine power has been perverted by unmanly tyrants. From Robin Hood to Rambo, captive or outlawed men revolt because the powerful subject positions within their societies have been usurped by male oppressors who don't qualify for them. (Hollywood ideology works to efface any suggestion that true masculinity could express itself undemocratically.) Thus, the usurpers often display characteristics not marked as signifiers of masculinity in the codes of male film performance at the time. They may for example be effete, overweight, short, foreign-accented, or disabled. The narrative trajectory in such films most often traces the male star-protagonist's liberation from his subjugated position to effect the restoration of appropriate patriarchal authority and the removal of the male-impersonator from power. In *Captain Blood* (1935), for example, Errol Flynn's Dr Peter Blood progresses from convicted traitor to enslaved laborer on the plantation of the Governor of Jamaica/the porcine Lionel Atwill to commander of a buccaneer ship to Atwill's successor as the new governor and husband to his niece (and Blood's former owner) Arabella.

Yet these narratives pose two uneasy questions. If the natural male position in patriarchy is to command the gaze, initiate exchanges, and articulate the law of the father, how do so many men whose masculinity is not fully constructed on-screen gain possession of these positions? And if patriarchy and capitalism in the wrong hands operate so oppressively, who is to say that the mere insertion of the 'correct' movie-star male icon into these systems will erase all oppression?

Spartacus, the epic about a gladiators' revolt against Rome in 73 BC, released in 1960 at the end of a decade of spectacular box office success for beefcake on display, provides an especially productive text through which to examine these questions. Its protagonist emerges from a system of institutionalized slavery – class difference at its most extreme – that, the film is at pains to articulate, deliberately excludes enslaved men from the subject positions granted their gender in the scopic and economic regimes of patriarchy. The experience of Spartacus (Kirk Douglas) as a gladiator combines marks of hypermasculinity – the training sequences feature enough phallic weaponry to send Freudians into sensory overload – with the feminine requirements to offer himself up as spectacle and acquiesce in the ultimate passivity demanded by his masters: 'Those who are about to die salute you.'[1] More importantly, the plot of *Spartacus* does not complete the 'natural' ascendancy of the oppressed male star into the usurper's place. While his revolt reaches the outlaw stage, he does not, like Captain Blood or Robin Hood, attain eventual reintegration into the power structure. His army is defeated and every man in it killed. Spartacus, who began the film condemned to starvation while chained to a cliff face, ends it crucified, a not dissimilar type of execution-as-spectacle. With the material failure of his struggle actually helping Crassus (Laurence Olivier) to cement his dictatorial sway over Rome, the signifying power of Spartacus's achievements in the interval of reprieve from this grisly destiny inevitably comes under scrutiny, in a way it would not had he escaped to become King of Thrace or marched starry-eyed into Christian martyrdom as do Marcellus and Diana in *The Robe* (1953).

With its masculine ego-ideal unable to retain his subjectivity within patriarchy, the film cannot fully recuperate patriarchal masculinity, despite the efforts of its second half to do so. Instead it reveals, without resolving, a dilemma of masculine subjectivity constantly shifting axes between material force and signifying practices, between sexual and class differences; ultimately the men in the film are caught between two unsatisfactory models of male power, which Spartacus distinguishes as 'animal' and 'Roman.' And every time the film answers the question, 'Can we define a human subjectivity independent of another's subjection?' affirmatively, sites of textual rupture whisper, 'Not here, not now.'

SITE OF SPECTACLE: THE ENSLAVED MALE

The first hour of *Spartacus*, which ends with the gladiators' revolt, rigorously details the spectacularization of the enslaved male and the systematic suppression of any move on his part to achieve subjectivity through mastery of the gaze. The gladiator is selected, groomed, and trained for the sole purpose of providing a worthy spectacle for 'ladies and gentlemen of quality who appreciate a fine kill.' The suitability of his body, both athletically and aesthetically, is the crucial criterion. Shopping in Libya, Batiatus (Peter Ustinov), slave dealer and proprietor of the gladiatorial school in Capua, rejects men whose rotten teeth signify bones like chalk and men who as Gauls are disposed to be disagreeably 'hairy.'

Once enrolled at the gladiatorial school, the slaves undergo bodily transformations. Batiatus encourages them with details of the more pleasurable aspects of this ritualistic eroticizing of their bodies: 'A gladiator is like a stallion. He must be pampered. You'll be bathed, oiled,

153

shaved, massaged, taught to use your heads. A good body with a dull brain is as cheap as life itself. You'll be given your ceremonial kowdahs – be proud of them . . . From time to time those of you who please me will be given the companionship of a young lady.'

The stallion simile encapsulates many of the contradictions the film assigns to its protagonist as enslaved male. It inaugurates the animal/human binary that he will invoke repeatedly to distinguish slave from free existence. However, in that a prize horse passively receives pampering and decoration – Batiatus tactfully omits reference to his pupils being branded like horses – so that empowered spectators may admire it, the stallion signifies less brute animality than femininity.[2] This becomes explicit when Claudia (Nina Foch) and Helena (Joanna Barnes) select the pairs they wish to fight to the death for their entertainment; the sequence serves as a parodic reversal of the many movie scenes in which a group of men ogle dancing girls, strip-tease artists, or other women on display. Motivated entirely by the amount of erotic stimulation a given body promises, the two 'capricious, over-painted nymphs' (as Batiatus later describes them) make their choices in near-orgasmic whispers after languorous gazings at the candidates. Helena insists on Draba (Woody Strode) because 'I want the most beautiful. Give me the big, black one.' Then she asks that the men be spared their 'suffocating tunics' and clothed only in enough 'for modesty.'

The stallion speech reveals Batiatus's insight that no slave would go through the grueling gladiatorial training if he clearly perceived himself as nothing more than a spectacle for Romans' desiring gaze. Indeed, the chronicler Appian of Alexandria speculated that the historical Spartacus 'persuaded about seventy [gladiators] to gamble for their freedom rather than be put on show at a public spectacle' (Bradley 1989: 98). So Batiatus tempts his recruits with the opportunity for male subjectivity. They will not be solely material good bodies with dull brains, 'cheap' bimbos; they will also be 'men' – stallions rather than fillies or geldings. They can have pride in the tiny pony-tail of the phallic kowdah; they can wield weapons; the most pleasing can have women. By transferring the term 'lady' from the Romans who will buy and watch the gladiators to the female slaves over whom alone they may be permitted mastery, Batiatus hopes to efface the humiliation of the enslaved male forced to make a spectacle of himself.

The promised subjectivity is, of course, a sham. The gladiators may use their weapons only on each other, with their masters dictating the choice of opponent. When Steve Neale groups the gladiatorial bout in *Spartacus* with other epic contests like the chariot race in *Ben Hur* (1959) as examples of male combat that 'are moments of spectacle . . . but they are also points at which the drama is finally resolved,' he overlooks the fact that Spartacus and Draba are fighting for nothing, except the titillation of spectators for whom there is definitely not the intention 'to disavow any explicitly erotic look at the male body' (Neale 1983: 14). The gladiators have no score to settle, as did Judah Ben-Hur and Messala; their combat has no narrative point for them.

Nor would their masters permit a fight that did. When the sadistic trainer Marcellus (Charles McGraw) hands Spartacus a sword and tries to goad him into striking, Spartacus knows that to wield it of his own volition would be fatal – his previous lashing out at Roman authority earned him a death sentence – and demurs. This indicates to Marcellus that Spartacus may have intelligence, a quality that, in direct contradiction to Batiatus's assertion, he proclaims 'dangerous for slaves.' The trainer promises, 'Everything you do, I'll be watching.'

As a corollary to this constant surveillance, entry into the symbolic order through language is prohibited. The gladiators are quartered in solitary cells, with talking forbidden in their communal areas. In the first hour of the film, Kirk Douglas speaks only twenty-one lines, all but one of them a phrase or sentence of six words or less. Spartacus's only power in relation to language is a negative one, to withhold speech when Romans demand it of him. Such a refusal to answer shakes Crassus from his icy detachment when he confronts Spartacus after the suppression of the revolt; metonymically prefiguring that moment is the condemned Spartacus's refusal to open his mouth on command so that Batiatus can poke his teeth, with which he has just hamstrung the guard.

Most problematic for the masculinity promised the gladiator, even his mastery of his female counterpart is subject to spectacularization. The key sequence occurs when Batiatus sends Varinia (Jean Simmons) to Spartacus's cell. Spartacus arrests her progress to his cot to touch her skin and hair, to pull down one sleeve of her dress to admire her naked shoulder, to tell her he has 'never had a woman before.' She disrobes, resignedly offering her body to his gaze and subsequent penetration. But Spartacus craves physical satisfaction far less than the entry into desire. Varinia is a mysterious object upon whom he looks with unabashed erotic pleasure. This entry into desiring subjectivity Rome cannot allow. Spartacus is already marked as a troublemaker in the first basic-training session when he looks Marcellus fiercely in the eye rather than lowering his gaze as the other slaves do.

Therefore Batiatus and Marcellus, voyeuristically spying on the proceedings through the barred ceiling, urge him to do something more than just look. The irony, that Batiatus and Marcellus, with a houseful of women (and men) at their disposal, would also rather look than rape, is precisely the point. The power of the gaze supersedes the power of the penis that is not a phallus. The scene represents a defining moment as to the meaning the film attributes to spectacle for Romans. The permission to become a spectator demarcates the master from the slave.

155

Figure 19 Peter Ustinov and Charles McGraw

Rome maintains and enforces its power through making spectacles of those it dominates. Just as, in psychoanalytic terms, the woman's body must become the phallus to assuage the threat posed by her failure to possess the phallus, so the gladiator must embody the very material domination that controls him in order to ease the threat to Roman mastery a slave's lack of self-determination signifies. Thus, forcing slaves to engage in phallic aggression against one another – in the arena or the bedroom – while Rome watches becomes homologous with a male making a fetishistic spectacle of woman. Spartacus's transgression here, as it is Draba's in the gladiatorial contest (also accompanied by tittering sexual innuendo from the spectators), is to refuse to penetrate a fellow slave for his master's visual/erotic pleasures.

Spartacus feels that to couple for pure physical stimulation, denied one's own subjectivity, while knowingly the object of another's detached gaze, robs the slave of humanity; 'Go away, I'm not an animal,' he shouts. When he repeats the claim to Varinia, she replies, 'Neither am I.' Objecting to his own spectacularization, Spartacus has not realized that he is in fact taking the Roman position in regard to Varinia. Throughout the film, the dangers of escaping the animal's objectification only to indulge in the Roman's passion for objectifying others haunt Spartacus's struggles to claim subjectivity for himself. The realm of sexual difference offers the most 'natural' place for such Romanization to occur. But Varinia's rebuke causes Spartacus immediately to disavow masculine tyranny. Relinquishing the gaze, he returns her dress, averts his eyes while she puts it on, and asks her name.

At this point, as signification is beginning for both slaves, Batiatus must intervene. Removing Varinia from the cell, he chides: 'You may not be an animal Spartacus, but this sorry show gives me very little hope that you will ever be a man.' Rome's hegemony would fall should its slaves inscribe themselves in a symbolic order. So it is necessary that male slaves acknowledge the primacy of material force over the desiring gaze. Throughout his confinement at Capua, Spartacus never gives up his mute courtship of Varinia through a mutual exchange of glances; the Romans never give up defining these yearning looks as marks of Spartacus's lack of manhood. In the scene in which Marcellus displays the slave's semi-naked body, slathered with different colors of paint to illustrate the consequences of variously placed sword thrusts. Marcellus catches Spartacus turning his head to gaze at Varinia. Rather than insist that Spartacus refrain from looking, he physically restrains him from abandoning the gaze: 'Since all you can do is look at girls, go ahead and look, slave.' A being forced to present his body for such passive display, Marcellus implies, can never gain power through the gaze. Such psychological attempts to castrate the gaze of the enslaved male complement the Romans' spectacularization of his body.

Yet spectacles offer little pleasure in *Spartacus*. Gazes are marked by their impotence, by a subjectivity whose object eludes it. Few point of view shots share the perspective of the voyeuristic Roman masters. What lingers in the mind are the glamour-lighted close-ups of characters in a state of despairing, unachievable desire, often staring into an empty quadrant of the wide-screen frame. A number of these shots feature Jean Simmons, appearing to offer her directly to the male spectator's erotic gaze, but even more present Douglas in this manner, and not a few Olivier. The visual style underlines the futility of the look rather than the erotic pleasure of looking, a notable instance being the intercut shots of Spartacus on the cross and Varinia in the cart straining to fix each other in their respective gazes while distance and death hurry them apart.

The film underscores its emphasis on troubled looks by frustrating the visual pleasures of the audience. For a wide-screen spectacular with a cast of thousands, it presents relatively few panoramic vistas or much visual excess: '. . . it is free of Christian martyrs being eaten by lions, has no chariot races, lacks the customary orgies in which dusky, semi-

Figure 20 Kirk Douglas and Charles McGraw

nude girls cram grapes into their mouths as fat, Roman nobles eye them lasciviously' (Alpert 1960: 32).

Spectacle becomes troubled within the diegesis because the spectacularized bodies repeatedly resist their assigned roles. Spectators can therefore assure themselves untroubled looking only when they have the body under stringent material control, when they stage a 'spectacle of the scaffold,' starring 'the body of the condemned' (Foucault 1977: 32; 3). 'The public execution is to be understood not only as a judicial, but also as a political ritual,' Foucault continues. 'It belongs, even in minor cases, to the ceremonies by which power is manifested' (Foucault 1977: 47). On three occasions in *Spartacus* Romans sentence rebellious slaves to death and display their bodies. For hamstringing the guard, Spartacus, stripped to a loincloth and riveted to a rock, is to be starved in full view of his fellows. After Draba's death during his attack on Crassus and his party, Marcellus hangs his body upside down at the entrance to the gladiators' cells 'until he rots.' The gladiators' uprising itself of course constitutes the most elaborate revolt and subsequent spectacular punishment the film portrays.

Prepared for the afternoon before, when Draba turned his weapon on the spectators instead of his defeated opponent, it occurs spontaneously at the moment Marcellus once again mocks Spartacus's gaze, telling him to take a 'last look' at the departing Varinia and reminding him of his lack of access to language – 'no talking in the kitchen, slave' – as Spartacus speaks his dismay. But the slave army's temporary success only makes its eventual subjugation the more terrible. Crassus promises the Roman citizenry 'the living body of Spartacus for whatever punishment you deem fit, this or his head.' He eventually lines the Appian way with the crucified bodies of Spartacus and six thousand of his followers. As Foucault observes: 'Justice pursues the body beyond all possible pain' (Foucault 1977: 34).

'I'M SPARTACUS': THE TRAP OF MALE SUBJECTIVITY

Spectacular displays of criminals even after they become corpses represent the body's translation from the material realm to that of signification. *Spartacus* also attempts to write the body out of its discourse, setting up a contrast between materiality and signification that will transform the rotting corpses of its male heroes into an eternal principle of brotherhood and freedom. The Saul Bass titles design, in which the credits appear over fragmented body parts from Roman statuary and inscriptions from Latin tablets, foregrounds this binary at the outset. As I will subsequently argue, this strategy derails because of a number of internal contradictions, primarily generated by a mismatch between the more than usually detailed and complex psychologies of the principal male characters, in what screenwriter Dalton Trumbo called 'this remarkably unstable script' (Manfull 1970: 521), and the narrative, ideological, and star functions the film requires them to fulfill.

Before considering what ruptures it in the two hours that comprise the uprising and its consequences, let me detail the ideological framework *Spartacus* intends to construct. The film announces its terms, already implicit in what has gone before, when Spartacus discovers Crixus and the others forcing two Romans they have captured to fight to the death. First contemptuously addressing the captives, 'Noble Romans! fighting each other like animals,' Spartacus then turns on his comrades: 'What are we becoming – Romans?' This is the crux. How does one escape animality, the purely material form of existence imposed upon the gladiators that constructed their masculinity in terms of bodily force and aggressive penetration, without becoming Roman, transcending materiality only by entrance into a system of desire and signification propped up by the objectification and oppression of the Other?

Spartacus invokes Draba as the model upon which to build a masculinity that is neither animal or Roman: 'I swore that if I ever got out of this place, I'd die before I watched two men fight to the death again. Draba made that promise, too. He kept it. So will I.' Here Spartacus

Figure 21 Kirk Douglas and Woody Strode

echoes the film's preceding depiction of Romanness as participation in coercive spectatorship. However, in doing so, he mistakes the nature of Draba's revolt. Draba made no statement about watching men kill; he vowed not to kill on another's command. Yet he could not maintain his choice to renounce phallic aggression; he could only redirect that aggression toward his masters, a move that brought his death at Crassus's hands, precisely the trajectory that the gladiators' revolt itself traces. To be truly free the slaves must both liberate themselves from spectacularization and gain the option to forswear the sword. Neither Rome nor Hollywood is ready for that.

David Denby notes in his review of the restored *Spartacus* re-release that when Draba turns his trident on the Romans 'the weapon comes flying at the camera – a real shock' (Denby 1991: 96). The shock is one of recognition; for movie audiences go to spectaculars to see what the Romans at Capua have demanded: athletic men fighting and killing each other, taking brief respites for lovemaking. Masculine ego-ideal stars like Kirk Douglas devote their careers to making spectacles of themselves for the entertainment of suspiciously Roman-like moviegoers.[3] And what kind of ego-ideal would Spartacus be if audiences didn't finally get to enjoy his repeated phallic mastery?

Consequently the sequences that portray the liberated slave encampment reveal that the gladiators spend their time doing the same things they did while enslaved. They use the training methods they learned to put recruits for Spartacus's army through their paces. After the waves of Roman legions come forth to challenge them, they are locked in a recurrent cycle of combat, much as they were at Capua. To be sure, these sequences replace the claustrophobic, walled and barred *mise-en-scène* of the gladiator school with mountain exteriors, the fragmented, taut montage with more fluid camera movements at wider angles, to imply that the slaves' former lives were repressively dehumanized only because of Roman control and spectacularization. To be an animal running free in the hills is indeed preferable to being an animal pulling a plow or displayed in a circus; but it is not to cease being an animal. Spartacus rightly intuits that the slaves' material activities must become linked to signifying practices if they are to transcend animality (or human narcissism). He therefore has urged them to act not as a 'gang of drunken raiders' but as an 'army of gladiators,' harnessing phallic aggression to the ideas of freedom, brotherhood, and home.

The problematic for Spartacus and his soldiers is to enter into signification without partaking of the tyranny subjectivity often authorizes. The film disingenuously elides the process by which the slaves amass a looted fortune of 50 million sesterces in order to buy transportation out of the country, only to be foiled by the far more practiced capitalistic machinations of Crassus. Not elided, however, is the establishment of conventional patriarchal gender relations between Spartacus and Varinia once they are free to become lovers – or as Varinia insists to Crassus with bourgeois prudishness, husband and wife. The Varinia Spartacus first encountered did not follow the Hollywood norm. Director Stanley Kubrick told his old employers, *Look* magazine: 'The way the scene was originally written, she was the typical movie heroine. She fought for her virtue; she beat her little fists against his chest and behaved in a cliché movie fashion. But when I did the scene, I realized that obviously she wasn't inexperienced – even if she was the heroine of the movie. It would be false for her to act this way' ('Spartacus' *Look* 1960: 88).

Once freed, however, Varinia quickly becomes that typical movie heroine.[4] At the moment they are celebrating their mutual attainment of liberation from others' control of their lives ('No one can ever sell you, or give you away'), she makes Spartacus her new master: 'Forbid me ever to leave you.' She casts herself as his adoring helpmeet, serving dinner and wine to his rowdy lieutenants, assuring him his weaknesses are strengths, swimming nude while he admires her from concealment, bearing the son – Spartacus never entertains any other possibility than that their baby will be a boy – whom she dubs her only reason for living once Spartacus is captured and killed. Batiatus's description of her to Gracchus (Charles Laughton) sums up this inconsistency: 'Proud, yes. The more chains you put on her, the less like a slave she looks. You feel she would surrender to the right man, which is irritating.' Varinia, then, anchors the typical recuperation of patriarchy in films of this genre through the 'right men' who star in them.

Such operations are so familiar that they might pass unnoticed if not for several sites of rupture within the text. First, characters from time to time admonish Spartacus for becoming too enamored of masculine subjectivity and phallic aggression. When he complains that a group of new converts to the rebellion contains 'too many women,' a feisty grandmother asks him where he would be if 'some woman hadn't fought all the pains of hell' to bring him into the world. His attempt to imprison the bird Antoninus's magic trick would release leaves him literally with egg all over his face.

Secondly, although typecast by both Rome and Hollywood in the role of narcissistic, phallic aggressor,[5] Spartacus from the beginning – if not consistently – distrusts such masculine power and gropes for a means to transcend it. Having slaved in the brutal, all-male world of the Libyan mines since before his thirteenth birthday has led him to conclude that the exercise of male sexuality may hurt women. (Unspeakable in a Hollywood film of this era, but hardly unimaginable, a violation of the young Spartacus by Roman guards or older slaves in the mines might explain this conclusion. Varinia was also first enslaved at thirteen, and the parallel may be drawn to suggest that on this cusp of puberty both became available to Roman rape.) Taunted with the knowledge that Varinia has been given to 'the Spaniard,' he whispers to her the next morning, 'Did he hurt you?' Subsequently he repeats that question when she announces her pregnancy in the midst of their love-play and when their son kicks in the womb. His sexist tone aside, Denby quite rightly points out that Spartacus 'treats his woman, Varinia . . . with so much respect that she urges him to get a little rougher' (Denby 1991: 95).

Spartacus eventually recognizes that although gaining the ability to employ phallic power for his own ends rather than a Roman's may grant him male subjectivity, this subjectivity is still an animal's. His awareness crystallizes when Antoninus (Tony Curtis) joins the rebels. Antoninus's 'work' as singer of songs and performer of magic tricks at first draws Spartacus's mockery, but soon he is urging the poet to abandon his desire to be trained as a soldier ('He wants to fight. An animal can learn to fight'); instead 'You won't learn to kill; you'll teach us songs.' The shift of Spartacus's primary male bond from the aggressive Crixus (who, unlike Draba, killed his opponent in the Capuan arena and 'always wanted to march on Rome') to the intellectual/poet Antoninus signals his dissatisfaction with a masculinity predicated on brute mastery alone.

Spartacus, then, yearns for a subjectivity beyond narcissism. He confesses his discomfort at his imperfect access to language – 'I can't even read' – and lack of abstract knowledge about the natural world. Even sleeping beside the woman he loves 'more than my life,' Spartacus feels so alone that he must 'imagine a god for slaves.' Resisting the oppressive patriarchy of the Roman symbolic order, hoping one day to abjure phallic aggression, he still desires entry into some symbolic system. Can such a system exist without deriving from difference and thereby producing subjection? (Is there a non-phallic human subjectivity?) Can it avoid the total effacement of the material body, the production of subjects who function in a realm of sterile contempt for physical life, who accept too readily the suffering and death of real bodies in pursuit of a transcendental signifier? Can Spartacus vie with the Romans on the level of signification without becoming a Spartacan?

Here *Spartacus* encounters its most stubborn internal contradictions. As its generic conventions dictate, it parallels Spartacus's 'healthy' exercise of male subjectivity with the perverse tryanny of the Romans. He, like Crassus and Marcellus, tends to ask a person's name at once. For him it is a 'friendly question,' a granting of reciprocal signifying power, while for the Romans, demanding a slave's name is a demand that he surrender that power. The cross-cutting between Spartacus addressing his followers and Crassus addressing the citizens of Rome is meant to illustrate the same contrast. Yet parallels tend to conflate as well as contrast, planting a seed of doubt that a Spartacus who mastered the symbolic order might evolve into no more than another Crassus. That history allows Spartacus to triumph only in the arena of signification further muddies the waters.

Films with a rebel/outlaw hero confronting a tyrannous political regime frequently utilize the split Neale notes in the contradiction, for cinematic constructions of masculinity, 'between narcissism and the Law, between an image of *narcissistic* authority on the one hand and an image of *social* authority on the other' (Neale 1983: 9). The narcissistic ego-ideal, given more to action than words, undermines the tyrant's hold on political power through physical rebellion until a proper enunciator of the law of the father can replace him. Thus King Richard's return 'relieves' Robin Hood; the Glorious Revolution deposes King James and allows Captain

Blood to serve England lawfully under King William. In the religious epic, while the male protagonist defies the tyrant, God or Christ redeems his struggle by supplanting the tyrant's pagan deities. Spartacus, however, must pull double duty, play Christ as well as Ben-Hur. The private, inarticulate Spartacus of the Capua scenes is joined by a public Spartacus who initiates the discourse of home, freedom, and brotherhood meant to define a symbolic that will supplant Rome's.[6] These two roles don't easily co-exist. Hollis Alpert observes that, since Kirk Douglas's scenes contain 'remarkably little talking,'

> It comes as something of a shock, then, when Spartacus finally speaks out for freedom and makes the point that it was worth fighting for. This doctrine was undoubtedly subversive at the time, even if it does seem like a truism now. But that is the message of the picture, and Spartacus is stuck with it.
>
> (Alpert 1960: 32)

Not only does it strain the film to reconcile these two roles for Spartacus, but neither is unproblematic in isolation. As we have seen, narcissistic power does not suffice the private Spartacus; it pulls him back into the animal. Furthermore the disavowal of the phallus as signifier of masculinity threatens to collapse gender difference and inflect slave brotherhood with the homoeroticism, implicit in the genre, that suffuses the film and is its primary site of textual anxiety. Spartacus may find in Antoninus a paradigm for an alternative masculinity, but Antoninus, well aware that his work as performer-on-view rather than soldier, coupled with his pretty-boy looks, codes him as feminine, a stimulus to Crassus's appetite for 'snails,' insists on his access to just the kind of phallic mastery Spartacus wishes to abandon.[7]

The realm of signification into which the public Spartacus inscribes his followers is caught in the paradox Alpert notes. A banal 'truism' for the 1960 American audience the film text addresses, it is an anachronism for Spartacus, who lived a century before Christ and two thousand years before American democracy.[8] Eventually he did himself become the signifier that authorizes his discourse, a signifier of the revolutionary Other whose vitality the very existence of *Spartacus* itself confirms. Unlike the successful slave liberator, DeMille's Moses, who receives God's Law from burning bushes and mountaintops, who can keep his hands free of blood while Yahweh takes care of the smiting, Spartacus must improvise a god for slaves who offers no divine intervention that would allow him to abandon phallic aggression while retaining his freedom.

In contrast to Spartacus, who masters neither materiality nor signification without misgivings, stands Crassus, the central figure of the last two-thirds of the film, in which the slave revolt becomes just one element of the struggle between patrician dictatorship and plebeian republicanism to define the signified of 'Rome.'[9] Untroubled by his rival's humanistic doubts, he commands both realms at the film's end, erasing Spartacus's material presence and serving as a warning of the darker implications of a Spartacan symbolic victory. Crassus identifies completely with the male position articulated by patriarchal capitalism. A patrician who constantly invokes his 'fathers,' he commands the 'money and words' (Mulvey 1975: 208) that mark the dominant patriarch. He repeatedly involves himself in the triangular transactions that derive from the practice of exogamy as discussed by Lévi-Strauss, where women serve as objects of exchange to enable the various relations between men that power patriarchal economy.[10] Luce Irigaray's detailed discussion of 'Women on the Market' in *This Sex Which Is Not One* postulates that women are mere commodities, 'the material alibi for the desire for relations among men . . . In order for a product – a woman? to have value, two men, at least, have to invest (in) her' (Irigaray 1985: 180; 181).

But as was the case with the spectacularized body in *Spartacus*'s scopic economy, so the mediating body in the film's economy of exchange does not have to belong to a female. Not only does Crassus enter into power relations with other men through the exchange of or rivalry for woman, in this case Varinia, who mediates his dealings with Spartacus, Batiatus, and Gracchus, but also through enslaved men (Antoninus) and even free Romans (Glabrus (John Dall), Caesar (John Gavin)). To underscore his extraordinary ability to commodify in the absence of sexual difference or disparities in class/economic status, the film draws parallels between Crassus's initial encounters with Varinia and with Antoninus – Crassus eyes each approvingly, asks their country of origin and 'employment history' while enslaved, and decides to take each home with him – and between the attempted sexual seduction of Antoninus and political seduction of Caesar, which both take place in bath houses.

Whatever his dealings with human beings, however, Crassus's desire is activated solely in contemplation of the phallus as signifier he calls Rome. Theirs is an intensely erotic relationship, whose eroticism he can maintain only by disassociating Rome from any traces of materiality. When Caesar agrees with Gracchus that 'Rome *is* the mob,' Crassus snaps back, 'No, Rome is an eternal thought in the mind of God.' It's no accident that the two Romans who hold out against Crassus's blandishments are the pragmatic sensualists Gracchus and Batiatus.

Yet, for someone so invested in the symbolic order and given to asserting the name of the father ('Gladiator, I am Marcus Licinius Crassus; you must answer when I speak to you'), Crassus is manifestly mired in the mirror stage of narcissism. Upon hearing rumors that Varinia has caused his opponent to fall 'in love for the first time,' Gracchus muses, 'It would take a great woman to make Crassus fall out of love with himself.' If we look at all those to whom Crassus is attracted sexually or politically – the two attractions are essentially the same for him – we notice that the actors (Simmons, Curtis, Dall, Gavin) share Olivier's classical features, dark hair, attractive physique. The two slaves have been to a certain extent Romanized, educated as companions for Roman children; Antoninus has in fact taught these children 'the classics,' has been a conduit for the replication of his masters' ideology. Glabrus, and especially Caesar, share Crassus's extended patrician pedigree: 'For 200 years your family and mine have been members of the equestrian order and the patrician party, servants and rulers of Rome.'

Crassus has fashioned an inventive structure of desire through which to achieve both narcissistic and social power. To maintain his narcissistic phantasy of omnipotence, he must efface sexual difference and the castration anxiety that accompanies it. He accordingly makes bisexual object choices which reduce gender difference to the distinction between 'oysters and snails.' He splits off the physical enjoyment of sex, now just a matter of taste, from the ecstasies of desire, which can only arise for him in relation to the signifier Rome. Thus Crassus's bantering tone in the first half of the seduction scene with Antoninus shifts to sado-masochistic fervor when he characterizes himself as avatar of Rome:

> There, boy, is Rome, the might, the majesty, the terror of Rome. There is the power that bestrides the known world like a colossus. No man can withstand Rome, no nation can withstand Rome – how much less a boy. There's only one way to deal with Rome, Antoninus. You must serve her, you must abase yourself before her, you must grovel at her feet, you must love her.

(Ironically, a nervous studio cut the oysters-and-snails bath scene from the original release print, but left in the more perverse passage I have just quoted.)

Crassus, then, takes no erotic pleasure in others' bodies *per se* but can use them to establish a desiring relation to Rome. The bodies themselves are, however, interchangeable. When Spartacus defeats and symbolically castrates Glabrus ('You and that broken stick are all that's left of the garrison of Rome'), Crassus coolly casts off his former protégé in favor of Caesar as his tool for securing military control of the city. When both Varinia and Antoninus run away rather than submit to his sexual domination, he does not obsessively pursue either.

Speaking to Antoninus, Crassus describes Rome as potently masculine, yet always female – the pronoun is 'her.' By contrast, when he had told Glabrus of his own plan for gaining political control of the Senate, in essence for making Crassus another signifier for Rome, his metaphor maintained heterosexual gender distinctions: 'I shall not violate Rome at the moment of possessing her.' On the one hand Crassus, whatever his bisexual appetites, defines himself as a dominating masculine subject with Rome as the object of his desire; on the other, the female Rome represents the phallus he must never use to conquer her. By analogy Crassus-as-Rome is always a seducer, never a rapist, more concerned with gaining his beloved's surrender than in physically consummating their union.[11] As he wishes Rome to receive him, so he writes himself for those whose submission he invites. He will stand phallic and erect but femininely passive rather than masculinely aggressive. They must, so to speak, rush forward to impale themselves upon him. This psychology underlies Crassus's response to the puzzled Varinia who, bedecked in jewels like one of the patrician nymphs he brought to Capua and courted via a nervous ritual that is half villainous sexual extortion and half the stumbling of an adolescent on a first date, reminds her owner, 'I belong to you; you can take me any time you wish': 'I don't want to take you. I want you to give. I want your love Varinia.'

The need for Varinia, fetishized as Rome, to submit to Crassus as eagerly as Rome has done, results from her union with Spartacus in the months that separated her initial defection from Crassus's final assumption of ownership. Realizing that she will not willingly surrender her love, Crassus is content to have her surrender instead her memories of Spartacus. At this point, she accurately diagnoses his obsession: 'You're afraid of him. That's why you want his wife. To soothe your fear by having something he had.'

Crassus's fear of Spartacus stems from the gladiator's having achieved signifying power. When Crassus had offered to spare the lives of the surviving rebels if they identified Spartacus to him, first Antoninus and then all the men rose to proclaim 'I'm Spartacus' to prevent their leader from sacrificing himself for them. Crassus recognizes the signifier 'Spartacus' rivalling the signifier 'Rome' for the power of making men surrender their subjectivities to it. Until he can have material possession of the body of the gladiator, he cannot annihilate the signifying power of his name ('What was he, was he a god?'). Varinia intuits that the willing defection of a body that Spartacus possessed, her own, would in fact only partially fulfill Crassus's need, that 'nothing can help' him.

What does help Crassus is the private spectacle he compels Spartacus and Antoninus to enact before him. An initial rebuff, when Spartacus refuses to answer to his name – signifier resisting linkage to captive body – drives Crassus to rare hysteria and physical violence. But in the end Crassus gets what he wants. By rigging the conditions of the fight so that to win is to lose, he recuperates Draba's refusal to kill Spartacus by forcing Spartacus to kill Antoninus. Twice Spartacus has been part of a spectacle in which a slave resisted Rome's command to penetrate another slave against his or her will. Now he is trapped into following that script.[12] Furthermore, his reaction to Crassus's revelation that Varinia and the child are alive and slaves in his household leaves no doubt that this last surviving slave, and he alone, is Spartacus.

Having thus identified, spectacularized, and crucified Spartacus, Crassus can regain his imaginary plenitude. He no longer needs Varinia, which perhaps explains the puzzling omission from the film of any scene that shows his discovery of her abduction by Batiatus and manumission by Gracchus. His masculinity, while marked as perverse and monstrous, nevertheless survives intact within the diegesis.

'COULD WE HAVE WON, SPARTACUS?'

Since classic Hollywood narratives dislike leaving the perverse and monstrous in the ascendant, *Spartacus* relies on its 'future perfect' strategy to counter Crassus's present victory. Crassus acknowledges his fears that Spartacus's legend may still threaten Rome's hegemony, 'even more' than Caesar's ambitions threaten Crassus's monopoly on political power. 'Here's your victory,' Spartacus has told his captors over Antoninus's body. 'He'll come back. He'll come back, and he'll be millions.' As a more immediate reversal of its protagonist's defeat, the film concludes with the escape of Varinia and their child, a seeming answer to Spartacus's prayer for a son who would be born free. As filmed, however, the sequence undercuts itself:

> Varinia's cart moves away from the camera down a path lined on both sides with crucified slaves. In Trumbo's version, of course, the audience would assume that she and Spartacus' child travel into a democratic future which gives value to his sacrifice; in Kubrick's, one barely [?] visible to this film's audience, they move into an indeterminate world where there exists only the certainty of death.
>
> (Nelson 1982: 57)

When coupled with the fact that the only male left to occupy the driver's seat beside Varinia, usually reserved for the bearer of privileged masculinity who will complete the heterosexual couple of classical Hollywood narrative closure, is the obese, craven, avaricious slave-dealer Batiatus – *pace* Peter Ustinov's delightful, Oscar-winning performance – this bleak landscape can represent a happy ending only as parody.[13]

'Could we have won, Spartacus?' Antoninus asks his comrade as they await their deaths. 'Could we ever have won?' Spartacus responds with the discourse of symbolic victory, slaves daring to say 'no' to tryanny, standing tall in the mountains, singing in the plains. Antoninus, however, plays materiality's trump: 'And now they're dead.' When Spartacus, following this exchange, answers Antoninus's query as to whether he is afraid to die with the glib 'No more than I was to be born' – especially as contrasted to Antoninus's simple 'Yes' in response to the same question –

we sense the inadequacy of the film's resort to signification to efface its material tragedy.

The true victory about which Antoninus speculates could only occur with the eradication of the binaries of signification and materiality, subjectivity and subjection, Roman and animal. While *Spartacus* allows its protagonists to oscillate among all these positions, it cannot imagine a space in which such binarism collapses. The future perfect solution to masculine subjectivity, unattainable within the diegesis, is no more possible for 1960 Hollywood than for 73 BC Rome. What might this alternative masculine space look like? It would be a space where Antoninus could sing his songs without forfeiting his manhood and his life, where Spartacus could find a subjectivity not limited to Crixus's short-sighted animality nor doomed to replicate Crassus's Roman will to power. The freedom into which Spartacus's son would be born would create spectators who do not subjugate and spectacles that do not degrade. The millions in whom Antoninus's spirit would be reborn would possess a radical new human consciousness liberated from the always-already of culture and unthreatened by difference of any type.

And does any place exist where one might locate such a consciousness? Let's just say that when director Kubrick, freed from the ideological constraints he faced on *Spartacus*, attempted to represent this consciousness, he could do so only in the most embryonic form, the Starchild; and he still had to utilize the future perfect tense, assigning it an origin beyond Jupiter in the year 2001.

NOTES

I would like to thank Steven Cohan and John Ower for helping me clarify the arguments expressed in this essay.

1 See Robyn Wiegman's essay in this volume for a discussion of the similar combination of feminization and hypermasculinity in the cultural portrayals of African American men. The overlapping of slavery and African heritage in the American experience probably accounts for the similar representation of the gladiators in *Spartacus*.

2 Kappeler's clever rewriting of John Berger's essay 'Why look at Animals?' by substituting the term *woman* for the term *animal* shows that the two identities need not be mutually exclusive. *Spartacus* insists on comparing feminized males to animals rather than women because of its massive textual anxiety about the homosexuality its male bonding evokes and Crassus overtly articulates.

3 *Spartacus* stops just short of overtly comparing the gladiatorial school to a film studio and the spectacularized combatants to actors. Executive producer/star Douglas's autobiography contains an undercurrent of unease about the feminization inherent in the position of the male film actor, especially in beefcake genres. He notes that he had to do 'what the starlets do' to convince the film-makers that he was physically right to play the boxer in *Champion* (1949): 'I took off my jacket and shirt, bared my chest and flexed my muscles.

They nodded approvingly, satisfied that I could play a boxer. I was probably the only *man* in Hollywood who's had to strip to get a part' (Douglas 1988: 129). He also twice refers to studio contracts as 'slavery.' Kubrick, asked if it daunted him, as a relatively inexperienced director, to work with a cast of so many established stars, replied: 'All stars, no matter how stubborn or opinionated they may be . . . are extremely vulnerable in front of the camera . . . so it's not hard to get them to do a scene the way you want it.' ('Spartacus' *Look* 1960: 88).

4 In contrast to the Capua and Rome scenes, the scenes representing the liberated slaves are as a whole conventional in both style and content. The taut intensity of the first hour gives way to slack, perfunctory editing rhythms. In place of narrative structure, the action moves forward via clichéd montage sequences that rely on sentimental representations of cute children, sturdy oldsters, and plucky dwarfs. A number of commentators have speculated that Kubrick, who subsequently disowned *Spartacus* because his author-ity extended *only* to directing the actors, composing the shots, and editing the picture (Phillips 1975: 85; Nelson 1982: 55), used these means to sabotage those parts of the script that were uncongenial to him (see Denby 1991: 96; Combs 1984: 258).

5 In his review of *Spartacus*, Dwight MacDonald comments: 'As an actor, Mr. Douglas has only one asset: extreme aggressiveness' (MacDonald 1961: 24).

6 Keith Bradley notes that the historical rebellion of Spartacus lacked any such symbolic aspirations and thus could not threaten the institution of slavery: 'it becomes impossible to view the Spartacan movement as being in any way dominated by abstract or ideological imperatives: freedom from slavery was the intent of the fugitives; the slavery system itself remained unaffected' (Bradley 1989: 101).

7 Any chance for the film to establish Antoninus as exemplar of a privileged, non-phallic masculinity was cancelled out by the fatal miscasting of Tony Curtis in the role (puzzling since the character was created for the express purpose of finding Curtis a part in the film so that he could discharge a commitment to Universal Studios (Douglas 1988: 286)). At 34, he was too old to play a character whom Crassus calls 'a boy' and Spartacus a surrogate son. Moreover, he recites poetry so that it sounds like prose in 'an accent which suggests that the ancient Tiber was a tributary of the Bronx River' ('The New Pictures' *Time* 1960: 102); he speaks the American urban ethnic idiom of the rest of the gladiators apart from whom he is supposedly marked as Other.

8 If the crucified Spartacus is meant as a precursor of Christ, his ideology is also meant to suggest that of twentieth-century American democracy. Michael Wood speculates that this latter project characterizes epics of the 1950s and 1960s generally (Wood 1975: 184–8). This American ideology sits uneasily upon the film since the US itself had permitted Negro slavery for several centuries – having the African Draba strike the first blow for freedom is supposed to defuse that issue – and since Crassus's political maneuverings link Romans to the Washington and Hollywood establishments' behavior during the McCarthy era. Audiences were unlikely to ignore the latter parallel because of all the publicity concerning Dalton Trumbo's screenwriting credit for *Spartacus* 'breaking the blacklist.' See Smith (1989: 75–100) for an analysis of the film in this context.

9 Crassus was the central character in the first versions of the script because Douglas felt he needed to snare Olivier in order for his Howard Fast Spartacus

project to beat out a rival one, based on Arthur Koestler's *The Gladiators*, proposed by United Artists to star Yul Brynner (see Douglas 1988: 283–5).

10 See Eve Kosofsky Sedgwick's *Between Men*, especially chapter 3, 'Gender Asymmetry and Erotic Triangles,' for a survey of applications of the Lévi-Strauss exogamy theory to narratology (Sedgwick 1985: 21–7).

11 Crassus throughout the film prefers to dominate in a way that requires others to undertake physical contact. He commands his legion in terms of strategy but never raises a weapon or goes near the chaos of the fighting. His scrupulous avoidance of the mess of materiality doubtless explains the disgust on his face when he must cut Draba's neck, becoming marked by the slave's blood as he will later be by Spartacus's spit. This fastidiousness is, I would assert, more complex than Nelson's dismissive 'Hollywood liberals have the illusion that all fascists are impotent proto-McCarthys' (Nelson 1982: 56).

12 If Spartacus had really wanted to deny the Romans the pleasure of a contest, he would have advised Antoninus that they should both simultaneously impale themselves on their swords – the Roman way Gracchus chose rather than become Crassus's stooge. But the star images of Douglas and Curtis would not have accommodated such a logical solution. Once again the Romans' desires and the film audience's coincide. Douglas jokes that he had Spartacus kill Antoninus to compensate for Curtis's Eric killing his Einar in *The Vikings* (1958) (Douglas 1988: 286). By this reasoning, Varinia rejects Crassus's romantic overtures to pay back Olivier's Hamlet for repudiating Simmons's Ophelia in 1948.

13 Fast summarizes the life led by 'young Spartacus' as follows: 'With this kind of a life, the son of Spartacus lived and died – died in struggle and violence as his father had' (Fast 1951: 363).

BIBLIOGRAPHY

Alpert, H. (1960) 'The Day of the Gladiator,' *Saturday Review*, October 1: 32.

Bradley, K. (1989) *Slavery and Rebellion in the Roman World, 140 B.C.–70 B.C.*, Bloomington: Indiana University Press.

Combs, R. (1984) 'Spartacus,' *Monthly Film Bulletin* 51: 257–9.

Denby, D. (1991) 'A Funny Thing Happened on the Way to the Baths,' *New York*, May 13: 95–6.

Douglas, K. (1988) *The Ragman's Son*, New York: Simon and Schuster.

Fast, H. (1951) *Spartacus*, New York: Crown.

Foucault, M. (1977) *Discipline and Punish: the Birth of the Prison*, trans. A. Sheridan, New York: Pantheon.

Irigaray, L. (1985) *This Sex Which Is Not One*, trans. C. Porter and C. Burke, Ithaca, NY: Cornell University Press.

Kappeler, S. (1986) *The Pornography of Representation*, Minneapolis: University of Minnesota Press.

MacDonald, D. (1961) 'Films,' *Esquire* 55: 24, 32.

Manfull, H., ed. (1970) *Additional Dialogue: Letters of Dalton Trumbo 1942–1962*, New York: M. Evans.

Mulvey, L. (1975) 'Visual Pleasure and Narrative Cinema,' rpt in Philip Rosen (ed.) *Narrative, Apparatus, Ideology: a Film Theory Reader*, New York: Columbia University Press, 1986.

Neale, S. (1983) 'Masculinity as Spectacle: Reflections on Men and Mainstream Cinema,' *Screen* 24, 6: 2–16.

Nelson, T. (1982) *Kubrick: Inside a Film Artist's Maze*, Bloomington: Indiana University Press.

'The New Pictures' (1960) *Time*, October 24, 76: 102.

Phillips, G. (1975) *Stanley Kubrick: a Filmmaker's Odyssey*, New York: Popular Library.

Sedgwick, E. K. (1985) *Between Men: English Literature and Male Homosocial Desire*, New York: Columbia University Press.

'Spartacus' (1960) *Look*, November 20: 85, 88.

Smith, J. (1989) ' "A Good Business Proposition": Dalton Trumbo, *Spartacus* and the End of the Blacklist,' *Velvet Light Trap* 23: 75–100.

Wood, M. (1975; rpt 1989) *America in the Movies*, New York: Columbia University Press.

9

FEMINISM, 'THE BOYZ,' AND OTHER MATTERS REGARDING THE MALE

Robyn Wiegman

When *Newsweek* featured the street smart hero of blaxploitation films, John Shaft, on its cover in October, 1972, it was marking a new era for Hollywood cinema: 'All over the country', the cover story exclaimed, ' "bad-ass niggers" are collecting dues with a vengeance – and, if you don't believe it, just head downtown for a movie' (October 23, 1972: 74). By the end of the decade, however, African American male stars were increasingly finding themselves the twilight figures in interracial male bonding films, and the high hopes of black cinema in the 1970s seemed at an end.[1] But now, *Newsweek* is heralding another revolution. 'With 19 films this year', it asserts, 'Hollywood fades to black' (June 10, 1991: 50).[2] And as anyone knows who has gone screening, the primary images issuing from these new films concern the historical complexity and contemporary conditions affecting the African American male, whose high rates of poverty, incarceration, and early death have coalesced in the startling appellation: 'an endangered species' (Gibbs 1988). At risk for extinction are several generations, and although cinema can certainly not be collapsed into a naive 'real,' these new films take quite seriously and self-consciously their representational role as modeling a future for today's young black men.

How do we understand the historical emergence of this 'New Jack Cinema', as *Newsweek* (June 10, 1991: 51) calls it, and what kinds of critical discourse can negotiate the political demands implicit in their narrative production? I ask these questions from an avowedly feminist position, foregrounding my political interests not in order to supplant the radical racial content and context of this cinematic production, but to approach, once again, the compelling critical issue of representation and what has been called, reductively and problematically, multicultural difference. It is perhaps no accident that the critical language in cinema studies surrounding issues of gender, race, class, and/or sexuality so clearly and easily betrays the asymmetry of cultural relations – reiterating 'difference' without the positivity of a critical analysis into its logical underpinnings, most often white, heterosexual, bourgeois, and male. But already, right here, we confront the political and theoretical difficulty of the whole difference dilemma, where the paradigms available for our articulation of the multiplicity of social subjectivity and (dis)empowerment too often fail to comprehend their inherent complexity. Simply positing the primary terms of each binary configuration does not make possible the many instances in which social positioning straddles the strict duality of oppressor/oppressed, where rights and privileges may be accorded along one particular axis but are circumvented and violently denied along others. Most importantly, the binary description of social positioning betrays the compounded production of identity and difference, their mutual and contradictory inscription not only across the social body, but at the specific corporeal sites where the meanings of categories of identity are literally and metaphorically imposed.

It is this situation, in which social positioning is often at odds within itself, that attends the cultural location of and tensions surrounding the category of identity defined as the African American male. For in his relation of sameness to the masculine and in his threatening difference to the primacy of white racial supremacy, the African American male is stranded between the competing – and at times overdetermining – logics of race and gender. Denied full admittance to the patriarchal province of the masculine through the social scripting of blackness as innate depravity, and occupying a position of enhanced status through masculine privilege in relation to black women, the African American male challenges our understanding of cultural identity and (dis)empowerment based on singular notions of inclusion and exclusion. The simultaneity of his position – to be at once inside and outside the definitional domains of hierarchical empowerment – demonstrates the difficulty of maintaining unified and disengaged readings of the structure and function of race, class, sexuality, and/or gender. Instead, we are impelled toward thinking of new ways to approach not simply relations of identity and difference but, most crucially, their embodied asymmetries as well. In doing so, various complexities within the race/gender nexus, in particular, can be revealed.

My critique of binary understandings of power relations takes its lead from recent developments in contemporary feminist theory, where questions about differences of race, class, and sexuality among women have increasingly dismantled the historical status of the category of Woman as a unified, homogeneous, and internally consistent whole.[3] But while the question of differences among women initiates a crucial rethinking of feminism's own paradigmatic assumptions, it is significant that in its quest for an all-encompassing framework devoid of exclusions, feminist theory has also contributed to the diffusion of distinct categories of difference, producing its own, now clichéd, polysyllabic referent 'genderraceclass'. Such a referent offers the pretense toward grappling with the difficult issue of multiple differences without providing critical models for understanding their various and historically shifting deployments. In the process, the attention to multiplicity (differences among women) plays a secondary role to homogeneity (the difference of woman as compared to man), thereby establishing women's differences from one another as a sub-category within an expanded, but still overarching sign of gender: 'women.'[4] In this way, multiple differences continue to be understood not as the compounded identity formation of all social subjects, but as the discrete categorical markings for those positioned as eccentric to feminism's historical rendition of woman as white, middle-class, and heterosexual.

By exploring differences in this way, feminism can maintain its historical commitment to the primacy of sexual difference as the epistemological ground for understanding women's varied social positioning – even as such a theoretical formulation risks the specificity of cultural organization that the turn toward multiple differences was to have revealed. For in positing women as multiple and heterogeneous – while still framing their positioning, as my language here indicates, through the category of gender – feminist theory discounts the way in which specific cultural determinants (such as race) may at times not only outweigh the significance of gender, but thoroughly shift the very productive grounds on which gender constitutes itself. Gender, as Hortense Spillers and others demonstrate, is itself multiply formed.[5] And its multiplicity does not reside, as feminism too often seems to assume, within the binarized realm of the feminine, but attends to those figurations of bodies that comprise the masculine as well.[6]

Because of this problem of paradigms in feminist thought, I want to approach in this paper the possibility of an antiracist feminist cinematic reading by shifting our frame of reference away from the scene of woman/women and towards the issue of racial differences among men, articulating such a reading within the historical nexus of race and gender through which black masculinity has been given meaning. Most importantly, I am interested in how the discourse of sexual difference has served to delineate the contours of African American male representation in the United States, providing the primary terms through which the contradictions inherent in a masculine 'raced' position have been – and continue to be – culturally mediated. A cursory glance at this historical terrain, even for the uninitiated, reveals a discursive production reliant on sexual difference: from nineteenth-century images of the bumbling, ineffectual minstrel 'coon' (and their twentieth-century servile and metaphorically castrated heirs) to the mythologized black male rapist of both centuries, whose hypermasculinization begets and nourishes the many cinematic trajectories of 'Shaft' and 'Superspade'.[7] But before turning to the historical fashioning of black male representation, it is necessary to begin with a more systematic exploration of feminist film theory, where the homogenizing tendencies of patriarchal discourses have been strangely reinscribed by feminist theory's own attraction to the monolithic logic provided by sexual difference. This logic renders secondary various hierarchical differences among men, reproducing within feminism's own political agenda the ahistorical account of cultural production that patriarchal discourses are themselves at pains to preserve.

PARADIGMATIC MATTERS

Because the question of cultural difference in feminist film theory has routinely emerged as a question of gender, the paradigmatic reading of the cinematic regime posits it as a visual territory in which the masculine affirms its dominance through the specular colonization of its opposition, the feminine. In her ground-breaking article, 'Visual Pleasure and Narrative Cinema,' Laura Mulvey explains, '[t]he paradox of phallocentrism in all its manifestations is that it depends on the image of the castrated woman to give order and meaning to its world . . . it is her lack that produces the phallus as symbolic presence, it is her desire to make good the lack that the phallus signifies' (1975: 57). In granting subjectivity through the power of the 'look,' the politics of visibility reiterate patriarchal organization, equating the male's position as activator of the gaze with the transcendent subjectivity of universalized meaning. In the process, as most readers of this volume well know, the female body is cast as spectacle, reaffirming the primacy of the visible by emphasizing the *sighting* of difference while producing her as signifier of the masculine. For Luce Irigaray, whose re-readings of Lacan have been influential to feminist film theory, the spectacle of woman, the scene of her body as the site of castration, acts to wed the masculine subject with himself. Captured in this closed circuit of masculine relations, woman is condemned to theoretical absence, reduced, as Irigaray says, '*to the economy of the Same*' (Irigaray 1977: 74).

Through this articulation of the feminine within the logic of the Same, patriarchal discourses – dominant cinema among them – render women indecipherable by denying them access to female subjectivity. Early feminist film theorists such as Pam Cook and Claire Johnston (1974) sought a way out of this dilemma, arguing that it is precisely through this incoherence that the female can subvert (albeit incompletely) the patriarchal logos of film. But such a prescription for a feminist counter-cinema, as Constance Penley has pointed out, encodes its own problematical assumption of the feminine not only as naturally disruptive but as natural in itself. 'There is no feminist advantage', she writes, 'in positing either a historically unchanging feminine essence or a monolithic patriarchal

176

repression of that essence. The very idea of an essence is ahistorical and asocial . . .' (Penley 1988: 5). In her work in the 1980s, Teresa de Lauretis would refashion these issues into the question, '[h]ow do we envision women as subjects in a culture that objectifies, imprisons and excludes, woman?' (de Lauretis 1984: 10), finding that the theoretical traditions of semiology and psychoanalysis from which feminist film theory had emerged seemed to negate the very possibility of female subjectivity. 'Like cinema', she writes, 'they posit woman as at once the object and the foundation of representation, at once telos and origin of man's desire and of his drive to represent it, at once object and sign of (his) culture and creativity' (de Lauretis 1984: 8). Through its claim that processes of cinematic representation depend on the mappings of sexual difference, early feminist work in film would offer a critical paradigm that seemed to exclude women from the very subjectivity that feminist theorists sought to claim.

Quite ironically, then, the models developed in early feminist film theory carry with them a burdensome potential to recontain women in the patriarchal logic of binary exclusions. Whether demonstrating the denial of female subjectivity in cinema's specular relations or insisting on resistance by asserting her potential for disruption from the space of the margin, feminist theory found itself torn between strategies of interpretation bounded by an ahistorical repression of woman on one hand and the naturalization of a feminine specificity on the other.[8] Either way, as de Lauretis would later describe in *Technologies of Gender*, feminist thought was constrained 'within the conceptual frame of a universal sex opposition . . . mak[ing] it very difficult, if not impossible, to articulate . . . differences among women' (de Lauretis 1987: 2). This movement from a theoretical paradigm that unwittingly reinscribed patriarchal logic to an increasing concern with differences among women enabled feminist theory not only to begin to question its own complicity with cultural hierarchies but to make possible a subjectivity no longer reduced to the monolithic dimensions of negativity. For many, this has meant a shift away from or problematizing of the psychoanalytic paradigm because of its often-cited conflation of material social relations with abstracted and universalized discursive constructions.[9]

For Jane Gaines, the emphasis on psychoanalysis in feminist film theory becomes especially inadequate for analyses that turn to the figuration of the African American subject. In 'White Privilege and Looking Relations: Race and Gender in Feminist Film Theory,' she criticizes the way in which the psychoanalytic paradigm, 'based on the male/female distinction . . . works to keep women from seeing other structures of oppression . . . lock[ing] us into modes of analysis which will continually misunderstand the position of many women' (Gaines 1986: 61, 65). Gaines bases this assessment on the apparent incongruity between feminist–psychoanalytic readings of looking relations and the US cultural context in which 'some groups have historically had the license to "look" openly while other groups have "looked" illicitly' (1986: 76). Because the binary opposition between masculine and feminine cannot account for ways in which racial difference constructs a 'hierarchy of access to the female image' (1986: 75) – both in terms of who looks and whose image is circulated as the object of that look – Gaines suggests that feminist film theory reframe 'the question of male privilege and viewing pleasure as the "right to look" ' (1986: 76). Such a reframing would make it possible to differentiate relations within the masculine, delineating the materiality of castration as not simply a metaphorical inscription but as a literal practice that has accompanied the historical deployment of the black male gaze.[10]

Placing the question of the male gaze within a historical context and subsequently differentiating the possibilities of spectatorship along lines other than gender begins to suggest a necessary paradigm shift for feminist film theory. But while Gaines's discussion locates a particularly powerful tension within the production of a masculine cinematic and cultural gaze, she tends to reduce the complexity of the cinematic apparatus by eliding it too quickly and thoroughly with the cultural gaze. In the process, materiality takes on the historicity of the literal, and the voyeuristic pleasures of cinema, however wrought through a system of identification based on white modes of masculinity, are seemingly denied almost wholly to African American men. But rather than a simple reimposition of the racially-coded caveat against looking, cinema actually may offer in however limited, distanced, and disembodied ways, black male access to the white female image denied elsewhere.[11] In this regard, cinematic narrative and the apparatus of spectatorial looking are not the same, and while the white female remains taboo to a sexualized black male gaze in most film narratives, this denial is not coterminous with the spectatorial apparatus.[12] Gaines's notion of the right-to-look that frames the historical relation governing the sexualized nexus of black men and white women needs to be explored further, so that the implications of masculine differences can be understood both in terms of filmic narrative and the cinematic apparatus of spectatorial looking.

This entails, as the essays in this volume indicate, an increasing concern for the articulation of the masculine that approaches it in less monolithic and historically homogeneous ways. Most importantly, the often exclusive attention in feminist film theory to the figure of woman as the grounds for instantiating and articulating the production and effect of the discourse of sexual difference must continue to give way. As we see in Gaines's analysis, the ultimate reliance on the spectacle of woman as the significatory precondition for the construction of masculine hierarchies means that the scene of gender continues to be inscribed on the female body.

Gender, in other words, circulates as the figure of woman, and while that figure may be read in terms of her racial positioning – and while we can subsequently articulate the racial binarity that underscores the trajectory of masculine looking – this is a formulation inattentive to the significance of sexual difference at work in representational contexts largely devoid of women. Because feminist theory's frequent return to the figure of woman and/or women has only recently yielded to interrogations aimed at revealing the deployment of the discourse of sexual difference in multifarious cultural configurations, the scene of differences among men has remained a rather static and unexplored location. What this means for feminist political theory has yet to be adequately charted, but one thing seems quite certain: as we continue to pressure the limits of feminism's own theoretical gaze, sexual difference will increasingly be unhinged from its purported grounding in the female body and traced instead in its many layered production.

In the process, the scene of differences among men may prove a particularly compelling location for an analysis of the cinematic production of sexual difference, especially as gender has proven to be a powerful means through which racial difference has historically been defined and coded. Perhaps the most crucial issue that will emerge here is precisely how feminist theory can negotiate the imbrication of race and gender without reducing or exchanging one for the other. This negotiation is particularly tricky because of feminist theory's investment in the binarity of sexual difference, an investment that may enable an articulation of both the representational and political affinities that tie African American men to both black and white women by reiterating the contours of the very production we seek to critique.[13] In this sense, it becomes immensely important that feminist theory not reinscribe the feminization of Uncle Tom that characterizes early feminist–abolitionist work as the means for approaching the problems of white supremacy.[14] For the African American male is not a symbolic woman, no matter how intense the process through which a chain of social and specular being is inscribed along the lines provided by sexual difference. If lack must be consigned, if the black male must be physically, psychologically, and/ or symbolically castrated, then his construction in the guise of the feminine evinces not simply an aversion to racial difference but a profound attempt to negate *masculine sameness*, a sameness so terrifying to the cultural position of the white masculine that only castration can provide the necessary disavowal.[15]

To understand the terrain of masculine differences in the context of masculine sameness necessitates a rethinking of feminism's commitment to patriarchal organization as, in Irigaray's words, an economy of the same. For such sameness does not necessarily produce a homogeneous cultural order, regardless of the extent to which certain social arrangements (such as the military) operate by and through the mythos of an undifferentiated masculine structure. Instead, we need to explore the processes and practices through which masculine sameness provides the very terms that construct and defend hierarchies of oppression and exploitation among men, serving as a historically shifting discursive apparatus for the negotiation of multiple social relations. In this sense, the discourse of sexual difference has a significance that exceeds the boundaries of gender's binary oppositions, even as it deploys those oppositions as the means for confirming and perpetuating the cultural dimensions of white racial supremacy. Most importantly perhaps, the logic of the gaze as the primary articulatory mechanism around which sexual difference is understood as encoded in filmic production needs to be suspended, so that other formations of gender (and other deployments of the discourse of sexual difference) can be more fully explored. It is only in this way, by refusing to reduce gender to the specular embodiment of woman, that we can begin not only to chart the multiplicity of gender's production, but its imbrication and shifting relation to race as well.

READING THE MALE

It is within this context that I want to read the emergence of the new black cinema of the 1990s, where we can approach some of the complexities of the race/gender nexus by understanding how the deployment of the discourse of sexual difference has functioned historically as the governing framework for representational productions of the African American male. For it is in the oscillation between feminization (buffoonish Uncle Tom) and hypermasculinization (well-endowed rapist) that the contradictory social positioning of the black male has been negotiated, providing the means for disavowing his sameness to the masculine on one hand, while marking his masculinity as racially produced excess on the other. Importantly, where the logic of white supremacy and the white masculine's pre-eminent cultural positionality are overtly secured in each of these scenarios, the relationship between the feminine and the black masculine is just as thoroughly opposed. In casting the feminine as either an internalized, effete consciousness or the externalized emblem of the black male's sexual threat, the discourse of sexual difference inscribes the relationship between the black masculine and the feminine (of any racial designation) as coterminous, in metaphor or material practice, with psychic dissolution and death. Not surprisingly, such an inscription engenders a political context of distrust, alienation, and paralysis, making affiliations across categories of identity and difference difficult to envision, let alone to articulate and sustain.

While the oscillation between feminization and hypermasculinization varies according to the specific economic, social, and political contexts defining the cultural terrain, it is possible nonetheless to mark the historical arrival of the mythology of the phallicized black rapist as engendered by African American emancipation in the late nineteenth century. Here, the minstrel figuration of the African American male as Sambo, Tambo, Bones, Uncle Remus, and Jim Crow is joined by a new, highly stylized disciplinary representation: the myth of the black male rapist, defiler of white womanhood. Through the guise of an aggressive, hyper-phallic masculinity, the symbolic feminization of the black male that characterizes the popular consumptive sphere is exchanged for a discursive scenario that begets literal castration. As Trudier Harris discusses, reconstruction signals a transition in the cultural meaning of lynch law, marking not only its articulation as a racially coded formulation, but defining that formulation as the symbolic linkage between lynching, castration, and an assumed black male sexual predilection for white women.[16] In casting the white male as defender of white female sexuality, the economic crisis wrought by the transformation from slavery to freedom is translated into gendered terms, offering the dominant culture a powerful means through which not only black men but the entire black population could be recontained as innately, if no longer legally, inferior. As Richard Wright would later depict in *Native Son*, even the acusation of rape serves as 'that death before death came' (1966: 214), a death whose frequent culmination in lynchings and castrations literalized the equation between the black male and the feminine.

Given this relationship between the male body and cultural power, and the historical features of black male representation as sexual and gendered, it is no coincidence that Black Power discourses would turn to the figuration of sexual difference as the means for making claims to black male empowerment in the 1960s. In 'Initial Reactions on the Assassination of Malcolm X', Eldridge Cleaver epitomizes the rhetorical method of depicting the struggle for Black Power: 'We shall have our manhood. We shall have it or the earth will be leveled by our attempts to gain it' (Cleaver 1968: 66). Such attempts to 'heal the wound of my Castration', as Cleaver writes, are necessary to right the deep wrong inflicted on black men through slavery and cultural dispossession, where '[a]cross the naked abyss of negated masculinity . . . I feel a deep, terrifying hurt, the pain of humiliation . . . and a compelling challenge to redeem my conquered manhood' (Cleaver 1968: 188–9). By defining the politics of race within a metaphorics of phallic power as a counter to cultural articulations of black male inferiority, Black Power rhetoric reiterates the parameters of black male representation provided by the discourse of sexual difference, simultaneously marking the political and economic as part of a naturalized realm of gender. Such a formulation significantly participates in the broader cultural articulation of racial exploitation and oppression as a problem within the structure of masculine relations themselves.

It is perhaps obvious that such images of an aggressively violent black male who poses a physical threat to 'white civilization' nourishes the cultural fascination with and fantasy of black male castration in the nineteenth century and our own. But while the scenario of seemingly unprovoked black violence is certainly not new, its proliferation since the dawning of Civil Rights and Black Power provides a context in which African American political activity can be defined and contained within the parameters of a socially delinquent, if not pre-eminently dangerous, masculinity. That African American writers and political theorists in the 1960s and 1970s – not only Cleaver, but Amiri Baraka, Ishmael Reed, and Malcolm X – each reiterated at one time the metaphorics of a threatening phallic power attests to the powerful deployment of sexual difference in US culture more generally, and provides the framework for understanding the emergence of Shaft, Superfly, Hammer, Willie Dynamite, Black Belt Jones, and other exceedingly masculine figures in the cinema of the 1970s.[17] The oscillation between feminization and masculinization described here not only marks the oppositional logic of sexual difference that underlies African American male representation for the past two centuries, but specifies the discursive context in which any discussion of contemporary black male cinema must be made.

It is my contention, in fact, that many of the recent films by black male directors seek to subvert and deny in various ways the paradigmatic exchange of activity for objectification, on the one hand, while struggling for a more culturally productive black masculinity on the other. John Singleton's *Boyz N the Hood* (1991) is a case in point, not only because of the narrative's concern for the life-threatening contours of black masculinity, but also because of the attention it has received for purportedly instigating audience violence (see *Newsweek*, July 29, 1991: 48). By displacing the socio-political issues surrounding black masculinity – issues that *Boyz N the Hood*, for one, is at pains to reveal – on to the panic-image of irrational black violence, the logic of white supremacy exchanges the complexities of contemporary US culture for the alternatively terrorizing and appealing phantasm of massive violence and death. But in wrenching the scenario of black masculinity from the more easily consumable images of incipient feminization and one-dimensional criminality, *Boyz N the Hood* grapples quite seriously – if not always satisfactorily – with the contradictions embedded in the black male's social positioning, offering an interesting negotiation of the historical (con)text of black male representation in US cinema and culture.

For feminists schooled in conventional film theory, the kinds of issues I will be highlighting in *Boyz N the Hood*, particularly its political agenda toward a mediated masculinity, might seem to displace the film's overt signs of sexism: its reliance on objectifying language, as well as cinematography, for defining and characterizing women; its binary inscription of masculine and feminine as oppositional personal and cultural encodements; and its figuration of male separatism as part of, and at times precondition to, a black nationalist aesthetic. Clearly, the failure of motherhood and the championing of the black father characterize the oppositional and hierarchical logic of sexual difference that governs the film, providing the terms through which the contemporary crisis of black masculinity is being both challenged and defined. But to point to these representational effects without the historicizing gesture that seeks to place them in the broader context of US cultural production not only reifies their political deployment, but risks the inscription of a feminist analysis inattentive to the multiplicity and overdetermining construction of race and gender. For this reason, while I do not want to dismiss the film's use of certain conventional means for affirming the primacy of the masculine, I also do not want to understand that masculine as simply coterminous with patriarchy itself. For it is patriarchy as well as white supremacy that must be held accountable for the prevailing conditions of destruction and disenfranchisement attending African American men.

Boyz N the Hood specifically highlights this destruction in its opening sequence with two full screen statements: first, 'One out of every 21 Black American males will be murdered . . . [and then] Most will die at the hands of another Black male,' followed by the camera's rapid focus on a Stop sign. In this half minute, the film delivers its most immediate context and its most overt message, and in doing so establishes a significatory framework through which those who contribute to this cultural undoing are targeted as the primary audience. For a black male to kill another black male, the film posits, is tantamount to killing oneself. But more importantly, it is to act out, to its logical extreme, the desire of white supremacy. Where Spike Lee's *Do the Right Thing* (1989) made cross-racial violence its primary concern, *Boyz* draws its most daring critique of power and the internalized processes of annihilation by foregrounding the trajectories of racism within members of the black community itself. An especially powerful example of this is the presentation of a black male Los Angeles police officer, whose desire to rid the streets of 'niggers' reveals his own sadistic pleasure in the harassment, torture, and destruction of other black men. To counter this kind of black male abandonment of one another, the film offers the primary characters, Furious Styles (Larry Fishburne) and his son, Tre (Cuba Gooding Jr.), whose relationship forges a paradigm of inter-generational bonding that functions in the film's narrative as the means for translating the past and present into a different future for young black men. Locating the significance and impact of white supremacy in broad strokes, the film's primary focus is thus on the structures of discipline turned inward by the African

Figure 22 Cuba Gooding, Jr. and Larry Fishburne

American subject, whose defense against racism is often, paradoxically, a reiterative devaluation of black life.

Defined as a classic coming of age story, *Boyz* moves between the philosophical underpinnings of Furious's approach to teaching his son 'how to be a man' and the codes of masculinity ushered in on the streets. With a mix of neo-nationalist and safe sex rhetoric, Furious wants his son to know 'any fool with a dick can make a baby but only a real man can raise his kids.' His nationalism is highlighted at various, often didactic moments in the film where the link between responsibility and reproduction is set within the overarching context of violence, drugs, and alcohol abuse. In pointing out the significance of gun shops and liquor

184

stores 'on ever corner' in African American neighborhoods, Furious explains to a group of onlookers (in a speech with scenic overtones of a sermon-on-the-mount): 'They want us to kill ourselves . . . The best way to kill a people is to destroy their ability to reproduce themselves.' The focus on the question of sex and reproduction throughout the film – and its relation to economic and cultural survival – provides an important rearticulation of what the narrative posits as the prevailing mythos of masculinity, where guns, women, and offspring circulate in a psychological and social nexus of increasingly ineffectual, indeed murderous, machismo. Here, the distance from the black cinema of the 1970s is at its most forceful, as the terrain of sexuality takes on a seriousness that implicitly critiques the iconography of masculine prowess epitomized by Shaft and his various characterological reincarnations. In Singleton's cinematic world, the super phallic imago of black masculinity is too often a self-fulfilling fantasy of a genocidal white supremacy.

The tension between phallicism and a mediated black masculinity is played out in the competing characterizations of young black men in the Styles's neighbourhood, from the troubled Doughboy (Ice Cube) who spends his youth in and out of reform school, to his brother Ricky (Morris Chestnut), a teenage father who is on course for a football scholarship to the University of Southern California, to the more peripheral figures, Monster, Dooky, and the wheel-chair-bound Chris, all participants in Doughboy's raucous circle. Doughboy is, of these players, most central to the narrative, for it is in his story that the primary failure of the masculine eventually emerges as the precondition not only for his own death, but for the revenge slayings he performs on three other young black men. On one level, the narrative too simplistically marks this failure as the absence of the black father (an issue I will return to), as in Furious's early explanation of his strictness to Tre: 'I'm trying to teach you to be responsible. Your little friends across the street, they don't have nobody to show them how to do that. We'll see how they turn out.' But at other discursive levels, the failure of the masculine is more complex, as the scene leading to Doughboy's first arrest for theft indicates. Here, the boys (Doughboy, Ricky, Tre, and Chris) are examining the corpse of a black male murdered and dumped behind an abandoned building when they become targets for harassment by a group of older males. In trying to defend his friends, Doughboy is knocked to the ground, kicked, and left muttering, 'I wish I could kill that motherfucker.' It is at this point that he decides to go to a nearby store, though he is clearly equipped with no money. By the time we see him again, he is under arrest for shoplifting.

I read Doughboy's response to this scenario within the double context of his ineffectuality and humiliation at the hands of other black men, and as part of the seemingly reduced significatory value of black male

Figure 23 Ice Cube

life in general. That this humiliation and physical assault is accompanied by the defunct gaze of the culturally abject dead body links Doughboy's transgressive performance to the tableau of racial expenditure that not only organizes but defines the subjective and social contours of contemporary African American culture in the film. His 'criminality' in this and subsequent scenes is part of a performative masculinity whose overdetermination can be envied only in so far as one can ignore its deeper psychological vacuity. This vacuity is evinced in Doughboy's final words of the film, when the deaths of those who killed his brother subtend his now even more intense alienation. In thinking about a local television discussion of increasing world violence, Doughboy notes the absence of any mention of his brother's murder; instead 'They showed all these foreign places . . . Either they don't know . . . or don't care what's going on in the Hood', he says. 'The shit just goes on and on. The next thing you know somebody'll try to smoke me. Don't matter though. We all have to go sometime.' Doughboy's resignation is the final performative strategy, and its cyclical undoing becomes manifest in an ensuing frame when we are told that 'two weeks later' Doughboy, too, meets his end at the hands of another black male.

But rather than close the film on this moment, Singleton offers the trajectory of Tre's life – his exodus from the Hood to attend Morehouse College – as the future-sustaining alternative, an alternative made possible by the presence of Furious as guide and mentor to his son. This emphasis, as I have mentioned above, is at times disturbingly simple because of the way it posits African American fatherhood as a necessary compensation for the inadequacies of the mother. The very narrative ploy that sanctions Tre's removal from his mother's home in the early moments of the film pivots on her lack: 'I can't teach him how to be a man', she says to Furious, 'that's your job.' And Ricky and Doughboy's mother is represented as so discriminatory in her love that even Doughboy admits at the end, 'I ain't got no brother, got no mother neither. She loved that boy more than she loved me.' But *Boyz N the Hood* does offer a contradictory reading to this overarching motif when Tre's mother, Reva, historicizes Furious's role: 'Of course you took in your son . . . and you taught him what he needed to be a man . . . What you did is no different than what mothers have been doing since the beginning of time . . . Don't think you're special.' While this speech does not have the authoritative weight of a developed characterization to carry off a more lasting narrative effect, it does provide a telling rupture of the filmic text, drawing in Furious's model masculinity from its often antiseptic and prophetic orbit, and figuring such masculinity as *within* and not opposed to the parameters of the maternal feminine. It is at such a moment that sexual difference and its historical relationship to race in US culture emerge as multi-layered, complex in their interconnections.

Perhaps the film's most sustained and successful tracing of the contradictions and difficulties within the masculine occurs in its depiction of Tre, a contemplative, still virginal young man whose negotiation of the pitfalls of black masculinity is significantly linked to his relationship with women. One of the few characters who does not routinely refer to women with the slang, 'bitch,' Tre not only evinces the tension I have discussed above between phallicism and a mediated masculinity, but embodies that tension in the contradiction between his sexual anxieties and his own falsified self-representation. This contradiction is made apparent in a scene between Furious and Tre where the possibilities for the traditional cinematic scene of masculine bonding across the body of woman are seemingly served up for the purpose of being subverted. When Furious asks his son if 'you got some pussy yet?' Tre concocts an elaborate story of affirmation, one that highlights his sexual performance and appeal. But Tre has misinterpreted the intent of Furious's question, presenting his prowess while Furious is far more concerned about the issue of birth control. The moment of disclosure, this manufactured image of woman as the sexualized object of masculine desire, is thus denied its ability to function as the pretext for closer masculine bonds. In response to Tre's assertion that she was on the pill, Furious reinforces his central lesson: 'If a girl tells you she's on the pill, use something anyway. Pill ain't going to keep your dick from falling off.' The issue of masculine responsibility for sexuality transforms the scene of male bonding into internal discord, and the significance of the body of woman disappears in its inability to fortify relations among men.

In addition, the cinematic construction of Tre's story of sexual bliss highlights the traditionality of this masculine scenario of union as a self-serving production. As Tre unravels his narrative, we are offered a seeming re-enactment of the encounter, from the moment the woman appears (with appropriate jeers and competition among Tre and his friends) to their subsequent sexual consummation at her house the next day. But as Tre tells the story and the woman begins to speak, it is his voice that issues from her mouth, marking in a rather interesting way the very denial of female subjectivity that Tre's narrative itself enacts. In this regard, Singleton's approach to the sexual conquest scenes feature both the significance of sexual confirmation within the mythos of masculine bonds while demonstrating their appropriate contours. In denying the woman the seeming authenticity of her own voice, these scenes reveal their own narrative reliance on a masculine point of view that constructs and defines the parameters of sexual desire. That such a construction is a wholesale fabrication – and that its effect leads to discord and not affirmation within masculine relations – demonstrates one of the particular power aspects of the negotiatory politics of *Boyz N the Hood* and its rearticulation of black masculinity.

For Tre, in fact, the narrative of sexual assertion emerges as a scene of betrayal, a guilt-inducing production that forces him to examine his own fears about sexuality more generally. When his teenage friend who is already a father, Ricky, inquires about his sexual inexperience, Tre admits, 'I was afraid . . . of being a daddy.' This fear is legitimized throughout the film, and the end of Tre's virginity is heralded not as a conquest of the masculine over the feminine but as the act of a self-conscious and responsible sexual subject. Indeed, the entire dimensions of masculinity as conquering imposition – whether in terms of sexuality or its metaphoric extension, life on the streets – are reconfigured in *Boyz N the Hood*, enabling an articulation of black masculinity that moves, albeit uneasily, in less than polarized ways within the discursive contours of race and sexual difference. Most importantly perhaps, the film challenges the binary figuration of the black masculine as feminization on one hand or hypermasculinization on the other, seeking a way beyond the representational impasse that oversees the political, economic, and sexual containment of black men. While the political agenda of *Boyz N the Hood* is often undermined, as I have discussed, by its representational effect, the questing gesture toward a different figuration doubles back on the earlier and much heralded black cinema of the 1970s, finding 'manhood' a more complicated and contradictory domain.

That the tenaciousness of such a masculine quest often lends itself rather quickly to feminist suspicion is beyond question. But the political imperative guiding this essay necessitates that we not dismiss, on that basis alone, the significance and implications of this cinema for excavations of the contextual history of race and sexual difference in US culture. I am rejecting, in other words, the notion that because they focus on issues of masculinity, contemporary films by black male directors are simply reinscriptions of the dominant patriarchal organization of US culture – as if attention to the field of masculine relations is in itself either inherently anti-feminist or transhistorically and essentially misogynist. Such a rejection is necessary, I believe, even as we may recognize and lament the startling absence of African American female film-makers, as well as the paucity of scripts concerned with issues affecting most specifically black women.[18] But to posit this absence or paucity as the result of the seeming success of black men in contemporary film is to forge a one-dimensional oppositionality whereby gender becomes the primary figuration of social relations, discounting once again the significance of differences among men in historical, political, and economic ways. These differences provide the broad cultural context through which the narrative of *Boyz N the Hood* in particular is made, establishing the racial dimensions of a competitive masculine order that routinely invests in the destruction of African American men.

While the film's desire to forge a different masculinity, to recognize the framework of masculine relations that underlie race in the US without eschewing the masculine altogether, does not invoke a post-gender utopian feminist vision, its significance lies in foregrounding this specific configuration of race and gender. For it is here that the crisis of race within feminism will continue to visit itself, posing crucial questions about the relationship between the masculine and patriarchal organization that we are as yet unable to adequately understand or answer. What does become clear, within this kind of historicizing discussion of race and sexual difference, is that any simple collapse of issues of the masculine into patriarchal organization sacrifices the very materiality of race and gender in US culture today. It is in this light that I wish to end by reiterating my own political desire in crafting this paper, which is not to appropriate black male cinema for feminism but to place the dilemma of feminism squarely within the discursive field of black masculinity. This means that one does not simply produce a context in which African American male representations are measured in terms of the political standards of feminism, but that their representations provide an important (though not the only) public moment through which the entire domain of sexual difference can be rethought in the cultural context of white racial supremacy. In negotiating this increasingly public moment of black masculine critique, feminism confronts itself precisely where it has been convinced it did not or could not exist, making possible a

universe of political alliance no longer reducible to the monolithic laws
of gender.

NOTES

1 For further discussion of the significance of the buddy configuration as the
primary mode for cinematic images of African American males in the 1980s,
see Bogle (1989: 271–6) and Wiegman (1989); for blaxploitation films of the
1970s, see Bogle (1989: 231–66).

2 Among the films, Mario Van Peebles, *New Jack City* (1991); John Singleton,
Boyz N the Hood (1991); Spike Lee, *Mo' Better Blues* (1990) and *Jungle
Fever* (1991); Matty Rich, *Straight Out of Brooklyn* (1991); Charles Burnett,
To Sleep with Anger (1990); Robert Townsend, *The Five Heartbeats* (1991);
Joseph Vasquez, *Hangin' With the Homeboys* (1991); Ernest Dickerson, *Juice*
(1991); Bill Duke, *A Rage in Harlem* (1991); Kevin Hooks, *Go Natalie* (1991);
and Charles Lane, *True Identity* (1991).

3 While it would be impossible to list the many contributions to this field of
inquiry, I draw readers' attention to Alcoff (1988), Bulkin et al. (1984),
Hooks (1981, 1984), Moraga and Anzaldúa (1981), Spelman (1988), and
more recently to Barrett's (1988) introductory essay which quite coherently
examines the impact of the question of differences among women for feminist
theory.

4 For a more lengthy discussion of the transmutation of differences under the
sign of woman, see my forthcoming article in *Bucknell Review*.

5 See Spillers (1987) and Berlant (1991).

6 In her 1985 study, Sedgwick transforms the kinds of questions feminist theory
in that decade thought to ask by taking as its project the processes through
which the discourse of sexual difference – and the economy of desire precipi-
tated by the spectacle of woman – work to demarcate and perpetuate masculine hierarchies based on the intersecting dimensions of sexuality and class.
Here, masculinity and our understanding of its relation to patriarchal values
and dominant social arrangements were importantly unleashed from a monolithic rendering, and the possibilities for enjoining a feminist and antihomo-
phobic reading of cultural relations pursued. Such a theoretical approach is
suggestive in its refusal to surrender to the segregatory logic of US cultural
production, and provides a political standard not only for the present discussion but for subsequent feminist work on masculinity and relations among
men. For a less affirmative discussion of the turn toward issues of masculinity
in contemporary feminism, see Modleski (1991).

7 While I will elaborate more fully on the historical terrain of black male
representation in the discussion that follows, I direct readers as well to Bogle
(1989), Boskin (1986), Davis (1981), and Leab (1975).

8 For further discussion on these dual consequences of early feminist figurations
of woman in film, see the introduction to Mellencamp et al. (1984).

9 In her prescient 1978 article, Christine Gledhill observed that 'although the
Lacanian subject accounts for different sexual locations in the symbolic order,
it . . . appears to displace the effectivity of the forces and relations of production in the social formation' (Gledhill 1984: 33–4). While Gledhill's concerns are predominantly with questioning further 'the relation of patriarchy to
capitalism and bourgeois ideology' (35), her critique of feminist film theory's
dangerous universalization of sexual difference via the psychoanalytic para-

digm argues for a more materialist feminist intervention into film, particularly as the feminist theorist considers how various cultural discourses situate female spectators differently not simply from men but from one another. For Gledhill, this does not mean a complete dismissal of psychoanalysis but greater attention to the interplay between the representational and material forms of cultural production.

10 Harris's work (1984) provides an important exploration of the centrality of castration and lynching in African American literature by tracing the ritual scenes of dismemberment to other kinds of cultural accounts. See also Davis (1981) and my forthcoming essay, 'The Anatomy of Lynching.'

11 One thinks of the early scene in Richard Wright's *Native Son* where Bigger Thomas and his friends are at the theater watching a film about a young, rich white woman (Wright 1966: 33–5). Here, the narrative encodes the distance and difference between their ability to look at the cinematic scene and the denial of that looking as a material reality of their lives in the segregated South.

12 The differentiation I am trying to forge here can also be found in film theory's discussion of the female spectator, whose position within the film and as its spectator are not, as much early feminist film theory seemed to assume, the same. The *Camera Obscura* special issue, 'The Spectatrix' (Bergstrom and Doane 1990), provides commentary on both the historical figuration of the spectator in feminist theory and contemporary rearticulations.

13 Hartsock (1990) evinces the problem of critical diffusion by constructing a paradigm of cultural power that establishes women, blacks, homosexuals, the poor, etc. in a massive deployment as the *others* against whom dominant power is imposed. While she clearly recognizes the differences between various cultural structures of hierarchy, I am unconvinced that feminist theory will be furthered by maintaining such a configuration of power. See Harding (1986: 163–96) for a slightly more deft discussion of the similarities and differences that mark the positionalities of white women and both African American women and men.

14 See Sanchez-Eppler (1988) and my forthcoming essay in *Bucknell Review*.

15 In an analysis of the career of actor and singer Paul Robeson, Richard Dyer describes the cultural logic and political effect of black male elisions with the feminine: 'It is no accident that there are similarities between how black men are represented and how women are depicted . . . it is common for oppressed groups to be represented in dominant discourses as non-active . . . their passivity permits the fantasy of power over them to be exercised, all the more powerful for being a confirmation of actual power; their passivity justifies their subordination ideologically . . . [for] their activity would imply challenge . . . to the dominant it would imply change' (Dyer 1986: 116). In aligning representations of African American men with the constructed position of women, cultural discourses are able to neutralize black male images, exchanging potential activity and aggression against white masculine power for the structurally passive realm of sexual objectification. For a suggestive discussion of the eroticization of the black male body in the context of the tradition of female sexualization in Western art, see Mercer (1987).

16 This is not to say that castration was unknown as ritualistic punishment for perceived black male sexual aggression prior to Emancipation (see Jordan 1968: 154–8), but that its use would become so intensified in the later nineteenth century that we must recognize it as a specific form of discipline in the context of slavery's economic demise.

17 All of these figures made their impact in the proliferating genre of black action film. See Bogle (1989) for a critical appraisal.
18 At the same time, however, any hierarchical ranking that would reinforce black female absence by arguing for the greater seriousness of the contemporary plight of black men has at its basis a faulty rendering of the political contexts of race and gender. For further discussion of the implications of such hierarchicalizing, see Lubiano (1970).

BIBLIOGRAPHY

Alcoff, L. (1988) 'Cultural Feminism versus Post-Structuralism: the Identity Crisis in Feminist Theory,' in M. R. Malson, J. F. O'Barr, S. Westphal-Wihl, and M. Wyer (eds) (1989) *Feminist Theory in Practice and Process*, Chicago, Il: University of Chicago Press.

Barrett, M. (1988) *Women's Oppression Today: the Marxist–Feminist Encounter*, rev. edn, London and New York: Verso Press.

Bergstrom, J., and Doane, M. A., eds (1990) *Camera Obscura* Special Issue 'The Spectatrix' 20–1, May–September, 1989.

Berlant, L. (1991) 'National Brands/National Body: *Imitation of Life*,' in H. Spillers (ed.) *Comparative American Identities: Race, Sex, and Nationality in the Modern Text*, London and New York: Routledge.

Bogle, D. (1989) *Toms, Coons, Mulattoes, Mammies & Bucks: an Interpretive history of Blacks in American Films*, rev. edn, New York: Continuum Publishing.

Boskin, J. (1986) *Sambo: the Rise and Demise of an American Jester*, New York: Oxford University Press.

Bulkin, E., Pratt, M. B., and Smith, B. (1984) *Yours in Struggle: Three Feminist Perspectives on Anti-Semitism and Racism*, Ithaca, NY: Firebrand Books.

Cleaver, E. (1968) *Soul on Ice*, New York: Dell.

Cook, P., and Johnston, C. (1974) 'The Place of Woman in the Cinema of Raoul Walsh' in Constance Penley (ed.) (1988) *Feminism and Film Theory*, London: Routledge.

Davis, A. (1981) *Women, Race and Class*, New York: Random House.

De Lauretis, T. (1984) *Alice Doesn't: Feminism, Semiotics, Cinema*, Bloomington: Indiana University Press.

—— (1987) *Technologies of Gender: Essays on Theory, Film, and Fiction*, Bloomington: Indiana University Press.

Dyer, R. (1986) *Heavenly Bodies*, New York, St Martin's Press.

Gaines, J. (1986) 'White Privilege and Looking Relations: Race and Gender in Feminist Film Theory,' *Cultural Critique* 4, fall: 59–79.

Gibbs, J. T. ed. (1988) *Young, Black and Male in America: an Endangered Species*, Dover, MA: Auburn House Publishing Company.

Gledhill, C. (1978) 'Recent Developments in Feminist Film Criticism' in P. Mellencamp et al. (eds) (1984) *Re-Vision: Essays in Feminist Film Criticism*, Fredrick, MD: University Publications of America.

Harding, S. (1986) *The Science Question in Feminism*, Ithaca, NY: Cornell University Press.

Harris, T. (1984) *Exorcising Blackness: Historical and Literary Lynching and Burning Rituals*, Bloomington: Indiana University Press.

Hartsock, N. (1990) 'Foucault on Power: a Theory for Women?' in L. Nicholson (ed.) *Feminism/Postmodernism*, London: Routledge.

Hooks, B. (1981) *Ain't I a Woman: Black Women and Feminism*, Boston, MA: Long Haul Press.

_____ (1984) *Feminist Theory: From Margin to Center*, Boston, MA: South End Press.

Irigaray, L. (1977) *This Sex Which is Not One*, trans. C. Porter (1985), Ithaca, NY: Cornell University Press.

Jordan, W. (1968) *White Over Black: American Attitudes Toward the Negro, 1550–1812*, New York: Norton.

Leab, D. (1975) *From Sambo to Superspade: the Black Experience in Motion Pictures*, Boston, MA: Houghton Mifflin.

Lubiano, W. (1990) 'When Boys Collide: Gender Negotiations in African-American Cultural Studies,' paper presented at MLA Convention, Chicago, December.

Mellencamp, P., Doane M. A. and Williams, L., (eds) (1984) *Re-Vision: Essays in Feminist Film Criticism*, Fredrick, MD: University Publications of America.

Mercer, K. (1987) 'Imaging the Black Man's Sex' in P. Holland et al. (eds) *Photography/Politics Two*, London: Comedia.

Modleski, T. (1991) *Feminism Without Women*, London: Routledge.

Moraga, C., and Anzaldúa G., eds (1981) *This Bridge Called My Back: Writings by Radical Women of Color*, Watertown, MA: Persephone Press.

Mulvey, L. (1975) 'Visual Pleasure and Narrative Cinema' in C. Penley (ed.) (1988) *Feminism and Film Theory*, London: Routledge.

Penley, C., ed. (1988) *Feminism and Film Theory*, London: Routledge.

Sanchez-Eppler, K. (1988) 'Bodily Bonds: the Intersecting Rhetorics of Feminism and Abolition,' *Representations* 24, fall: 28–59.

Sedgwick, E. K. (1985) *Between Men: English Literature and Male Homosocial Desire*, New York: Columbia University Press.

Spelman, E. (1988) *Inessential Woman: Problems of Exclusion in Feminist Thought*, Boston, MA: Beacon Press.

Spillers, H. J. (1987) 'Mama's Baby, Papa's Maybe: an American Grammar Book', *Diacritics* 17, summer: 65–81.

Wiegman, R. (1989) 'Negotiating AMERICA: Gender, Race, and the Ideoliogy of the Interracial Male Bond,' *Cultural Critique* 13, fall: 89–117.

_____ (forthcoming) 'Toward a Political Economy of Race and Gender,' *Bucknell Review*.

_____ (forthcoming) 'The Anatomy of Lynching,' *Journal of the History of Sexuality*.

Wright, R. (1940; rpt 1966) *Native Son*, New York: Harper and Row.

10

THE BUDDY POLITIC

Cynthia J. Fuchs

This white obscenity, this escalation of transparence, reaches its
peak in the collapse of the political scene.

(Jean Baudrillard, *Fatal Strategies* (1990))

There's too much testosterone here.

(Tyler, *Point Break* (1991))

Heart Condition (1990) ends with a freeze frame of a snapshot wedding
portrait. Initially, the image reifies a prototypically happy family: glowing
bride Crystal (Chloe Webb), her infant son, and her smiling husband
Mooney (Bob Hoskins). However, as the photo dissolves from color to
black and white to end the film, we see that Mooney's smile is not
directed at his new wife and child. Rather, he beams at an empty space
delineated by his own outstretched arm, a space slowly filled by the
figure of Stone (Denzel Washington), Mooney's ghost buddy.

This remarkably incoherent image exposes what has been the movie's
preoccupation all along: the exciting, troubling relation between two
male bodies. That this bond occurs over Stone's dead one denotes the
film's paradoxical project, to simultaneously represent and efface differences which threaten the buddy alliance. While the plot device that
transplants upscale lawyer Stone's heart to racist cop Mooney's chest is
extreme, it also points out spiraling ideological and cultural tensions that
structure the generic buddy film.

First, the men's literally shared heart figures a masculine hegemony
which appears to subsume such tensions, an all-male unit transcending
race and class distinctions to produce stable self-identity. But second,
another tension remains unresolved by the film's snapshot conclusion,
suspended and disembodied like Stone's phantom self. The buddy movie
typically collapses intramasculine differences by effecting an uncomfortable sameness, a transgression of boundaries between self and other,
inside and outside, legitimate and illicit.

Conceived in paradox – in/outside various properties – the cop–buddy
team must always deny and fulfill what Eve Sedgwick terms 'male homo-

social desire,' the continuum from homosexuality to homophobia and back again (Sedgwick 1985). Such paradox is rehearsed in the buddy film's movement from conflict to resolution (between the two men or between them and a hostile command structure), a narrative continuum which contains initial axes of racial, generational, political, and ethnic difference under a collective performance of extraordinary virility. Again and again, these movies conclude with the partners triumphantly detonating all villains and nearby vehicles. The profusion of these psychosexual displays (as expensive special effects and formulaic repetitions) demonstrates by unsubtle metaphor the incongruous nature of the buddy politic. Too much and never enough, the final catharsis remains untenable.

Yet again, the problem of male self-identity is exacerbated by its apparent resolution. For this conspicuous discharge situates the male couple between the representational poles of homoeroticism and homophobia, in love with their self-displays and at odds with their implications. Caught inside conventions of 'male bonding' and outside racist, heterosexist norms, the buddy politic can only implode. Recent buddy films' responses to this apocalyptic scenario are predictably hysterical. This essay will examine efforts to efface homosexuality by recuperating racial otherness in the following cop–buddy films: *Off Limits* (Christopher Crowe, 1988), *Lethal Weapon* and *Lethal Weapon 2* (Richard Donner, 1987 and 1989), *The Rookie* (Clint Eastwood, 1991) *New Jack City* (Mario Van Peebles, 1991), *Black Rain* (Ridley Scott, 1989), and *Heart Condition* (James D. Parriott). Mapping the formula's evolution from the cultural trauma of Vietnam through the farce of the Reagan–Bush drug wars, these films efface the intimacy and vulnerability associated with homosexuality by the 'marriage' of racial others, so that this transgressiveness displaces homosexual anxiety.

FREEZE FRAMES

The cinematic male bond might best be described as an unresolvable process that (re)produces freeze frames on the order of the last image in George Roy Hill's *Butch Cassidy and the Sundance Kid* (1969). This famous image of disastrous ejaculatory excess – Paul Newman and Robert Redford run toward the camera, shooting and being shot, dying and dead – exemplifies the paradox of the buddy formula. Built on the bankability of two male stars, the buddy film negotiates crises of masculine identity centered on questions of class, race, and sexual orientation, by affirming dominant cultural and institutional apparati.

The dominant masculine context and accompanying identity crises are hardly new. The textual strategies by which men form intimate partnerships have evolved, though, from what Joan Mellen calls 'an adolescent bonding of young males' (Mellen 1977: 15) in early cowboy serials, the war movie *What Price Glory?* (1926) and the romantic adventure *Beau Geste* (1939), to more sophisticated mechanisms by which homosexuality is repressed. Coming of age during the late 1960s, the buddy film responded to the political advent of sex and race issues, through Women's Lib and the Civil Rights movement. Molly Haskell describes this period as 'a time when men, released from their stoical pose of laconic self-possession by the "confessional" impulse and style of the times, discovered each other' (Haskell 1974: 362). With women increasingly omitted from movie plots, Haskell writes, men could 'live out relationships and feelings that had remained below the surface' (Haskell 1974: 363).

Such 'relationships' reconfirmed white male self-identity within radically shifting social and political frames; these men without women defined themselves in opposition to the (absented) other. *Midnight Cowboy* (1969), *M*A*S*H* (1970), and *Carnal Knowledge* (1972) constructed male partners by virulent misogyny. At the same time, however, the exclusion of women compelled overt condemnation of implicit and even explicit homoeroticism, as the texts worked precisely to keep such frightening feelings 'below the surface.' (Even *Dog Day Afternoon's* (1975) sympathetic bisexual protagonist is delimited by his criminal status.) This homophobia was again reframed during the 1980s, as the buddy film developed more specific, less inflammatory narrative parameters. Gay characters (for instance, William Hurt in *Kiss of the Spider Woman* (1985) were named victims of familial, political, and social confusions.

By the same token, contemporary cop–buddy movies emphatically heterosexualize their homosocial protagonists (through off-screen ex-wives or girl friends who die on-screen) while settling other differences. Significantly, the transition from Reagan to Bush has yielded ever more formulaic buddy films, featuring higher body counts, larger numbers of interracial and cross-class buddy teams, and increasingly homophobic comedy. The escalating popularity and predictability of the genre parallel broader cultural trends. For instance, the legacy of the Reagan Administration – its injunction to 'get government off our backs,' massive arms build-up, and expansion of racism – has given way to Bush's even more centralized executive branch, the Gulf War 'victory,' and a simultaneous denial and further expansion of institutional racism (represented in Bush's flagrantly false declaration that Clarence Thomas was the 'best' candidate for Supreme Court Justice).

As Michael Rogin argues, the relation between the spectacle of Reagan's presidency and Bush's covert operations is deceptively oppositional (Rogin 1990: 101). The creation of this virtual non-space between spectacle and secrecy, Rogin observes, depends on their mutual support. The post-Vietnam War interplay of public and covert performances produces a powerful 'political amnesia' (Rogin 1990: 103) that enables official, (il)legal movement 'outside the law' to appear heroic. As the interracial cop–buddy film sustains its extralegal, politically progressive veneer, it also represses and recuperates the most threatening, invisible (non)difference of homosexuality.

VIETNAM, VIETNAM

The post-Vietnam popularity of buddy movies elaborates and builds on mythic wartime male camaraderie as a kind of last bastion against otherness. If, as Susan Jeffords argues, the 'remasculinization of America' was enacted through the framework of gender in Vietnam representations (Jeffords 1989: 1), the buddy formula reifies this process inside and outside the masculine context of war, reinscribing oppositions between a white male 'America' and racial others. *Off Limits*, for instance, sustains the paradox of homophobia and homoeroticism as a kind of performative hysteria, a battered masculine identity ironically (and never fully) recovered through beaten, bloodied, and fetishized star bodies. Consider the perfect and racially complementary musculature of Buck McGriff (Willem Dafoe) and Albaby Perkins (Gregory Hines). Sergeants in the Joint Services' Criminal Investigations Detachment (CID), they cruise the mean streets of Saigon in a plainly hopeless attempt to keep order, at odds with the South and North Vietnamese and their own superiors.

As in many buddy movies, the front seat of their car situates McGriff and Babe's bond, delineating their incorruptible morality as proximity and loyalty to one another. (It also locates their mutual erotic desire which is, again typically, displaced by comedy: when they discuss sex in the car, Babe has a banana in his mouth and McGriff picks at a health-food seed mixture in his lap.) Their black–white racial difference is suppressed by a more immediate concern in Saigon 1968, racial difference rewritten as one of language and nationality. Released in 1988, deep into the Bush Administration's disarticulation of race issues, the film ignores its own (off-screen) excuses of stateside racism and Civil Rights. Rather, it offers the US military invasion (clearly articulated by McGriff's diatribe against 'gooks' and 'slopes').

Both isolated and interdependent, McGriff and Babe adhere to a moral order by tracking the sign of transgressive difference, a serial murderer of Vietnamese prostitutes with Amerasian children. Their first suspect, a black enlisted man, is killed by an assassin's bomb blast, but not before his denunciation of Babe ('What do you want, Rochester?') highlights Babe's precarious historical position, partnered with a white man in a racist war. Yet the buddy loyalty prevails against the notoriously corrupt US military command structure, embodied by the real killer, who turns out to be their immediate superior, the aptly named Colonel Dix (Fred Ward).

McGriff and Babe's moral mission outside this system exacerbates their mutual vulnerability. Pursuing their prime suspect, Colonel Armstrong (Scott Glenn) to a brothel, McGriff watches, unseen from a window, as the officer ties a Vietnamese woman's limbs to four bedposts and pulls out a riding crop. McGriff's alarm is cut short when he is captured by Armstrong's men. The sequence inscribes conventional structures of heterosexual pornography and power: the Asian woman's barely disclosed nudity italicizes her vulnerability, while McGriff's voyeurism insinuates his 'guilt' by association with the immoral Armstrong, and, more broadly, the US invasion of Vietnam.

Significantly, the prostitute's body is displaced in the following scene by ('feminized') Viet Cong suspects whom Armstrong also abuses. Inside the chopper with Armstrong and the three suspects, McGriff and Babe are forced to conduct their interrogation of the Colonel as he conducts his own. The transformative issue is language. The buddies' powerlessness is revealed as an inability to ask the right questions; Armstrong moves beyond their legal juridiction and the film's moral frame. After throwing all suspects from the helicopter, Armstrong asserts his innocence by leaping out the door himself.

Pornography, according to Linda Williams, describes gendered power relations. Arguing that hard-core heterosexual pornography investigates the relation of invisible female pleasure and excessive male visibility, Williams develops a vocabulary that allows discussion of porn's broader cultural ramifications (Williams 1989). Thus the difference between the crop scene and the scene where Armstrong leaps from the helicopter is not based in sex, but in power. Armstrong's impotence is exposed when he jumps out after the VC suspects. In fact, the buddies who watch helplessly serve as the film's register of moral autonomy and masculine authority.

The long shot of the Colonel's plummeting body signals a profound rupture of ethical and narrative boundaries. Guilt and innocence become suddenly relative, unstable, and no longer oppositonal. Like the distinctions between self and other or ally and enemy subverted by the buddy formula, this collapsed difference now signifies only the failure of the military and social system. Matching the previous shots of the murdered suspects, the shot of Armstrong's fall links them all as 'victims,' killers officially paid and trained to do so. Guilt in this war is profoundly uncategorizeable. The futile mark of Armstrong's masculinity is his assumption of responsibility.

The combined spectacle of Armstrong's death and the partners' shared impotence draws and undermines various frames – of language (Vietnamese and English, the military jargon that effaces crimes which define the US mission in Vietnam), of bodies (the daily 'counts' designating the war of attrition), and of loyalties (to the US military ideology which prescribes such excess). The descent that figures this particular spectacle (and looks forward to Dix's fatal plunge from a church window) suggests what Jean Baudrillard calls the 'superficial abyss,' the inauthenticity and artifice that define 'seduction' (Baudrillard 1990: 3). *Off Limits* suggests that dissimulation is interchangeable with excessive simulation and further, that such seduction (read: victimization) is culturally gendered. Declaring his innocence with his dead body, Armstrong magnifies the war's seductive spectacles of penetration and excess.

Their encounter with Dix is triggered by just such a paradox, when their car is exploded. This time Babe is caught and removed by men in uniforms, and McGriff escapes, bloodied, exhausted, and bare-chested, to the nun's apartment. (Her alarm is dispelled when he falls asleep.) McGriff is urgently called away from her safe and starkly domestic space by Babe's hyperconventional performance outside the window. Miraculously (and improbably) escaped from the military police, Babe acts out his dream of being a star basketball player, complete with crowd noises and the 'whoosh' of the ball. When McGriff joins him, they pledge loyalty, find the final clue, and eventually shoot down Dix as he threatens to kill the nun. The partners' double shooting of Dix (in slow motion) incarnates the seductive, overtly moral (they are saving a nun) excess of penetration.

A similar image of double shooting closes *Lethal Weapon*, a text which is rife with homophobic verbal ejaculation. Here homoerotic tension is displaced most obviously on to race and class. *Off Limits*'s self-defined project is to cross limits and realign loyalties especially germane to its Vietnam context). By displacing the most visible and therefore deceptive difference on to Asian bodies (for the enemy was in fact a white man) the film privileges the buddy bond. In the final credits scene, Babe describes his letter from a woman with 'big tits,' as they drive off in their battered car, declaring and negotiating their heterosexuality. *Lethal Weapon* more vehemently displaces its homoerotic subtext even as it focuses more intensely on its protagonists' beautiful male bodies.

SECRET SPECTACLES

Consider the erasure and conflation of character and actor bodies constructed by its poster: Gibson looks straight at us, while Glover is slightly profiled, his face turned toward us, with his gun raised within the frame. 'Glover carries a weapon,' the ad copy reads, 'Gibson is one. He's the only LA cop registered as a *Lethal Weapon*.' If Glover's gun is prominently displayed, Gibson needs no such sublimation. The film itself redresses this glossy disembodiment by its introduction of Riggs (Mel

Figure 24 Danny Glover and Mel Gibson in *Lethal Weapon*

Gibson) and Murtaugh (Danny Glover) as naked bodies. Riggs wakes up alone and undressed in his unkempt house trailer, revealing his buttocks; Murtaugh examines his 50-year-old body, more discreetly below the frame linc of his bathtub, while his family sings 'Happy Birthday.' As Robyn Wiegman observes, this bourgeois black body exhibits 'the commodified heterosexual norm' from which the recently widowed Riggs is alienated (Wiegman 1991: 322). But the connection is here clearly defined as masculine body anxiety.

Where the borderline psychotic Riggs would kill himself, Murtaugh is concerned with self-preservation. This anxiety, though, is exacerbated and portrayed as masculine by their histories as Vietnam veterans. As in *Off Limits*, 'Vietnam' is here recirculated as history and sign of the process of male bonding and betrayal: the drug-dealing villains are ex-CIA fliers; Murtaugh's white 'Vietnam buddy' generates the mystery by requesting his help, and Riggs repeatedly invokes his weapons expertise to assert authority over his older partner. The men's individual pasts shape their current relation and recode it in terms of performance and desire. That is, Riggs stages his performance in the war and after (his target-shooting) as desirable object for Murtaugh's look. In return, Murtaugh offers an undesirable object, his 'wife's cooking.'

As Tania Modleski suggests, the running joke in both *Lethal Weapon* films about Trish Murtaugh's cooking and her husband's subsequent potential 'thinness' is related to a 'masculine fear of the body . . . combated by turning the body into a machine' (Modleski 1991: 141–2). Riggs's machine-body ironically becomes both films' focus of anxiety, frustration, and anger. Such focus is ironic for two reasons: first, as I have already mentioned, Riggs's body is significantly overcoded as Mel Gibson's 'sex-object' body. And secondly, Murtaugh's body is in fact the one more at risk, in both texts, given that he is black, older, and more vulnerable by virtue of his 'old' gun and less precise aim.

In other words, the films stage this body vulnerability both as audience seduction and process of male bonding. In *Lethal Weapon*, for instance, after a self-brutalizing 'Three Stooges' routine that intimidates and out-wits drug dealers, Riggs returns home to sob over his dead wife's portrait and place his revolver in his mouth; he imagines self-implosion. (However, in this regard, Riggs is immediately redeemed by his comparison to the film's other white lunatic, Mr Joshua (Gary Busey), who exhibits a G. Gordon Liddy-ish zest, for holding his arm in a fire.) Enacting a prototypical male aggression while resituating it as self-destructive, Riggs's hysteria also conflates Post-Traumatic Stress Disorder (PTSD) with weepy, melodramatic depression, a 'feminine' frailty and overpresence. Jeffords suggests that Vietnam narratives 'serve as the most straightforward means of gaining access to the fracture of gendered ideology because of their foregrounded logic of sexual differences' (Jeffords 1989: 84). We might also consider this 'fracture' as it informs the buddies' same-sex relationship, which grants a somewhat less than straightforward access to the same problematic of gendered ideology.

For example, the effect of Riggs's potential gender 'shifting' – his hysteria – is vigorously overlaid with what Lynne Joyrich has termed 'hypermasculinity,' a reaction against perceived incursions of the feminine (Joyrich 1990). Here the buddies' hypermasculine resurrection is produced by the heavy cultural coding of 'Vietnam,' *the* experience by which (sexual) difference is determined 'in country' and perpetuated back in 'the World.' When Murtaugh invites Riggs home for dinner, their bonding occurs after dinner, aboard Murtaugh's boat and then looking at each other across the bed of Riggs's truck. Thus ritualized, their homosocial loyalty excuses all other transgressions. That is, a 'secret spectacle' of hypermasculinity informs Riggs and Murtaugh's bonding. Their first day together climaxes with Riggs's memory of his part in the CIA's Phoenix Program. Crushing his beer can. Riggs says, 'When I was 19 I did a guy in Laos from 1000 yards out with a rifle shot in a high wind.' Murtaugh responds, 'Did you really like my wife's cookin'?' 'No,' says Riggs.

As this elliptic exchange secures and 'naturalizes' the male bond over the wife's burned roast, it also suggests the intimacy of male violence: to 'do a guy' is clearly a shared experience for vets and cops. Further, the reference to Phoenix (which targeted and 'neutralized' some twenty thousand individuals during the war) redoubles a relation between history and myth, in that Phoenix was indeed a top-secret spectacle. If, as Rogin writes, 'spectacle and secrecy define the political pecularities of the postmodern American empire,' one of the more visible secrets of that empire is the simultaneously displayed and denied violent excess that defines its masculine images (Rogin 1990: 103). Further, Rogin argues, 'political amnesia' produces and reproduces white heroes and mythologies. Such amnesia creates the paradox whereby Riggs alerts his black partner to South African villainy in *Lethal Weapon 2*.

Moreover, it is the white male body which assumes and displaces the first movie's most lethal violence, through a staged 'death.' Shot down by the villains, Riggs is resurrected like a phoenix; by virtue of a bullet-proof vest, his body remains unpenetrated, virginal. When the partners rescue Murtaugh's kidnapped daughter, Riggs surprises the villains. He shoots at them unseen and apparently invulnerable. His capture prolongs the narrative but also allows the eventual face-to-face cathartic battle with his counterpart psycho, Mr Joshua. More to the point of the film's politics of racial difference, Riggs's capture also allows his bare-chested, electroshock torture by a thug named Chin. This self-display and Riggs's deadly assault on Chin suggest, as Modleski points out, 'a defeat of the Asian enemy we were unable to accomplish twenty years ago' (Modleski 1991: 143).

Thus Riggs's 'resurrection' and the film's political amnesia function together as historical revision, such that the white hero performs all roles. The rescue of Murtaugh and his daughter (who has earlier registered her attraction to Riggs) enables Riggs to play noble white man *and* savage, virile hero and object of sexual desire, loyal police detective and illegitimate rogue. The partners' joint shooting of the 'albino' Joshua enacts, in slow motion, penetration and excess at once, an image 'too much' for standard speed, a release 'too much' for the subsequently depleted partners. Sealing their partnership in spite of their previous antagonism, this explosive discharge dispels race and class and represses the homoerotic charge which motivates it. As they exchange post-explosive glances, conflating viewing and acting subjects, the image delineates the process in which, as Jeffords notes, 'the subject can come to recognize itself only through/as spectacle' (Jeffords 1989: 16).

The anxiety that motivates this spectacle conflates sex and violence, but more emphatically displaces homosexuality by that violence. The explicit homophobia exhibited in *Lethal Weapon* (as Murtaugh pats out flames on his back, Riggs says, 'What are you, a fag?!') is recontained by comic punchlines, even a comic 'gay' character named Leo (Joe Pesci), in the sequel. Paradoxically, *Lethal Weapon 2* contains Riggs's homophobic (and more generally insane) excess through more intensive focus on the buddies' interracial masculine intimacy. The homoerotic charge that is expressed as anger in the first film here mediates violence. For example, Riggs rescues Murtaugh from a toilet rigged with a bomb: Murtaugh's pants are down, Riggs says, 'I know' as they look into each other's eyes. When the bomb explodes and the toilet flies out the window, they leap into a bathtub, whereupon Riggs tells Murtaugh to get off him before someone sees them.

This embrace reappears with the final image of Murtaugh cradling the near-dead Riggs in his arms. If impending death allows these exaggerated images of male-on-male contact, such images also link violence and sexuality, to the point that women are simply ejected from the script. Murtaugh's family leaves town, Riggs's heterosexual partner (a secretary for the South Africans) is murdered, and, amazingly, he learns that the same man murdered his wife, for whom he grieves so intensely in the first movie. When Murtaugh puts away his badge in order to help Riggs 'fuck' the villains, they name penetrable otherness rather than legal boundaries as the limit of male self-identity. After killing all available South African villains, Murtaugh embraces the wounded Riggs, until the sirens sound, that is, and Riggs tells Murtaugh to let go, because 'I don't want anyone to see us like this.'

GROUP SEX

The secrecy of masculine intimacy and vulnerability is sustained in these films by the 'marriage' of racial others, such that the transgressiveness of black–white difference displaces homosexual anxiety. In *The Rookie*, male penetrability is exacerbated by both partners' encounters with Latina women, first the villain Lisle (Sonia Braga), and in the final scene a new partner. Even when she is white, in the case of rookie David Ackerman's (Charlie Sheen) girl friend, upper-class Sara (Lara Flynn Boyle), the woman's threat to the male bond becomes the film's central and eventually unresolvable problem.

Racked with guilt over his brother's accidental death (analogous to the dead buddy often left behind in Vietnam War films), David suffers from nightmares. When Sara asks him, 'Why do you do this to yourself?' the answer is clear. Driven to self-redemption, he has disowned his wealthy father (Tom Skerritt) in favor of the police force. To cite David's adolescent need for masculine order and a father would be reductive; that he finds both in the figure of Nick (Eastwood) is both cataclysmic and consummate. Ironically, however, the connection between these buddies occurs as an exceedingly perverse 'feminization' of Nick *and* Eastwood. But if this process seems a demasculinization, it also results in Nick's assumption of a kind of 'hypergender,' a transgressive capacity to embody all roles, vulnerabilities, and authorities.

Beginning as a cigar-chomping, working-class retro-male, Nick's shifting position *vis-à-vis* David is variously constructed as nurturing, domineering, and abusive. The difference between them, most clearly readable as age and class, is soon transferred to sexuality, or the violent body penetration that signals 'homosexual' weakness. Part of the Los Angeles Grand Theft Auto unit, Nick and David track a vile and successful thief named Strom. That Strom has recently murdered Nick's previous partner, a black man, compels Nick's original resentment of David and his desire for vengeance. (That the Puerto Rican Raul Julia plays the German Strom also confuses issues of racial and ethnic identity.)

The shifting power relation between Nick and David is initiated in a bar, where the younger partner is brutally beaten by more experienced locals. Looking over David's body, Nick responds, 'I didn't know you were into group sex like this.' The scene cuts to the partners drinking beers and discussing motorcycles at Nick's house, David's first entry into the older man's narrative and formal space. This process of bonding is simultaneously interrupted and enhanced when the 'amateur' David is shot in the back by Lisle, Strom's partner, during the cops' botched stakeout. Strom and Lisle kidnap Nick, leaving David for dead.

The film proceeds to complicate the notion of 'group sex.' Like Riggs in *Lethal Weapon*, David is wearing body armor, so that his death is illusory. As he searches for Nick, the latter is bound in a warehouse which is equipped with a bank of video monitors. David's rescue is not in time to prevent Nick's ostensible 'rape' by Lisle. Denoting a certain vulnerability (and recalling Eastwood's similar plights in *Play Misty for Me* (1971) and *The Beguiled* (1971), the 'rape' is more clearly constituted as perversion, which, according to Baudrillard, is 'to pretend to be seduced without being seduced, without being capable of being seduced' (Baudrillard 1990: 22). The question is, which of Lisle or Nick is the more perverse? Dressed in spike heels and a black lace dress, she forces his erection by threatening him with her knife. This display of performative and penetrative power is redoubled when she turns on the video camera, so that their black and white image appears on multiple monitors.

'Now I'll have something to remember you by when you're dead,' she says. 'You think you're a real man, don't you?' she continues as she straddles him, cuts his forehead, and licks the blood. 'A real American tough guy?' The irony of her description signals the unreality of the image, collapsing Nick's sudden vulnerability on to Eastwood's heroic persona. But his exposure, like David's 'death,' is performative, false, perverse; her penetration is no match for his 'real' one. The reciprocity of their performances designates the scene's perversion, its investment in the representational power of bodies rather than any intrinsic 'realness.' Forcing him to bite a silver bullet she wears on a chain around her neck, Lisle sighs, 'Don't lose it.' But in fact this problematic construction of

Nick's 'rape' begins with the idea of such 'loss' as betrayal, a loss which is multiplied when both Strom and David see the tape running and interpret it differently.

David's rescue of Nick is delayed in part because he must first rescue Sara from one of Strom's men. He literally drives through the (amazingly flimsy) front door on Nick's bike, just in time to drag the villain off Sara. After the men fight for some minutes, she picks up David's gun and drills the Latino thug's chest with all six bullets, the film's second display of excessive interracial, female penetration. And indeed David reacts with horror, furious because the dead man knew Nick's location: 'If I wanted him dead I woulda shot him myself!' That he does find Nick anyway, in time to see the videotape, links these images of violation as self-loss through performance. The repeated 'rape' as image combines the threat and titillation of fluid identity – implied by Baudrillard's gender-bound delineation of the 'inscrutable' feminine which represents such transgression – that is absorbed by Nick's excessive masculinity. And indeed, as he drives his and David's getaway car through a second floor window as the building explodes around them, Nick is surreal, aflame, in ecstatic, slow-motion flight.

The image suggests a strange serenity, a stability relocated in Nick's body as they crash-land: he's ready to go, ever-virile. Yet the male bodies in *The Rookie* remain profoundly untenable, despite *and* because of such extraordinary narrative efforts to contain them. David's seduction by Nick parallels Nick's by Lisle (and as well, hers by the idea of him as Eastwood, the 'real American tough guy,' a seduction effaced by this particular narrative). To be a 'real' man means to 'keep it up.' By film's end, Nick is rescued twice by David, now fully redeemed for his brother's off-screen death and his own weakness. Promoted to Captain, Nick assigns David a new partner, Heather Torres, whose nationality and uniform serve to recuperate and domesticate the unruly Lisle, suggesting that her excessive discontinuity is indeed 'only' performative, while the male bond endures *as* incongruity.

IT'S A DEATH THING

Such instability is amplified in *Black Rain*, where the partner is replaced not at the end, but halfway through the movie. As in *Off Limits*, the process of bonding is defined and compelled by the cop-partners' alienation from the surrounding culture. New York detectives Nick (Michael Douglas) and Charlie (Andy Garcia) escort and lose a criminal to Tokyo, an outrageous display of neon, corruption, and hyper-technology. The connections among heterosexism and violence emerge in this film *as* representation, just as they do in *New Jack City*. What is unrepresentable in these texts is to the point of their concerns with male vulnerability and transgression. Atypically, these buddy films focus specifically on race. But both films retreat from this apparently radical premise to the less traumatic and more familiar crisis of masculine identity. Indeed, *New Jack City* effaces race with a return to the body and its penetration by drugs: 'It's not a black thing. It's not a white thing. It's a death thing.'

As structured by the buddy film, this 'thing' is also male (or, as Denzel Washington puts it in Spike Lee's *Mo' Better Blues*, 'It's a dick thing'). If they seem to be 'about' race (Asian and white in the unfortunately titled *Black Rain*, and African American and white/Italian American in *New Jack City*), these films are in fact obsessed with surfaces, displacing race on to color. Fragmented and disengaged from linear narrative, the films construct surfaces, representing male bodies as sexual objects, penetrated corpses, anxious paradoxes. Each text features multiple and shifting pairs of partners, and in each reciprocal violence legitimizes new sexual and moral parameters, repressing and reproducing homosexual panic as composite hypermachismo. *Black Rain* represents the threat of homosocial desire as a transgression of cultural differences between masculine ideals. In the incomprehensible glitz and clamor of Tokyo, Nick and Charlie are at once confused subjects surrounded by alien structures and customs, and conspicuous objects of curious Japanese looks. The Tokyo cops appears as a tractable, anonymous herd. One of them, Mas (Ken Takakura), tells Nick, 'I am part of a group,' a fidelity incompatible with the Americans' apparently inbred individualism.

Similarly, the partners in *New Jack City* redefine themselves according to their shifting urban environment. Originally the cop-partners Scotty (Ice T), and Nick Parretti (Judd Nelson) despise each other because of their cultural (read: racial) difference. The only white man in a black-centered movie, Parretti continually removes himself from the other officers (including a Chinese American) and dismisses their discourse as 'some kind of black thing.' This difference, however, is soon voided by the buddies' moralized muscle: their union against the uniformly black drug lords recontains masculinity as ethical spectacle. By contrast, the black gangster-partners, Nino (Wesley Snipes) and Gee Money (Allen Payne) name themselves the Cash Money Brothers (CMB) and their crackhouse the Enterprise, immediately commodifying their self-identity.

In *Black Rain*, the surface also belies cultural difference which is reproduced as sameness. That Nick and Charlie pursue a counterfeiter suggests not only the ephemeral nature of reality and appearances, but as well the collapse of desire on to consumption. Nick is himself a fake, a cop on the take who rationalizes his immorality as a reaction to an oppressive system, which is indicated by the close, dark brown office of the superior who chastises him. But his illusion is a reaction to the domesticizing threat against his 'real' masculinity. Like Eastwood's Nick, Douglas's Nick is a man defined by standard iconography. The film opens with Nick's motorcycle race against waterfront thugs, but his too-sensational machismo is honorable, because he competes to make money for child support payments. It is exactly his dissipation and vulnerability which force him to renegotiate his masculine identity. Initially aggressive and short-tempered, Nick is three times rendered impotent as a spectator: once with Charlie, he watches a murder in a New York restaurant, then when their prisoner is abducted in Tokyo, and the third time when Charlie is murdered by Japanese punks on motorbikes.

Nick's new partner, Mas, is essentially Charlie resurrected and transformed, assuming his role as Nick's moral conscience. Adrift and suddenly alone in this foreign world, Nick needs Mas to translate the language of the law he consistently ignores or thwarts. Nick's excess is mediated not only by Mas, but as well by the film's construction of a more monstrous enemy, the young villain Sato, who slices off his own finger in observance of Japanese ritual. This body mutilation and Charlie's decapitation mark the limits of a 'moral' masculinity, a savage, self-destructive, and irrecuperable excess, different in kind from the recuperative excess that orders the male bond.

Nick's rage is familiar, comprehensible, a result of other-perpetrated violence. He reacts vehemently. Mas, who practices martial arts in a structured environment, initially resists embracing Nick's cause. Following Charlie's murder, however, Mas accepts the dead man's badge, emblem of organized morality, whereas Nick takes the gun, emblem of his hysteria and his partner's castration/decapitation. Due to his earlier bonding with Charlie as spectacle (in a nightclub they drunkenly sing on stage, and Mas reveals an informal, 'American' side), Mas is infected, or penetrated, with what might be termed the 'virus' of Nick's self-righteous anger.

New Jack City also stages male bonding over a dead body of an undercover black agent, Pookie (Chris Rock). Scotty and Nick's mutual frustration over his death reshapes their racial conflict as justified, even noble, masculine excess. Where Scotty feels responsible, Nick reveals that he was once 'a Pookie, a poor white trash Pookie.' Drinking themselves into a competitive fury, the miserable and newly affirmed partners decide to 'get' Nino whatever the cost. Immediately following this scene, the absolutely corrupt male body, Nino, is revealed in bed with Gee Money's girl; that this image focuses on Nino's well-developed chest rather than hers suggests his unconventional obsession with his body and appearance (underlined throughout the film by his brightly-colored costumes, jewelry, and flashy haircut). Plainly, Nino's rupture of the homosocial CMB partnership is displaced by his betrayal of his 'brother's' body in order to satiate his own. As Gee Money says, 'You forgot about me, man, your brother.'

Nino's ultimate betrayal – his murder of Gee Money – occurs when he learns that his partner has unknowingly invited one of the other partners, the cop Scotty, into the CMB circle. As they face each other on an urban bridge, Nino laments Gee's betrayal by drugs, 'this glass dick you been suckin' on.' In turn, Gee pleads, 'Let's do us, man, me and you. Let's be a family again.' At this point, reconciliation is impossible. Nino agrees to once more 'be his brother's keeper,' then shoots Gee through the head.

Such betrayal in *Black Rain* is, in effect, avoided because Charlie dies. In his place, Mas complicates the film's performance of gender and allows Nick's redemption. 'Feminized' by virtue of his Asian features, soft-spokenness, and reluctance to act independently, Mas absorbs the memory of Charlie. As such, he is also model for the development of Nick's moral sensibility and his eventual decision to return Sato to the Japanese authorities rather than kill him in a fit of vengeful fury. At film's end Nick relinquishes the stolen counterfeiting plates to Mas, wrapped in a button-down shirt bestowed as a gift. This display of civilization confirms Nick's change of character, as well as Mas's Westernization. Their shared hysteria is legitimated and subverted by this act, 'saving face' for both.

New Jack City also offers the interracial couple's bonding by mutual redemption, so that their erotic frustration is displaced on to the violence of a third party. The generally peripheral 'Old Man,' representing an unspoken public anger at Nino's continual evasion of the law, assassinates him on the courtroom stairway. Scotty looks away, knowing that the black man will suffer for his vigilantism; Nick, however, smiles uncontrollably at the sight of the dead villain, a white man who can afford to love violence.

Their brief exchange of looks on the stairway recalls an earlier, bloodier spectacle, a warehouse shootout in which each partner saved the other. Nick hangs from a scaffold with the overweight, stuttering Duh-Duh-Duh Man (Bill Nunn) clinging to his legs. Nick seems doomed until Scotty shoots the villain, allowing the crucial freedom of Nick's lower body (he can ascend the scaffold). Just as Scotty smiles up at Nick, the latter fires his weapon at Duh-Duh-Duh Man, the monstrous body miraculously revived and aiming his gun at Scotty. When the thug is finally dead, the partners exchange cursory nods.

Like other cinematic male couples, this one is erected on and violates structures of desire, aggression, and spectatorship. The assertion of Scotty and Nick's shared identity depends on the dead body of the other, produced by their double shooting as exchange rather than simultaneous ejaculation. Instead of affirming a valiant and victimized manhood, in fact the process of male bonding here demonstrates its precarious nature, the impossibility of a stable masculinity when the oppositions that would define it are in flux. Baudrillard writes that 'the power of metamorphosis is at the root of all seduction . . . and the body is the first object caught in the game' (Baudrillard 1988: 46). Unhinged by process, the male buddy bodies drift into metamorphosis, 'dispersed' in appearances (Baudrillard 1988: 47).

Such death and dispersion continually circulate within the buddy movie as we enter the 1990s. The paradoxes posed by increasingly repressable racism and homophobic homoeroticism continue to break down and through cinematic surfaces at points like *Hear Condition*'s snapshot. But the family portrait fails to account for Stone's death and life, not to mention his sexual relationship with Crystal. The father of her son, he cannot hold the child, only 'feel' it through Mooney. The marriage to Crystal seals the men's bond of shared sexuality, at the cost of the black man's body, now a heart without a penis.

Straddling a tenuous boundary between presence and absence, Stone's body exists only as excess, a non-presence negotiated by his black son cradled by Crystal. Further, the photo's seeming self-reduction from full color differences to monochromatic two-dimensionality annuls agency, presenting itself as simulated 'history,' without agency. Despite its offer of a heterosexually coupled resolution, the photo posits a 'space-off . . . not visible in the frame but inferable from what the frame makes visible' (De Lauretis 1987: 26). Secret and transparent, the interracial male bond exceeds its visual and ideological frames.

The preceding image further confuses the film's homosocial representation. For this previous scene insinuates Mooney's death as well, following the buddies' assault on Crystal's drug-dealing pimp/Stone's murderer. A shot of Mooney lying on the beach situates him with Crystal crying over his body and a shotgun erect from his groin area, suggesting quite clearly his function in the upcoming exchange of vows. From here this scene cuts to a church, suggesting Mooney's funeral and then 'resurrecting' him as husband. Indeed, the recuperational contortions of this film are remarkable: Mooney's racism dissolves into deathless buddy loyalty and Crystal's life as a prostitute gives way to her newlywed glow. Yet amid this celebration of white masculine self-recovery, the disembodied black man marks the limit of the buddy politic.

BIBLIOGRAPHY

Baudrillard, J. (1988) *The Ecstasy of Communication*, trans. B. and C. Shutze, New York: Semiotext(e).

_____ (1990) *Seduction*, trans. B. Singer, New York: St Martin's Press.

De Lauretis, T. (1987) *Technologies of Gender: Essays on Theory, Film and Fiction*, Bloomington, Indiana University Press.

Haskell, M. (1974) *From Reverence to Rape: the Treatment of Women in the Movies*, New York: Penguin.

Jeffords, S. (1989) *The Remasculinization of America: Gender and the Vietnam War*, Bloomington. Indiana University Press.

Joyrich, L. (1990) 'Critical and Textual Hypermasculinity' in P. Mellencamp (ed.) *Logics of Television: Essays in Cultural Criticism*, Bloomington: Indiana University Press.

Mellen, J. (1977) *Big Bad Wolves: Masculinity in the American Film*, New York: Pantheon.

Modleski, T. (1991) *Feminism Without Women: Culture and Criticism in a 'Post-feminist' Age*, New York: Routledge.

Rogin, M. P. (1990) ' "Make My Day!"': Spectacle as Amnesia in Imperial Politics,' *Representations* 29: 99–123.

Sedgwick, E. K. (1985) *Between Men: English Literature and Male Homosocial Desire*, New York: Columbia University Press.

Wiegman, R. (1991) 'Black Bodies/American Commodities: Gender, Race, and the Bourgeois Ideal in Contemporary Film' in L. D. Friedman (ed.) *Unspeakable Images: Ethnicity and the American Cinema*, Urbana: University of Illinois Press.

Williams, L. (1989) *Hard Core: Power, Pleasure, and the 'Frenzy of the Visible,'* Berkeley: University of California Press.

Part IV

MUSCULAR MASCULINITIES

Figure 25 Arnold Schwarzenegger in *The Terminator*

11

MASCULINITY AS MULTIPLE MASQUERADE

The 'mature' Stallone and the Stallone clone

Chris Holmlund

Since the early 1980s feminist theorists have often drawn on Joan Riviere's essay, 'Womanliness as a Masquerade,' and Jacques Lacan's article, 'The Meaning of the Phallus,' to argue that femininity is a performance anxiously enacted for – and/or sadistically flaunted in defiance of – an audience of men. Within film studies, Mary Ann Doane's work on the masquerade has been particularly influential. In Doane's version, the masquerade of femininity compensates for women's 'lapse' into a subjectivity defined *a priori* as masculine. Women pretend to 'be' what they lack: they seem to embody the phallus. As a result, says Doane, women are positioned on the side of spectacle, in cinema and in society.

Yet though the masquerade of femininity conflates woman and spectacle – as Riviere puts it, 'womanliness and masquerade are one and the same' (Riviere 1929: 38) – this conflation is only an appearance. Its effects, nevertheless, are very real. Looking for a way out from what is a sorry state of affairs, for women at least, Doane suggests that the very fact that femininity *is* a masquerade indicates the existence of a gap 'between the woman and the image of femininity' (Doane 1988: 48–9). She urges female spectators to use this gap to highlight the artificiality of gender and expose the patriarchal 'network of power relations' (Doane 1982: 87) which limits and defines femininity and women.

Recently other film critics have begun to investigate masculinity and male spectacle. Some argue masculinity is a performance. Rarely, however, do they discuss masculinity as a masquerade, an oversight I find surprising. After all, Lacan explicitly states that men can 'have' the phallus just as little as women can ever 'be' it, even labelling masculinity a display (Lacan 1958: 85). Moreover, as Stephen Heath notes, for Lacan male masquerade is more intimately tied to power structures than female masquerade is: 'the trappings of authority, hierarchy, order, position make the man' (Heath 1986: 56).[1]

The failure to study men and masculinity in terms of masquerade

213

has serious consequences: (1) masculinity remains the untouched and untouchable ground against which femininity figures as the repressed and/or the unspoken;[2] (2) the differences between masculine and feminine masquerade and their various connections to power go unexamined; (3) the compulsory heterosexuality organizing masculinity and femininity as complementary if unequal opposites is left unchallenged; and, too often, (4) other matrices of masquerade are bypassed altogether.

If our analyses are to challenge dominant power structures, it is crucial we not allow masculinity to stand apart from femininity, and imperative we not think about gender separately from sexuality, race, region, age, and class. While I realize that in psychoanalytic circles it is customary to distinguish *male* fetishism from *female* masquerade, I am claiming both sexes masquerade in order to break down rigid gender-bound dichotomies.[3]

In the first section of this essay, therefore, I survey previous discussions of masquerade and show that, in different ways and with different objectives in mind, Riviere, Lacan, Doane, Judith Butler, Frantz Fanon and Homi Bhabha all intimate that masculinity as well as femininity can be thought of as a series of interlocking masquerades. For the most part, however, these theorists overlook the multiple masquerades of ambiguous figures like the gay butch clone, the lesbian femme, or the passing black, preferring to focus on the visible differences presented by other figures: the (white heterosexual) woman, the black (heterosexual man), the lesbian butch and the drag queen. I will argue, in contrast, that the butch clone's, lesbian femme's and passing black's masquerades of heterosexual white masculinity and femininity disguise subversive racial and/or sexual identities, and that the ways these masquerades overlap and interlock constitute specific links to power, conflict, and struggle. In no way are their masquerades 'benign variations' on an eternal, universal, originary theme.[4]

To delineate more precisely how masquerades of masculinity function in film today, in a second section I measure my model against two Sylvester Stallone movies from 1989, *Lock Up* (John Flynn) and *Tango and Cash* (Andrei Konchalevsky). Stallone is an especially fit figure for such an analysis: for audiences the world over he incarnates unquestioned virility, unassailable heterosexuality, and a US might and right which is, most decidedly, white. *Lock Up* and *Tango and Cash* both allude to and pump up Stallone's established tough guy image, built on muscles as a masquerade of proletarian masculinity, yet they shift this image significantly. Crucially, in both these films Stallone is no longer a loner, no longer a little Rocky or a big Rambo fighting unbeatable odds and winning impossible battles all by himself. Now he is joined by another man, a figure so like Stallone I call him the Stallone clone.

By naming this second man the Stallone clone I do not just mean he

Figure 26 Sylvester Stallone and Kurt Russell in *Tango and Cash*

looks, talks, and acts like Stallone. In these films, Stallone and the clones are very fond of each other, so for me, 'clone' evokes the butch clone, the homosexual who passes as heterosexual because he looks and acts 'like a man.' Admittedly, my reading of these films is a 'queer' reading, but it is a 'queer' reading the films themselves propose. Thanks to the clones, moreover, in both *Lock Up* and *Tango and Cash* sexuality is more easily grasped as separate from yet allied with gender, and the national, racial, and class differences used to constitute 'good' as opposed to 'bad' male couples are more obvious as well.

In conclusion, and still using the Stallone films as foils, I suggest directions for further research, and signal political limitations in thinking about masquerade solely or primarily as parodic performance or subversive spectacle. Although resistance through masquerade is not the only answer, I find arguing that masculinity and femininity are both masquerades polemically useful, because it makes it easier to question, understand, and enjoy popular mainstream representations like *Lock Up* and *Tango and Cash*.

DRESSING UP, PUTTING ON, AND STEPPING OUT: THEORIES OF MASQUERADE

I find looking at the secondary characters on which analyses of masquerades depend makes theoretical *partis pris* more visible. For masquerades change according to who is looking, how, why, at whom. If we are to assess how they are linked to power, and to resistance, we must think about how they function, and unravel the ways they are interconnected. We need, in other words, to distinguish dressing up (embellishment) from putting on (parody, critique), from stepping out (affirmation, contestation).

Riviere's essay, for example, is broadly interested in 'intermediate types' (Riviere 1929: 35). In passing she compares her academic women subjects to three different sets of homosexuals: (1) gay men who 'exaggerate their heterosexuality as a "defence" against their homosexuality' (Riviere 1929: 35); (2) 'homosexual women who, while taking no interest in other women, wish for "recognition" of their masculinity from men and claim to be the equals of men, or in other words to be men themselves' (Riviere 1929: 37); and (3) a single gay man who finds sexual satisfaction by disguising himself as his sister, then looking at himself in a mirror.

Because Riviere thinks of sexuality only in relation to gender, she sees all these various masquerades as motivated by a similar need to disguise the desire to be heterosexual men. Throughout, she speaks only of 'womanliness' as a masquerade. In her view, no active female desire or lesbian eroticism exists. Gay male desire, too, is silenced. [5]

Had Riviere voiced the term she represses in each comparison, however, she might have mentioned the gay 'mirror' man's homosexual and feminine masquerades, the butch lesbian's homosexual and masculine masquerades, and the butch clones' heterosexual and masculine masquerades. All these people, it seems to me, are busy dressing up, if not necessarily putting on or stepping out.

The case histories Riviere recounts present other matrices of masquerade as well. The first suggests class and racial masquerades are entwined with feminine masquerade. As a child, Riviere's client, a wealthy Southern woman, dreamt of disguising herself as a domestic in order to kill her mother and father and steal their money. She also fantasized about seducing a black man, then masking her provocation by saying it was necessary to avoid rape. Surely this woman is engaging in multiple masquerades, dressing up to step out in style, even though Riviere never says so.[6]

Lacan, in contrast, recognizes that dressing up is a necessary part of stepping out as a sexual being, for both men and women. 'In 'The Meaning of the Phallus,' he maintains that, since both sexes lack and desire the phallus, both find pleasure and protection in disguise. Heterosexual men cover up their lack by projecting it on to women. In order to find a replacement part on their lover's body for what they know they do not have, heterosexual women willingly if unwittingly suspend all disbelief that the penis is not the phallus. Heterosexual desire is thus predicated on both sexes' tacit agreement to remain unconscious of how comic each finds the other's posturings. In Lacan's framework, as a result, these masquerades can never be parodies or put-ons.

And what of homosexual men and women? Like Riviere, in this essay Lacan sees lesbians as asexual, as suffering from a 'disappointment' in heterosexual love.[7] In a companion piece, 'Guiding Remarks for a Congress on Feminine Sexuality,' he is more open to lesbian sexuality, admitting that lesbians are more interested in femininity than in masculinity. Nevertheless he continues to speak of lesbianism as transvestism, noting 'we still have to take up the naturalness with which such women appeal to their quality of being purely men' (Lacan 1966: 97). Whether this lesbian 'dressing up' refers only to the butch, and whether it can be seen as 'putting on,' as challenging the alignment of masculinity and femininity with heterosexuality, is unclear.

Lacan is less concerned in 'The Meaning of the Phallus' with male homosexuality, presumably because gay men share with straight men the same desire for possession of the phallus. For both dressing up and display are essential. Indeed, Lacan's most provocative remark, made just after his discussion of homosexuality, obliquely links heterosexual masculinity with homosexual masculinity. Because in his framework the phallus is necessarily veiled, it is difficult to know where difference begins and where it ends.[8] As a result, Lacan notes that 'in the human being virile display itself appears as feminine' (Lacan 1958: 85). For all their cocky, self-assured, flaunting of masculinity, therefore, straight men and butch clones both are merely masquerading.

Unlike both Riviere and Lacan, Doane pointedly mentions race and region. Briefly, she describes masculinity as a masquerade as well. Nowhere, however, does she mention homosexuality or explore the possibility that feminine masquerade might be pleasurable as well as anxious.[9] She says she wants to distinguish feminine masquerade from cross-dressing and transvestism. Yet homosexuality is not reducible to fetishistic transvestism. As Robert Stoller points out, the lesbian butch is erotically excited by the men's clothes she wears: she does not deny she

217

'is a female, knows she is a homosexual, does not wish for sex change and does not try to pass as a man' (Stoller 1985: 150).

Butler's discussions of gender trouble, in contrast, revolve around the dressing up, putting on, and stepping out of butch lesbians and drag queens. Butler excels at uncovering the homosexuality repressed in Riviere's and Lacan's discussions of femininity, maintaining that 'gay is to straight not as copy is to original, but rather as copy is to copy' (Butler 1990: 31). In her view, neither homosexual nor heterosexual performances are purely apprehensive or defensive. There is room for laughter and pleasure too.

Yet although Butler acknowledges, with Lacan, that 'the masculine subject only *appears* to originate meanings' (Butler 1990: 45), she too speaks only of femininity in terms of masquerade, referring to homosexual cross-dressing as parody or performance. Because she rarely refers to the lesbian femme or the gay butch clone, she unwittingly continues the concentration on cross-dressing Doane decries.[10] Most problematic, however, given her goal of destabilizing the body as ground, is her failure to consider class and, especially, race.[11]

Focusing specifically on racial masquerade in *Black Skin, White Masks*, Fanon unhooks both blackness and whiteness from male and female bodies. Although, he says, blacks must don white masks if they are to achieve success in colonial societies, this does not guarantee authenticity or essence: 'the Negro is not, anymore than the white man' (Fanon 1967a: 231). The white masks of the book's title disguise whites as well as black. As Stephan Feuchtwang observes, in Fanon's understanding of race, skin color thus becomes a kind of 'psychic interface' with social, political, and economic consequences (Feuchtwang 1985: 458).

But the ambivalence which haunts whites as well as blacks is not equivalent. Other blacks often see through masquerades of speech, dress, and carriage adopted by passing and/or educated blacks.[12] Whites, however, tend to type all blacks as 'black', and to dismiss them as inferior by treating them as children.[13]

Bhabha continues Fanon's project of examining racial masquerades. Drawing on Lacan, he argues that the sexual fetish and the racial stereotype are similarly structured around recognition and disavowal, pleasure and anxiety. Like Fanon, he sees racial masquerades as potentially subversive. On the one hand, he says, mimicry of colonial authority exposes this authority as hollow.[14] On the other hand, 'the effect of mimicry is camouflage . . .' (Bhabha 1984: 125): 'the veil [of the Algerian woman freedom fighter] conceals bombs' (Bhabha 1986: xxiii). Thus, while the ultimate threat of masquerade may be that under the mask there is *nothing*, there is always also a fear that the costume hides *something*. In the case of the Algerian woman, different contexts produced different perceptions: Europeans saw only the veil; Algerians 'saw' the masquerade *and* the bombs.

Yet Bhabha's decision to posit racial difference as *analogous* to sexual difference makes it hard to think the two categories together and against each other. His insistence on ambivalence makes it difficult to distinguish dressing up, putting on, and stepping out. Indeed, as Robert Young says, Bhabha's work is so dense that it becomes difficult to know 'who "the colonizer," "the colonized," or "the native" actually is' (Young 1990: 151).

The uncertainty over how to interpret an ambiguous figure like the veiled Algerian woman is particularly acute. Not only does who she 'is' depend on who is looking, who she 'is' is obviously tied to a specific historical moment. The identities of the butch clone, the lesbian femme, and the passing black seem to me similarly connected to resistance and power. Yet where the Algerian woman freedom fighter relies on her veil for disguise, the clone, the femme, and the passing black use their bodies as masks, making it impossible to refer to the body as ground. The passing black, as Fanon shows, destabilizes whiteness as well as blackness. The clone and the femme upset the delicate balance of heterosexuality and gender 'truth,'[15] and offer an escape from the transvestite trap Butler and Doane confront. For the problem with looking at the drag queen, the lesbian butch, or the cultural cross-dresser,[16] is that it is all too easy to invoke a 'true' gender or racial identity under the clothes.

The butch clone's muscles and macho attire, in particular, ensure he looks 'like a man,' and a working-class man at that.[17] He is living proof that, as Lacan hints, masculinity, not just femininity, is a masquerade. Yet for those who know where and when to look, his homosexuality, seemingly so invisible, is unmistakable. Like the femme, moreover, he demonstrates that dressing up, putting on, and stepping out can be fun. Their masquerades, unlike those Doane and Riviere describe, are pleasurable, not just anxious.

No matter what figure we choose to look at, however, if we really want to question the body as base, we must acknowledge all matrices of masquerade, and study 'specific discursive form[s], in . . . particular historical conjuncture[s]' (Bhabha 1983: 204). As one contribution to this project, I offer the following 'queer' examination of Stallone and his clones' muscular macho masculinity.

THE 'MATURE' STALLONE AND THE STALLONE CLONE

Many male genre films contain homoerotic elements. But because most center on a single man or a group of men, it is relatively easy, as Steve Neale and Paul Willemen argue, to displace, diffuse, and/or deny the homoerotic overtones of male bonding.

Lock Up and *Tango and Cash* make such denial difficult. Both are far more overtly homoerotic, if also more homophobic, than the Rocky or the Rambo series, *F.I.S.T.* (Jewison, 1979), *Rhinestone* (Clark, 1984), or *Cobra* (Cosmatos, 1986). Both are in part prison films, a sub-genre where homosexuality is more openly acknowledged than in most.[18] Both also draw on the *doppelgänger* sub-genre, and therefore 'enact the shifting relationships of men to masculinity and femininity, heterosexuality and homosexuality, sadism and masochism,' in much the same ways the literary doubles Otto Rank studied do (Holmlund 1986: 33).

Most importantly, however, *Lock Up* and *Tango and Cash* feature male heroes who are *bona fide* buddies. True, Stallone sometimes had male friends in his earlier films, but these men were his helpers, never his equals, let alone his clones. *Lock Up* and *Tango and Cash*, in contrast, valorize, even glamorize, male friendships and relationships through the constant reflection of beautiful male bodies.

Lock Up tells the story of model prisoner Frank Leone's (Stallone) transfer to Gateway, a maximum security prison run by his old arch-rival, Warden Drumgoole (Donald Sutherland). The Warden is out to break Leone once and for all. The film chronicles Leone's resistance and his adoption of a young white male prisoner, First Base (Larry Romano). When First Base is murdered by the Warden's goons two-thirds of the way through the film, Leone's resolve hardens. After several spectacular torture scenes featuring a scantily clad Stallone, Leone exposes the Warden's villainy and obtains his own release.

Tango and Cash is more consistently a buddy movie. Tango (Stallone) and Cash (Kurt Russell) are rival California cops who join forces to fight a drug czar named Perret (Jack Palance). They begin to threaten his business; he, in return, has them framed and imprisoned for murder. Again we see Tango and Cash's prison tortures, then their death-defying escape, and finally their righteous retribution.

In both films masculine masquerade is doubled, for the clones masquerade as and mimic Stallone. In *Lock Up*, First Base is a younger, thinner, shorter, more naive but only slightly less muscular version of Frank Leone. Their hair color and cuts, speech patterns and movements, are identical. In *Tango and Cash*, Cash is less well dressed and more outspoken than Tango, but the two are almost equally muscular and almost equally 'bad'. The reflection of Stallone in the clones, combined with their constant framing, muscles bulging, in doors, mirrors, newspaper photos, and TV screens, leaves no doubt that these are men who are meant to be looked at, by men as much as if not more than by women. Clearly they are spectacles as well as actors.

Omnipresent two shots and frenetic cross-cutting indicate the force of Stallone and his clones' emotional bonds, even though they rarely touch. Tango and Cash, especially, look at each other long and hard and, although their looks signal competitiveness, they convey more than a little affection, admiration, and appreciation as well.[19] The shower scene in particular suggests that for these men, heterosexuality may be merely a macho pose. Here the looks are particularly 'meaningful,' the dialogue full of double entendres. Stallone's and Russell's biceps, calves, pecs, abs, and butts are displayed for their – and our – gaze as they stand naked in the prison shower. They look each other up – and down. Cash drops the soap. 'What are you doing?' Tango asks. 'Relax, soap up and don't flatter yourself, peewee,' Cash replies. Tango is nervous, but pretends he is shy: 'I don't know you that well.'[20]

In both films Stallone and his clones talk to each other a lot, in simple sentences and using one and two syllable words, of course.[21] Frequently, as in the shower scene, their teasing signals the possibility of a homosexual relationship. An example from *Lock Up*: after spraying each other with water and paint, First Base asks Leone if he is married. 'Are you proposin' to me? You're not my type,' Leone coyly replies. And how to convey in print the delight these inarticulate men take in their shared secret words – in *Lock Up*, 'DTA' ('don't trust anyone'), in *Tango and Cash*, 'FUBAR' ('fucked up beyond all recognition')? Constant explosions and grunts create a super-charged and definitely male sonic atmosphere, while shadowy blue tunnels and steamy rooms set the stage for heated half-lit passion. Not coincidentally, both films include torture by electricity. As we watch these big men twitch involuntarily, we suspect a certain orgasmic pleasure lurks alongside the obvious threat of death.

Both films, it is true, attempt to contain the homoeroticism generated by the display of male bodies and male bonding by positioning Stallone and the clones as 'family' and by designating Stallone as the more 'mature' of the two, labelling him the dad and the older brother-in-law, respectively, of First Base and Cash. Both films also portray the clones as slightly more effeminate, more naive, or more wild than Stallone. Right before he is killed, for example, First Base is made to hold a broom and sweep up. Often, as Neale and Willemen argue, the direct looks of one man at another are coded as sadistic and attributed to an enemy: both Sutherland and Palance watch Stallone on video screens, and Sutherland, his face half in shadow, often looks down on Stallone in the prison yard below. To safeguard still further Stallone's heterosexuality, in *Lock Up* he is given a girl friend, Melissa (Darlanne Fluegal); in *Tango and Cash* he ultimately gives his sister, Kiki (Teri Hatcher), not himself, to Cash. Melissa is clearly part of the 'normal' world outside the prison gates. Gateway is 'hell': the religious lyrics of the final song only underline the obvious. God would hardly approve of Tango's sister, Kiki, however: she works as an erotic dancer. We see plenty of her body, and especially, of course, of her tits and ass.

But these careful restructurings of hints of homosexuality according to binary oppositions of gender betray the nervousness which underlies masquerades of masculinity: desire between men, the overt enjoyment of another man's body and especially of his penis, must be denied. A man who is a 'real man' does not acknowledge that 'having' a penis is insufficient, that it is *not* the same thing as 'having' the phallus. Fear and narcissism thus permeate masquerades of masculinity as well as masquerades of femininity, even though the two occupy different positions *vis-à-vis* power.

Cut-aways in both these films from moments of spectacle to chase scenes and fire fights only momentarily displace the anxiety accompanying male display, an anxiety which is even more acute in *Tango and Cash* than in *Lock Up* because here Stallone is so clearly aging, and so clearly a yuppie. Unlike *Lock Up*, where Stallone always wears fewer clothes than anyone else, in *Tango and Cash* Stallone's body is relatively rarely seen. As in *Rocky IV*, where in the first part of the film Stallone was also rich and 'soft,'[22] in *Tango and Cash* costume and props (glasses, Armani suits, the *Wall Street Journal*) link masculinity with power.

As Yvonne Tasker details in her analysis of *Tango and Cash* in this volume, Stallone consciously tried to shift his image in this film – a phenomenon he continued in *Rocky V* (Avildsen, 1990) and *Oscar* (Landis, 1991). Unfortunately, his verbal reference to Rambo – 'Rambo is a pussy' – at the beginning of the film is not enough to prove his toughness or compensate for his switch of class allegiance. We want to see the body. In Stallone's case, muscles are costume enough. In clothes, and especially in business suits, he looks overdressed. His attempts at being 'classy' only demonstrate how much masculine masquerades are shaped by class expectations.[23] As one reviewer put it: 'Stallone doesn't wear suits well – he's simply too big. . . . Stallone and *Tango and Cash* only really get rolling when he strips down to his muscle-tee and beats up bad guys. This, to his credit, he does extraordinarily well' (Fiorillo 1990: 301).

But the hyper-spectacle of muscular masculinity both films offer in some ways only compounds the problem. For what's a musclebound straight guy to do when, as Lacan maintains, the very 'exaggeration of masculinity appears feminine' (Lacan 1958: 85)? Because 'having' the phallus (masculinity) and 'being' the phallus (femininity) are both performances disguising the same lack of the phallus, 'having' may even tip over into 'being.' The spectacle of Cash in full female drag on the arm of Tango's sister, herself disguised as a motorcycle-riding bull dyke, demonstrates just how tenuous appearances can be: homosexuality always lurks beside heterosexuality. Indeed Butler suggests 'the very notions of masculinity and femininity . . . [are] rooted in unresolved homosexual cathexes' (Butler 1990: 54).

But homosexuality and heterosexuality are not the only matrices which structure masculinity and femininity. In *Lock Up* and *Tango and Cash*, homoeroticism and homophobia are always threaded together with racial, class, and national stereotypes to create 'good' masculinities opposed to 'bad' masculinities. The principal characters of both films are white, opposed along ethnic rather than racial lines and, in *Lock Up*, along class lines as well. In both films Stallone plays a version of the sexy family-oriented Italian he made famous in *Rocky*. Admittedly, he insists less on his ethnicity here: hints of 'Italianness' are enough to evoke the whole package, as, for example, Leone's approving comment to his girl friend, 'Now that's Italian!', when she gives him a big kiss, or Tango's teasing of Cash with 'Ciao bella!' Loyalty to family is still a key component, however: Leone passes on to First Base the lessons he has learned in the school of hard knocks ('always be ready to move first'; 'you gotta respect something 'cuz you don't get much, and what you got you gotta protect'), and Tango jealously safeguards his sister's reputation, a losing battle to be sure. Significantly, in both films his enemies are well-to-do and northern European: the Warden Anglo-Saxon, the drug czar, Perret, French.

Lock Up is the more progressive of the two films, at least where race is concerned. Male doubles are everywhere, distinguished primarily by race and class. Sadistic poor white prisoners and staff threaten Stallone and his clone with homosexual rape and/or torture, shouting things like 'hey punk, when you gonna paint your nails and answer the name bitch?' Good blacks, on the other hand, become Stallone's allies, even part of his family. Two, Lt Meissner (John Amos) and Mr Braden (William Allen Young), are prison officials. Unlike the Warden, Meissner plays by the rules. His impartiality is evidenced by his dark sunglasses and impassive expression. Of the prisoners, Eclipse (Frank McRae) is the most important. A huge black, he is pitted against Chink Weber (Sonny Landham), the biggest and 'baddest' of the white prisoners. In many ways Eclipse is also the reincarnation of Stallone/Leone's first white adoptive father: both take him under their wings and welcome him into their garages. Stallone's initiation of First Base into the joys of dipsticks and purring engines is but another link in an Oedipal chain premised on interracial and homosexual adoptions.[24]

In *Tango and Cash*, in contrast, the only real doubles are Tango and Cash. Here 'bad' masculinities are defined through racial and/or national stereotypes. Perret's gang includes blacks, Asians, and a working-class Brit known as Ponytail (Brion James). As in *Lock Up*, references to homosexual rape abound. When Cash walks into prison, for example, someone threatens to 'tear him a new ass' and someone else promises to 'pour brown sugar into [his] hole.' Undaunted, Tango and Cash respond to these 'bad' masculinities with equally homophobic, xenophobic, and racist insults. In the prison electrocution sequence, Ponytail

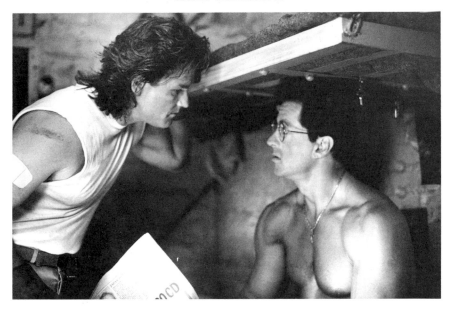

Figure 27 Sylvester Stallone and Kurt Russell in *Tango and Cash*

tries to intimidate Cash: 'You're a pretty boy, aren't you? I'm going to yank your thing out of your 'ole and tie it in a knot.' Cash explodes: 'I don't wanna be killed by this Limey immigrant jerk-off. I wanna be killed by an American . . . jerk-off.'

But Tango and Cash always prefer fighting to talking. The finale is especially spectacular, combining a dazzling display of weaponry – tanks, cars, tractors, machine guns, grenades, dynamite, and more – with a dazzling display of muscles. When the smoke clears, however, Tango, Cash, and Kiki are quite literally the only people left. No longer need we worry about the fate and status of these bulky buddies or their bodies: white masculinity and the family have triumphed with a vengeance.

CONCLUSION

The insistence in both films on the inviolability of heterosexual masculinity has a hysterical ring to it. The doubling and hyping of masculinity in these films only highlights how much masculinity, like femininity, is a multiple masquerade.

But it would be a mistake to underestimate how much and how often spectators, and performers too, see masquerade as reinforcing hegemonic power relations, precisely because masquerade suggests there may be something underneath which is 'real,' and/or 'normal.' As Lacan has shown, masquerade is inherently nostalgic, an appearance which gestures toward a lack perceived as originary. It is not coincidental, then, that Stallone's fans are so often conservatives: his mask of healthy, happy, heterosexual, white masculinity is eminently reassuring to the Right. Indeed, Stallone's reflection in and love for the Stallone clones of *Lock Up* and *Tango and Cash* may only increase this reactionary appeal. The butch clone is, after all, an ambiguous figure. Like the lesbian femme and the passing black, his identity is fluid, and the spectator in many ways holds the key which unlocks the meaning of his performance and spectacle, interpreting it variously as dressing up, as putting on, or as stepping out.

Thus, though I may talk about Stallone and the clones' masculinity and heterosexuality as masquerades, most people do not see them as such. The kind of perverse interrogation of box office blockbusters I have engaged in here has another drawback as well: there is always the risk that the specificity of homosexual pleasures will disappear within speculation about homoeroticism in what are, in this case, basically heterosexual male genre films.[25] This risk increases astronomically, it seems to me, if as critics we fail to notice or downplay the films' homophobia. It's like thinking *Soul Man* (Steve Miner, 1986), where a white man masquerades as black to beat Harvard Law School's affirmative action quotas, could ever tell us the whole truth about race and racism.

Still, I think, 'queer' analyses like this one are useful, because as Riviere hints, with the concept of masquerade we do not have to divorce critique from identification: dressing up, putting on, and stepping out are all possibilities. And since, in Butler's words, 'appearances become more suspect all the time' (Butler 1990: 47), the question of what, if anything, masquerade masks need not produce answers which are mutually exclusive. What are decisive, as Fanon and Bhabha insist, are the concrete effects masquerades have.

As film critics, we may want to look with particular attention at a new sub-genre of action adventure films I call the 'buddy body movie.' Popularized in the 1980s, this sub-genre includes not just *Lock Up* and *Tango and Cash* but also the *Beverly Hills Cop* (Brest, 1984, and Donner, 1989), *Lethal Weapon* (Donner, 1987 and 1989) and *Die Hard* (McTiernan, 1988, and Harlin, 1990) films, *Twins* (Reitman, 1988), *Internal Affairs* (Figgis, 1990) and more – the list grows longer every day. All combine male action with male spectacle, and foreground matrices of sexuality, class, and race in ways the male genre films Neale and Willemen studied do not.

After all, admitting that masculinity is a multiple masquerade 'does not constitute a denial of its forcefulness, its effectivity' (Doane 1988: 45). Masculinity may be only a fantasy, but as the success of Sylvester Stallone's films, including their invocation by right-wing politicians like

Reagan and Bush, so amply demonstrates, masquerades of masculinity are eminently popular, and undeniably potent.

NOTES

Thanks to Dale Watermulder and Jon Jonakin for their help.

1 Eugenie Lemoine-Luccioni is more snide. She says, 'if the penis were the phallus, men would have no need of feathers or ties or medals' (Lemoine-Luccioni 1983: 34).
2 See also Doane (1988: 47).
3 Marjorie Garber adopts a similar strategy when she argues that both sexes experience 'fetish envy.' Garber does not consider racial fetishes and masquerades in her discussion of 'the triangulated relationship between Michael Jackson, Diana Ross and Madonna,' however, an oversight I find troubling. See Garber (1990: 55).
4 The expression is Chandra Mohanty's, in an article which eloquently denounces the silencing of race in academic analyses. See Mohanty (1990: 180).
5 Butler makes much the same argument, though she skips over Riviere's analyses of gay men. See Butler (1990: 50–4).
6 Riviere's assessment neatly sidesteps class, age, race, and region: the black man becomes merely 'the man,' the wealthy Southern woman just 'the woman' (Riviere 1929: 37–8). Riviere says nothing about her client's class-based masquerade as a servant or her imaginary transformation of herself from child to adult, and fails to comment on her client's desire for a black man.
   A second case revolves around class. Here Riviere describes an acquaintance, a 'capable' 50-year-old housewife, who habitually 'act[s] a part' with workmen, the butcher, and the baker, making herself out to be an 'uneducated, foolish and bewildered woman' while 'rul[ing them] in reality with a rod of iron' (Riviere 1929: 39). Yet in her analysis Riviere again reduces all difference to gender difference: working-class men become merely 'potentially hostile father figures' (Riviere: 39). See further Holmlund (1989: 109–10) and Doane (1988: 48.)
7 See Lacan (1958: 85) and Butler (1990: 49).
8 See Garber (1990: 54) for a similar observation.
9 See further Holmlund (1991) and Straayer (1990: 51).
10 Butler mentions the femme and the clone only three times. See Butler (1990: 51, 122, and 123).
11 Except for nods in the introduction and conclusion to the need to 'describe their convergencies within the social field,' these matrices of masquerade disappear entirely (Butler 1990: 13; see also 145).
12 See Fanon (1967b: 17–27), especially 17–18.
13 In *Black Skin, White Masks* Fanon angrily notes that 'a white man addressing a Negro behaves exactly like an adult with a child and starts smirking, whispering, patronizing, cozening' (Fanon 1967a: 31). See also Fanon (1967b: 102).
14 See Bhabha (1984: 129, 131).
15 On the femme, see Holmlund (1991).
16 On cultural cross-dressing see, for example, Ching-Liang Low 1989 and Silverman 1989.

17 See Humphries (1985: 77–8).

18 Yvonne Tasker argues rightly, however, that prison films associate homosexuality with punishment: heterosexuality is not an option.

19 Steve Neale, in contrast, maintains that 'the male body cannot be marked explicitly as the erotic object of another male look: that look must be motivated in some other way, its erotic component repressed. . . . [T]he male body must be disqualified, so to speak, as an object of erotic contemplation and desire' (Neale 1983: 8). Willemen, too, sees Mann's Westerns as permeated by 'fundamentally homosexual voyeurism (almost always repressed)' (Willemen 1981: 16). See also Neale (1980) and Smith (1989).

20 Penis jokes like this one are found throughout 1970s and 1980s Hollywood films. As is the case in *Tango and Cash*, however, the penis itself is rarely seen because, as Peter Lehman notes, 'the awe we attribute to the striking visibility of the penis is best served by keeping it covered up. . . . [It] may, much of the time, be unconscious homoeroticism.'

21 Their chatter distinguishes them from the silent, solitary hunks Neale studied. See Neale (1983: 7).

22 For a detailed discussion of aging, class, and masculinity in *Rocky IV* see Holmlund (1990: 88–91).

23 In a study of *Rocky II*, Valerie Walkerdine stresses that 'masculinity is always lived as class specific, in relation to the body and the mental/manual division of labour' (Walkerdine 1986: 198). Stallone's scrappy macho masculinity is identifiably working-class: for his characters, as for many of his fans, she says, fighting represents a 'bid for mastery, a struggle to conquer the conditions of oppression, which remain as terror' (Walkerdine 1986: 177).

24 The extent to which this Oedipal chain is forged in a homoerotic fire is more than usually obvious in *Lock Up*, since Leone and First Base function both as father and son and as butch clone. As Butler says, 'the resolution of the Oedipal complex affects gender identification through not only the incest taboo, but, prior to that, the taboo against homosexuality. The result is that one identifies with the same-sexed object of love, thereby internalizing both the aim and object of the homosexual cathexis' (Butler 1990: 63).

25 On the overuse of the term 'homosexual' in film studies, see further Green (1984: 47): 'contemporary concerns should require us to differentiate this [homosocial bonding] from some kind of gay eroticism, as I imagine many gay men will find little interest in what are manifestly heterosexual phantasies about heterosexual men (together).'

BIBLIOGRAPHY

Bhabha, H. (1983a) 'Difference, Discrimination, and the Discourse of Colonialism' in F. Barker et al. (eds) *The Politics of Theory*, Colchester: University of Essex.

_____ (1983b) 'The Other Question,' *Screen* 24, 6: 18–35.

_____ (1984) 'Of Mimicry and Man: the Ambivalence of Colonial Discourse,' *October* 28: 125–33.

_____ (1986) 'Foreword: Remembering Fanon,' in F. Fanon *Black Skin, White Masks*, London: Pluto Press.

Butler, J. (1990) *Gender Trouble*, London: Routledge.

Ching-Liang Low, G. (1989) 'White Skins/Black Masks: the Pleasures and Politics of Imperialism,' *New Formations* 9: 83–104.

Doane, M. (1982) 'Film and the Masquerade: Theorising the Female Spectator,' *Screen* 23, 3–4: 74–87.

–––––– (1988) 'Masquerade Reconsidered: Further Thoughts on the Female Spectator,' *Discourse* 11, 1: 42–53.

Fanon, F. (1952; rpt 1967a) *Black Skin, White Masks*, New York: Grove Press.

–––––– (1964: rpt 1967b) *Toward the African Revolution*, New York: Monthly Review Press.

Feuchtwang, S. (1985) 'Fanon's Politics of Culture: the Colonial Situation and its Extension,' *Economy and Society* 14, 4: 450–73.

Fiorillo, C. M. (1990) '*Tango and Cash*,' *Films in Review* 41: 301–2.

Garber, M. (1990) 'Fetish Envy,' *October* 54: 45–56.

Green, I. (1984) 'Malefunction: a Contribution to the Debate on Masculinity in the Cinema,' *Screen* 25. 4–5: 36–49.

Heath, S. (1986) 'John Riviere and the Masquerade,' in V. Burgin, Donald, J., and Kaplan, C. (eds) *Formations of Fantasy*, London: Routledge.

Holmlund, C. (1986) 'Sexuality and Power in Male Doppelgänger Cinema: the Case of Clint Eastwood's *Tightrope*,' *Cinema Journal* 26, 1: 31–42.

–––––– (1989) 'I Love Luce: the Lesbian, Mimesis and Masquerade in Irigaray, Freud, and Mainstream Film,' *New Formations* 9: 105–23.

–––––– (1990) 'New Cold War Sequels and Remakes: *Down and Out in Beverly Hills, Rocky IV, Aliens*,' *Jump Cut* 35: 85–96.

–––––– (1991) 'When Is a Lesbian Not a Lesbian? the Lesbian Continuum and the Mainstream Femme Film,' *Camera Obscura* 25–6: 96–119.

Humphries, M. (1985) 'Gay Machismo,' in Metcalf and Humphries (eds) *The Sexuality of Men*, London: Pluto Press.

Lacan, J. (1958) 'The Meaning of the Phallus,' trans. J. Rose, in J. Mitchell and J. Rose (eds) (1982) *Feminine Sexuality*, New York: Norton.

–––––– (1966) 'Guiding Remarks for a Congress on Feminine Sexuality,' trans. J. Rose, in J. Mitchell and J. Rose (eds) (1982) *Feminine Sexuality*, New York: Norton.

Lehman, P. (1991) 'Penis-Size Jokes and Their Relation to Hollywood's Unconscious' in A. Horton (ed.) *Comedy/Cinema/Theory*, Berkeley: University of California Press.

Lemoine-Luccioni, E. (1983) *La Robe: Essai Psychanalytique sur le Vetement*, Paris: Editions du Seuil.

Mohanty, C. (1990) 'On Race and Voice: Challenges for Liberal Education in the 1990s,' *Cultural Critique* 14: 179–208.

Neale, S. (1980) *Genre*, London: British Film Institute.

–––––– (1983) 'Masculinity as Spectacle,' *Screen* 24, 6: 2–16.

Riviere, J. (1929) 'Womanliness and the Masquerade' in V. Burgin, Donald, J., and Kaplan, C. (eds) (1986) *Formations of Fantasy*, London: Routledge.

Silverman, K. (1989) 'White Skin, Brown Masks: the Double Mimesis, or With Lawrence in Arabia,' *differences* 1, 3: 3–54.

Smith, P. (1989) 'Action Movie Hysteria, or Eastwood Bound,' *differences* 1, 3: 88–107.

Stoller, R. (1985) *Observing the Erotic Imagination*, New Haven, CT: Yale University Press.

Straayer, C. (1990) 'The Hypothetical Lesbian Heroine,' *Jump Cut* 35: 50–8.

Walkerdine, V. (1986) 'Video Replay: Families, Films and Fantasy,' in V. Burgin, Donald, J., and Kaplan, C. (eds) *Formations of Fantasy*, London: Routledge.

Willemen, P. (1981) 'Anthony Mann: Looking at the Male,' *Framework* 15–17: 16–20.
Young, R. (1990) *White Mythologies*, London: Routledge.

12

DUMB MOVIES FOR DUMB PEOPLE

Masculinity, the body, and the voice in contemporary action cinema

Yvonne Tasker

The status of masculinity within Hollywood's representational system is explored here through an analysis of four films and their stars: Bruce Willis in *Die Hard* (1988) and *Die Hard 2* (1990), Sylvester Stallone in *Lock Up* (1989), Stallone and Kurt Russell in *Tango and Cash* (1989). These films and stars exemplify, in different ways, a tendency of the Hollywood action cinema toward the construction of the male body as spectacle, together with an awareness of masculinity as performance. Also evident in these films is the continuation and amplification of an established tradition of the Hollywood cinema – play upon images of power and powerlessness at the center of which is the male hero.

Within this structure suffering – torture, in particular – operates as both a set of narrative hurdles to be overcome, tests that the hero must survive, and as a set of aestheticized images to be lovingly dwelt on. Whilst numerous studies have commented on the construction of woman as victim within the American cinema, sometimes speculating on the masochistic pleasures this may offer to female viewers, few studies seem to comment in any depth on the figure of the male hero in this context, pursued and punished as he so often is. It is in thinking about such questions that a consideration of the action film may also allow a wider discussion of masculinity and sexuality within the Hollywood cinema, particularly in thinking through the significance of what critics have increasingly come to see as its performative status.

Indeed talking about men in the Hollywood cinema as 'performing the masculine' seems to be *de rigueur* these days, a critical vogue that is both fruitful and intensely problematic. In quite another context, that of commenting on the self-representations of academic Frank Lentricchia, Lee Edelman poses a question: 'might it not be useful,' he asks, 'to inquire just what, if anything, is getting subverted here or to ask how the miming of heterosexual privilege by a heterosexual male differs from the persistently oppressive enactment of that privilege in the culture at large?' (Boone and Cadden 1990: 44). Rather arch this, but Edelman's impatience, his irritation with a criticism vaguely based in the terms of supposedly self-reflexive 'performance,' does indicate the importance of, if not refusing an optimistic address to the cinema, then retaining an awareness of the complexities of representations, of their operation within wider systems than the cinematic. I'm not so bold as to seek for subversion here, being in any case unsure as to what it might look like. Paradox and contradiction though, with which Hollywood has always been replete, do come into the equation.

PERFORMING MASCULINITY

That masculinity can be seen as performative, as insistently denaturalized, has been something of a touchstone in recent discussions of the Hollywood cinema. A variety of formulations of postmodernism and postmodernity have been invoked in this critical development. Suspicious critics have tended to perceive postmodernism and its associated buzzwords as providing a depoliticized catch-all framework for cultural analysis. This is an important qualification given the tendency, sometimes manifest in models constructed within the framework of postmodernism, to forget about the operations of power.

It does seem important to ask what is the status of this performativity, a quality which some are keen to embrace and others to refute. How would we account, for example, for the undoubtable marketability of the male body in the 1980s? One context is offered by the changing definitions, within a shifting economy, of the roles that men and women have been called upon to perform, particularly in that crucial arena of gender definition, the world of work.

Richard Dyer notes the tendency of male stars such as Clint Eastwood and Harrison Ford 'either to give their films a send-up or tongue-in-cheek flavour . . . or else a hard, desolate, alienated quality.' Dyer speculates that in a world 'of microchips and a large scale growth (in the USA) of women in traditionally male occupations' the adoption of such tones suggests that the 'values of masculine physicality are harder to maintain straightfacedly and unproblematically' (Dyer 1987: 12).[1]

Scott Benjamin King's analysis of the American cop show *Miami Vice*, a series which has attracted much critical attention and is perhaps the original 'Armani with a badge,' echoes Dyer's comments on the world of work. King offers a critique of those who understood the stylized visual beauty of the show and of its male protagonists, via postmodernism, as a narrative emptiness, seeing such perspectives as, at worst, a rather alarmingly literal interpretation of the 'end of narrative.' Instead of seeing the show as pure spectacle, as a refusal of narrative, King points out that *Vice* offered the repeated re-enactment of narratives of failure, the significance of which he locates within the context of contemporary articulations of masculinity. A reorientation of the relationship between men, masculinity, and consumption in the West necessarily affects those definitions of male identity achieved through production. King surmises that 'if postmodernism is a crisis of the excess of consumption, and, further, a crisis related to shifting definitions of masculinity, it is also a crisis in the concept of work' (King 1990: 286). In particular King signals the importance, in the construction of Sonny Crockett's character, of failure within the realm of work. Crockett's work consists of getting the bad guys, work that he is unable to perform effectively, work that is carried out in a context over which he has no control. It is such a lack of control that is in turn crucial to the scenario of the two *Die Hard* films, where the hero finds himself in impossible situations controlled by incompetent bureaucracies.

Barbara Creed situates the pin-up muscleman star within the critical frameworks of postmodernism in her comments on the tendency of images and texts in the 1980s to 'play with the notion of manhood.' Creed suggests that Stallone and Schwarzenegger, the muscular stars of the decade, could only be described as 'performing the masculine.'

> Both actors often resemble an anthropomorphised phallus, a phallus with muscles, if you like . . . They are simulacra of an exaggerated masculinity, the original completely lost to sight, a casualty of the failure of the paternal signifier and the current crisis in master narratives.
>
> (Creed 1987: 65)

The 'current crisis in master narratives' is seen by Creed not as the inability to tell a good story, but in terms of the failings of the key terms around which stories are constructed, terms which include a coherent white male heterosexuality along with the rationality and binary structures it is often taken to propose. For Creed it is the sheer physical excess of the muscular stars that indicates the performative status of the masculinity they enact, an excess quite different, indeed rather more obvious, to the qualities of tone, say a sense of parody or of alienation, that Dyer refers to in passing.

Muscles raise a familiar paradox over the coming together of naturalness and performance which Dyer has characterized in terms of the way in which muscles can function as both a naturalization of 'male power and domination' and as evidence precisely of the labor that has gone into that effect (Dyer 1982: 71). The 'strain' that Dyer identifies in the male pin-up stems from this paradox, from the self-conscious performance of qualities assumed to be natural. Dyer warns us against the dangers of 'causal logic,' the temptation to read images of men in terms

232

only of male power. The performance of a muscular masculinity within the cinema draws attention to both the restraint and the excess involved in 'being a man,' the work put into the male body and the poses that it strikes. But if the cinematic hero is in the business of performing manliness not only at the level of physique, what is the significance of this performance, and what is the nature of the charade that he is acting out? The movies considered here insistently work through a set of motifs related to sexuality and authority, motifs which are mapped on to both narrative structure and the body of the male hero. Linking the questions of the male hero's effectivity at work, the embodiment of an excessive physical performance and an anxious narrative of male sexuality, is the crisis of the paternal signifier to which Creed refers.

'RAMBO IS A PUSSY': STARS AND MASCULINITY

The phenomenon of stardom provides a useful starting point for thinking about the performative aspects of masculinity in the cinema, perhaps because spectacle, performance, and acting all function as both constitutive components of stardom and significant terms in those writings concerned with the sexual politics of representation. Within the action cinema the figure of the star as hero, larger than life in his physical abilities and pin-up good looks, operates as a key aspect of the more general visual excess that this particular form of Hollywood production offers to its audience. Along with the visual pyrotechnics, the military array of weaponry and hardware, the arch-villains and the staggering obstacles the hero must overcome, the overblown budgets, the expansive landscapes against which the drama is acted out, and the equally expansive soundtracks, is the body of the star as hero, characteristically functioning as spectacle.[2]

Richard Dyer locates the 'central paradox' of stardom as the instability of 'the whole phenomenon' which is 'never at a point of rest or equilibrium, constantly lurching from one formulation of what being human is to another' (Dyer 1987: 18). Particular star images are no more stable than the phenomenon as a whole. Embracing contradictory elements and constantly shifting the ground, star images present themselves as composed of so many layers, as so many slippages. Performances in films, gossip in newspapers and magazines, publicity that is both sought and unlooked for: all these elements work to constantly displace and reconfirm our understanding in an endlessly played out revelation of 'the truth behind the image.'

In this sense the territory of the star image is also the territory of identity, the process of the forging and reforging of ways of 'being human' in which a point of certainty is never ultimately arrived at. Inevitably the ongoing formulation and reformulation of ways of 'being a man' constitutes an important part of this process. Paradoxically this process sits alongside the absolute certainty with which we often feel able to identify a particular type and to speak about what it may mean – in the context of debates around masculinity John Wayne provides perhaps the most longstanding and oft-cited example, a figure whose meaning seems absolutely fixed.

The two Stallone pictures considered here are more than exemplary since, while any film redefines and works over star images, these movies set out, more or less explicitly, to rewrite their hero/star. Both *Tango and Cash* and *Lock Up* operate in part as attempts to shift the grounding of Sylvester Stallone's star image. The star's publicity began to use new strategies after a series of dents to his public persona: *Rambo III* (1988), something of a disaster with the 'untimely' Russian withdrawal from Afghanistan where the film was set, the break-up of his marriage to Brigitte Nielsen, and a wave of bad publicity about being a wimp over his failure to turn up at Cannes, allegedly through fear of becoming a target for terrorism, as well as the accusations that Stallone dodged the draft during the Vietnam War. With a spectacular economy Stallone's image absorbed the wimp tag, using the associations to distance the star from his Rambo persona and present him as a softer, more likeable guy both in 'real life' and his films. *Lock Up* was to be an 'action picture with heart,' something it was felt *Rambo III* hadn't been, whilst *Tango and Cash* was to emphasize a more sophisticated Stallone. His character, Ray Tango, wears suits and spectacles, deals in stocks and early on sets out the terms of a new image by delivering the joke line 'Rambo is a pussy.'

An attempted redefinition of Stallone's star image in these films is conducted through both the body and the voice. A shift away from the physical, the body as the central component of Stallone's image, is also a move into the verbal and this emphasis, basically the shock value of the fact that the hulk could talk, was echoed and exploited in the surrounding publicity. An *American Film* feature sets about this sort of renegotiation, suggesting that although 'you think of Stallone as a heavyweight, up close he appeared more of a middleweight, with quick moves and a light, almost spritely grace.' We also learn that for the interview Stallone 'spoke quickly,' that he wore glasses, was 'well-tailored, well-barbered and very smooth of face,' and that his voice 'was a little higher pitched than usually heard in his movies.' The smaller build, the clothed body, the higher pitched voice – all these aspects of Stallone's dress, speech, body, and his new movies are used in this feature-interview in order to distance the star from the macho roles and physical display which made him famous. That these marks of a new image are distinctly feminizing provides a significant gloss on how to sell a male star as something other than a hunk/hulk. With more or less degrees of cynicism and humor, magazine features laid the pitch of a new sensitive Stallone who appeared as an art collector and as an artist, exhibiting and selling his paintings. Within the terms of pop discussions of masculinity at the time the shift can be expressed as one from Neanderthal man to New man.

Tango and Cash sets out to be humorous, taking swipes at Stallone's he-man image within a buddy movie format. The film can work with such a redefinition of Stallone's seemingly well-established strong silent type persona, partly because of the presence of Kurt Russell, and also because of its comic tone. *Tango and Cash* plays off two male types in its buddy pairing from the 'bad cop, worse cop' scene which serves partly to tell us that, despite the glasses, Tango is no softy, to the boldly (or crudely, depending on your point of view) drawn contrast between the two men's styles. Russell plays out a well-established persona, the macho slob sent up in Carpenter's *Big Trouble in Little China* (1986), worshipped in *Backdraft* (1991). An extraordinary but regular guy, Russell retains a tough guy aura whilst exuding those qualities that pass for normality. The opening sequences of *Tango and Cash* are concerned to establish the differences between the two cop heroes – their offices, guns, clothes, appearance, eating habits, and social graces. Both Ray Tango and Gabriel Cash are media stars, cops who get very public results and who, whilst they have never met, maintain a rivalry over their respective press coverage. Cash dismisses Tango, whose picture is featured in the newspaper, as 'Armani with a badge,' and Tango's captain paraphrases the press coverage as 'Down Town Clown versus Beverly Hills Wop,' which about sums it up.

As the film progresses Tango and Cash move from rivalry to friendship, partly drawn together by the plot to frame them, and partly through the character of Kiki/Katherine, Tango's sister. They survive the ordeal of prison together, escape together, and proceed to unmask the conspiracy of drug dealers orchestrated by arch-villain Perret. From the separate press photos we see at the beginning of the film they progress to the final newspaper image, a take-off of *Desperately Seeking Susan*, with the two clasping raised hands. By the end of the film they are finishing each other's sentences. Russell's presence allows for repartee between the two tough guys, swapping jokes in the shower and so on. Giving Stallone a chance to talk and dress up, it is Russell who gets his shirt off within the first few minutes of the film. And it is also Kurt Russell who ends up in female drag, posing as the butch 'property' of Tango's sister in order to make a getaway from the club where she is a dancer. Because this is a comic film and there is thus an implicit promise that nothing too 'dreadful' is going to happen, there is a space for male and female drag and for jokes about the male image and sexuality which are not permissible within the earnest prison drama of *Lock Up*. Playing upon notions of dressing up and acting out different star images, Tango and Cash are offered as good to look at, 'two of the department's most highly decorated officers.'

MEN WITHOUT WOMEN: *LOCK UP*

Of course 'men without women' is somewhat misleading since there is a woman in *Lock Up* – there is a woman in all four films, a figure who seems to be necessary even if she has little to say or do. Anxieties to do with difference and sexuality increasingly seem to be worked out over the body of the male hero – an economy in which the woman has little space or function. In *Die Hard 2* Holly McClane (Bonnie Bedelia) is literally suspended in the air until the final minutes of the film, trapped in a stranded plane which circles the airport where the action takes place. If we are seeing the performance of masculinity in these films, the action cinema for the most part prefers all-male environments as the stage for such a performance, arenas such as sport, prison, and the world of work, including the military and the police force. The family is generally avoided, only rarely occupying much screen time.

Lock Up works through some of the most privileged sites for the performance of masculinity, sites which are also charged with homo-eroticism. The opening sequence maps out these sites. We see Stallone as Frank Leone at home, a popular local figure with a loving girl friend, Melissa. Light in tone, the opening sequences joke with images of Leone going 'to work,' his friendly repartee with the prison guard at Norwood playing off what we already know from the film's publicity – that his role in the film is that of a convict rather than a prison guard. The opening credits offer us both Leone's past and his present as he cleans up old framed photographs which offer a nostalgic history of his place within male arenas – messing around with cars, playing football, drinking beer, father and son poses. Through these pictures we see Leone growing up as a regular guy. The activities imaged here are all reprised, in distorted form, on the inside.

Lock Up sets out to dramatize brutality and the conflict between desire and the law. Leone, a model prisoner, is abruptly transferred from the relatively open regime of Norwood to the monstrous Gateway prison run by Warden Drumgoole (Donald Sutherland), an old adversary. Drumgoole declares that 'You have no rights unless I give them to you. You feel no pleasure unless I tell you you can.' Defining hard time as 'hell' he promises Leone the 'guided tour.' A demanding and irrational father, Drumgoole asserts his complete control over the situation. The narrative from this point consists of Drumgoole's attempts to push Leone to the edge, looking for a violation that will keep him in prison, as state (and as Drumgoole's) property. Much of the film consists of outlining

236

Figure 28 Bruce Willis in *Die Hard*

Leone's physical and psychological torture, his struggle against this regime and the rules of prison life. One familiar cinematic definition of masculinity constructs restraint, a control over the emotions, as providing a protective performance. Such a pattern quickly becomes apparent in *Lock Up* in which the rules of prison life involve not betraying emotion, looking away – refusing, for the sake of survival, the challenge that a look proposes.

If anxieties to do with sexuality and difference are increasingly worked out over the male body and its commodification as spectacle, then there seem to be two dominant strategies in the action cinema. Resorting either to images of physical torture and suffering or to comedy, the body of the hero, his excessive 'masculinity,' is subjected to humiliation and mockery at some level. In this sense action movies which echo with straightfaced sincerity and those which resort to comedy may well be operating on similar terrain. *Tango and Cash* and the two *Die Hard* films incorporate comedy, as do action films such as *Lethal Weapon* (1987) and its sequel or those in which Arnold Schwarzenegger dispenses his notorious one-liners. *Lock Up*, by way of contrast, relentlessly stresses the hero's suffering, amplifying a tendency evident in many of Stallone's films.

Within the walls of Gateway the sequences which opened the film and which defined Leone's 'normality' are grotesquely reprised. A football game played with the neighborhood kids becomes the vicious game in the prison yard, not a game but a lesson. Leone's work as a car mechanic, signaled both in the photos and in the garage location in which he cleans them, is paraphrased in the cons' loving restoration and the warden's destruction of an old Mustang. It is not the gruesome spell in solitary that finally drives Leone into an escape attempt, but the threats to those he loves. In Gateway the role of Melissa is taken up by the character of First Base – so named because of his naivety in relation to the prison system, but not without a sexualized overlay. Indeed given the scenario – pin-up bodybuilder type in jail – it's hardly surprising that *Lock Up* draws heavily on homoeroticism. Yet in the action movie the threat of prison is, more or less explicitly, the threat of a homosexuality expressed in terms of violence, rather than the tenderness seen in Leone's friendship with First Base. Spotting a sign of weakness, Drumgoole attempts to use this affection, employing a group of convicts to kill First Base. The scene for this drama is the gym where First Base has his chest crushed by a set of weights. The threatening aspects of these masculine arenas – the football field, the gym – are brought out. With First Base dead, Melissa resumes her role as threatened object. Whilst the film borrows from homoeroticism, delighting in lingering shots of the star's body, physical contact is something else, and Leone can only bring himself to walk around First Base's dead body, reaching out to touch him and pulling away.

Emphasizing the visual at the expense of dialogue – the body of the hero and the prison environment rendered in dramatic lighting, bright and artificial or filtering through from the world outside, with rapid editing, extreme close-ups, and long lingering shots – creates a space in which to enact an intensified emotional drama. One reviewer smirked over Stallone's 'fatal fondess for naff montage,' referring to the central section in which the cons fix up an old motor car, and the scene in which it is destroyed, both of which are rendered through music and montage. It is only within the montage that Leone and First Base get to touch each other, playing games and spraying each other with water as they work together. One wonders, however, what there is to say within this situation, and also what is unsayable.

PROBLEMS OF PLACE: *DIE HARD*

The primacy of the body and of the voice, and the different masculine identities they propose, are played off against each other in these four films. In conceptualizing the relationship between masculinity and power the ability to speak is fundamental. Securing a position to speak from is crucial in order to invest the voice with authority. It is in part the search for such a position, one that John McClane ultimately usurps, that is enacted in both *Die Hard* and *Die Hard 2*.

In the action cinema struggles over position and authority, military rank for example, serve metaphorically as a space for the problematics of class. Such an articulation is reasserted and modified through the body of the hero, a uniform which may protect him. In this sense the body of the hero, produced as spectacle, is invested with potent signifiers of class. Commenting on Stallone's *Rocky* cycle of films, Valerie Walkerdine speaks of boxing as turning 'oppression into a struggle to master it, seen as spectacle' (Burgin et al. 1986: 172). This production of both struggle and labor as spectacle is central to the articulation of a class-based definition of masculinity in the action cinema. If muscles are signifiers of both struggle and traditional forms of male labor, then for many critics the muscles of male stars seem repulsive and ridiculous precisely because they seem to be dysfunctional, 'nothing more' than decoration, a distinctly unmanly designation. The body of the hero may seem dysfunctional, given a decline in the traditional forms of labor that he is called on to perform, but also essential in a last stand, operating as both affirmation and decoration. A paradox is played out through the figure of the powerful hero who operates in a situation beyond his control, in which he is in many senses powerless.

A rather different set of negotiations is at work over Bruce Willis's star image in *Die Hard*, a film which capitalizes on the wise-cracking persona derived from his role in the hit TV series *Moonlighting*. This comedy/drama/detective series centered on the Blue Moon detective agency, though little in the way of detection ever happened, and the action consisted mostly of verbal confrontations between Willis and Cybill Shepherd in a variety of guises. Whilst *Die Hard* gives us Bruce Willis as action hero pin-up, his persona is very much defined through the voice, more wise-guy than tough-guy. Willis scored a huge success, for example, as the voice of baby Mikey in *Look Who's Talking* (1989). Indeed the particular type of masculine identity that Willis enacts as John McClane in these films has something childlike about it, a trait shared with his role in *Moonlighting*. A perpetual adolescent, even if a knowing one, there is a sense in which he seems to be playing games (cops and robbers, cowboys and Indians). *Die Hard* has Willis/McClane cracking jokes to himself along with a facial expression which carries a sense of surprise and confusion that these explosive events are happening to him.

For much of the film he communicates with both the 'terrorists' and the world outside through a radio taken off one of the bodies. Not wishing to reveal his name over the air, he is asked to choose an identity for himself. The chief 'terrorist,' Hans Gruber (Alan Rickman), taunts McClane in an attempt to discover his identity – 'Just another American who saw too many movies as a child. An orphan of a bankrupt culture who thinks he's John Wayne, Rambo, Marshall Dillon?' – before finally settling on a contemptuous 'Mr Cowboy.' Searching for an appropriate reference point, and refusing those that are offered to him, McClane styles himself as Roy Rogers, the singing cowboy. McClane acts out this role and keeps up a running commentary at the same time – a variety of self-aware performance which fits well with Willis's image, his self-mocking macho bravado.

It is perhaps the failure of work, the lack of effectivity with which his efforts are greeted that, as much as anything, allows an understanding of the cynical vision of the populist hero that emerged in the 1960s and 1970s and which is crucial to the characterization of John McClane in the two *Die Hard* films. This characterization is marked by both the hero's frustration and his ultimate triumph. In *Die Hard* John McClane is a New York cop in Los Angeles and, while he has transferred to the LAPD for *Die Hard 2*, the drama is enacted in Washington. In both cases he has no official place, as a stream of officials and bureaucrats insist on pointing out.

The narrative of *Die Hard* operates around the terms of performance with a miscrecognition at its heart. The film centers on the Nakatomi Corporation's building in Los Angeles which is taken over by a group of assorted European 'terrorists.' McClane happens to be in the building attempting a reconciliation with his wife, Holly, who is Nakatomi's number two executive. McClane's interventions are unwelcome not only to the 'terrorists' but to the Los Angeles police and the FBI gathered outside. The terrorists' entire plan revolves around their faith in the FBI machine. Sticking to a well-worn operational routine for dealing with a hostage situation, the FBI cut all power to the building, thus breaking the final time-lock on the company safe which the gang can't crack from within. The FBI, assuming the gang are terrorists, act according to the book and in the process play their part in the heist. Both groups attempt a double-cross, and the lone cop hero is stranded in the middle. Such a structure is also used in McTiernan's earlier film *Predator* (1987) in which Schwarzenegger's crack military squad, thinking they're being tracked by enemy agents as they plough through an unspecified jungle location, act accordingly. Not realizing that they are in a science-fiction movie and that what's killing them off is a chameleon-like monster, they are unable to take effective action.

Die Hard 2, set in Dulles International Airport, continues the double bluff used by its predecessor, so that the crack military team brought in to deal with the evolving terrorist crisis are themselves in on the caper. The plot centers on the attempts of a military group led by Col. Stewart to prevent the film's Noriega figure from being put on trial in the United States. Once more bureaucracy seems to present insurmountable obstacles for the hero. The airport police and authorities exclude him from their discussions; having him removed from the center of operations by security guards, they effectively attempt to prevent him from being heroic. McClane needs the help of the janitor, located in a private subterranean realm below the airport itself, to save the day. After his exploits at Nakatomi McClane is now a media star, as is his opponent Col. Stewart, and he is told not to 'believe his own press,' articulating a suspicion that McClane is acting up to a fabricated image of himself as hero. In a further layer of complexity the head of the anti-terrorist unit, Major Grant (John Amos), initially gains McClane's trust precisely by playing the anti-bureaucracy card so effectively as a cover, presenting himself as a no-nonsense soldier. McClane himself uses the jargon in order to fingerprint a corpse, telling the bemused orderlies that he's 'Got a new SOP for DOA's from the FAA.'

By and large the hero of the recent action cinema is not an emissary of the State or, if he is, the State is engaged in a double-cross, as in *Rambo* (1985). The hero may be a policeman or a soldier but he more often than not acts unofficially, against the rules and often in a reactive way, responding to attacks rather than initiating them. The hero recognizes that he is, as Rambo puts it, 'expendable.' Representatives of the State utter myriad variants on the line, 'this mission never existed.' In the *Die Hard* films McClane, like so many action heroes, opposes himself to authorities that are both bureaucratic and duplicitous.

The body of the hero, though it may be damaged, represents almost the last certain territory of the action narrative. In hits like *Robocop* (1987) and *Total Recall* (1989) neither the body nor the mind is certain, both being subject to State control within a science-fiction dystopia. There is a moment in *Total Recall* when Schwarzenegger's character is asked to step back and consider his position – is he an intergalactic spy caught up in an intergalactic conspiracy as he claims, or is he just an ordinary manual laborer with paranoid delusions as they claim? The moment is funny partly because we don't know very certainly as viewers ourselves, though we can guess what Arnie's reaction is likely to be, but also because as a star and as a character within the film Schwarzenegger inhabits both positions – an extraordinary ordinary guy caught up in a nightmare narrative.

Similar problems of identity afflict Murphy/Robocop in Verhoeven's earlier film. Such images draw on the generic currency of science fiction, and whilst the films considered here emerge from the tradition of the war film and the political thriller, they are similarly conspiratorial. When all else fails, the body of the hero, and not his voice, his capacity to make a rational argument, is the place of last resort. That the body of the hero is the sole narrative space that is safe, that even this space is constantly under attack, is a theme repeatedly returned to within the action cinema.

PERFORMANCE, IDENTITY, AND THE CINEMATIC:
SOME CONCLUSIONS

The action cinema is often seen as the most 'Neanderthal,' the most irredeemably macho of Hollywood products. I've tried to argue that the films considered here work out a series of problematics to do with class and with sexuality, and that this is situated within a cultural context in which masculinity has been, to an extent, denaturalized. The psychoanalytic notion of homeovestism, defined as 'a perverse behaviour involving wearing clothes of the same sex,' is useful in this respect (Zavitzianos 1977: 489). In the cases Zavitzianos describes the use of garments associated with paternal authority, and most particularly uniforms associated with sports and the military, provides a way to stabilize body image, to relieve anxiety and to raise self-esteem. Of course Zavitzianos, in an all too familiar clinical tone, tells us that with treatment 'the homeovestite may improve and evolve from a homosexual object to a heterosexual one.' Maybe it is precisely because the boundaries between different categories come so close in this structure that talk of improvement is felt to be necessary. The paraphernalia of masculine uniforms and identities is nonetheless seen as part of a fantasy structure which is invented. Psychoanalysis, at least potentially, offers a structure which allows for the possibility of moving beyond any simple opposition between perversion and normality as they are commonly construed.

A less pathologizing version of this notion is to be found in Lacan's concept of male parade, in which the accoutrements of phallic power, the finery of authority, belie the very lack that they display. In a similar way the muscular male body functions as a powerful symbol of desire and lack, heroism as a costume. Within the narratives which I have discussed here the position of the father, a position of authority, lacks credibility in various ways. This lack of credibility is part of a denaturalization of masculinity and its relation to power, a shift that can be seen to be enacted in the virtually woman-free zone of the action narrative. Whilst it is played out on a huge stage, McClane's despairing struggle is also a small drama, a family drama. Both *Die Hard* and *Die Hard 2* draw to a close with McClane searching for his wife amongst the debris, covered in blood and crying out her name, seeming like nothing so much as a child. Indeed while Holly McClane provides the term which holds the narrative together, since neither the job of cop nor patriotism provides the hero's motivation, they are rarely together, the moment of reunion constantly postponed. Only once, in the first film, do we see the family together, with McClane as a father – glimpsed as an image, a frame photograph in Holly's office.

Postmodernity, whatever else it is taken to designate, signals significant shifts in the definition of work and the masculine identity that it proposes.

Postmodernism also calls into question the production and status of knowledge and categories of truth. These developments help to situate and historicize the shifts in Hollywood's representation of the male hero. In turn Andy Medhurst has characterized postmodernism as the hetero-sexual version of camp, a discourse in which both the play of multiple identities and acts of appropriation are fundamental. Sincerity, says Med-hurst, is 'the ultimate swearword in the camp vocabulary' since while it 'implies truth; camp knows that life is composed of different types of lie' (Medhurst 1990: 19).

This suggestion returns me to those suspicions that cast doubt on the possibility of making a distinction between a parodic performance of masculinity and the oppressive enactment of that performance. To say that the enactments of masculinity seen in the action cinema seems like nothing so much as a series of exercises in male drag could well fall foul of such a criticism, since it is the awareness of performance that distin-guishes the masquerade from sociological conceptions of social roles. Yet, within the cinema, whose awareness are we speaking about – the producers', the stars', the audience's? When Rae Dawn Chong, watching Schwarzenegger strut his stuff in *Commando* (1985), sighs 'I don't believe this macho bullshit,' whom is she speaking to? There are a whole range of experiences and identities – those of lesbian and gay audiences, of black and Asian audiences, of all the margins that make up the center – that are rarely addressed directly by the Hollywood cinema in the way that white men seem to be.[3] Yet the enactment of a drama of power and powerlessness is intrinsic to the anxieties about masculine identity and authority that are embodied in the figure of the struggling hero.

NOTES

My thanks to Val Hill for all her help in thinking through these ideas.

1 Obviously these comments apply most particularly to big-budget action movies.

2 Though it is important to note that the success of action pictures, such as the *Rambo* series, is not limited to the West.

3 Of course Hollywood doesn't constitute the totality of cinema, though it provides the focus for this essay. We should also note that there is an important tradition of black American action narratives, made both within Hollywood formulas and in modes derived from the Hong Kong cinema. The Hong Kong martial arts tradition itself, as well as the white western versions of it that have appeared through the 1980s, remain immensely popular. In my experience these films are often only accessible through the video market. Generally made on relatively low budgets and often falling foul of the British censors, such films nevertheless provide an important counterpoint to Holly-wood's action entertainment tradition.

BIBLIOGRAPHY

Boone, J. and Cadden, M., eds (1990) *Engendering Men: the Question of Male Feminist Criticism*, London: Routledge.

Burgin, V., Donald, J. and Kaplan, C., eds (1986) *Formations of Fantasy*, London: Routledge.

Creed, B. (1987) 'From Here to Modernity: Feminism and Postmodernism,' *Screen* 28, 2: 47–67.

Dyer, R. (1982) 'Don't Look Now,' *Screen* 23, 3–4: 61–73.

——— (1987) *Heavenly Bodies: Film Stars and Society*, London: BFI/Macmillan.

King, S. B. (1990) 'Sonny's Virtues: the Gender Negotiations of *Miami Vice*,' *Screen* 31, 3: 281–95.

Medhurst, A. (1990) 'Pitching Camp,' *City Limits*, May 10–17: 19.

Zavitzianos, G. (1977) 'The Object in Fetishism, Homeovestism and Transvestism,' *International Journal of Psycho-Analysis* 58: 487–95.

13

CAN MASCULINITY BE TERMINATED?

Susan Jeffords

US masculinity in Hollywood films of the 1980s was largely transcribed through spectacle and bodies, with the male body itself becoming often the most fulfilling form of spectacle. Throughout this period, the male body – principally the white male body – became increasingly a vehicle of display – of musculature, of beauty, of physical feats, and of a gritty toughness. External spectacle – weaponry, explosions, infernos, crashes, high-speed chases, ostentatious luxuries – offered companion evidence of both the sufficiency and the volatility of this display. That externality itself confirmed that the outer parameters of the male body were to be the focus of audience attention, desire, and politics.

But there is already evidence that this emphasis on externality and the male body is shifting focus. In the 1990s, externality and spectacle have begun to give way to a presumably more internalized masculine dimension. In contrast to the physical feats of Sylvester Stallone in the *Rambo* films, the determined competitiveness of Bruce Willis's John McClane in the *Die Hard* films, the confrontations of Clint Eastwood's Dirty Harry, the whip-cracking of Harrison Ford's Indiana Jones, the steely authority of Robocop, and Michael J. Fox's time-traveling dualities in *Back to the Future*, recent Hollywood male star/heroes have been constructed as more internalized versions of their historical counterparts. More film time is devoted to explorations of their ethical dilemmas, emotional traumas, and psychological goals, and less to their skill with weapons, their athletic abilities, or their gutsy showdowns of opponents.

By seeming to step back from their own spectacle, these men are presumably leaving space for Hollywood's version of 'difference,' or what it prefers to characterize as 'justice' and 'equality.' What Hollywood culture is offering, in place of the bold spectacle of male muscularity and/as violence, is a self-effacing man, one who now, instead of learning to fight, learns to love. We can include here such recent box office items as *Field of Dreams* (1989), *Robin Hood* (1991), *The Doctor* (1991), *Regarding Henry* (1991), *Switch* (1991), the new Disney *Beauty and the Beast* (1991), even *Boyz N the Hood* (1991). What I want to do here is

245

interrogate the 'new' man of the 1990s, and find out what complications await viewers who acknowledge his existence.

As part of a widespread cultural effort to respond to perceived deteriorations in masculine forms of power, Hollywood films of the 1980s – in conjunction with the premiere politician produced by that system, Ronald Reagan – highlighted masculinity (and Reagan's collaborative nationalism) as a violent spectacle that insisted on the external sufficiency of the male body/territory. Very little film time is devoted, for example, to Rambo's internal feelings. The most memorable scene here is Rambo's impassioned outburst at the end of *First Blood* (1982), in which he indicts US society for abandoning him and his fellow Vietnam veterans. But because of the fact that the speech is largely unintelligible and occurs in a brief moment at the end of the series of explosions, the focus of the scene is less on John Rambo's emotional state than upon the externalization of those emotions as violent and destructive actions, as he goes on a rampage around the gun shop where he has sought refuge from the police. And the effect of the scene is less to comment on Rambo's state of mind than to transfer guilt for his mistreatment from the small-town sheriff who harasses him to the society at large.

In the Rambo sequels, it is as if these brief moments of emotional insight have been forgotten, or consigned to what Michael Rogin has called the 'amnesia' of US political spectacle (Rogin 1990). In *Rambo: First Blood II* and *Rambo III* emotional expression is largely reserved for those who heroize Rambo. The most audiences see of Rambo's 'internal' workings are the times when his body is opened through wounds that he incurs. In these films, Rambo *is* externalization, so much so that his body is made indistinguishable from its surrounding environs. It is not simply that Rambo is shown principally outdoors that emphasizes his externality, but that he *is*, quite literally in *Rambo II*, that outdoors, as his body merges into mud, water, and rocks to defeat his Soviet pursuers.

This pattern of internal amnesia is typical of male action film sequences of the 1980s – the *Rambo*s, *Lethal Weapon*s, and *Die Hard*s come most readily to mind. Where the first film in a sequence is likely to reveal some emotional content of its hero – Rambo's Post-Traumatic Stress Disorder, Riggs's depression about his wife's death, or John McClane's distress over his wife's career – the second is likely to abandon even the momentary internal character developments that dotted these first films in favor of the externalized spectacle itself. Sequels of the 1980s offer more explosions, more killings, and more outright violence. (In the most extravagant shift, Rambo expertly kills no one in *First Blood* and then turns to killing 44 people in *Rambo II* and an uncountable number in *Rambo III* (Van Biema 1985: 37).) Even the most developed emotional subplot, Riggs's suicidal guilt over his wife's death in *Lethal Weapon 1*, is not only explained but externalized in *Lethal Weapon 2* when he has sex with another woman *and* kills his wife's murderer.

The popularity and financial success of these films suggests that sequentiality itself was one of the mechanisms for Hollywood responses to crises in the representations and marketing of US masculinities in this period. It is, most directly and insistently, the question of whether and how masculinity can be reproduced successfully in a post-Vietnam, post-Civil Rights, and post-women's movement era. One of the answers that these films provide is through spectacular repetition, or, more specifically, through the repetition of the spectacles of the masculine body, a body that, in this case, includes the male hero, his weapons, and his environment.

In order to get at how this repetition works, I'd like to examine here two of the best-selling serial films of this period, James Cameron's *The Terminator* (1984) and *Terminator 2: Judgment Day* (1991), films whose narratives center on masculinity and repetition, or, more concisely, the reproduction of masculinity. But because the second of these films dips into the 1990s, I hope to use this film sequence to comment on both the transitions and the ambiguities that are now taking place between that externalized male body and its internalized progeny.

MASCULINITY AND/AS REPETITION

As with so many male action films of the 1980s, and as with so much of Hollywood's altered marketing and production strategy of the same period, repetition is at the heart of both Cameron films. In writing about *The Terminator*, Karen Mann and Constance Penley argue for the importance of repetition in the film. Mann suggests that at both a structural and a thematic level, the story of the film depends upon repetition as self-reproduction, as the future steps back to re-write the past. Of the future John Connor, leader of the rebel humans fighting the machines that are out to kill them in the year 2029, she argues: 'He satisfies the fantasy of reaching back in time to control those who control him – his parents – by choosing who they are to be. . . . His choice [of his own father] provides the illusion of self-generation' (Mann 1989–90: 21). Penley takes on this same theme of re-writing the past, except that she reads it in terms of psychoanalytic categories: 'the fantasy of time travel is no more nor less than the compulsion to repeat that manifests itself in the primal scene fantasy' (Penley 1989: 47). Again, the re-writing of reproduction under the control of the male child fulfills the primal scene fantasy of being present at the moment of one's conception. In either case, both Mann and Penley recognize the importance of repetition as reproduction in these films, where the future son reaches back to the past, in effect, by choosing the father to give birth to himself (it is John

Connor who decides that Kyle Reese – his father – should return to the past to 'protect' his mother, and, coincidentally, to father himself).

Much of the plot of *The Terminator* revolves around this form of repetition as self-reproduction. *Terminator 2* takes this repetition self-consciously, knowingly re-working the plot, themes, and spectacles of its predecessor. Clearly, there is a certain financial intuitiveness about repeating as much as possible about a successful film, so that the sequel can try to replicate its audience appeal and box office receipts. But Cameron does more than merely repeat in *T2*; he self-consciously reworks elements of the first plot into the second, not simply explaining or answering some of them (by finally showing us John Connor's face, for example, or narrating how Sarah Connor learned the military skills that her son was later to put to such good use against the machines), but inverting them, so that nothing in the film gets repeated *exactly*. Everything is altered, if only slightly (even Schwarzenegger's chest size is somewhat diminished), in a way that offers clues about how repetition, reproduction, and self-production are working in the shift from the masculinity of the 1980s to the 1990s, how, in other words, masculinity is currently reproducing itself, i.e through inversion rather than duplication.

T2's early trailers and commercials clued audiences in to the most obvious form of reworking in the film, the shift in the character of the Terminator: 'Once he was programmed to destroy the future. Now his mission is to save it.' The very act for which this machine got its name in the first film – the relentless hunting and killing of human targets – is the key to its changed personality in the second. In *T2*, the human-killing task is left to the newer and sleeker machine model Terminator, the liquid metal T2000, while the original Terminator, now re-programmed by the future adult John Connor to protect his 11-year-old childhood self, is instructed not to kill humans any more. (Though the plot suggests that it is young Connor who gives the Terminator this instruction, from the time of its return to the present, the Terminator has already distinguished itself from its earlier counterpart by only injuring and not killing the people it meets; it's as if not killing people was somehow now its 'nature.') Instead of being the source of humanity's annihilation, the Terminator is now the *single* guarantor of its continuation. If, in the first film, the Terminator were to kill Sarah Connor, John Connor would not be born, and he would not be able to lead the human rebellion against the machines, leaving the machines to accomplish their goal, the extermination of all human life. Now, in the second film, the Terminator is the only one capable of protecting the young Connor from the more efficient and sophisticated T2000. And here's the biggest reworking that comes from this shift: freed from its mission of destroying humanity, the Terminator can now become not simply the protector of human life, but its generator. By 'giving' John

Connor his life, the Terminator takes, in effect, Sarah Connor's place as his mother. In one of the film's most astounding inversions, the Terminator can now be said to give birth to the future of the human race.

But if the Terminator is now responsible for human futures, what has happened to Sarah Connor, the woman whose tough fighting terminated the Terminator in the first film, and whose future held out the birth of a son who would save the human race? Like the Terminator, Sarah Connor's character is repeated and inverted in the second film. Where in the first she was uncertain, frightened, and weak, in her rebirth she is tough-minded, fearless, and strong (the first shot is of Sarah Connor doing chin-ups in her room at the mental hospital). This 'new' Sarah Connor looks like the mercenary she has trained to be through all the intervening years, wearing military fatigues, toting heavy weapons, and having a mission to perform. As final proof of her new hard character, she even forgets to love her son, chewing him out for rescuing her from the hospital: 'You can't risk yourself, even for me! You're too important. . . . I didn't need your help. I can take care of myself.' It's as if she's not a mother at all, but only a soldier for the future.

Sarah Connor does remember that she's a mother, once. When she tries to kill Miles Dyson – the man responsible for developing Skynet, the computer system that will take on the task of eliminating humans – thinking thereby to change the future, she fails. Cracking off the first few rounds of her high-powered rifle, it seems that she will take the Terminator's place and do what it no longer can do – kill human beings. But when she comes face to face with Dyson lying on the floor with his wife and son crying over him, she breaks into tears and can't do it. Then, when John Connor arrives, she finally tells him that she loves him, as if her admission of failure at being a tough combatant releases her to still have the feelings of a mother.

In *The Terminator*, Sarah Connor was told that she would be, in effect, the mother of the future. That would seem, in the logic of this film, to be a pretty important job, since it's Sarah Connor who teaches her son all of the skills he will use to save humanity. Yet in the second film Sarah is effectively locked out of having any real role in the future. First, John tells the Terminator that he learned information about weapons, machines, and fighting from mercenaries his mother took him to meet, not directly from her. And secondly, for some years, she was not present for him as a mother at all, being locked away in a mental ward where she was not allowed to see him. He was left with foster parents who taught him that everything his mother said about the future was a crazy illusion of her deranged and obsessed mind. Thirdly, as an audience, we are witness to how Sarah ignores her son for most of the film. The excuse, that she's concentrating on keeping him alive, puts her in direct

Figure 29 Arnold Schwarzenegger and Edward Furlong in *Terminator 2*

competition for the Terminator's role, a job – and a body – that she just can't fit. And while she's focusing on being a super-soldier, the Terminator is working on being a better mom, listening to and playing with the son that Sarah hardly notices for all the weapons she's carrying. Sarah Connor even acknowledges that the Terminator is doing a better job than she and consciously decides to leave her son in its care when she goes on what promises to be a suicide mission to kill Dyson. While John is teaching the Terminator how to give high-fives, the camera pulls back to Sarah's point-of-view shot, and her voiceover reasons:

Watching John with a machine. It was suddenly so clear. The Ter-

Figure 30 Linda Hamilton in *Terminator 2*

minator would never stop. It would never hurt him. It would never leave him or get impatient with him. . . . . It would die to protect him. Of all the would-be fathers who came and went over the years, this machine, this thing, was the only one who measured up. And in an insane world, it was the sanest choice.

Though Sarah refers to the Terminator as John's father here, it is apparent that, with her disappearance, it would be his sole parent, since, in the odd logic of this film, John's father was both killed in the past and hasn't even been born yet. And though Sarah calls it a father, it's clear that the Terminator doesn't do things that the mercenary father-figures

251

did. This father doesn't teach John about weaponry or survival skills, and doesn't freak out, like the others did, about John's role in the future. And unlike Sarah, it will always stay with him. The Terminator is thus not only a father but a mother as well to John Connor – to the hope of a human future. What had been its most frightening feature in the first film – Reese tells Sarah, 'It will *never* stop!' – is now in Sarah's words its most admirable feature: it will never stop caring for John.

From the second film's outset then, Sarah Connor has been gently delegitimized in her role as the mother and protector of the human future. Though she, better than any human, understands the consequences that await unchanged human actions, and would seem as a result to be an important source of knowledge, and her survival skills and patience are admirable, she is not presented as cool and clear-thinking. Instead, as Linda Hamilton chooses to play the part, Sarah Connor is more an animal than a human, or, better yet, a human whose animal instincts have been brought out in the face of death. As one film reviewer puts it: 'She is an animal. She bares her teeth. She snarls . . . She has an animal voice. Like an animal, she does anything to protect her young. That is her strongest emotion' (Baumgold 1991: 26). So not only does Sarah not have the machine body or efficiency to compete with the Terminator as a protector for her son, her emotions as a mother are primitive, stemming more from her animal instincts than from any loving relationship between two people. When she is shown as a mother, her maternity is of the most brutish and unreflective kind.

Her final delegitimization is accomplished by none other than John Connor himself, showing how he has been able to surpass his mother's animal tendencies to remain human, even in the face of the future he knows he will confront. Importantly, the scene in which he does this succeeds all of the other deteriorations of Sarah's role as mother – her brusque treatment of her son, her mental instabilities, her emotional breakdowns, her abandoning of her son to the care of a machine – and marks the final separation of Sarah and John, or, more precisely, the termination of his final dependence on her and new alliance with the Terminator. After she has failed to kill Dyson, the Terminator sits down to narrate for Dyson the history of the future and the role he will play in it. When Dyson responds, 'How were we supposed to know?', animal Sarah attacks: 'Fucking men like you built the hydrogen bomb! Men like you thought it up. You think you're so creative. You don't know what it is to create a life, to feel something growing inside you.' But just when her feminist critique of masculine birth compensation gets rolling, John Connor calmly interrupts: 'Mom. We need to be a little more constructive here.' Seated beside the Terminator, already taking command, John's retort relegates Sarah to the crouching, chain-smoking background bundle she becomes. He and his future-self-programmed private Terminator are in control.

MASCULINITY AS FATHERING

To 'flesh out,' as it were (the Terminator is a machine chassis with a flesh coating), the Terminator's change in function from killer to protector, from stranger to parent, audiences are shown not only the Terminator not killing people (its strategy now is to shoot them in the legs, *à la* the Rambo of *First Blood*), but shown as well its altered personality. It asks questions (when young John Connor tells it not to kill anyone, the Terminator asks 'Why?'; and it later asks Connor, 'Why do you cry?'), it uses slang ('No problemo'), and it plays with children (it and Connor exchange high fives).[1] Perhaps most importantly, it learns (rather than break into the starter on every stolen automobile, it learns from Connor that people usually put their keys in the car's visor). As it tells John Connor, 'The more contact I have with humans, the more I learn.' This learning is, in fact, one of the key thematic foundations of the film, since it is the Terminator's ability to learn that leads it to sacrifice itself for the survival of humanity: since humans once learned from its predecessor's computer chips how to produce the machines that would destroy the world, it must self-destruct, even though it's now a good Terminator, to prevent people from repeating that past mistake.

The Terminator offers the ostensible explanation for why men of the 1980s are changing their behavior: they learned that the old ways of violence, rationality, single-mindedness, and goal-orientation (there is no one more goal-oriented than the first Terminator; as Reese says to Sarah Connor, 'He'll never stop. Not until he kills you!') were destructive, not only for individual men, but for humanity as a whole. And the solution to this dilemma? According to this film, for the 1980s man to learn from his past (future?) mistakes to produce a change in character, a 'new,' more internalized man, who thinks with his heart rather than with his head – or computer chips.

But to show that 'learning' is a non-discriminatory attitude of the 'new' masculinity, the Terminator is not the only male in *T2* to change his behavior. Miles Dyson is the African American scientist who, *T2*'s future history recalls, constructs Skynet, the computerized military defense network responsible for starting the nuclear devastation that almost ends human existence. When Sarah Connor, the Terminator, and John Connor tell Dyson about how his current research will lead to a nuclear apocalypse, he volunteers to help them destroy all of his files, finally sacrificing his own life to set off the bomb that will explode the research institute he heads. (True to the new masculine ideal of non-killing, Dyson warns the police officers who have come to stop the break-in that they should leave before he sets off the bomb.) And like the Terminator, Dyson leaves behind him not only a woman and her son, but the future of the entire human race. The message here is clear: in this narrative, masculinity transcends racial difference, suggesting that the forces of change – killing to non-killing, silence to speech, indifference to love, external display to internal exploration, absent to active paternalism – not only cross racial boundaries but draw men together. What more unlikely alliance than a white-fleshed killing machine from the future and a dark-skinned benevolent scientist from the present? And yet, these 'men' work together to preserve human futures; together, they give human life to the world.

The single key feature that solidifies the alliance of Dyson and the Terminator is not simply that they both believe in the Terminator's future, or that they understand the potential destructive power of Skynet, but that they are both 'fathers' – both to young male children and, by narrative implication, to the future. The scene immediately prior to Sarah Connor's attack on Dyson is the one in which she effectively turns her son over to the Terminator father. Dyson also has a son; in fact, he is the first member of the family we see besides Dyson, as the son's robot-controlled car drives into his father's computerized study. It is also the son who saves his father's life. While the wife cowers in terror at Sarah Connor's rifled commands ('Stay on the floor, bitch!'), the son cries over his father's body. It is this act which seems to draw Sarah to a halt and prevent her from terminating Dyson, as if Sarah knows that killing *any* son imperils the future. The alignment of Dyson and the Terminator is effected through the close proximity in which both men are shown as fathers. Their comparison is not, as it was between the African American police chief and the Terminator in the first film, one of human versus machine, or protector versus killer, or even black versus white, but instead one of sacrificing fathers who want to preserve a human future for their sons against the inhuman systems (mechanized or flesh) that are bent on carrying out a plan that will destroy all human life. Where humanity was the common denominator that erased racial difference in the first film, now fatherhood erases the difference between all 'new' men, whether they are machines or human.

The introduction of Dyson serves not only to show that the new masculinity transcends racial and class difference, but that the vehicle for that transformation is fathering, the link for men to 'discover' their 'new' internalized selves. Throughout the late 1980s, fathering was a key characterization and narrative device for displaying the 'new' Hollywood masculinities. In films such as *Three Men and a Baby, Look Who's Talking, One Good Cop* (1991), *Regarding Henry, Boyz N the Hood*, and others, fathering became the vehicle for portraying masculine emotions, ethics, and commitments, and for re-directing masculine characterizations from spectacular achievements to domestic triumphs. But *Terminator 2* shows that this characterization is more than a simple warming of the individual male cold heart and an improvement of father–child relations, but instead a wholesale social patterning, in which these men become not only the replacements for women whose work has interfered with their ability to mother their children (an indictment that links otherwise diverse films like *Terminator 2* and *Boyz N the Hood*), but fathers for an entire human future. While mothers might lay claim to giving biological birth to children, these fathers insure that there will be a world for these children to live in. And they accomplish this, not with bombs and bombast, but with love and protection.

MASCULINITY AND/AS INDIVIDUALISM

In looking at discourses about nuclear warfare, Gillian Brown focuses in on the emphasis on sequentiality in discussions of both nuclear warfare and nuclear disarmament, suggesting that this interest in sequence is an indication of the preoccupation of both factions with continuity, futures, and reproduction, or what she phrases 'the ideology of sequential self-extension.'

> When the antinuclear chain letter enjoins us to take a stake in futurity, or when the nursery rhyme reconstructs our self-extension in the world, they epitomize our familiarity with and reliance on a notion of projection in which we ourselves *are* our (possible) futures.
>
> (Brown 1989: 294)

As she astutely goes on to say, this ideology of self-extension is dependent upon a certain notion of individualism, in which the individual not only owns the narrative and therefore the sequence that it articulates, but through that narrative, owns the self as well:

> antinuclear thematics of affiliation and associationism share with pronuclear survivalism this desire for sequence and the narrative of possessive individualism it reprises. Thinking about the nuclear, then, is itself a sequence in the history of liberal humanism, a sequence that foregrounds the dynamic of disappearance and reappearance in the logic of self-proprietorship.
>
> (Brown 1989: 292–3)

The particular thinking about the nuclear that is narrated in *The Terminator* and *Terminator 2: Judgment Day* is equally based upon a narrative of individualism that explains the apparent contradictions between the films' seemingly left-wing antinuclear conclusions and their star's right-wing Republican endorsements. What finally resolves this narrative spectacle of violence, technology, and mechanical genocide is

the even greater spectacle of male individualism in the act of self-sacrificing fathers. For what greater and more powerful act of *individual* self-
determination can there be than the *rational*, willing, and determined
decision to end one's own life, not in the despair of defeat but in the
triumph of birth? of being the generator of the human future?

And this is what makes *T2* so disarmingly dangerous a narrative. The
first film, like most Hollywood films before it, had to separate its male
egos into good – Kyle Reese, Sarah Connor's protector/lover and father
of John Connor, leader of the future – and evil – the Terminator,
automated vehicle for the destruction of human life – largely as a result
of a pattern of masculinity that necessitates defining men not by content
but by opposition to an other. *T2* works by a similar pattern, with the
old Terminator validating itself by protecting John Connor against the
T2000 and showing itself by contrast to be more 'human.' But this second
film plays with so many oppositional reversals that this familiar pattern
manages to slip in a few interesting realignments.

The most obvious reversal is that of goodness and authority, represented in *T2* primarily by the police. Whereas the first film showed police
officers as ineffectual but well-intentioned – they tried to protect Sarah
Connor from the Terminator, but didn't believe her or Reese about its
power, a failure that cost the officers their own lives – in the second, it
is the police who are the greatest threat to both Connors and the Terminator. The T2000 disguises itself as a police officer, thereby not only
gaining access to automated police information but also winning the
confidence of unwitting citizens like John Connor's foster parents. But
it is also the police who try to stop Sarah, John, Dyson, and the Terminator from destroying the Cyberdyne research lab where the computer
chips and records about the first Terminator are being studied. Where
in the first film the police are shown protecting people, in the second,
they are shown protecting only property, principally the property of the
very corporation that will decide on a path of human genocide in the
future. And where the Terminator does not kill in the second film, the
police do; they are responsible for the death of Dyson, and are clearly
trying to kill both Connors.

It is important to look not only at what reversals take place in the
depictions of the police, but what shifts these reversals imply about the
oppositional definitions of masculinity in each film. In *The Terminator*,
Kyle Reese was most obviously defined against the Terminator: he was
human, it was a machine; he wanted to protect Sarah, it wanted to kill
her; he wanted to save the human future, it wanted to prevent it; he
made love to her, it hurt her; he gave her a son, it gave her a nightmare.
But Reese was also opposed to the police. While they too wanted to
protect Sarah, they finally could not. And against everything Sarah
Connor and, by then, the audience, knew, the police did not believe

Reese's story about the future. In that film, the police functioned to show that it was not enough simply not to be a machine; people had to be resourceful, have access to important information (what the future held; how to make pipe bombs; how to detect Terminators), and, most importantly, had to be able to act (the thematic anchor of masculinity in the 1980s). While the police stood around firing handguns at the Terminator (even the audience knew by this time that this was a laughable excuse for action), Reese helped Sarah escape from the Terminator. What *The Terminator* told its audiences was that if you wanted to be able to *father the future* – for this is literally what Reese did – you had to be more than good-hearted and human; you had to be strong, decisive, and powerful (through knowledge) – to not only *want* to protect the mother of the future, but to be able to do it.

In the second film, the police serve again to show that being human is not enough. But here, they are opposed, not to an even more protective human (the cameras keep panning across the mottoes written on the LA police cars: 'to serve and protect'), but to a more human protector. While the Terminator is opposed to the T2000 for purposes of the thematic battle of good and evil – the survival or destruction of humanity – it is more effectively opposed to the police officers in terms of its character: the police disdain John Connor (he is a delinquent), it cares for him; they kill Dyson, it repaired his wounds after Sarah first shot him; they hide behind faceless machines, it is a machine with a face. But most importantly, in this second film, while the Terminator protects humans (not just John Connor, but through him, all humanity), the police protect machines. They amass their greatest force to protect an empty corporate building that houses the most sophisticated computer technology in the world. In contrast, the Terminator's most forceful act was re-powering itself to save Sarah and John Connor from a machine, the T2000.

These reversals of authority and oppositional presentations of police power are less a critique of institutional oppressions (the police mean well but are misinformed), and more an effort to distinguish individual actions from organized institution. By presenting the police as inefficient but well-meaning in *The Terminator* and ineffective and misguided in *Terminator 2*, individual men – Reese and the Terminator – are made to seem not only effective but *necessary*, both to the protection of women and children and to the survival of humanity. In the face of a society that is perceived as increasingly technologized, mechanized, routinized, and anonymous, the power of individual decision-making and individual action is drawn as paramount in these films. Male viewers – particularly white male viewers – who may feel increasingly distanced from what they understand to be traditional male forms of power and privilege can be empowered through the assertions of the role male individualism must play in the future of humanity. *Terminator 2* can offer to these viewers not only a panacea for their feelings of disempowerment, but it can reinforce the culturally-designated culprits of that scenario in the guise of technology, machines, non-passive women, and managerial blacks as well.

Most importantly, the film accomplishes this through one of the simplest and most reassuring frameworks available to many male viewers: individualism as fathering. In a slick re-writing of the traditionally gender-marked division between public and private, the Terminator films are offering male viewers an alternative realm to that of the declining workplace and national structure as sources of masculine authority and power – the world of the family. It is here, this logic suggests, that men can regain a sense of their expected masculine power, without having to confront or suggest alterations in the economic and social system that has led to their feelings of deprivation. Throughout the 1980s, the Yankelovich Monitor of US social attitudes recorded that men's primary definitions of masculinity rested in their sense of a man being 'a good provider for his family' (Faludi 1991: 65). The Terminator films capitalize on this sensibility – one that is becoming economically and socially obsolete – by implying a relationship, not between men and the partners, but between masculinity and future generations, an abstract and inverted repetition of both the public and private realms within which many US men are sensing a deterioration of their abilities to define their identities and/as their privileges. And *T2* accomplishes this goal through the portrayal of a father's relationship with his son.

MASCULINITY AND/AS SELF-PRODUCTION

In another narrative of nuclear apocalypse, Christa Wolf speaks about the same kind of 'male rationalism' that Sarah Connor seemed to be criticizing in her attack on Dyson, saying,

> This in turn raises the question of what today could possibly still represent 'progress' . . ., now that the masculine way has almost run its course – that is, the way of carrying all inventions, circumstances, and conflicts to extremes until they have reached their maximum negative point: the point at which no alternatives are left.
>
> (Wolf 1984: 244)

As if Cameron had read this book, the characters of *Terminator 2* seem to have 'learned' the lesson Wolf was trying to impart about the inevitability of warfare within the framework of a 'rational' way of thinking. Both the Terminator and Dyson seem to have understood that their forms of 'progress' – computerized technologies, advanced weaponries, enhanced defense strategies, and increasingly efficient assessments of 'life' – will lead nowhere, at least, to a human nowhere, in which the destruction of all life is the logical end-product of their programming/ thinking. Wolf even anticipates the characters of these 'new' men when her protagonist, Cassandra, tells a Greek chariot driver that 'in the future there may be people who know how to turn their victory into life' (Wolf 1984: 116).

This of course seems to be the most astonishing lesson that men of the Terminator's future have learned by looking at their own futures: that the continuation of their success and powerful accomplishment of goals leads only and inevitably to the destruction of the future itself. *Terminator 2* seems to have rightly earned its label as an 'anti-nuclear' (James 1991: H9) film, one that short-circuits the nuclear nightmare by 'learning' about the limitations of male mechanization. In this way, *T2* seems more than a direct response to 1980s male characters like Rambo or Robocop, whose hardbodies imitated or integrated indestructible machines that led to the downfall of evil. Those 1980s machine-men get tossed into the steel melting pot at the end of *T2* along with the T2000 and the self-sacrificing Terminator, leaving behind the young John Connor, bearer of a new and more human future.

But what Wolf didn't anticipate was the agility of US culture to find venues for 'alternative' masculinities. Rather than acknowledge an end point at which masculinity must recognize its own negation – what seems on the surface to be the conclusion of *T2* – the film's complex reasonings supply a 'new' way for masculinity to go: not, as in the 1980s, outward into increasingly extravagant spectacles of violence and power (as Rambo and Ronald Reagan showed, these displays had become their own forms of parody), but inward, into increasingly emotive displays of masculine sensitivities, traumas, and burdens. Rather than be impressed at the size of these men's muscles and the ingenuity of their violences, audiences are to admire their emotional commitments and the ingenuity of their sacrifices, sacrifices that are being made, *T2* reminds its viewers, for their future.

T2 reveals the ways in which this link between masculinity and futures is so problematic. Donald Greiner, in his discussion of the traditions of masculine representations in the American novel, identifies the two main 'enemies' of men in these novels: space and time:

> Time is always the enemy of spaciousness for the bonded male in the American novel because, if possible immortality is associated with space, certain mortality is equated with time. . . . If men are to fulfill the destiny of America . . . then they must avoid the reality of time for the illusion of space.
>
> (Greiner 1991: 13)

What *T2* offers is an alternative way to resolve these anxieties about the

Figure 31 Can masculinity be terminated?

ends of masculinity/territory through the manipulation of space and time via the male body. As John Connor not only chooses his own biological father in Kyle Reese (fathers himself, as it were), but also programs his mechanical father into the 'kinder and gentler' Terminator, he seems to have conquered the restrictions of time, not by expanding into external territories (the solutions of Natty Bumppo, Huck Finn, or Theodore Roosevelt), but by territorializing the interior of the male body.

It is thus John Connor and not Sarah Connor or the Terminator who holds the real power of these films, and marks himself as the hero of Hollywood sequels, for it is he who survives the destruction of the 'old' masculinity, witnessing teary-eyed the Terminator's destruction. As he stands above the melting Terminators, audiences are to recognize in John Connor not only the father of his own and the human future, but the new masculinity as well.

But in one of *T2*'s most remarkable inversions, the film manages not only to reveal the 'new' masculinity/father, but to excuse the 'old' one as well. For though the Terminator must sacrifice itself in order to prevent a destructive future, the film's plot makes it clear that *it's not his fault*. Because the mechanized body from the movie's past has been shown, largely through the oppositional framework of the script, to be a 'good Terminator,' its elimination is constructed to be not vengeful but tragic. The Terminator had to sacrifice itself, not because it was 'bad' or harmful or even useless, but because others around it misused its components. Comparably, audiences can conclude that the aggressive and destructive 1980s male body that became the target for both ridicule and hatred may not have been *inherently* 'bad,' but only, in some sociologically pitiful way, misunderstood. And who, finally, does *Terminator 2* suggest *does* understand this obsolete but lovable creature? None other than John Connor, the 'new' man himself.

So, while *T2* may present John Connor as the savior of the human race, John Connor is finally saving something else, something far more immediate than a mechanized future and something far more dangerous than a personally-targeted mechanized killing machine. He is saving masculinity for itself, not only embodying the 'new' future of masculinity, but rescuing its past for revival. Because, after all, there will have to be another movie.

NOTE

1 This re-characterization is reinforced by one of Schwarzenegger's intervening Hollywood hits, *Kindergarten Cop*, in which viewers are treated to the spectacle of Arnold frollicking with 5-year-olds.

BIBLIOGRAPHY

Baumgold, J. (1991) 'Killer Women,' *New York*, July 29: 24–30.
Brown, G. (1989) 'Nuclear Domesticity: Sequence and Survival' in H. M. Cooper, A. A. Munich and S. M. Squier (eds) *Arms and the Woman: War, Gender and Literary Representation*, Chapel Hill: University of North Carolina Press.
Faludi, S. (1991) *Backlash: the Undeclared War Against American Women*, New York: Crown Publishers.
Greiner, D. J. (1991) *Women Enter the Wilderness: Male Bonding and the American Novel of the 1980s*, Columbia: University of South Carolina Press.
James, C. (1991) 'A Warmer, Fuzzier Arnold,' *The New York Times*, July 14: H9.

Mann, K. B. (1989–90) 'Narrative Entanglements: *The Terminator*,' *Film Quarterly* 43, 2: 17–27.
Penley, C. (1989) 'Time Travel, Primal Scene, and the Critical Dystopia' in J. Tagg (ed.) *The Cultural Politics of 'Postmodernism*,' Binghamton, NY: Department of Art History, SUNY.
Rogin, M. (1990) ' "Make My Day!": Spectacle as Amnesia in Imperial Politics,' *Representations* 29: 99–124.
Van Biema, D. H. (1985) 'With a $100 Million Gross(out), Sly Stallone Fends off *Rambo*'s Army of Adversaries,' *People* 24, 2: 34–8.
Wolf, C. (1984) *Cassandra*, trans. J. Van Heurck, New York: Farrar, Straus and Giroux.

INDEX OF FILMS

Act of Vengeance (Bob Kelljam) 113
Alien (Ridley Scott) 129
Alley Cat (Edward Victor) 103, 105, 108, 109
Altered States (Ken Russell) 128
American in Paris, An (Vincente Minnelli) 65
American Werewolf in London, An (John Landis) 125, 131
Angels with Dirty Faces (Michael Curtiz) 74

Back to the Future (Robert Zemeckis) 245
Backdraft (Ron Howard) 235
Band Wagon, The (Vincente Minnelli) 49, 62, 65, 67n
Barkleys of Broadway, The (Charles Walters) 67n
Beau Geste (William Wellman) 196
Beauty and the Beast 245
Beguiled, The (Don Siegel) 204
Ben Hur (William Wyler) 18, 154
Beverly Hills Cop (Martin Brest) 225
Big Trouble in Little China (John Carpenter) 235
Birth of a Nation (D. W. Griffith) 101n
Black Rain (Ridley Scott) 195, 205–8
Blood on the Sun (Frank Lloyd) 75
Blue Skies (Stuart Heisler) 59
Bolero (Wesley Ruggles) 43n
Border Incident (Anthony Mann) 14
Boys from Brazil, The (Franklin Schaffner) 122
Boyz N the Hood (John Singleton) 6, 182–92 *passim*, 245, 254, 255
Broadway Melody (Harry Beaumont) 46

Brood, The (David Cronenberg) 122
Butch Cassidy and the Sundance Kid (George Roy Hill) 195

Captain Blood (Michael Curtiz) 152
Carnal Knowledge (Mike Nichols) 196
Carrie (Brian de Palma) 131
Cat Chaser (Abel Ferrara) 114
Cat People (Jacques Tourneur) 124
Champion (Mark Robson) 169n
Cheat, The (Cecil B. de Mille) 41n
City of Dim Faces (George Melford) 29
Cobra (Joseph Henabery) 39
Cobra (George Pan Cosmatos) 220
Commando (Mark L. Lester) 243
Coogan's Bluff (Don Siegel) 89
Creature from the Black Lagoon, The (Jack Arnold) 131
Curse of the Werewolf (Terence Fisher) 126

Dancing Lady (Robert Z. Leonard) 50
Dead Ringers (David Cronenberg) 6, 129, 134–47 *passim*
Death Wish (Michael Winner) 114
Desperately Seeking Susan (Susan Seidelman) 235
Die Hard (John McTiernan) 7, 225, 230, 232, 237, 238–41, 242, 246
Die Hard 2: Die Harder (Renny Harlin) 7, 225, 230, 232, 236, 237, 238–41, 242, 246
Dirty Harry (Don Siegel) 101
Do the Right Thing (Spike Lee) 183
Doctor, The (Randa Haines) 245
Dog Day Afternoon (Sidney Lumet) 196

Dracula (Tod Browning) 123
Dracula (John Badham) 122, 123
Dressed to Kill (Brian dc Palma) 5,
  119, 120, 122

Eagle, The (Clarence Brown) 37, 39,
  42n
Easter Parade (Charles Walters) 63,
  64, 65, 67n
El Cid (Anthony Mann) 12
Exorcist, The (William Friedkin) 122,
  131
Eyes of Youth (Albert Parker) 29

F.I.S.T. (Norman Jewison) 220
Fall of the Roman Empire, The
  (Anthony Mann) 18
Fatal Attraction (Adrian Lyne) 92
Field of Dreams (Phil Alden
  Robinson) 245
First Blood (Ted Kotcheff) 246
Fistful of Dollars, A (Sergio Leone) 12
Five Heartbeats, The (Robert
  Townsend) 190n
Fly, The (Kurt Neumann) 136–7
Fly, The (David Cronenberg) 6, 128,
  129, 134–47 *passim*
Footlight Parade (Lloyd Bacon) 74
For a Few Dollars More (Sergio
  Leone) 12
Four Horsemen of the Apocalypse, The
  (Rex Ingram) 28–34, 40
Frankenstein (James Whale) 128
Funny Face (Stanley Donen) 59, 62

G-Men (William Keighley) 74
Gentlemen Prefer Blondes (Howard
  Hawks) 46
Go Natalie (Kevin Hooks) 190n
Good, the Bad, and the Ugly, The
  (Sergio Leone) 12
Guns in the Afternoon (Sam
  Peckinpah) 15

Hangin' with the Homeboys (Joseph
  Vasquez) 190n
Hannie Caulder (Burt Kennedy) 103
Heart Condition (James D. Parriott)
  194, 209
Homicidal (William Castle) 119
Howling, The (Joe Dante) 125
Hunger, The (Tony Scott) 131

I Spit on Your Grave (Meir Zarchi)
  103–9 *passim*, 116, 129
Internal Affairs (Mike Figgis) 225

Johnny Come Lately (William K.
  Howard) 74–5
Juice (Ernest Dickerson) 190n
Jungle Fever (Spike Lee) 190n
Junior Bonner (Sam Peckinpah) 18

Kindergarten Cop (Ivan Reitman) 261
King Kong (Merian C. Cooper and
  Ernest Shoedsack) 131
Kiss of the Spider Woman (Hector
  Babenco) 196

Let There Be Light (John Huston) 79,
  80
Lethal Weapon (Richard Donner) 195,
  199–203, 204, 225, 237, 246
Lethal Weapon 2 (Richard Donner)
  195, 202, 225, 246, 247
Lock-Up (John Flynn) 7, 214–26, 230,
  234–8
Look Who's Talking (Amy
  Heckerling) 239, 254

M*A*S*H (Robert Altman) 196
Mad Max (George Miller) 12
Major Dundee (Sam Peckinpah) 15
Man of the West (Anthony Mann) 18
Man Who Shot Liberty Valance, The
  (John Ford) 15, 112, 116n
Midnight Cowboy (John Schlesinger)
  196
Million Dollar Mermaid (Mervyn
  LeRoy) 66n
Mo' Better Blues (Spike Lee) 190n, 206
Moran of the Lady Letty (George
  Melford) 33
Ms 45 (Abel Ferrara) 103, 104, 109,
  114, 116n

Naked Vengeance (Cirio H. Santiago)
  107, 129
New Jack City (Mario Van Peebles)
  190n, 195, 205–8
North by Northwest (Alfred
  Hitchcock) 10

Off Limits (Christopher Crowe) 195,
  197–9, 200, 205

Officer and a Gentleman, An (Taylor Hackford) 141
Omen, The (Richard Donner) 122
One Good Cop (Heywood Gould) 254
Oscar (John Landis) 222

Pat Garrett and Billy the Kid (Sam Peckinpah) 15
Peeping Tom (Michael Powell) 109
Pirate, The (Vincente Minnelli) 65
Play Misty for Me (Clint Eastwood) 5, 87–102, 204
Point Blank (John Boorman) 18
Predator (John McTiernan) 240
Psycho (Alfred Hitchcock) 5, 119, 131
Public Enemy, The (William Wellman) 74–6, 80

Rage in Harlem, A (Bill Duke) 190n
Raging Bull (Martin Scorsese) 114, 115
Rambo: First Blood Part II (George Pan Cosmatos) 241, 243n, 245, 246, 253
Rambo III (Pcter MacDonald) 234, 246
Reflection of Fear (William A. Fraker) 119, 122
Regarding Henry (Mike Nichols) 245, 254
Repulsion (Roman Polanski) 131
Rhinestone (Bob Clark) 220
Right Stuff, The (Phil Kaufman) 141
Roaring Twenties, The (Raoul Walsh) 74
Robe, The (Henry Koster) 153
Robin Hood, Prince of Thieves (Kevin Reynolds) 245
RoboCop (Paul Verhoeven) 241, 245
Rocky (John Avildsen) 223, 239
Rocky II (Sylvester Stallone) 227n
Rocky IV (Sylvester Stallone) 222
Rocky V (John Avildsen) 222
Rookie, The (Clint Eastwood) 203–5
Royal Wedding (Stanley Donen) 50, 51, 55, 63

Samourai, Le (Jean-Pierre Melville) 12
Saturday Night Fever (John Badham) 18
Searchers, The (John Ford) 112, 113, 116n
Sheik, The (George Melford) 31

Silence of the Lambs, The (Jonathan Demme) 5, 126–8
Silk Stockings (Rouben Mamoulian) 48, 58, 62, 67n
Sisters (Brian de Palma) 130
Son of the Sheik, The (George Fitzmaurice) 35, 39
Soul Man (Steve Miner) 225
Spartacus (Stanley Kubrick) 6, 18, 151–71
Steel and Lace (Ernest Farino) 109–13, 115, 116
Straight Out of Brooklyn (Matty Rich) 190n
Sudden Impact (Clint Eastwood) 103, 106, 107, 108, 109
Superman (Richard Donner) 12
Superman 2 (Richard Lester) 12
Switch (Blake Edwards) 245

T-Men (Anthony Mann) 14
Tango and Cash (Andrei Konchalevsky) 7, 214–16, 230, 234–8
Task Force (Delmer Daves) 79
Terminator, The (James Cameron) 7, 247–61 *passim*
Terminator 2: Judgment Day (James Cameron) 7, 247–61 *passim*
Texas Chainsaw Massacre, The (Tobe Hooper) 104
That's Entertainment II (Gene Kelly) 67n
Thelma and Louise (Ridley Scott) 106, 116n
Thief of Bagdad, The (Raoul Walsh) 42n
Three Men and a Baby (Leonard Nimoy) 254
Tightrope (Clint Eastwood) 87, 88, 99–100
Time of Your Life, The (H. C. Potter) 75
To Sleep with Anger (Charles Burnett) 190n
Top Gun (Tony Scott) 141
Top Hat (Mark Sandrich) 56
Total Recall (Paul Verhoeven) 129, 241
True Identity (Charles Lane) 190n
Twins (Ivan Reitman) 225

Videodrome (David Cronenberg) 129, 147

Werewolf of London (Stuart Walker) 126
What Price Glory? (Raoul Walsh) 196
White Heat (Raoul Walsh) 4, 66, 70–84
Wild Bunch, The (Sam Peckinpah) 15

Wolf Man, The (George Waggner) 125, 126

Yankee Doodle Dandy (Michael Curtiz) 74, 75
Young Rajah, The (Philip Rosen) 37

GENERAL INDEX

action film 7–8, 194–209, 214–16, 219–27, 230–43, 245–60
Adrian 37
Allan, Maude 40
Allen, Nancy 119
Allyson, June 67n
Alpert, Hollis 158, 164
Altman, Rick 49–50
Amos, John 223, 241
Appian of Alexandria 154
Astaire, Adele 50
Astaire, Fred 4, 46–69, 75
Atwill, Lionel 152

Banky, Vilma 35
Baraka, Amiri 182
Barker, 'Ma' (Arizona Clark) 73
Barnes, Joanna 154
Bass, Saul 159
Baudrillard, Jean 194, 199, 204, 208–9
Bedelia, Bonnie 236
Bellour, Raymond 10
Berger, John 169n
Berkeley, Busby 46
Bhabha, Homi 214, 218, 219, 225, 226n
Bingham, Dennis 101n
Boone, Pat 66n
Bowker, Benjamin 77–9, 83n
Boyd, Stephen 18
Boyle, Lara Flynn 203
Bradley, Keith 154, 170n
Braga, Sonia 203
Briffault, Robert 123
Bronson, Charles 101
Brown, Gillian 255
Browning, Tod 123
Brownlow, Kevin 42n
Brynner, Yul 171n

buddy film 6–7, 194–209, 225; *see also* action film
Bujold, Geneviève 137
Busey, Gary 201
Bush, George 7, 195–7, 226
Butler, Judith 214, 218–19, 222, 225, 226n, 227n

Cagney, James 4, 70–83
Caine, Michael 119
Cameron, James 247–8, 258
Castle, Irene 25–6
Castle, Vernon 25–6, 39, 40, 43n
castration 2, 12–13, 15–16, 66, 81, 105, 110–11, 118–19, 121, 127, 129–30, 139–41, 143–5, 147, 166, 175–6, 178–9, 181–2, 191n, 207
Chaney, Lon, Jr. 126
Charisse, Cyd 47–9, 56, 58–9, 66, 67n
Chestnut, Morris 185
Chodorow, Nancy 147n
Chong, Rae Dawn 243
Churchill, Sarah 50, 52, 54
Clark, Thomas 83n
class 3, 26, 32, 108, 112, 173, 175, 190n, 194–6, 203, 215, 218–19, 223, 225, 227n, 239, 242, 254
Cleaver, Eldridge 181–2
Close, Glenn 91
Cobb, Stanley 71
Conley, Tom 72, 77
Cook, Donald 74
Cook, Pam 176
Cooper, Gary 18
Corey, Arthur 37
Crane, Mr and Mrs Douglas 25
Crawford, Joan 50
Creed, Barbara 232–3

Croce, Arlene 62
Cronenberg, David 6, 134–47
Crosby, Bing 62
Crowther, Bosley 71, 73
Curtis, Tony 162, 166, 170n, 171n

Dafoe, Willem 197
Dailey, Dan 62
Dall, John 165–6
dance 4, 23–43, 46–68, 75–6
d'Arville, Madeleine 26
Davis, Geena 137
de Lauretis, Teresa 177, 209
de Palma, Brian 119–20, 130
Delameter, Jerome 64, 67n
Delon, Alain 12
DeMille, Cecil B. 41n, 164
Denby, David 160–2, 170n
Diaghilev, Sergei 23, 29, 33, 37
Dietrich, Marlene 18
Dijkstra, Bram 123
Doane, Mary Ann 79, 213, 217–19,
    225, 226n
Douglas, Kirk 152, 155, 157, 161, 164,
    169n, 170n, 171n
Douglas, Michael 205–6
Dyer, Richard 66n, 191n, 231, 232, 233

Eastwood, Clint 5, 12, 70, 87–103, 106,
    109, 195, 203–4, 206, 231, 245
Ebert, Roger 103–4
Edelman, Lee 230–1
Edens, Roger 64
Ellis, John 10, 17, 19n
Elsaesser, Thomas 100–1
Erikson, Erik 78–9, 81
ethnicity see race
Evans, Walter 124–5

Fairbanks, Douglas 39, 42n
Fanon, Frantz 214, 218, 225, 226n
Farnham, Marynia 81–2
Fast, Howard 170n, 171n
Fawcett, Farrah 103
feminism 1, 5–6, 9, 27, 81–2, 98–9, 137,
    146, 173–90, 196, 213, 247, 252
feminization of men 33–4, 37–9, 46–66
    passim, 70–83 passim, 94, 121–32,
    135–7, 141–3, 151, 164, 169n, 179,
    180–2, 188, 191n, 198, 203, 208, 234
Ferrara, Abel 114
fetishization 2, 15, 17–19, 55, 62, 91,

104, 143–5, 151, 156, 167, 197,
    217–18, 226n
Feuchtwang, Stephen 218
film noir 16, 65–6, 68n
Finley, William 130
Fischer, Lucy 66, 66n
Fishburne, Larry 183
Flack, Roberta 95
Fluegel, Darlanne 221
Flynn, Errol 152
Flynn, John 214
Foch, Nina 154
Ford, Harrison 231, 245
Foster, Jodie 127
Foucault, Michel 151, 158–9
Fox, Michael J. 245
Frank, Marcie 146n
Frawley, William 43n
Freed, Arthur 64
Freud, Sigmund 114–15, 120–1, 124,
    126–7, 139–43

Gaines, Jane 177–8
Galen 118
Gamman, Lorraine 2
gangster films 3–4, 71–83 passim, 151
Garber, Marjorie 226n
Garcia, Andy 205
Garland, Judy 65, 66n
Gavin, John 165–6
gaze, the 1, 3, 10, 13, 15–19, 47, 60,
    92–5, 99, 131, 151, 154–9, 169n,
    176, 178–80, 200, 221, 237
Getz, John 136, 139
Gibson, Mel 199–200
Gill, David 42n
Glass, Bonnie 25
Gledhill, Christine 190n, 191n
Glenn, Scott 198
Glover, Danny 199–200
Goff, Ivan 76
Goldbeck, Willis 34–5
Goldblum, Jeff 136
Gooding, Cuba Jr. 183
Gordon, Keith 119
Gottfredson, Michael 73
Grant, Cary 10
Graven, P. S. 71
Greiner, Donald 259

Hamilton, Linda 252
Hanna, Judith Lynne 29
Hansen, Miriam 25, 30, 33, 41n, 42n

Hantover, Jeffrey 34
Harris, Trudier 181
Hartung, Philip 71
Haskell, Molly 196
Hatcher, Teri 221
Hawks, Howard 12
Hayakawa, Sessue 29, 41n
Heath, Stephen 213
Hepburn, Audrey 59–60
Herman, Pee-Wee 70
Heston, Charlton 12, 15
Higashi, Sumiko 25
Hines, Gregory 197
Hirschi, Travis 73
historical epic film 3, 6, 12, 18, 151–71
Hitchcock, Alfred 16–17
Hoffman, Gertrude 23
Holden, William 15
Holmlund, Chris 87, 99, 101n, 226n
Homans, Margaret 146n
homoeroticism 107, 152, 164, 195, 197,
    202, 209, 219, 221, 223, 227n, 238
homosexuality 6–7, 9, 13, 19, 34, 42,
    75, 88–9, 98, 105, 114–16, 169n,
    195–7, 202–4, 206, 214–25, 226n,
    227n, 238, 242–3; see also
    feminization of men, homoeroticism
homosociality 194–6, 201, 207
Hopkins, Anthony 127
Horney, Karen 130
horror film 5–6, 118–32, 134–47; see
    also science-fiction film
Hoskins, Bob 194
Howe, Herbert 39
Hudson, Rock 18
Hull, Edith M. 30
Hurley, Neal 71, 74, 79
Hurt, William 196
hypermasculinity 70, 152, 175, 180,
    188, 201

Ice Cube 185
Ice-T 206
Irigaray, Luce 165, 176, 179
Irons, Jeremy 134, 139

Jackson, Michael 226n
James, Brion 223
Jeffords, Susan 197, 201–2
Johnston, Claire 176
Joyrich, Lynne 201
Julia, Raul 204

Kaplan, E. Ann 143
Kappeler, Susanne 151, 169n
Karpis, Alvin 73
Kaye, Danny 62
Kelly, Gene 62, 64–5, 68n
Kendall, Elizabeth 23
Kidder, Margot 130
King, Scott Benjamin 231
Kittay, Eva 135, 138
Knight, Arthur 90–1
Koestler, Arthur 171n
Kosloff, Theodore 37
Kracauer, Siegfried 146
Kristeva, Julia 5, 118, 121–2, 127–8,
    132
Kristofferson, Kris 15
Kubrick, Stanley 161, 168, 169, 170n

Lacan, Jacques 101n, 134, 140, 143,
    146n, 176, 190n, 213–14, 217–19,
    222, 224, 226n, 242
Landham, Sonny 223
Langella, Frank 122
Laughton, Charles 162
Lawford, Peter 50, 52, 63
Lee, Spike 183, 190n, 206
Lehman, Peter 113, 116n, 227n
Lemoine-Luccioni, Eugenie 226n
Lentricchia, Frank 230
Leone, Sergio 12, 17
Lerner, Alan Jay 51
Lévi-Strauss, Claude 123, 165, 171n
Liddy, G. Gordon 201
Locke, Sondra 103, 107
Lombard, Carole 43n
looking see gaze, the
Lundberg, Ferdinand 81–2

McCarten, John 75, 77
McCrea, Joel 15
MacDonald, Dwight 170n
McGilligan, Patrick 73–7, 83n, 91
McGraw, Charles 155
MacGregor, Helen 37
McRae, Frank 223
McRobbie, Angela 24
Madonna 59, 226n
male body, the 4, 5–8, 15, 29, 40, 54,
    62, 68n, 163, 167–8, 174–5, 186,
    194–5, 197, 199–202, 204, 206, 209,
    220, 222, 224–5, 227n, 236–8, 241,
    243, 260–1; damaged 15, 90, 105–7,
    110, 116, 118–32, 142, 152, 159–60,

163, 167, 197, 204, 237, 246; on display 1, 3, 17–18, 23–4, 26, 33–4, 46–8, 60, 63, 151, 153–5, 159–60, 176, 230–4, 239, 245–7, 259; in relation to female body 1, 17, 29, 33–4, 59, 66n, 71, 134, 136, 142, 145, 159–60, 176, 178–9, 187–8, 217–18, 250, 252
Maltin, Leonard 104
Mann, Anthony 13–14, 16, 227n
Mann, Karen 247
Marchand, Roland 43n
Marchon brothers 37
Marshment, Margaret 2
Martin, Mick 104, 116n
Marvin, Lee 18
masochism 32, 70, 113–14, 118–32 *passim*, 140, 230; and sadism 2, 4–5, 13, 16, 30–1, 104–6, 134, 152, 166, 220, 230
masquerade 3, 7, 48, 63, 119, 213–26, 243
Mastrosimone, William 103
Mature, Victor 67n
Mayne, Judith 87, 101n
Medhurst, Andy 243
Mellen, Joan 195
Melville, Jean-Pierre 12
Mercer, Beryl 74
Miller, Ann 63
Mills, Donna 88
Mix, Tom 12
Modleski, Tania 19n, 190n, 200–2
Mohanty, Chandra 226n
Monahan, Michael 27
Mordkin, Mikhail 41n
Moreno, Antonio 37
Morris, Michael 42n
Mouvet, Maurice 25–6, 29, 31
Mueller, John 49, 67n, 68n
Mulvey, Laura 1–4, 10–11, 13–15, 17, 46–7, 60, 143, 151, 165, 176
Murray, Nickolas 37
musical film 4, 18, 46–69, 74–5

narcissism, 2, 6, 10–12, 13–15, 48, 63, 116, 162–3, 165–6, 222
Neale, Steve 3–4, 46–7, 55, 66n, 75, 121, 154, 163, 219, 221, 225, 227n
Nelson, Judd 206
Newman, Paul 195
Nielsen, Brigitte 234

Nijinsky, Vaslav 24, 34, 37, 41n, 42n
Nunn, Bill 208

O'Brien, Edmond 73
O'Connor, Donald 62
Olivier, Laurence 123, 153, 157, 166, 171n
Ouspenskaya, Maria 126

Paige, Janis 59
Palance, Jack 220–1
patriarchy 2, 4, 9, 11, 14, 31, 47, 55, 82, 123, 134, 137–9, 153, 162–3, 165, 174, 176–7, 179, 189, 190n
Pavlova, Anna 37
Payne, Allen 206
Pearce, John 72
Peckinpah, Sam 15
Penley, Constance 70, 176–7, 247
Pesci, Joe 202
Plummer, Christopher 18
Polan, Dana 61, 70–1
Porter, Cole 48
Porter, Marsha 104, 116n
Powell, Jane 47, 50–3, 56
Presley, Elvis 66n
Propp, Vladimir 14–15
Pruette, Lorine 27

race 4, 6–8, 23–43 *passim*, 88–9, 96, 98, 108, 170n, 173–90, 194–209, 214–19, 223, 225, 226n, 243, 253–4, 257–8
Radway, Janice 30–2, 35–6
Raft, George 43n
Rains, Claude 126
Rambova, Natacha 36–7, 42n
Rank, Otto 220
rape-revenge film 5, 103–16
Reagan, Ronald 7, 195–6, 226, 246, 259
Redford, Robert 195
Redgrove, Peter 123
Reed, Ishmael 182
Reeves, Steve 12
Reid, Wallace 37
Richard, Cliff 66n
Richards, Renee 70
Rickman, Alan 239
Riviere, Joan 213–14, 216–17, 219, 225, 226n
Roberts, Ben 76
Robeson, Paul 191n
Robinson, Edward G. 75

Rock, Chris 207
Rodowick, D. N. 13
Rogers, Ginger 56–8, 64–5, 67n
Rogin, Michael 196–7, 202, 246
Romano, Larry 220
Roosevelt, Theodore 25, 40n
Roshanara 23
Ross, Diana 226n
Russell, Kurt 220–1, 230, 235

Sacco and Vanzetti, 25
Sacks, Oliver 71
sadism see masochism
St Denis, Ruth 23
St John, Adela Rogers 27, 41n, 42n
Sawyer, Joan 25
Schatz, Thomas 61, 76
Schwarzenegger, Arnold 7, 8, 232, 237, 240–1, 243, 248
science-fiction film 12, 241, 129, 134–47, 151
Scott, Randolph 14
Sebald, Hans 80, 82
Sebastian, Carlo 25
Sedgwick, Eve Kosofsky 171n, 190n, 194–5
Shawn, Ted 26, 34, 41n, 42n
Sheen, Charlie 203
Shepherd, Cybill 239
Showalter, Elaine 82, 147n
Shuttle, Penelope 123
Siegel, Don 92
Silver, Alain 123
Silverman, Kaja 145–6
Simmons, Jean 155, 157, 166, 171n
Simon, William 83n
Sinatra, Frank 62
Singleton, John 182, 186, 190n
Sirk, Douglas 18
Skerritt, Tom 203
Smith, Dwight C., Jr. 71
Smith, Paul 70, 87, 101n, 141, 227n
Snipes, Wesley 206
Spaeth, Sigmund 23
spectacle 2–4, 7, 9–19 passim, 33, 46–8, 68, 106, 151–9, 160–1, 165, 167–8, 176, 196, 198–9, 202, 207–8, 213, 216, 220, 222, 224–5, 230–1, 233, 237, 239, 245–6, 255–6, 259
spectatorship 2–5, 18, 24–5, 31–2, 35–6, 46–7, 52, 59, 61, 65, 104–6,

109, 116, 131, 144, 151, 155, 158–61, 178, 213, 224, 225
Spillane, Mickey 65
Spillers, Hortense 175
Stallone, Sylvester 7, 214–27, 230, 232, 234–9, 245
Stewart, James 15
Stoller, Robert 217
Stowitts, Hubert 37
Strauss, Richard 23
Strecker, Edward 80, 82
Strode, Woody 154
Studlar, Gaylyn 113
subjectivity 1–2, 6, 136, 142, 144, 153–4, 156–7, 161–3, 167, 169, 174, 176–7, 213
Sutherland, Donald 220–1, 236

Takakura, Ken 206
Tasker, Yvonne 222, 227n
Terry, Alice 29
Thomas, Clarence 196
Thurston, Carol 30
Travolta, John 18, 66n
Trumbo, Dalton 159, 168, 170n
Tudor, Andrew 123
Twitchell, J. B. 125
Tyler, Carole-Anne 70

Ursini, James 123
Ustinov, Peter 153, 168

Valentino, Rudolph 4, 23–43
voice, the 5, 7, 92, 95–8, 155, 164, 188, 234, 238–41
von Sacher-Masoch, Leopold 113
von Sternberg, Josef 17–18, 113

Walker, Alexander 37
Walkerdine, Valerie 227n, 239
Waller, Willard 77–8
Walsh, Raoul 76, 83n
Walter, Jessica 88
Washington, Denzel 194, 206
Wayne, John 8, 15, 234, 239
Webb, Chloe 194
Wecter, Dixon 79
Welch, Raquel 103, 107
western film 3, 5, 8, 12, 14–15, 17–18, 151, 239–40
Wiegman, Robyn 169n, 200
Willemen, Paul 13–14, 16–18, 19n, 219, 221, 225, 227n

Williams, Esther 66n
Williams, Linda 55, 104, 121, 130–1, 198
Willis, Bruce 239, 245
Winship, Mary 42n
Wolf, Christa 258–9
Wollen, Peter 33–4
Wood, Michael 170n
Wood, Robin 114, 140
Wright, Richard 181, 191n

Wycherly, Margaret 73, 83n
Wylie, Philip 80–2

X, Malcolm 182

Young, Robert 219
Young, William Allen 223

Zavitzianos, G. 242
Ziegeld, Florenz 46